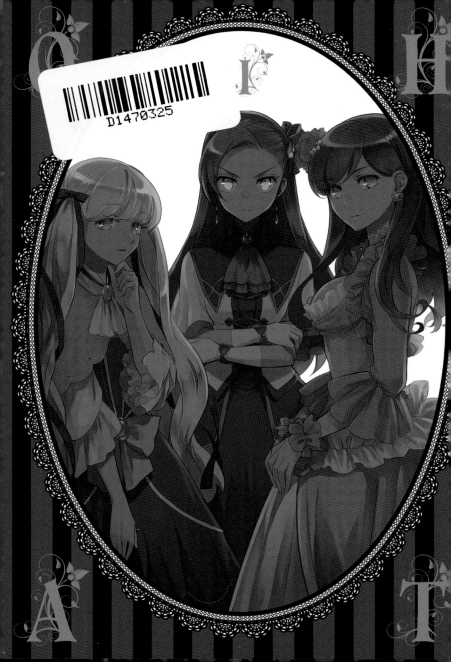

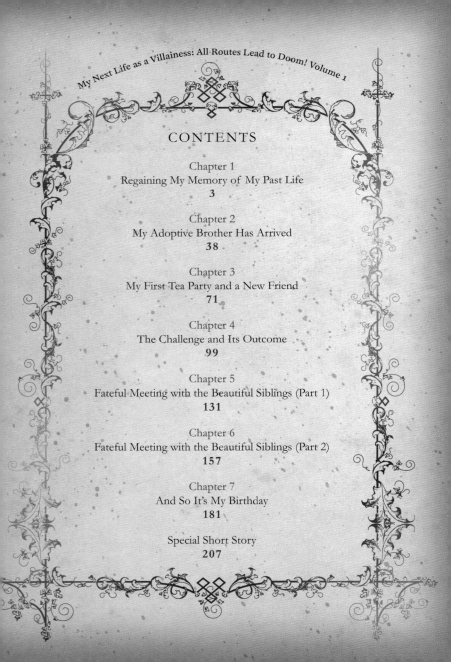

CONTENTS

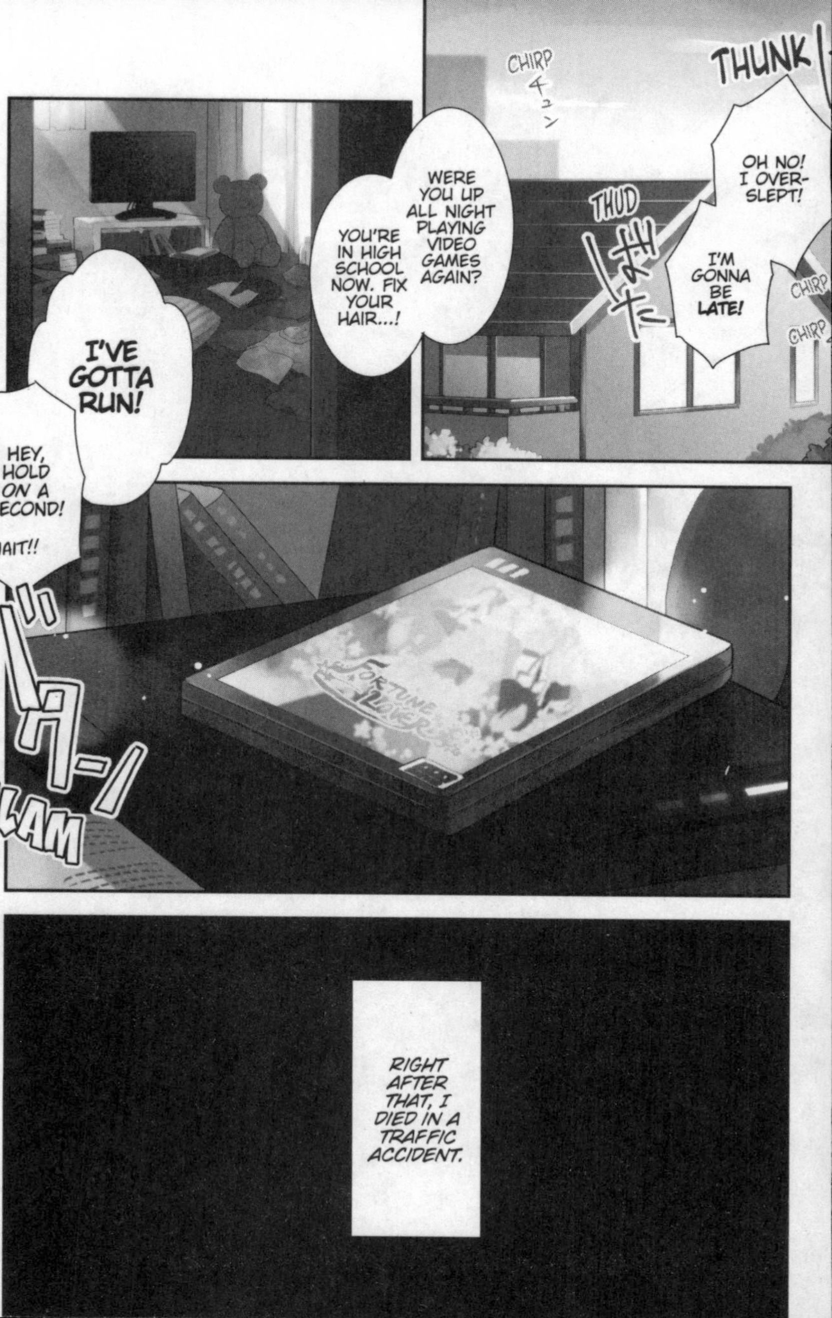
THUNK
CHIRP
チュン
OH NO! I OVER-SLEPT!
I'M GONNA BE **LATE!**
THUD
CHIRP
CHIRP
WERE YOU UP ALL NIGHT PLAYING VIDEO GAMES AGAIN?
YOU'RE IN HIGH SCHOOL NOW. FIX YOUR HAIR...!
I'VE GOTTA RUN!
HEY, HOLD ON A SECOND!
WAIT!!
SLAM
FORTUNE LOVER
RIGHT AFTER THAT, I DIED IN A TRAFFIC ACCIDENT.

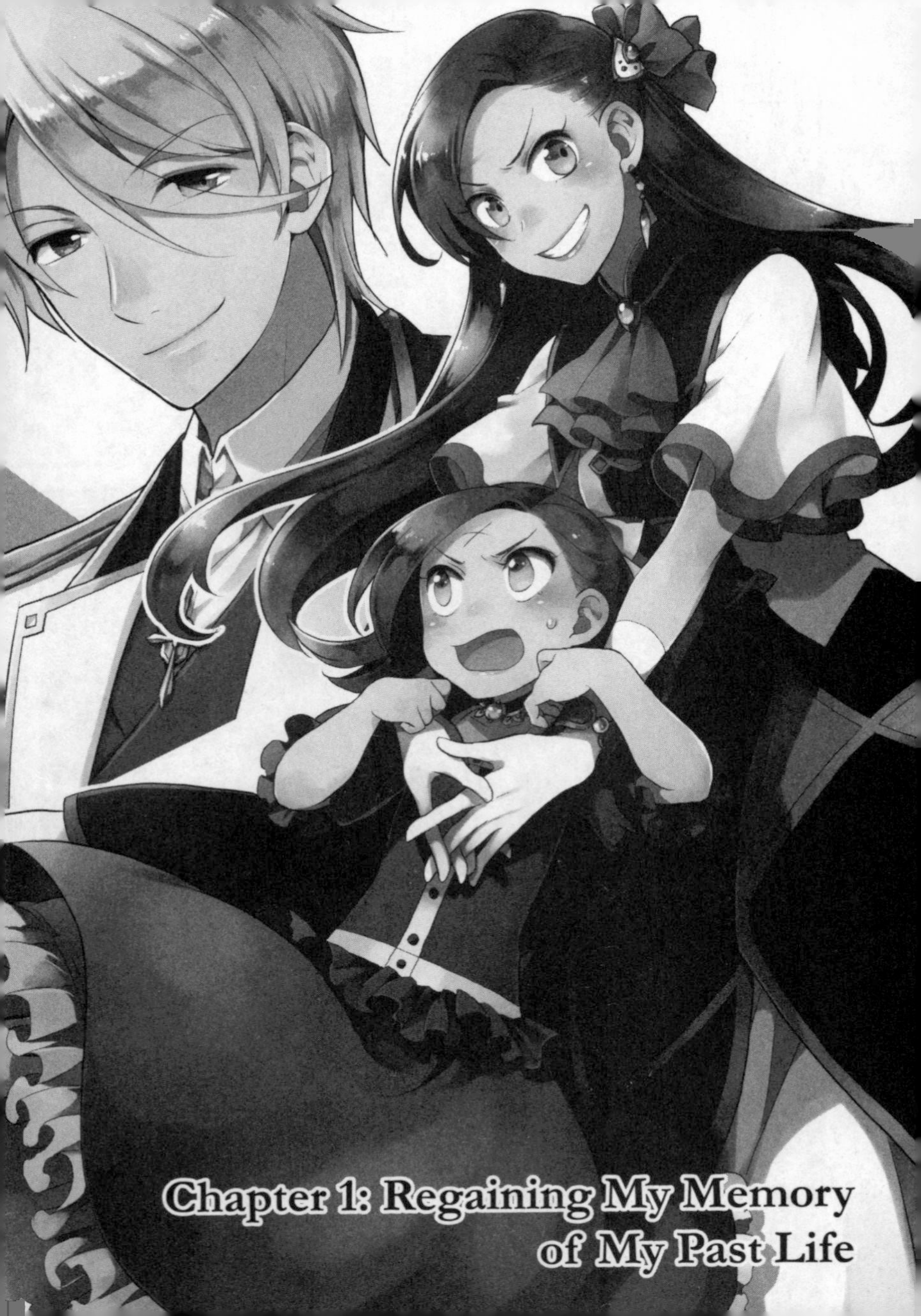

Chapter 1: Regaining My Memory of My Past Life

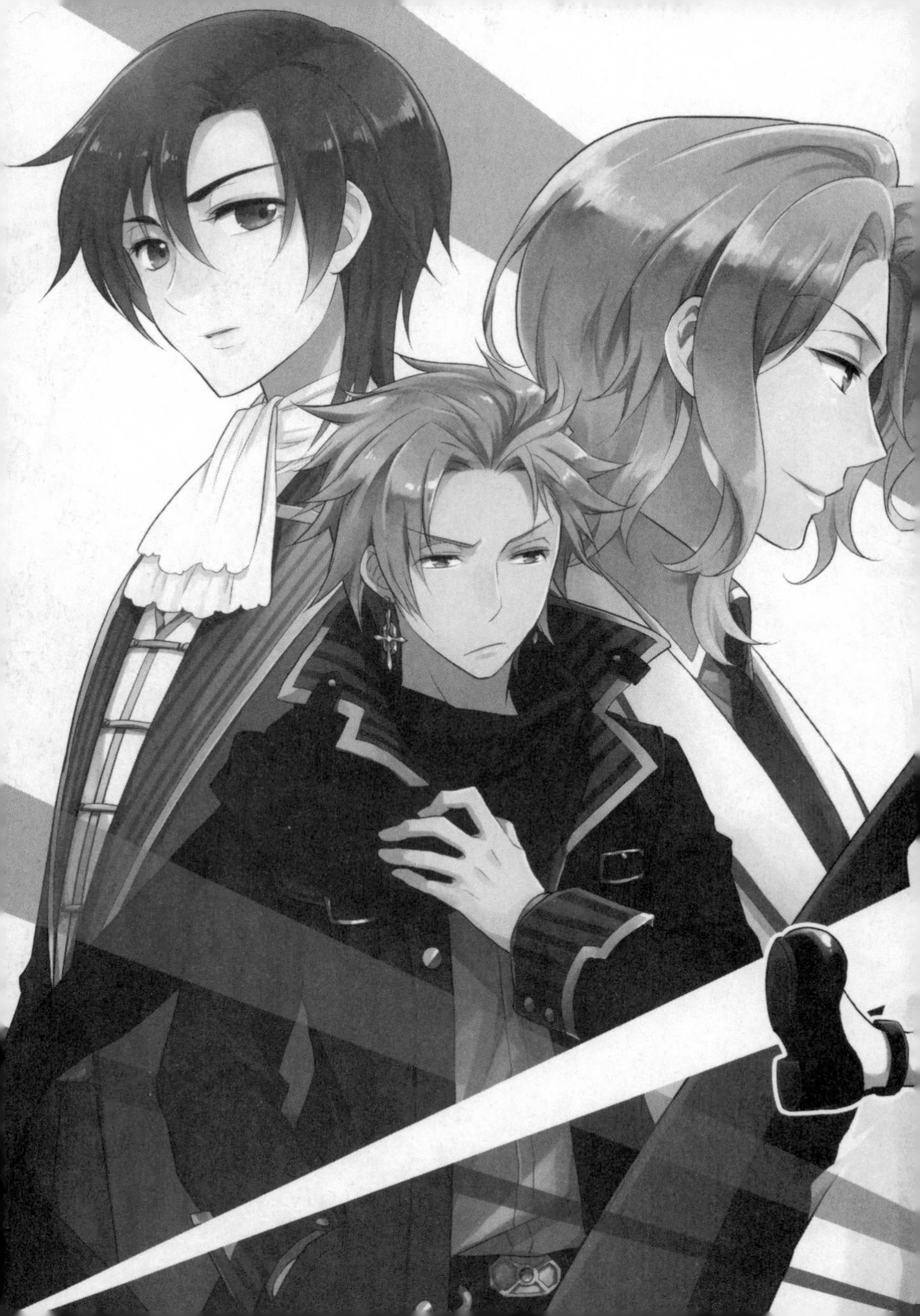

My Next Life
as a VILLAINESS:
ALL ROUTES
LEAD TO DOOM!

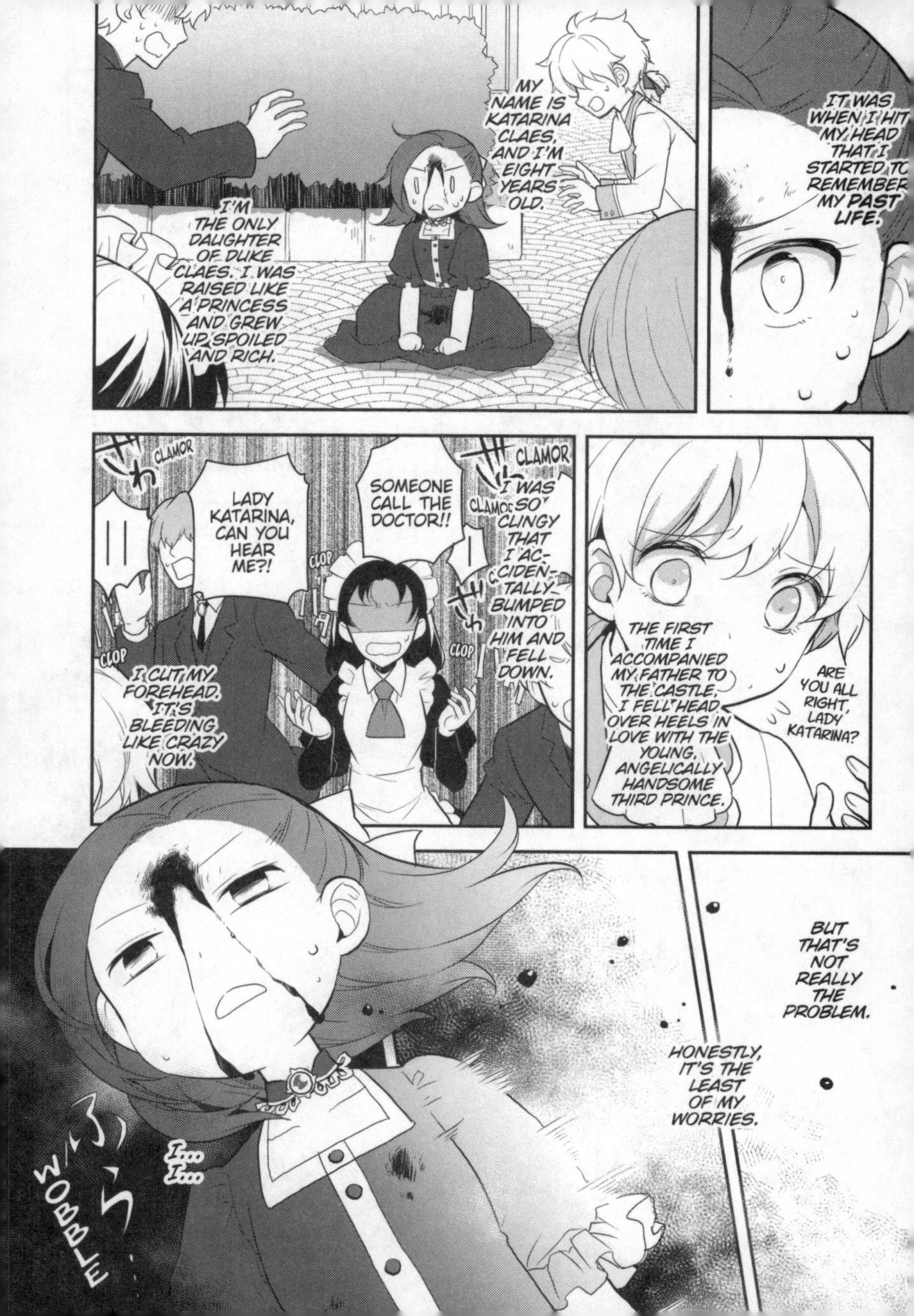
IT WAS WHEN I HIT MY HEAD THAT I STARTED TO REMEMBER MY PAST LIFE.
MY NAME IS KATARINA CLAES, AND I'M EIGHT YEARS OLD.
I'M THE ONLY DAUGHTER OF DUKE CLAES. I WAS RAISED LIKE A PRINCESS AND GREW UP SPOILED AND RICH.
THE FIRST TIME I ACCOMPANIED MY FATHER TO THE CASTLE, I FELL HEAD OVER HEELS IN LOVE WITH THE YOUNG, ANGELICALLY HANDSOME THIRD PRINCE.
ARE YOU ALL RIGHT, LADY KATARINA?
CLAMOR
I WAS SO CLINGY THAT I ACCIDENTALLY BUMPED INTO HIM AND FELL DOWN.
SOMEONE CALL THE DOCTOR!!
CLOP
CLAMOR
LADY KATARINA, CAN YOU HEAR ME?!
CLOP
I CUT MY FOREHEAD. IT'S BLEEDING LIKE CRAZY NOW.
CLOP
BUT THAT'S NOT REALLY THE PROBLEM.
HONESTLY, IT'S THE LEAST OF MY WORRIES.
I... I...
WOBBLE

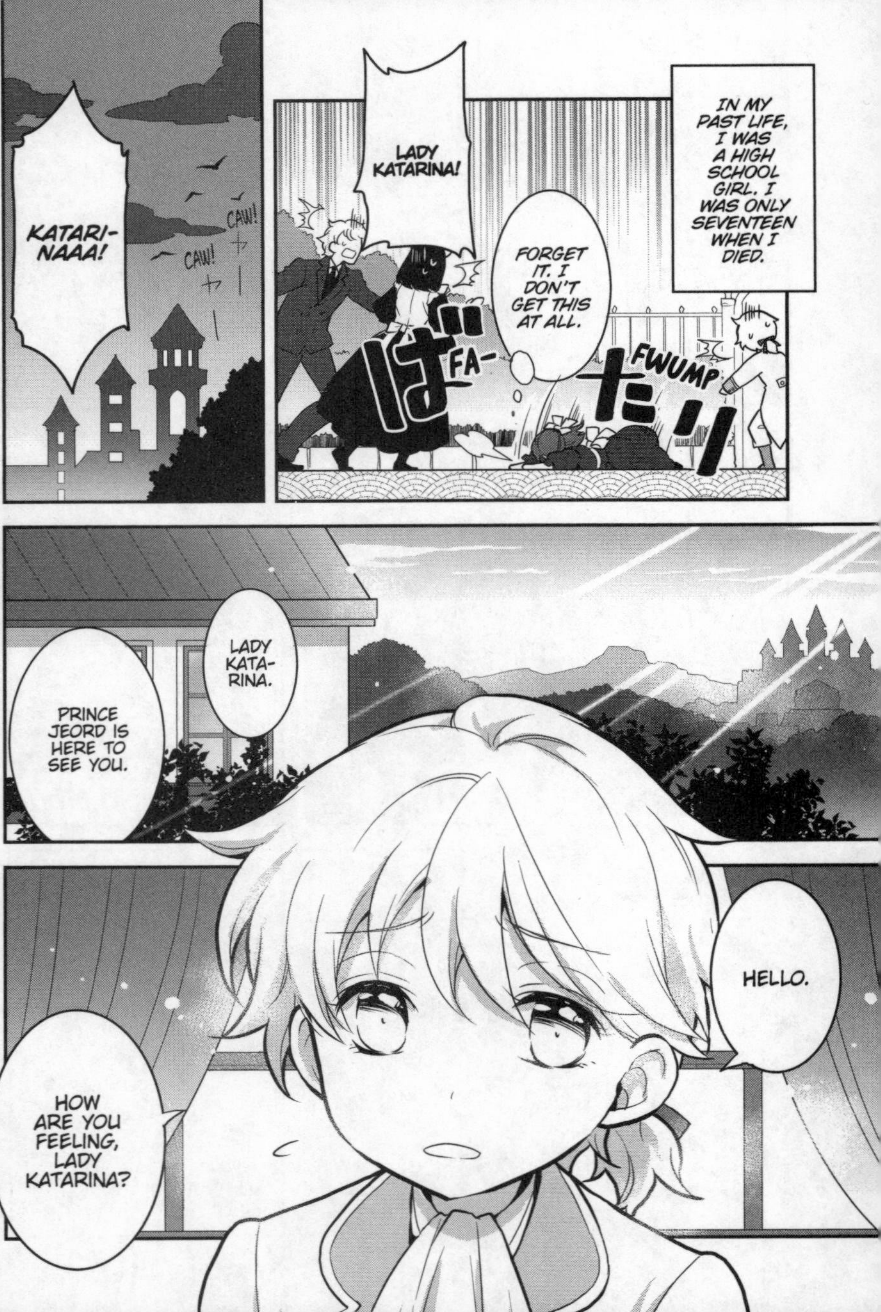

IN MY PAST LIFE, I WAS A HIGH SCHOOL GIRL. I WAS ONLY SEVENTEEN WHEN I DIED.
LADY KATARINA!
FORGET IT. I DON'T GET THIS AT ALL.
FWUMP
FA-
KATARI-NAAA!
CAW!
CAW!
LADY KATA-RINA.
PRINCE JEORD IS HERE TO SEE YOU.
HELLO.
HOW ARE YOU FEELING, LADY KATARINA?

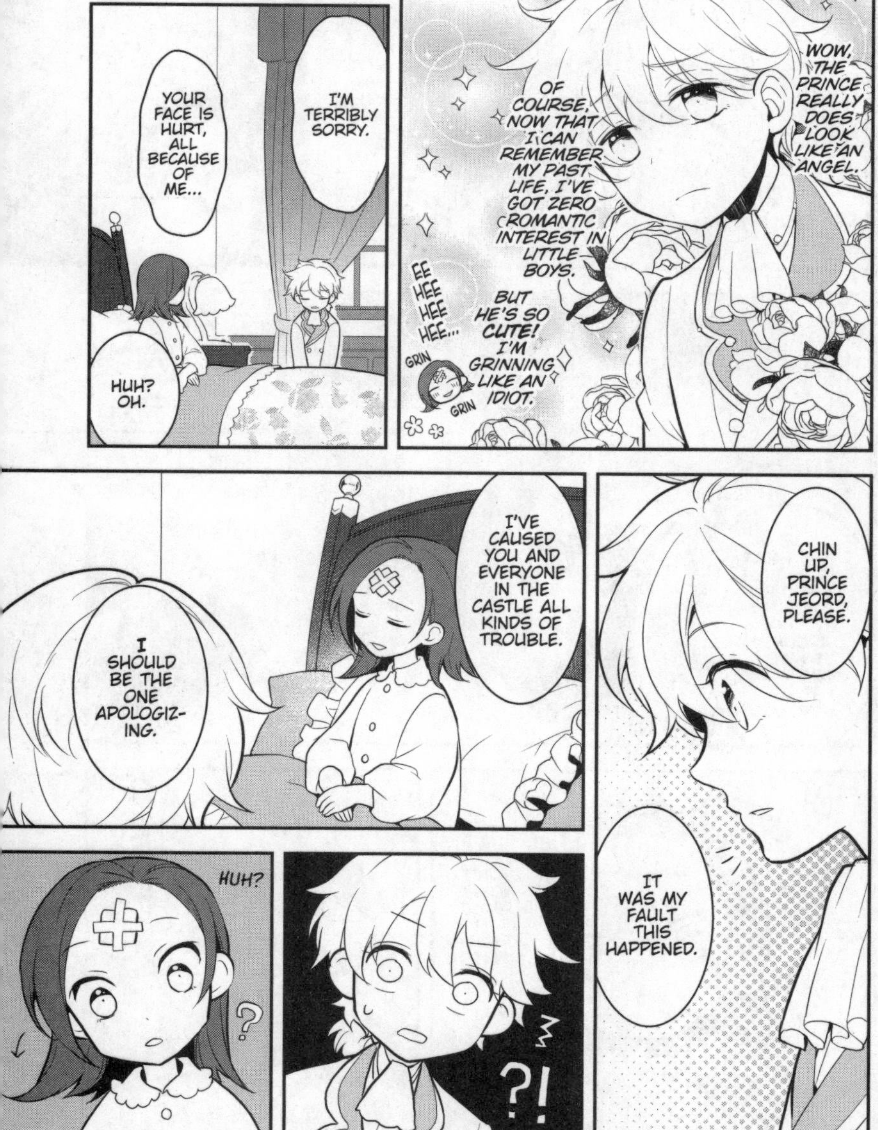
WOW, THE PRINCE REALLY DOES LOOK LIKE AN ANGEL.
OF COURSE, NOW THAT I CAN REMEMBER MY PAST LIFE, I'VE GOT ZERO ROMANTIC INTEREST IN LITTLE BOYS.
BUT HE'S SO CUTE! I'M GRINNING LIKE AN IDIOT.
EE HEE HEE HEE...
GRIN
GRIN
I'M TERRIBLY SORRY.
YOUR FACE IS HURT, ALL BECAUSE OF ME...
HUH? OH.
CHIN UP, PRINCE JEORD, PLEASE.
IT WAS MY FAULT THIS HAPPENED.
I'VE CAUSED YOU AND EVERYONE IN THE CASTLE ALL KINDS OF TROUBLE.
I SHOULD BE THE ONE APOLOGIZING.
?!
HUH?
?

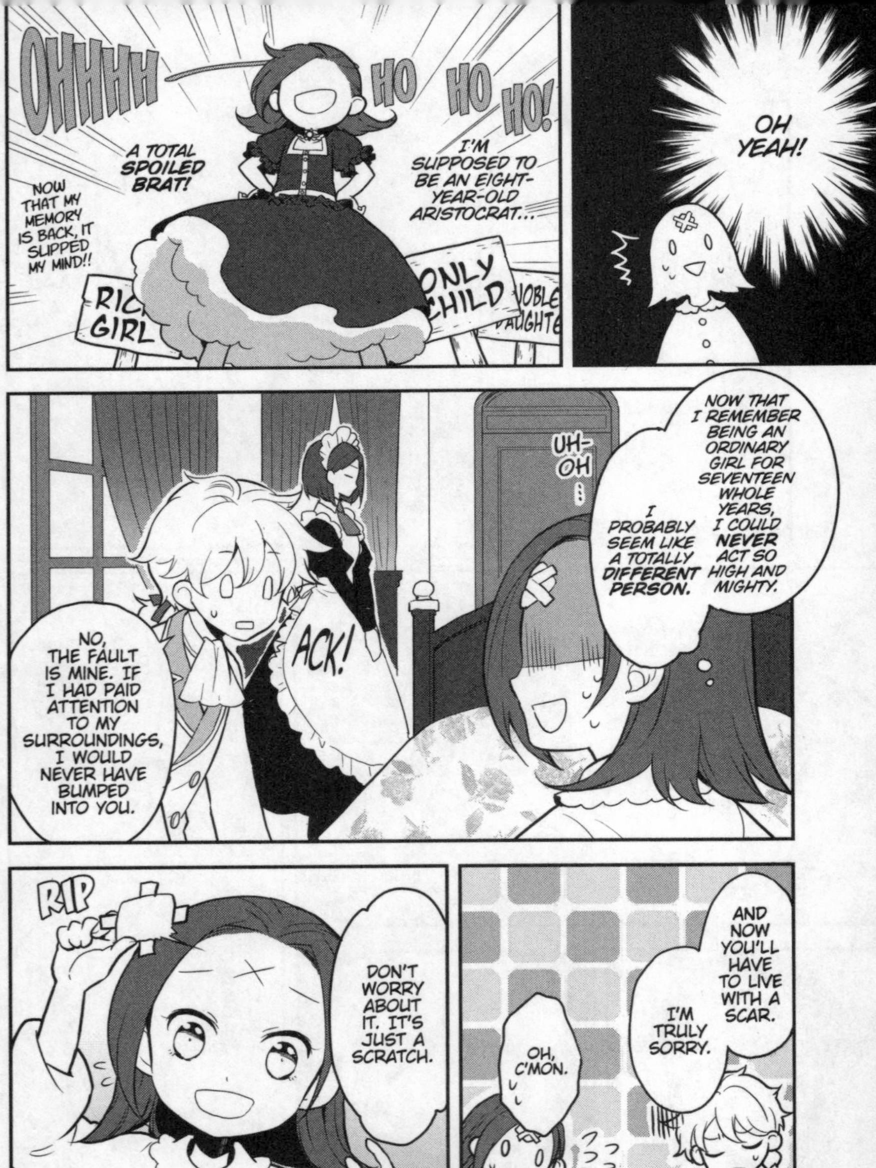

OH YEAH!
OHHHH HO HO HO!
I'M SUPPOSED TO BE AN EIGHT-YEAR-OLD ARISTOCRAT...
A TOTAL SPOILED BRAT!
NOW THAT MY MEMORY IS BACK, IT SLIPPED MY MIND!!
ONLY CHILD
OBLE DAUGHTE
RIC GIRL
NOW THAT I REMEMBER BEING AN ORDINARY GIRL FOR SEVENTEEN WHOLE YEARS, I COULD NEVER ACT SO HIGH AND MIGHTY.
I PROBABLY SEEM LIKE A TOTALLY DIFFERENT PERSON.
UH-OH...
ACK!
NO, THE FAULT IS MINE. IF I HAD PAID ATTENTION TO MY SURROUNDINGS, I WOULD NEVER HAVE BUMPED INTO YOU.
AND NOW YOU'LL HAVE TO LIVE WITH A SCAR.
I'M TRULY SORRY.
OH, C'MON.
RIP
DON'T WORRY ABOUT IT. IT'S JUST A SCRATCH.

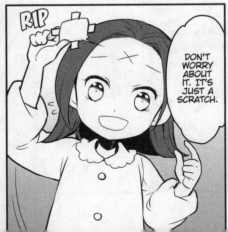

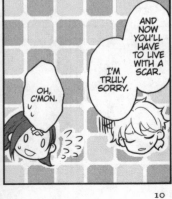

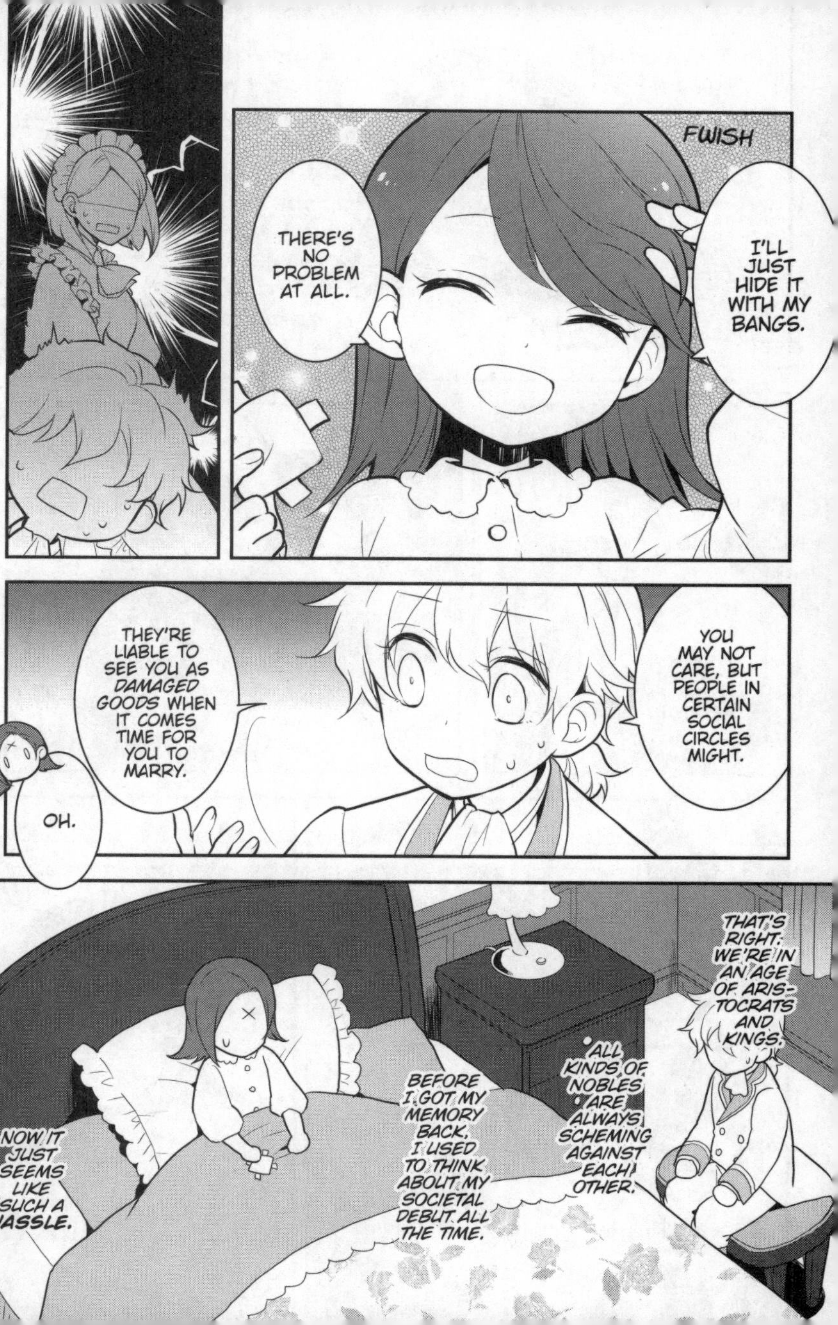
FWISH
I'LL JUST HIDE IT WITH MY BANGS.
THERE'S NO PROBLEM AT ALL.
YOU MAY NOT CARE, BUT PEOPLE IN CERTAIN SOCIAL CIRCLES MIGHT.
THEY'RE LIABLE TO SEE YOU AS *DAMAGED GOODS* WHEN IT COMES TIME FOR YOU TO MARRY.
OH.
THAT'S RIGHT. WE'RE IN AN AGE OF ARIS-TOCRATS AND KINGS.
ALL KINDS OF NOBLES ARE ALWAYS SCHEMING AGAINST EACH OTHER.
BEFORE I GOT MY MEMORY BACK, I USED TO THINK ABOUT MY SOCIETAL DEBUT ALL THE TIME.
NOW IT JUST SEEMS LIKE SUCH A **HASSLE**.

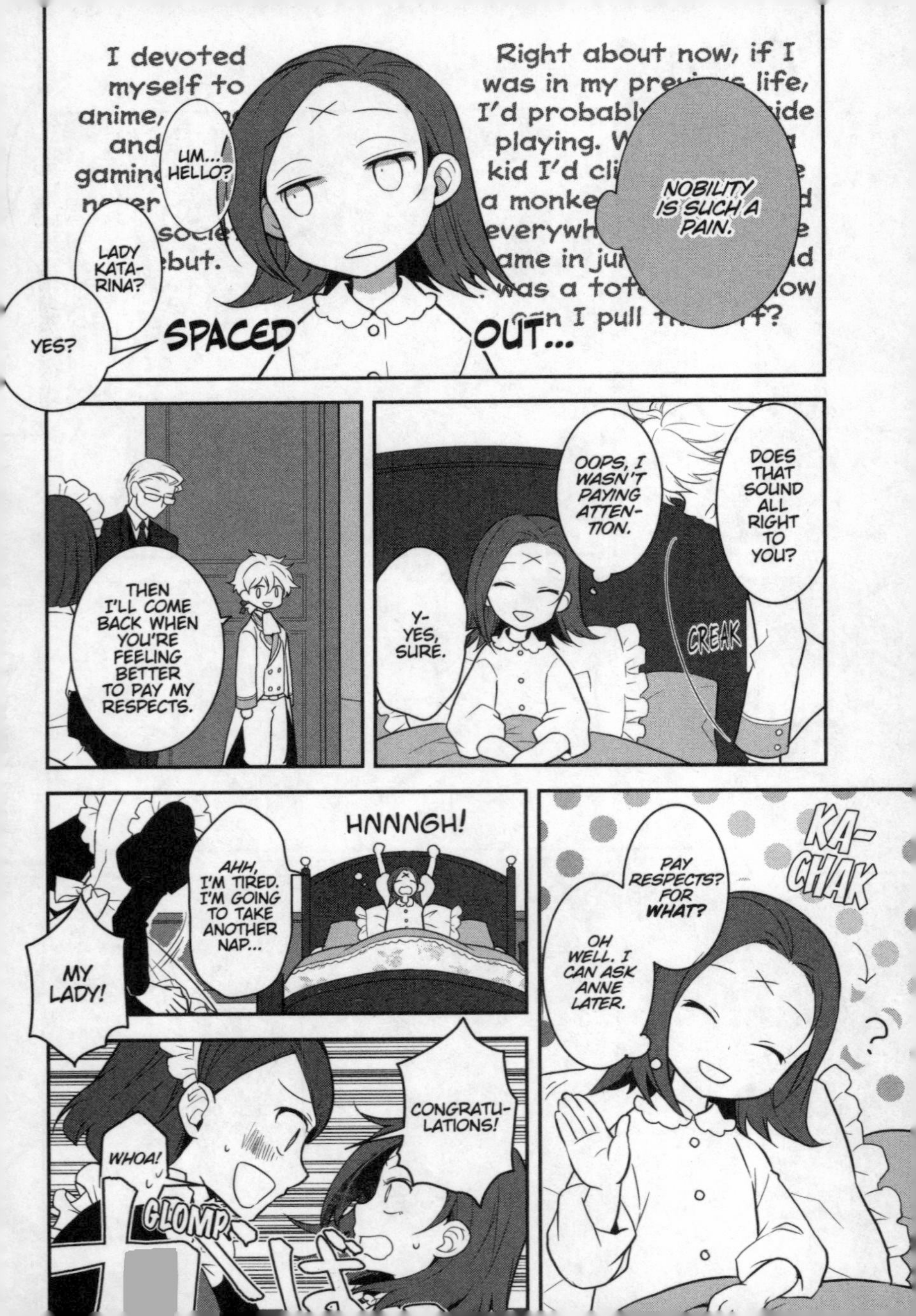
Right about now, if I
was in my previ life,
I'd probabl ide
playing. W
kid I'd cli
a monke
everywh
ame in ju
was a tot ow
can I pull f?
NOBILITY IS SUCH A PAIN.
I devoted
myself to
anime,
and
gaming
never
socie
ebut.
UM... HELLO?
LADY KATA-RINA?
SPACED OUT...
YES?
DOES THAT SOUND ALL RIGHT TO YOU?
OOPS, I WASN'T PAYING ATTEN-TION.
CREAK
Y-YES, SURE.
THEN I'LL COME BACK WHEN YOU'RE FEELING BETTER TO PAY MY RESPECTS.
KA-CHAK
PAY RESPECTS? FOR WHAT?
OH WELL. I CAN ASK ANNE LATER.
HNNNGH!
AHH, I'M TIRED. I'M GOING TO TAKE ANOTHER NAP...
MY LADY!
CONGRATU-LATIONS!
WHOA!
GLOMP

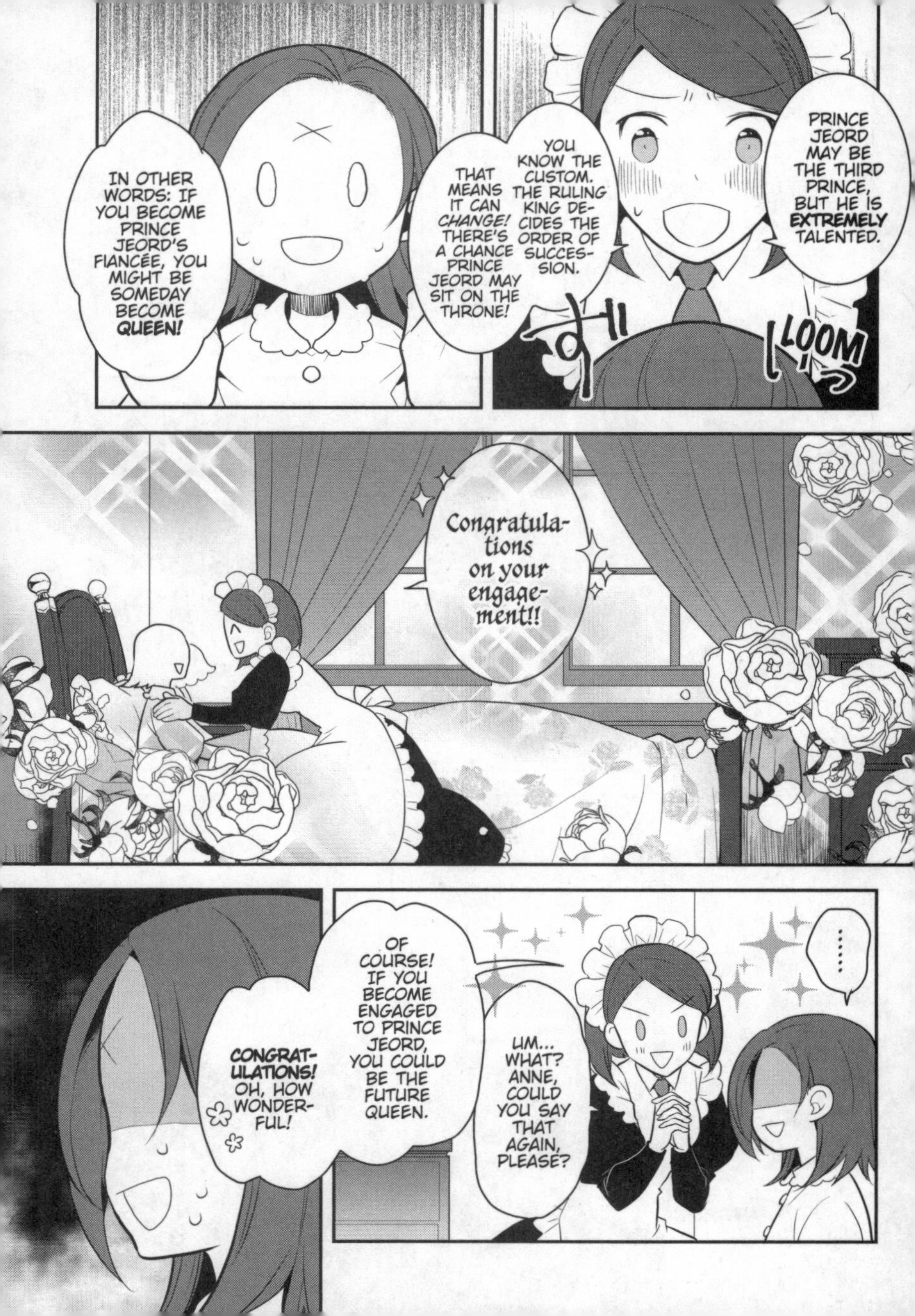
PRINCE JEORD MAY BE THE THIRD PRINCE, BUT HE IS **EXTREMELY** TALENTED.
YOU KNOW THE CUSTOM. THE RULING KING DECIDES THE ORDER OF SUCCESSION.
THAT MEANS IT CAN *CHANGE!* THERE'S A CHANCE PRINCE JEORD MAY SIT ON THE THRONE!
LOOM
IN OTHER WORDS: IF YOU BECOME PRINCE JEORD'S FIANCÉE, YOU MIGHT BE SOMEDAY BECOME **QUEEN!**
Congratulations on your engagement!!
......
UM... WHAT? ANNE, COULD YOU SAY THAT AGAIN, PLEASE?
OF COURSE! IF YOU BECOME ENGAGED TO PRINCE JEORD, YOU COULD BE THE FUTURE QUEEN.
CONGRATULATIONS! OH, HOW WONDERFUL!

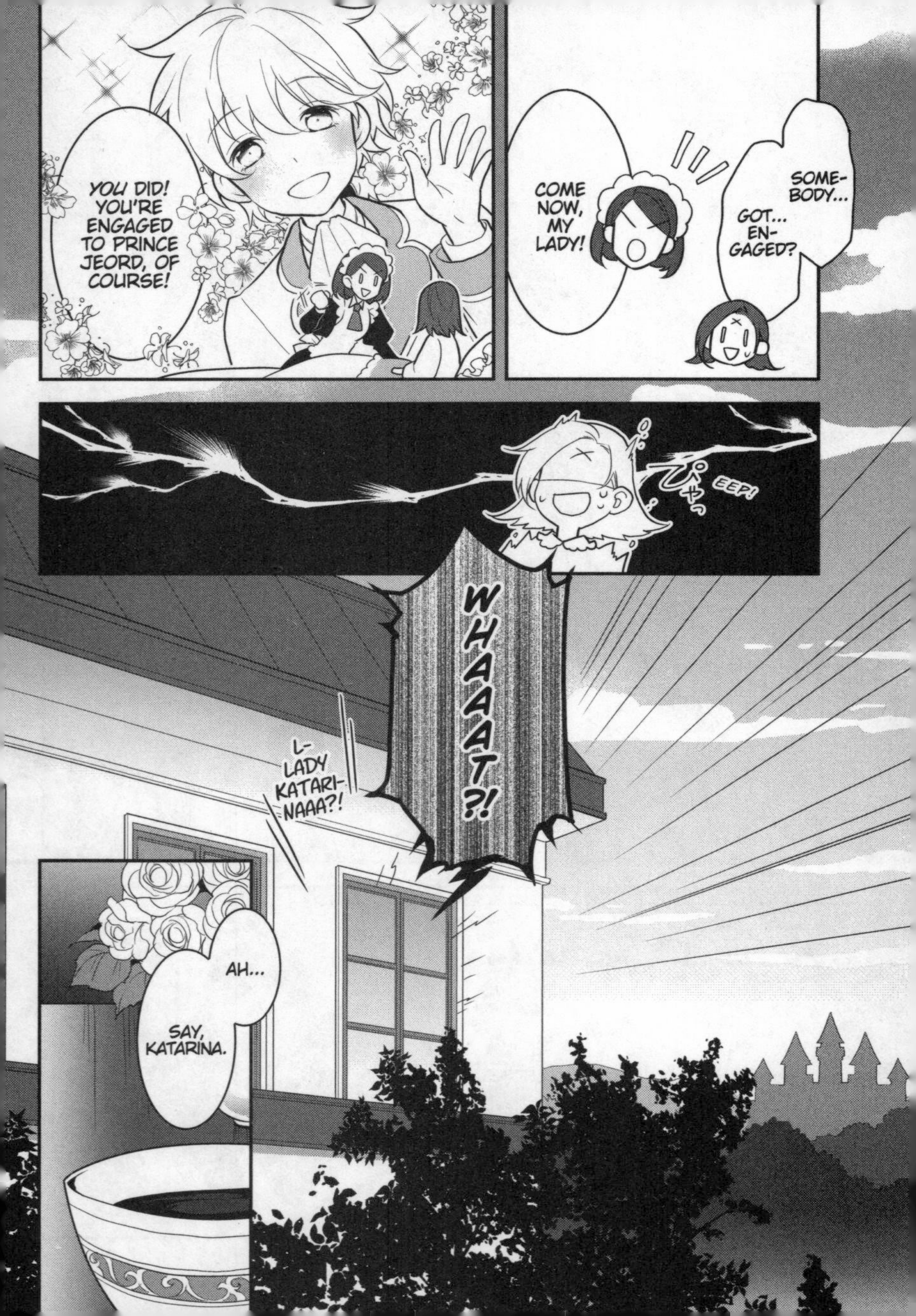
SOMEBODY... GOT... ENGAGED?
COME NOW, MY LADY!
YOU DID! YOU'RE ENGAGED TO PRINCE JEORD, OF COURSE!
ぴゃっ
EEP!
WHAAAAT?!
L-LADY KATARI-NAAA?!
AH...
SAY, KATARINA.

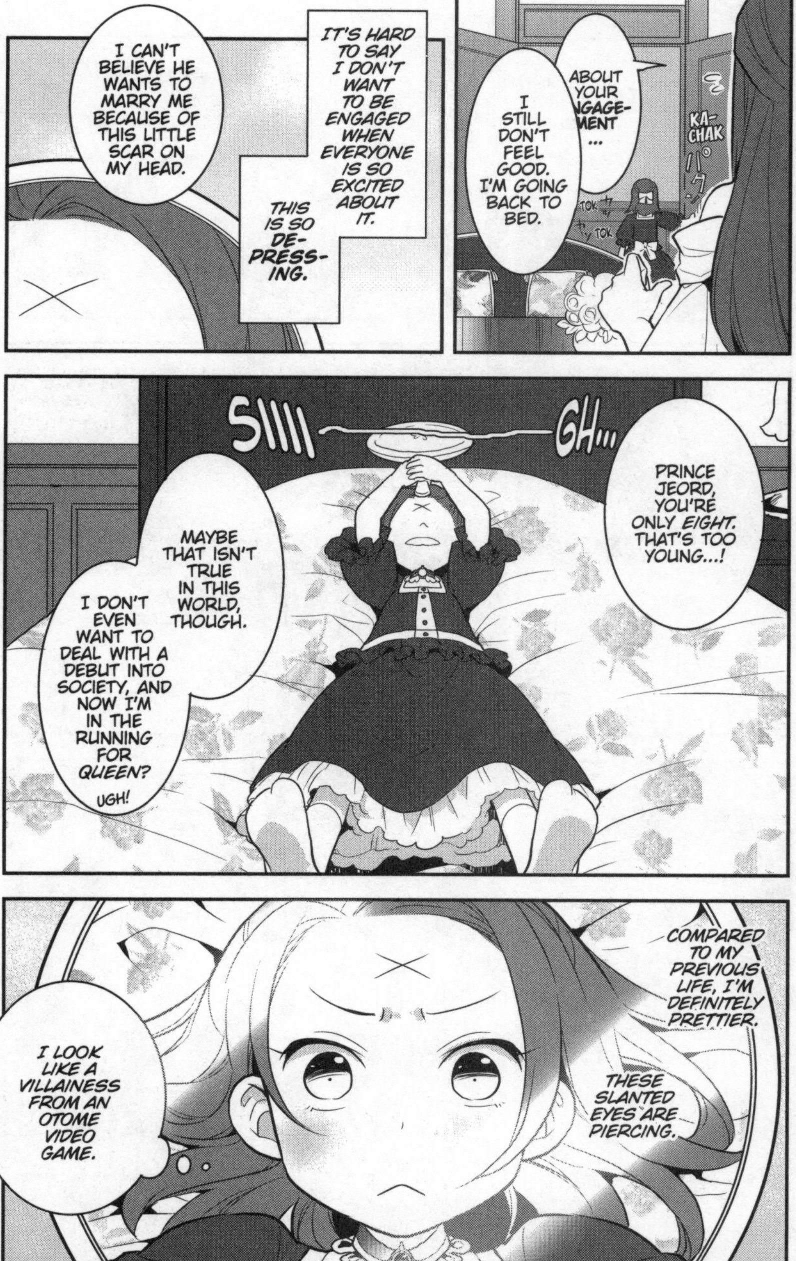
ABOUT YOUR ENGAGEMENT...
I STILL DON'T FEEL GOOD. I'M GOING BACK TO BED.
KA-CHAK
TOK
TOK
IT'S HARD TO SAY I DON'T WANT TO BE ENGAGED WHEN EVERYONE IS SO EXCITED ABOUT IT.
THIS IS SO DE-PRESS-ING.
I CAN'T BELIEVE HE WANTS TO MARRY ME BECAUSE OF THIS LITTLE SCAR ON MY HEAD.
SIIIII—GH...
PRINCE JEORD, YOU'RE ONLY EIGHT. THAT'S TOO YOUNG...!
MAYBE THAT ISN'T TRUE IN THIS WORLD, THOUGH.
I DON'T EVEN WANT TO DEAL WITH A DEBUT INTO SOCIETY, AND NOW I'M IN THE RUNNING FOR QUEEN?
UGH!
COMPARED TO MY PREVIOUS LIFE, I'M DEFINITELY PRETTIER.
THESE SLANTED EYES ARE PIERCING.
I LOOK LIKE A VILLAINESS FROM AN OTOME VIDEO GAME.

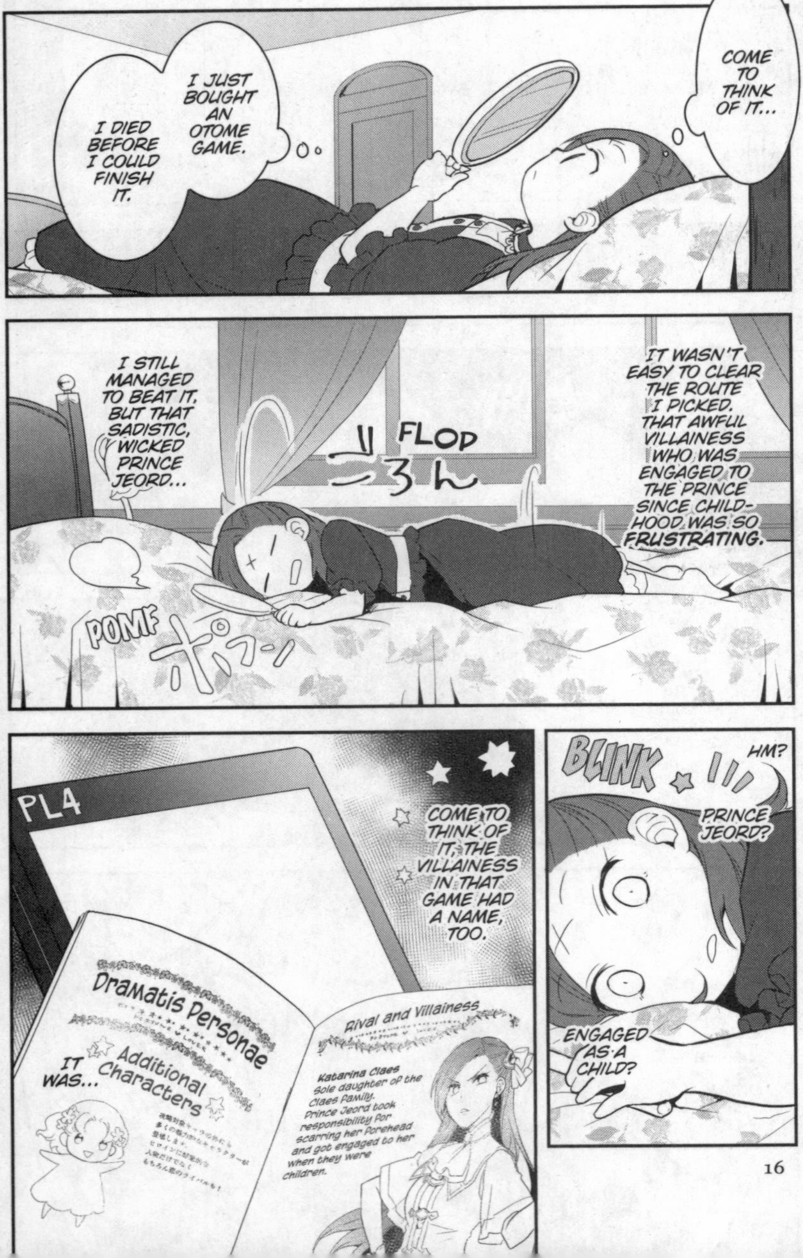
COME TO THINK OF IT...
I JUST BOUGHT AN OTOME GAME.
I DIED BEFORE I COULD FINISH IT.
IT WASN'T EASY TO CLEAR THE ROUTE I PICKED. THAT AWFUL VILLAINESS WHO WAS ENGAGED TO THE PRINCE SINCE CHILD-HOOD WAS SO FRUSTRATING.
FLOP
I STILL MANAGED TO BEAT IT, BUT THAT SADISTIC, WICKED PRINCE JEORD...
POMF
BLINK
HM?
PRINCE JEORD?
ENGAGED AS A CHILD?
COME TO THINK OF IT, THE VILLAINESS IN THAT GAME HAD A NAME, TOO.
PL4
Dramatis Personae
Additional Characters
IT WAS...
Rival and Villainess
Katarina Claes
Sole daughter of the Claes Family. Prince Jeord took responsibility for scarring her forehead and got engaged to her when they were children.

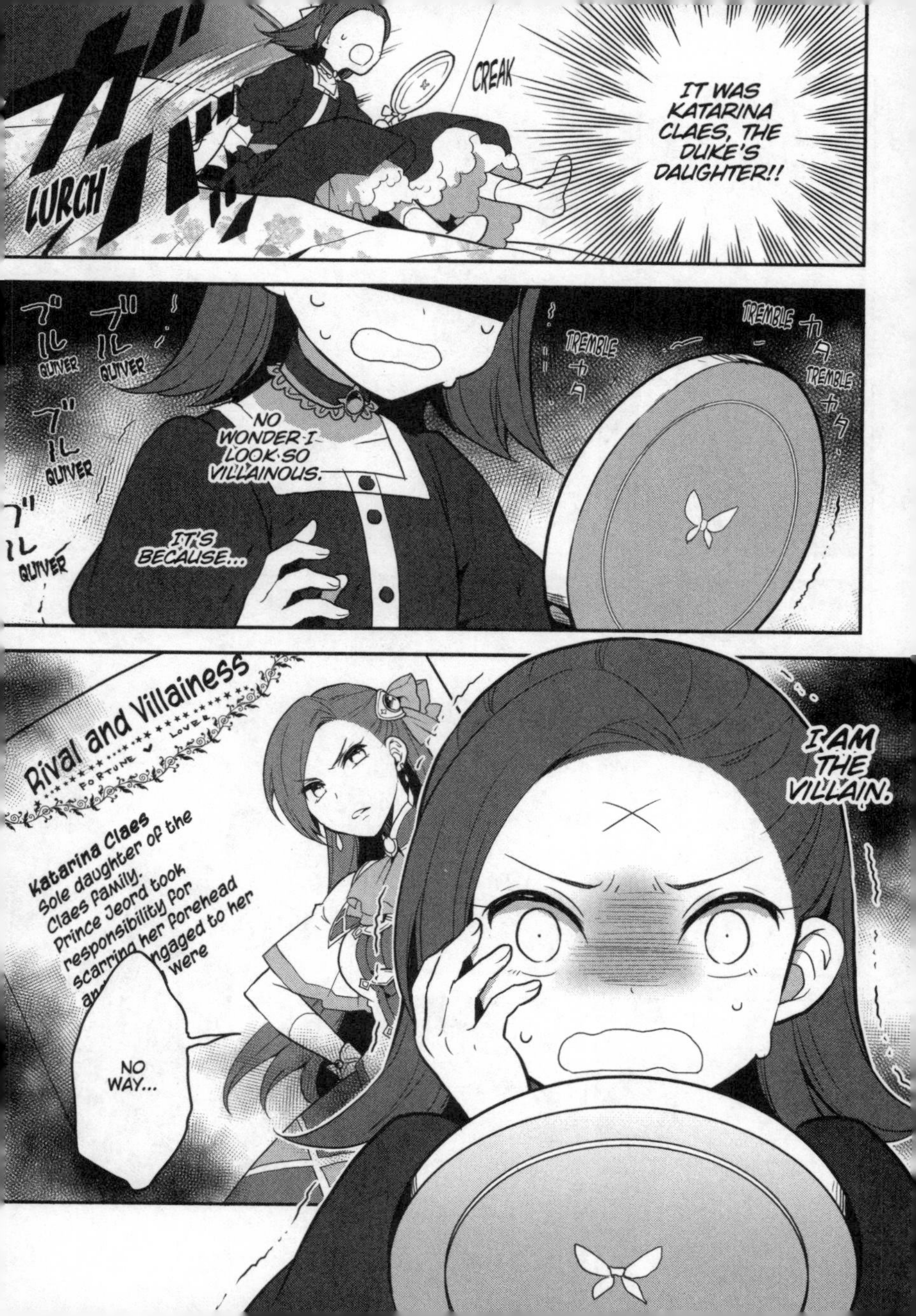
IT WAS KATARINA CLAES, THE DUKE'S DAUGHTER!!
CREAK
LURCH
カタ
TREMBLE
カタ
TREMBLE
カタ
TREMBLE
NO WONDER I LOOK SO VILLAINOUS.
IT'S BECAUSE...
ブル
QUIVER
ブル
QUIVER
ブル
QUIVER
ブル
QUIVER
I AM THE VILLAIN.
Rival and Villainess
FORTUNE ♥ LOVER
Katarina Claes
Sole daughter of the Claes family.
Prince Jeord took responsibility for scarring her forehead
NO WAY...

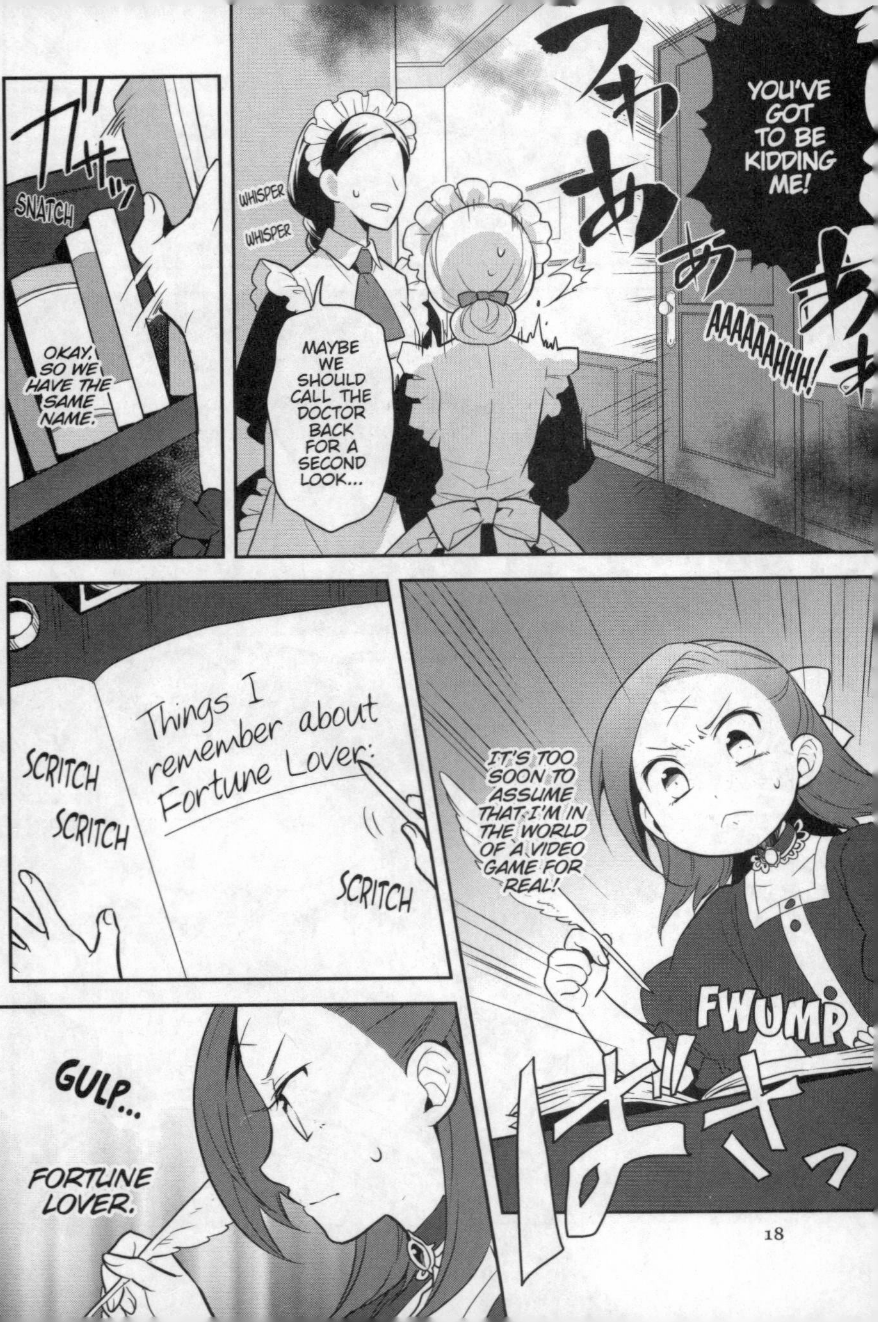
YOU'VE GOT TO BE KIDDING ME!
AAAAAAHHH!
WHISPER
WHISPER
MAYBE WE SHOULD CALL THE DOCTOR BACK FOR A SECOND LOOK...
SNATCH
OKAY, SO WE HAVE THE SAME NAME.
IT'S TOO SOON TO ASSUME THAT I'M IN THE WORLD OF A VIDEO GAME FOR REAL!
FWUMP
Things I remember about Fortune Lover:
SCRITCH
SCRITCH
SCRITCH
GULP...
FORTUNE LOVER.

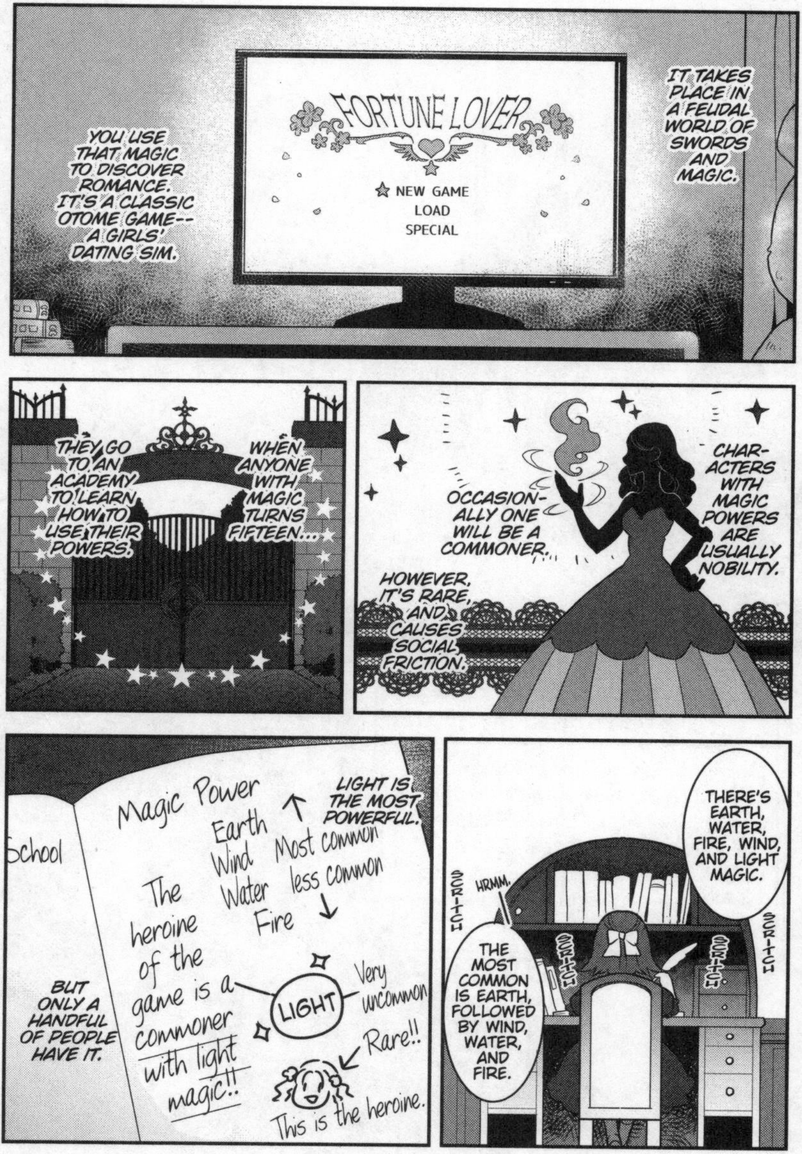
IT TAKES PLACE IN A FEUDAL WORLD OF SWORDS AND MAGIC.
FORTUNE LOVER
NEW GAME
LOAD
SPECIAL
YOU USE THAT MAGIC TO DISCOVER ROMANCE. IT'S A CLASSIC OTOME GAME--A GIRLS' DATING SIM.
CHAR-ACTERS WITH MAGIC POWERS ARE USUALLY NOBILITY.
OCCASION-ALLY ONE WILL BE A COMMONER.
HOWEVER, IT'S RARE, AND CAUSES SOCIAL FRICTION.
WHEN ANYONE WITH MAGIC TURNS FIFTEEN...
THEY GO TO AN ACADEMY TO LEARN HOW TO USE THEIR POWERS.
THERE'S EARTH, WATER, FIRE, WIND, AND LIGHT MAGIC.
SCRITCH
SCRITCH
HRMM.
SCRITCH
SCRITCH
THE MOST COMMON IS EARTH, FOLLOWED BY WIND, WATER, AND FIRE.
LIGHT IS THE MOST POWERFUL.
Magic Power
Earth
Wind
Water
Fire
Most common
less common
School
The heroine of the game is a commoner with light magic!!
LIGHT
Very uncommon
Rare!!
This is the heroine.
BUT ONLY A HANDFUL OF PEOPLE HAVE IT.

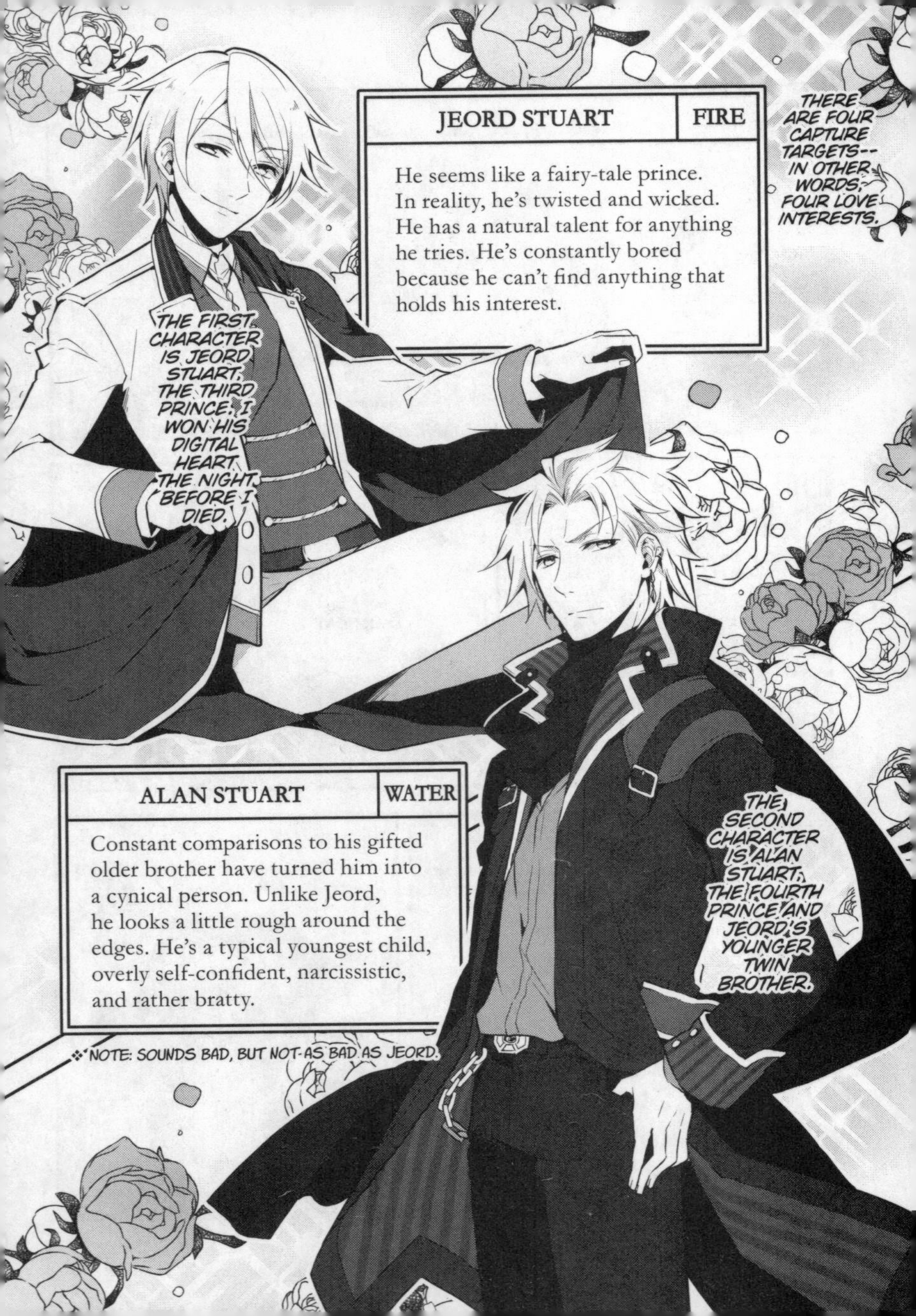
THERE ARE FOUR CAPTURE TARGETS-- IN OTHER WORDS, FOUR LOVE INTERESTS.
JEORD STUART
FIRE
He seems like a fairy-tale prince. In reality, he's twisted and wicked. He has a natural talent for anything he tries. He's constantly bored because he can't find anything that holds his interest.
THE FIRST CHARACTER IS JEORD STUART, THE THIRD PRINCE. I WON HIS DIGITAL HEART THE NIGHT BEFORE I DIED.
THE SECOND CHARACTER IS ALAN STUART, THE FOURTH PRINCE AND JEORD'S YOUNGER TWIN BROTHER.
ALAN STUART
WATER
Constant comparisons to his gifted older brother have turned him into a cynical person. Unlike Jeord, he looks a little rough around the edges. He's a typical youngest child, overly self-confident, narcissistic, and rather bratty.
❖NOTE: SOUNDS BAD, BUT NOT AS BAD AS JEORD.

THE THIRD GUY IS KEITH CLAES, AN ADOPTIVE BROTHER TO JEORD'S FIANCÉE, KATARINA CLAES.

KEITH CLAES	EARTH

He was adopted from a distant relative of the Claes family because of his powerful magic. However, he was ignored by his adoptive mother and sister and became a playboy to get attention.

THE LAST CHARACTER IS NICOL ASCART, JEORD AND ALAN'S OLD FRIEND AND SON OF THE PRIME MINISTER.

NICOL ASCART	WIND

The son of the prime minister, he grew up together with Jeord and Alan. He is the most practical person out of the four men. He's both bold and quiet.

BESIDES THE INDIVIDUAL ROUTES WITH THESE MEN, THE GAME ALSO FEATURES A "REVERSE HAREM" ROUTE WHERE YOU CAN WIN THE HEARTS OF ALL FOUR.

MOST IMPORTANTLY, THERE'S THE RIVAL CHARACTER, KATARINA CLAES.

AND...

SCRITCH

HER FATE IN THE GAME IS...

JEORD AND THE HEROINE GET MARRIED!

リンゴーン

BA-BING

Jeord Route

Good ♡ End

| Ends up exiled. | ← | Stripped of her rank for the crime. | ← | Extreme harassment of the heroine. |

Bad End

| Dies. | ← | Ends up defeated by Jeord in the fight. | ← | Attacks the heroine with a knife in a fit of jealousy. |

❖ NOTE: EVEN THOUGH IT WAS TO SAVE THE HEROINE'S LIFE, JEORD STILL KILLED HIS FIANCÉE. HE SPLITS UP WITH THE HEROINE AND LEAVES THE COUNTRY TO SEEK ATONEMENT.

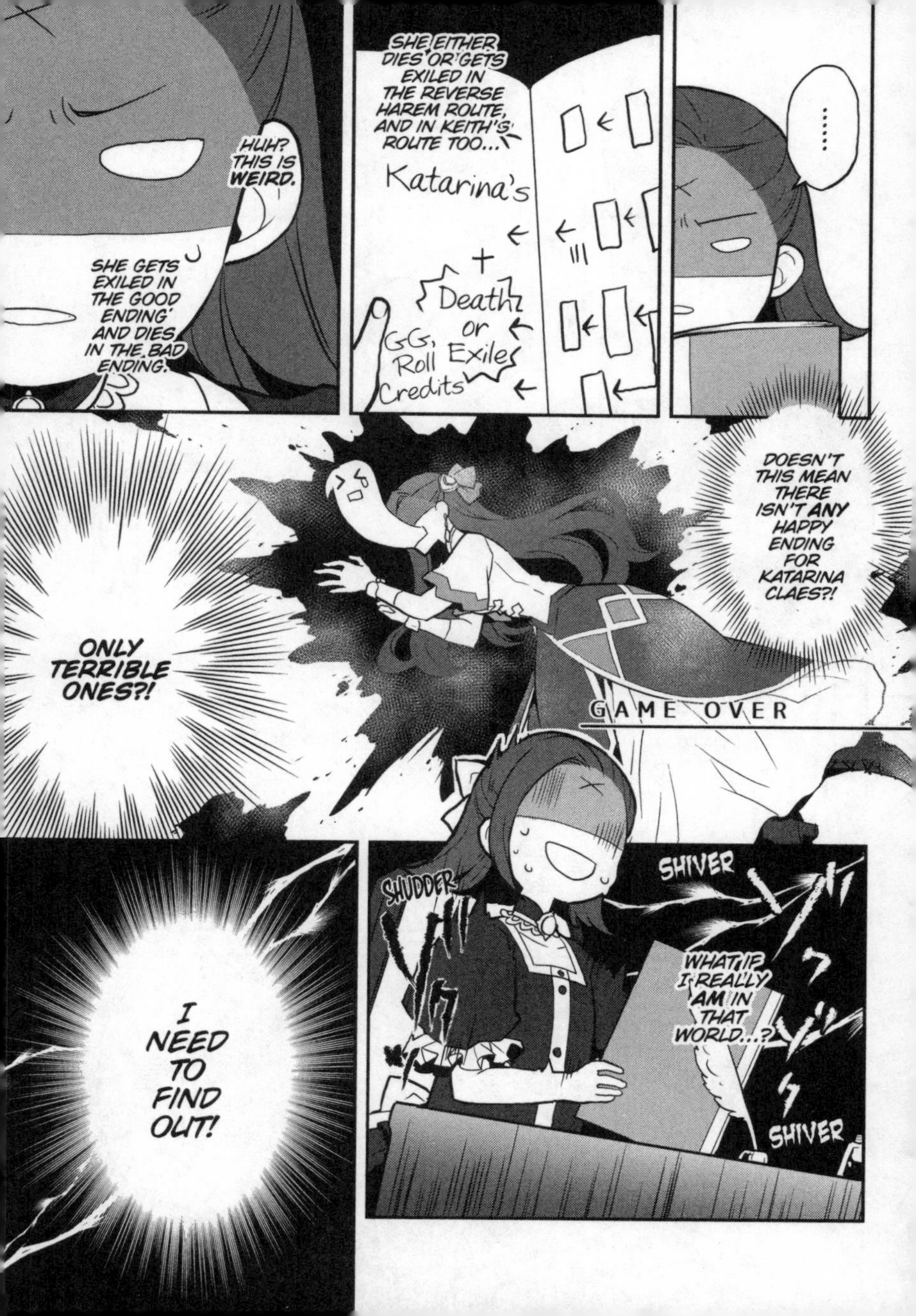
......
SHE EITHER DIES OR GETS EXILED IN THE REVERSE HAREM ROUTE, AND IN KEITH'S ROUTE TOO...
Katarina's
Death or Exile
GG, Roll Credits
HUH? THIS IS WEIRD.
SHE GETS EXILED IN THE GOOD ENDING AND DIES IN THE BAD ENDING.
DOESN'T THIS MEAN THERE ISN'T ANY HAPPY ENDING FOR KATARINA CLAES?!
GAME OVER
ONLY TERRIBLE ONES?!
SHIVER
WHAT IF I REALLY AM IN THAT WORLD...?
SHUDDER
SHIVER
I NEED TO FIND OUT!

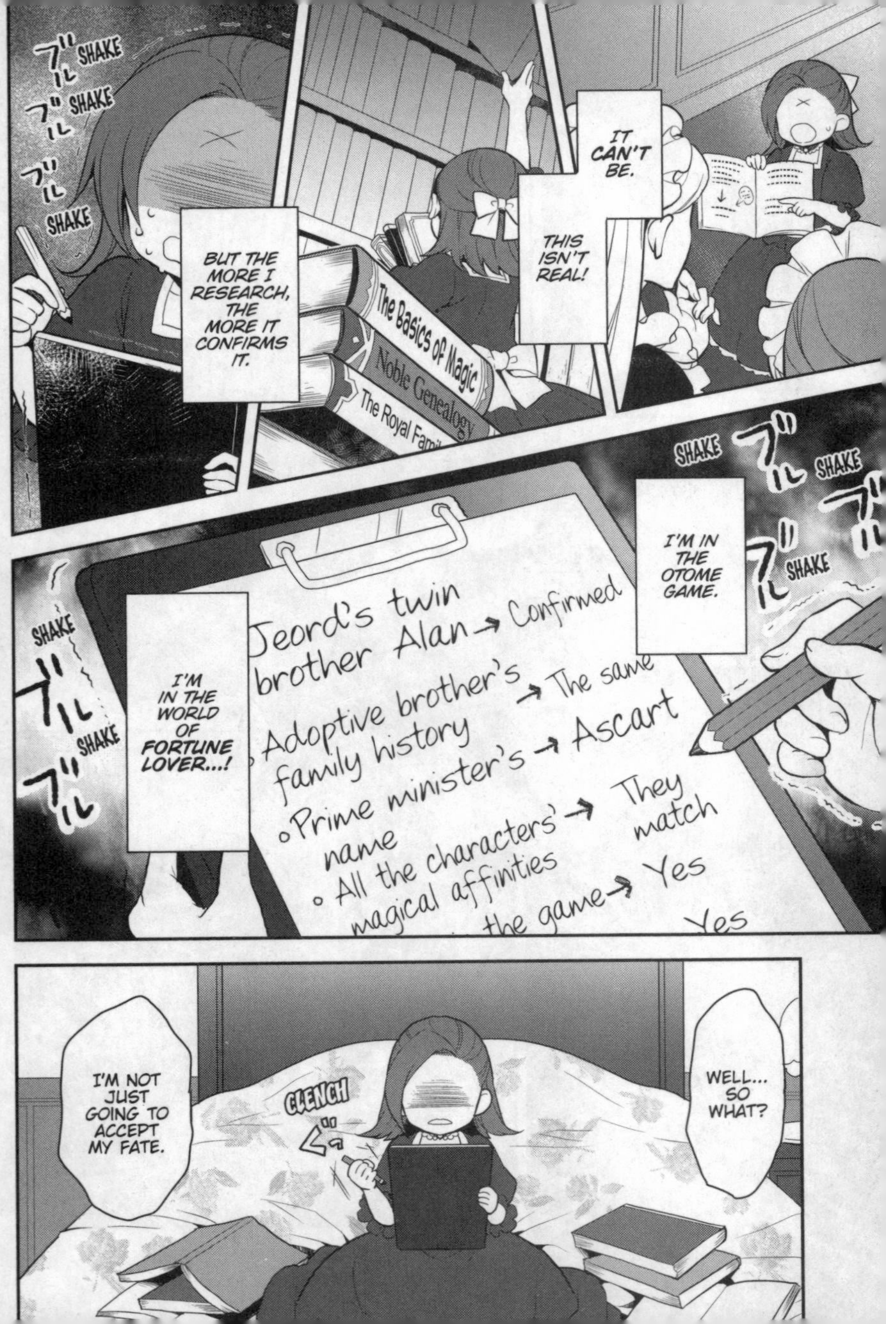
IT CAN'T BE.
THIS ISN'T REAL!
The Basics of Magic
Noble Genealogy
The Royal Famil
BUT THE MORE I RESEARCH, THE MORE IT CONFIRMS IT.
SHAKE
SHAKE
SHAKE
SHAKE
SHAKE
SHAKE
I'M IN THE OTOME GAME.
Jeord's twin brother Alan → Confirmed
∘ Adoptive brother's family history → The same
∘ Prime minister's name → Ascart
∘ All the characters' magical affinities the game → They match
Yes
Yes
I'M IN THE WORLD OF FORTUNE LOVER...!
SHAKE
SHAKE
WELL... SO WHAT?
CLENCH
I'M NOT JUST GOING TO ACCEPT MY FATE.

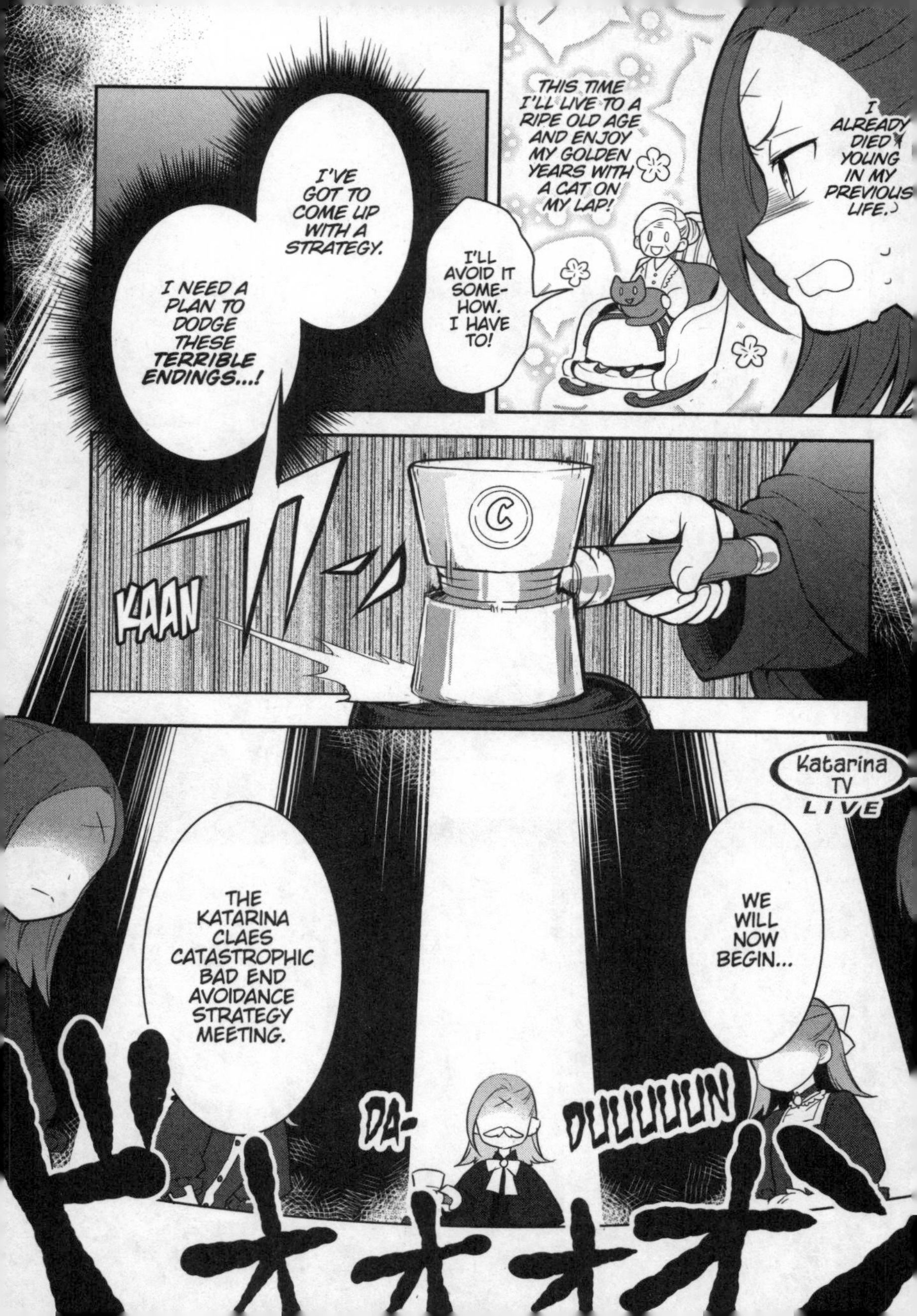
I ALREADY DIED YOUNG IN MY PREVIOUS LIFE.
THIS TIME I'LL LIVE TO A RIPE OLD AGE AND ENJOY MY GOLDEN YEARS WITH A CAT ON MY LAP!
I'LL AVOID IT SOMEHOW. I HAVE TO!
I'VE GOT TO COME UP WITH A STRATEGY.
I NEED A PLAN TO DODGE THESE TERRIBLE ENDINGS...!
KAAN
Katarina TV LIVE
WE WILL NOW BEGIN...
THE KATARINA CLAES CATASTROPHIC BAD END AVOIDANCE STRATEGY MEETING.
DA- DUUUUUN

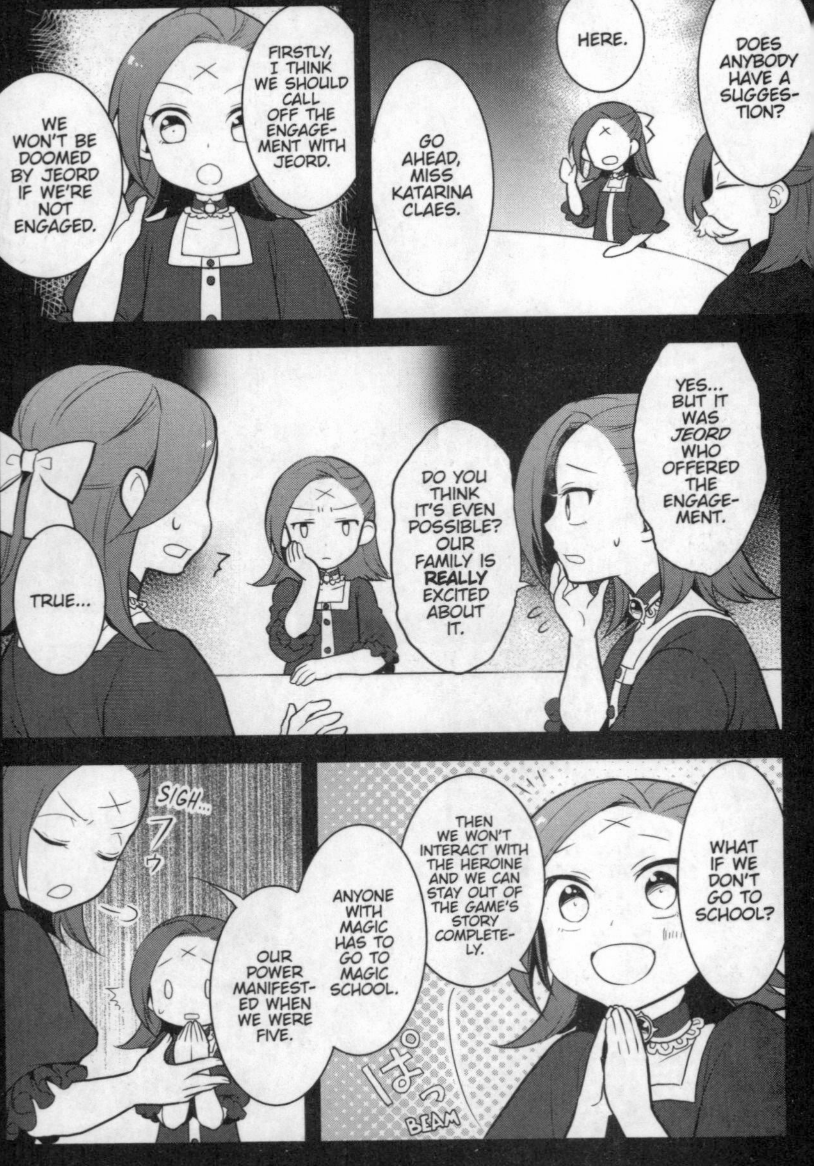
DOES ANYBODY HAVE A SUGGESTION?
HERE.
GO AHEAD, MISS KATARINA CLAES.
FIRSTLY, I THINK WE SHOULD CALL OFF THE ENGAGEMENT WITH JEORD.
WE WON'T BE DOOMED BY JEORD IF WE'RE NOT ENGAGED.
YES... BUT IT WAS *JEORD* WHO OFFERED THE ENGAGEMENT.
DO YOU THINK IT'S EVEN POSSIBLE? OUR FAMILY IS **REALLY** EXCITED ABOUT IT.
TRUE...
WHAT IF WE DON'T GO TO SCHOOL?
THEN WE WON'T INTERACT WITH THE HEROINE AND WE CAN STAY OUT OF THE GAME'S STORY COMPLETELY.
ぱっ
BEAM
SIGH...
フゥ
ANYONE WITH MAGIC HAS TO GO TO MAGIC SCHOOL.
OUR POWER MANIFESTED WHEN WE WERE FIVE.

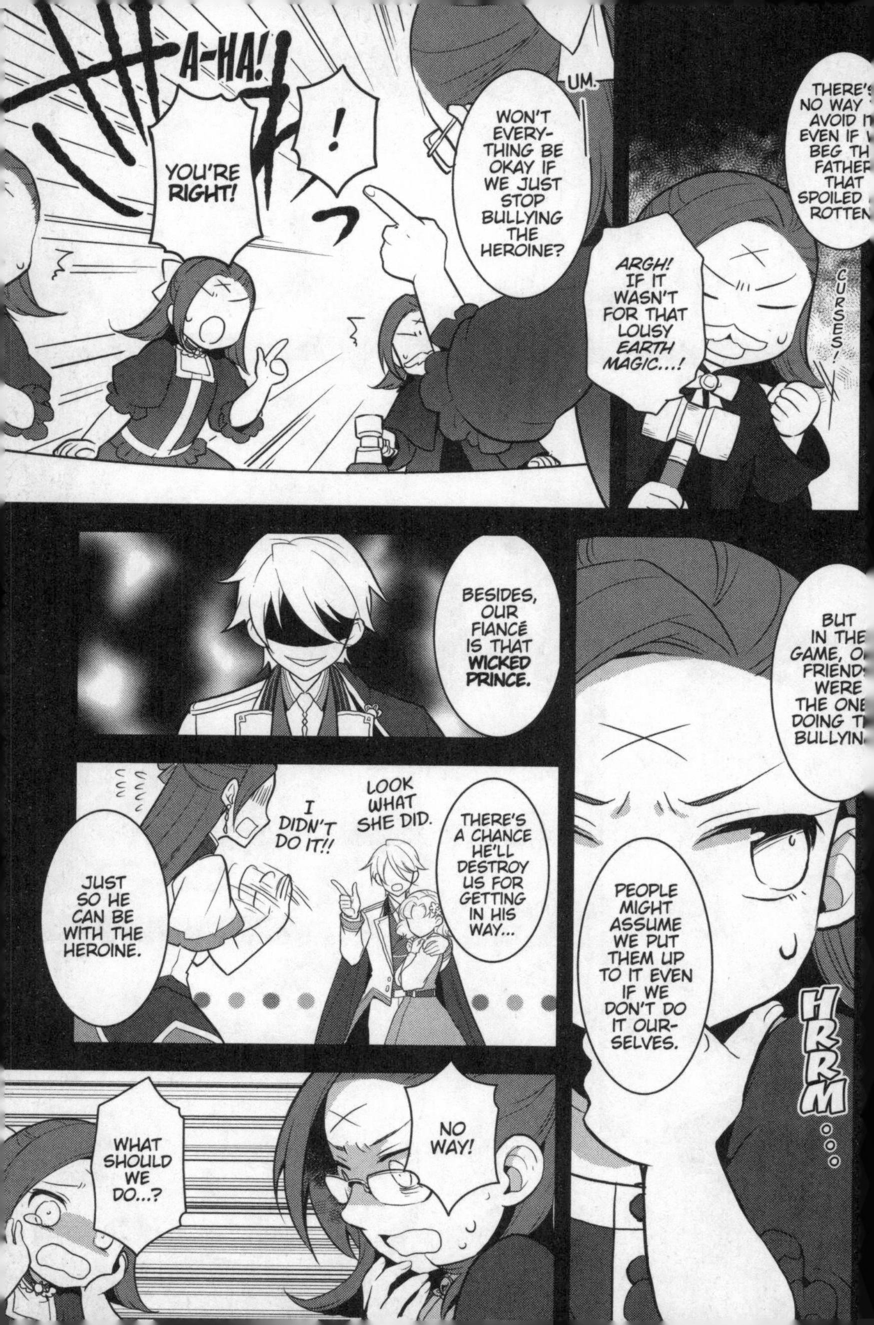
THERE'S NO WAY T AVOID IT EVEN IF W BEG TH FATHER THAT SPOILED ROTTEN
CURSES!
ARGH! IF IT WASN'T FOR THAT LOUSY EARTH MAGIC...!
UM.
WON'T EVERYTHING BE OKAY IF WE JUST STOP BULLYING THE HEROINE?
!
A-HA!
YOU'RE RIGHT!
BUT IN THE GAME, O FRIEND WERE THE ONE DOING T BULLYIN
PEOPLE MIGHT ASSUME WE PUT THEM UP TO IT EVEN IF WE DON'T DO IT OURSELVES.
HRRM...
BESIDES, OUR FIANCÉ IS THAT WICKED PRINCE.
THERE'S A CHANCE HE'LL DESTROY US FOR GETTING IN HIS WAY...
LOOK WHAT SHE DID.
I DIDN'T DO IT!!
JUST SO HE CAN BE WITH THE HEROINE.
NO WAY!
WHAT SHOULD WE DO...?

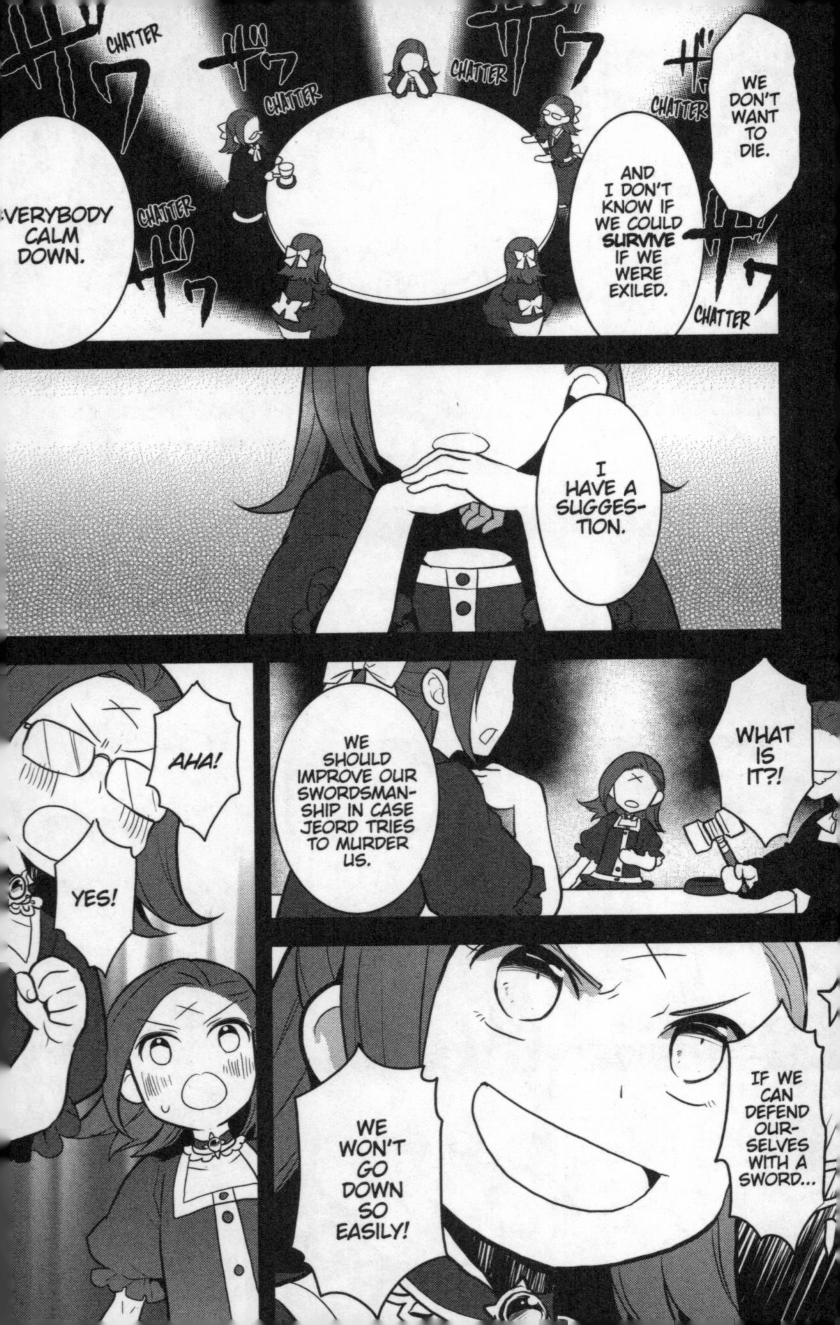
CHATTER
WE DON'T WANT TO DIE.
CHATTER
AND I DON'T KNOW IF WE COULD SURVIVE IF WE WERE EXILED.
CHATTER
CHATTER
CHATTER
CHATTER
CHATTER
EVERYBODY CALM DOWN.
I HAVE A SUGGES-TION.
WHAT IS IT?!
WE SHOULD IMPROVE OUR SWORDSMAN-SHIP IN CASE JEORD TRIES TO MURDER US.
IF WE CAN DEFEND OUR-SELVES WITH A SWORD...
WE WON'T GO DOWN SO EASILY!
AHA!
YES!

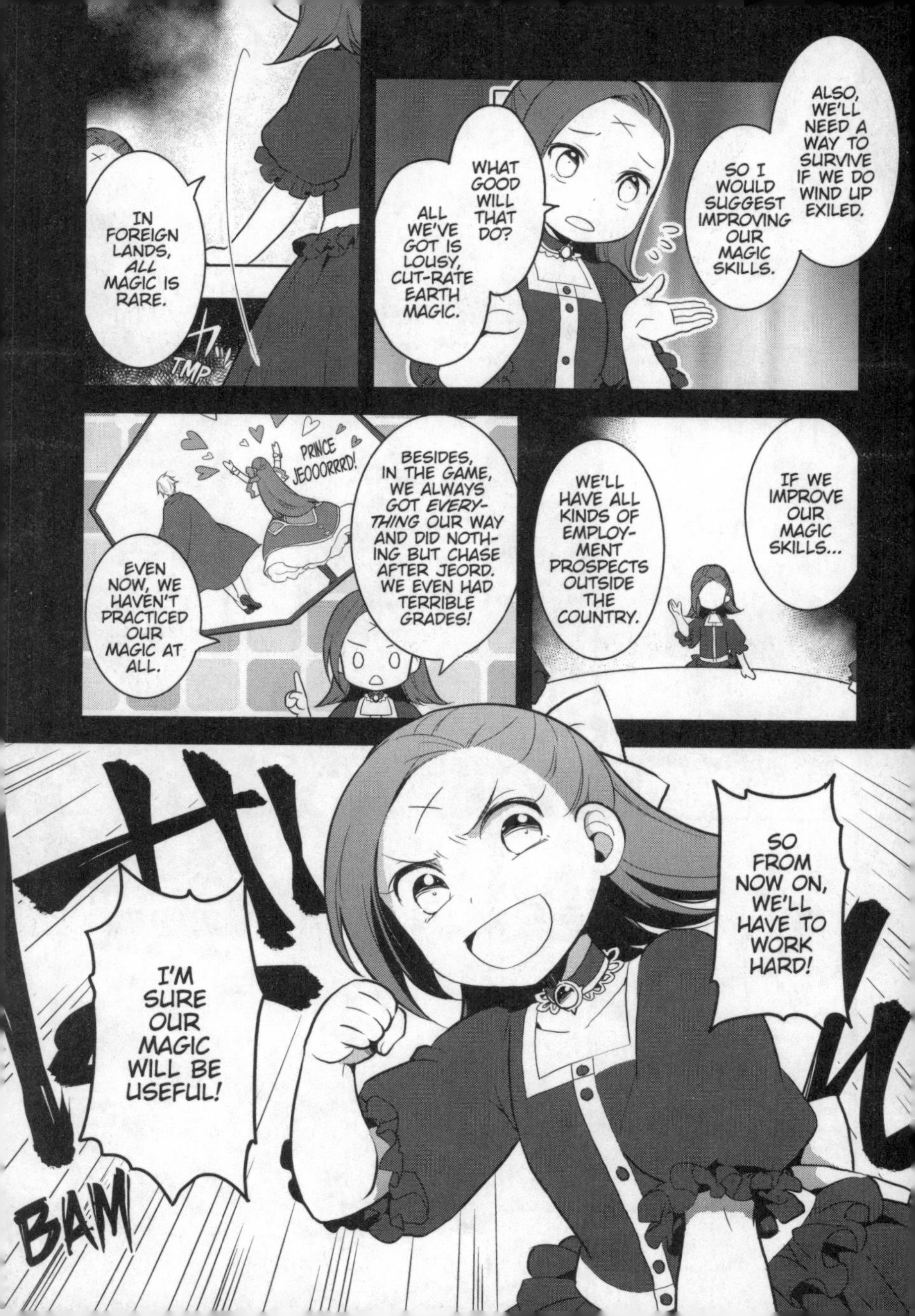

ALSO, WE'LL NEED A WAY TO SURVIVE IF WE DO WIND UP EXILED.
SO I WOULD SUGGEST IMPROVING OUR MAGIC SKILLS.
WHAT GOOD WILL THAT DO?
ALL WE'VE GOT IS LOUSY, CUT-RATE EARTH MAGIC.
IN FOREIGN LANDS, *ALL* MAGIC IS RARE.
TMP
IF WE IMPROVE OUR MAGIC SKILLS...
WE'LL HAVE ALL KINDS OF EMPLOYMENT PROSPECTS OUTSIDE THE COUNTRY.
BESIDES, IN THE GAME, WE ALWAYS GOT *EVERYTHING* OUR WAY AND DID NOTHING BUT CHASE AFTER JEORD. WE EVEN HAD TERRIBLE GRADES!
PRINCE JEOOORRRD!
EVEN NOW, WE HAVEN'T PRACTICED OUR MAGIC AT ALL.
SO FROM NOW ON, WE'LL HAVE TO WORK HARD!
I'M SURE OUR MAGIC WILL BE USEFUL!
BAM

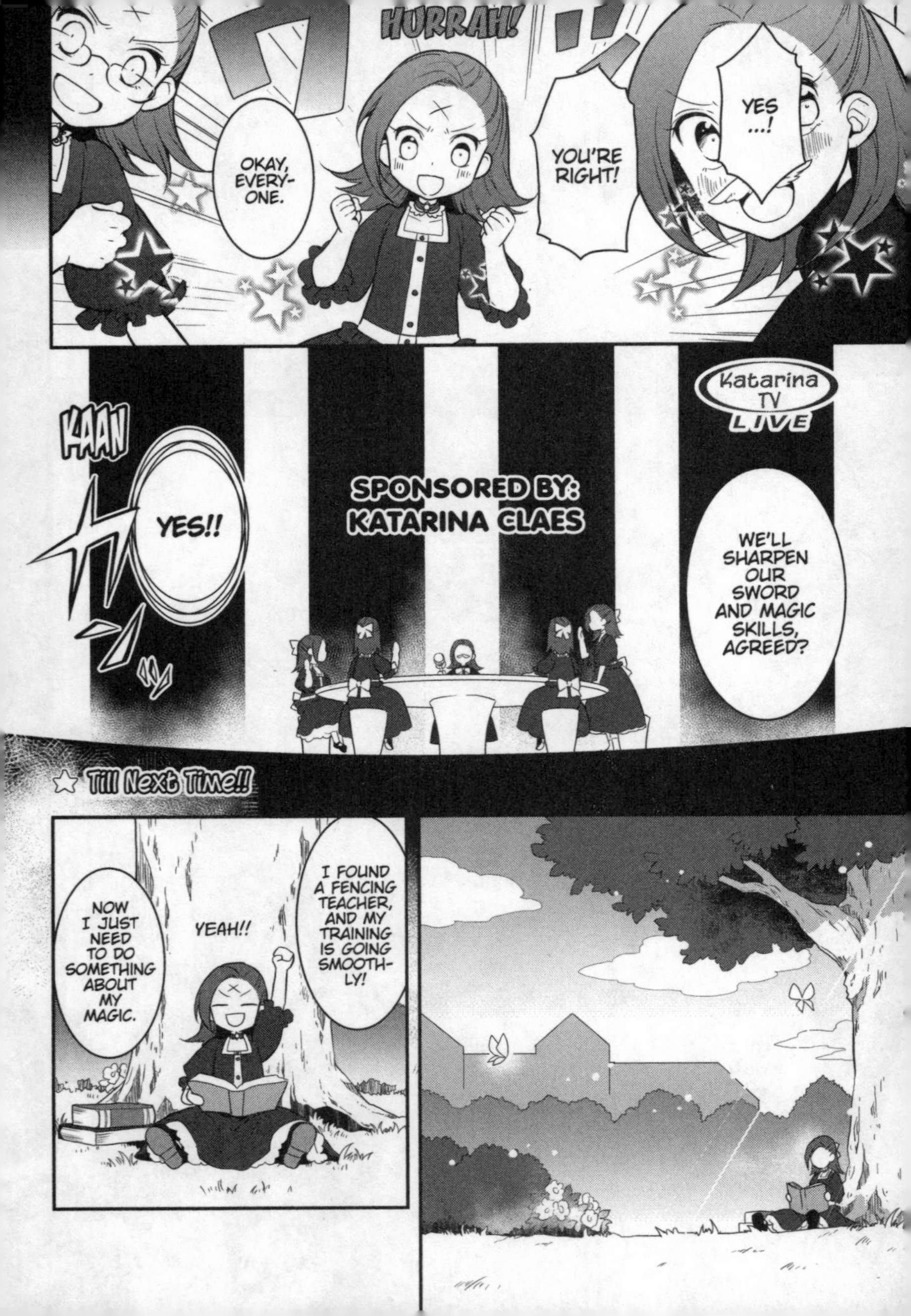
YES ...!
HURRAH!
YOU'RE RIGHT!
OKAY, EVERY-ONE.
Katarina TV LIVE
WE'LL SHARPEN OUR SWORD AND MAGIC SKILLS, AGREED?
SPONSORED BY: KATARINA CLAES
YES!!
KAAN
Till Next Time!!
I FOUND A FENCING TEACHER, AND MY TRAINING IS GOING SMOOTH-LY!
YEAH!!
NOW I JUST NEED TO DO SOMETHING ABOUT MY MAGIC.

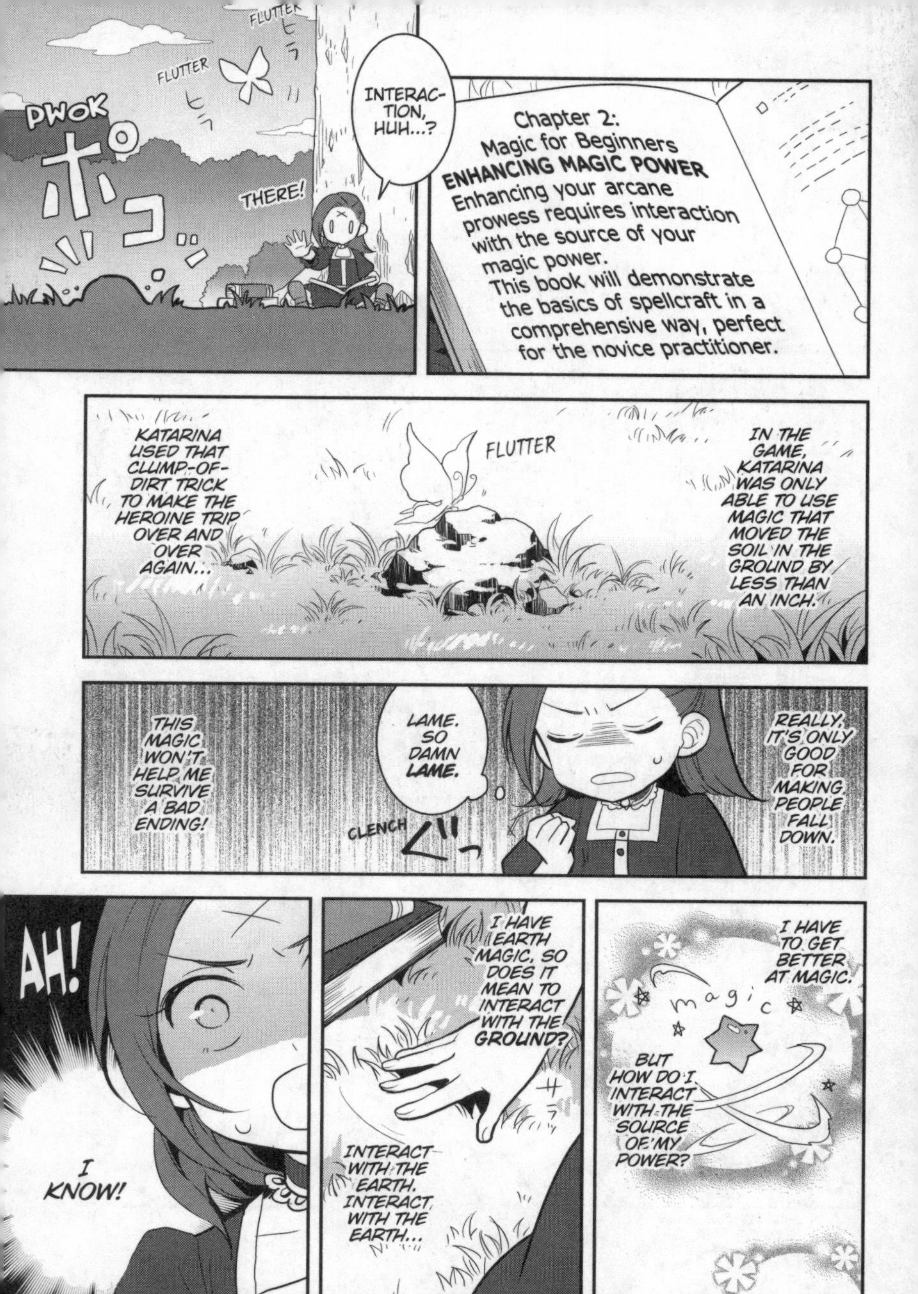
Chapter 2:
Magic for Beginners
ENHANCING MAGIC POWER
Enhancing your arcane prowess requires interaction with the source of your magic power.
This book will demonstrate the basics of spellcraft in a comprehensive way, perfect for the novice practitioner.
INTERACTION, HUH...?
FLUTTER
FLUTTER
THERE!
PWOK
IN THE GAME, KATARINA WAS ONLY ABLE TO USE MAGIC THAT MOVED THE SOIL IN THE GROUND BY LESS THAN AN INCH.
FLUTTER
KATARINA USED THAT CLUMP-OF-DIRT TRICK TO MAKE THE HEROINE TRIP OVER AND OVER AGAIN...
REALLY, IT'S ONLY GOOD FOR MAKING PEOPLE FALL DOWN.
LAME. SO DAMN LAME.
THIS MAGIC WON'T HELP ME SURVIVE A BAD ENDING!
CLENCH
I HAVE TO GET BETTER AT MAGIC.
magic
BUT HOW DO I INTERACT WITH THE SOURCE OF MY POWER?
I HAVE EARTH MAGIC, SO DOES IT MEAN TO INTERACT WITH THE GROUND?
INTERACT WITH THE EARTH. INTERACT WITH THE EARTH...
AH!
I KNOW!

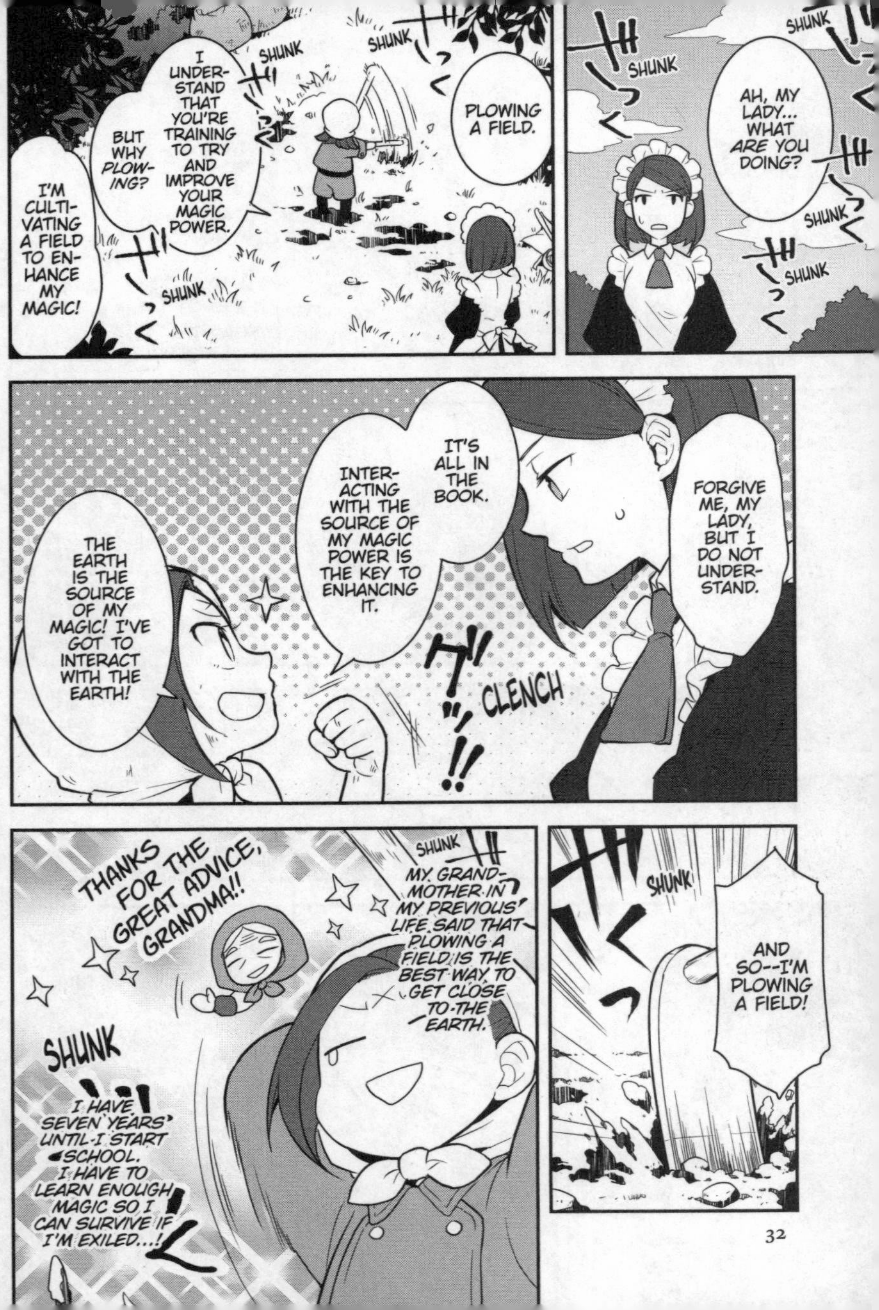
SHUNK
SHUNK
AH, MY LADY... WHAT ARE YOU DOING?
SHUNK
SHUNK
SHUNK
SHUNK
PLOWING A FIELD.
SHUNK
I UNDERSTAND THAT YOU'RE TRAINING TO TRY AND IMPROVE YOUR MAGIC POWER.
BUT WHY PLOWING?
I'M CULTIVATING A FIELD TO ENHANCE MY MAGIC!
SHUNK
FORGIVE ME, MY LADY, BUT I DO NOT UNDERSTAND.
IT'S ALL IN THE BOOK.
INTERACTING WITH THE SOURCE OF MY MAGIC POWER IS THE KEY TO ENHANCING IT.
THE EARTH IS THE SOURCE OF MY MAGIC! I'VE GOT TO INTERACT WITH THE EARTH!
CLENCH
SHUNK
AND SO--I'M PLOWING A FIELD!
SHUNK
MY GRANDMOTHER IN MY PREVIOUS LIFE SAID THAT PLOWING A FIELD IS THE BEST WAY TO GET CLOSE TO THE EARTH.
THANKS FOR THE GREAT ADVICE, GRANDMA!!
SHUNK
I HAVE SEVEN YEARS UNTIL I START SCHOOL. I HAVE TO LEARN ENOUGH MAGIC SO I CAN SURVIVE IF I'M EXILED...!
SHUNK

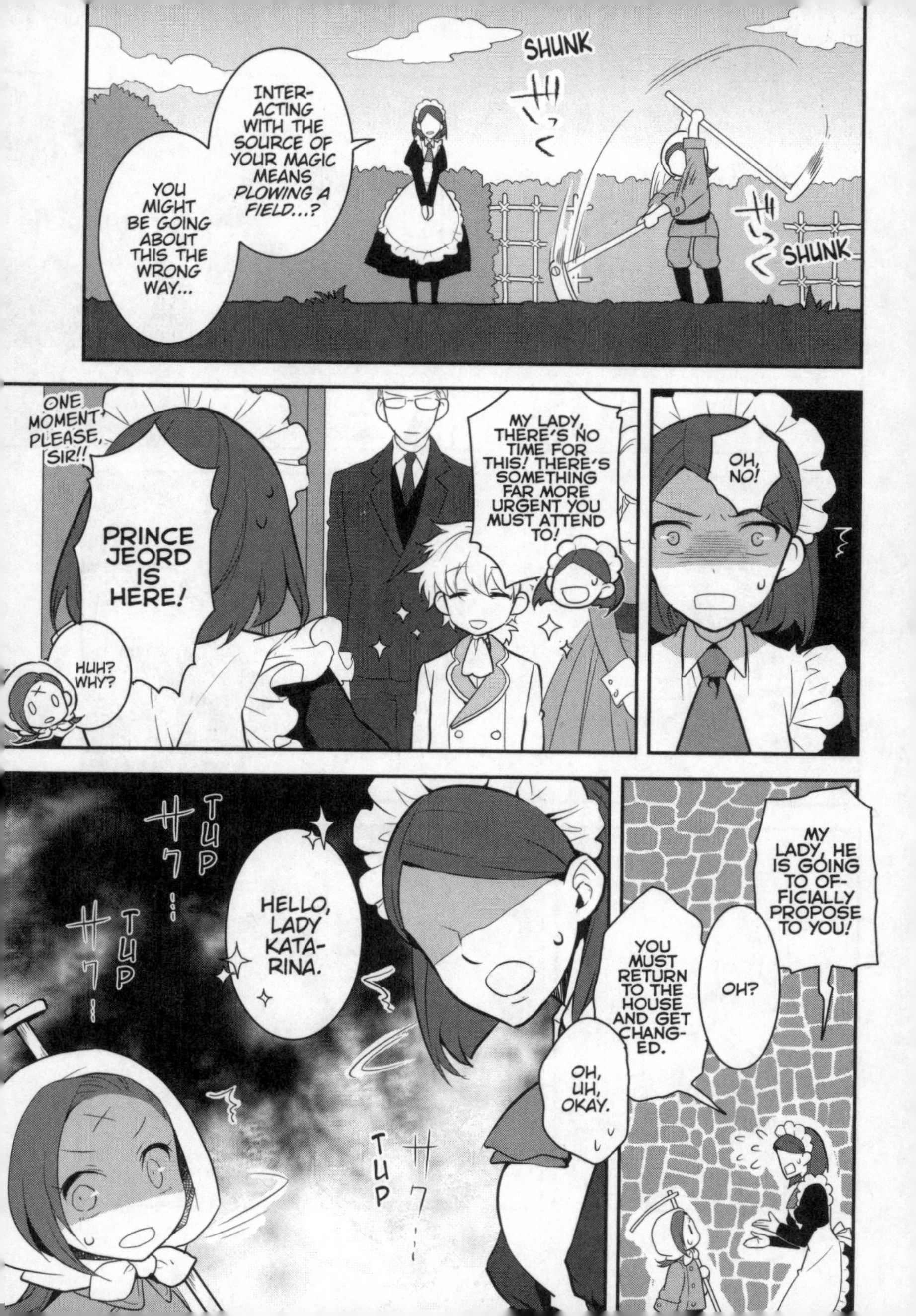
SHUNK
INTER-ACTING WITH THE SOURCE OF YOUR MAGIC MEANS PLOWING A FIELD...?
YOU MIGHT BE GOING ABOUT THIS THE WRONG WAY...
SHUNK
OH, NO!
MY LADY, THERE'S NO TIME FOR THIS! THERE'S SOMETHING FAR MORE URGENT YOU MUST ATTEND TO!
ONE MOMENT PLEASE, SIR!!
PRINCE JEORD IS HERE!
HUH? WHY?
MY LADY, HE IS GOING TO OF-FICIALLY PROPOSE TO YOU!
OH?
YOU MUST RETURN TO THE HOUSE AND GET CHANG-ED.
OH, UH, OKAY.
TUP
TUP
HELLO, LADY KATA-RINA.
TUP

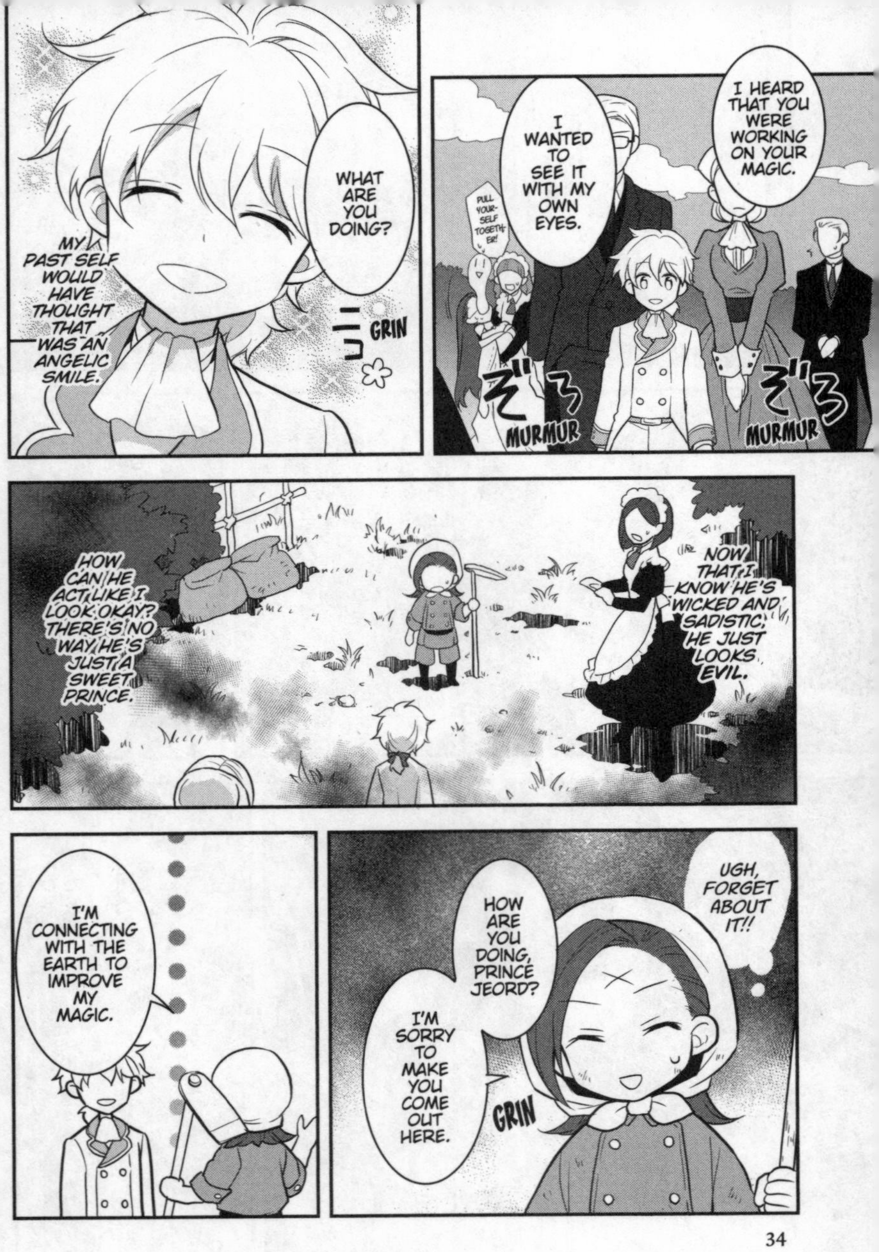
I HEARD THAT YOU WERE WORKING ON YOUR MAGIC.
I WANTED TO SEE IT WITH MY OWN EYES.
PULL YOURSELF TOGETHER!
ぞろ
MURMUR
ぞろ
MURMUR
WHAT ARE YOU DOING?
MY PAST SELF WOULD HAVE THOUGHT THAT WAS AN ANGELIC SMILE.
ニコ
GRIN
NOW THAT I KNOW HE'S WICKED AND SADISTIC, HE JUST LOOKS EVIL.
HOW CAN HE ACT LIKE I LOOK OKAY? THERE'S NO WAY HE'S JUST A SWEET PRINCE.
UGH, FORGET ABOUT IT!!
HOW ARE YOU DOING, PRINCE JEORD?
I'M SORRY TO MAKE YOU COME OUT HERE.
GRIN
I'M CONNECTING WITH THE EARTH TO IMPROVE MY MAGIC.

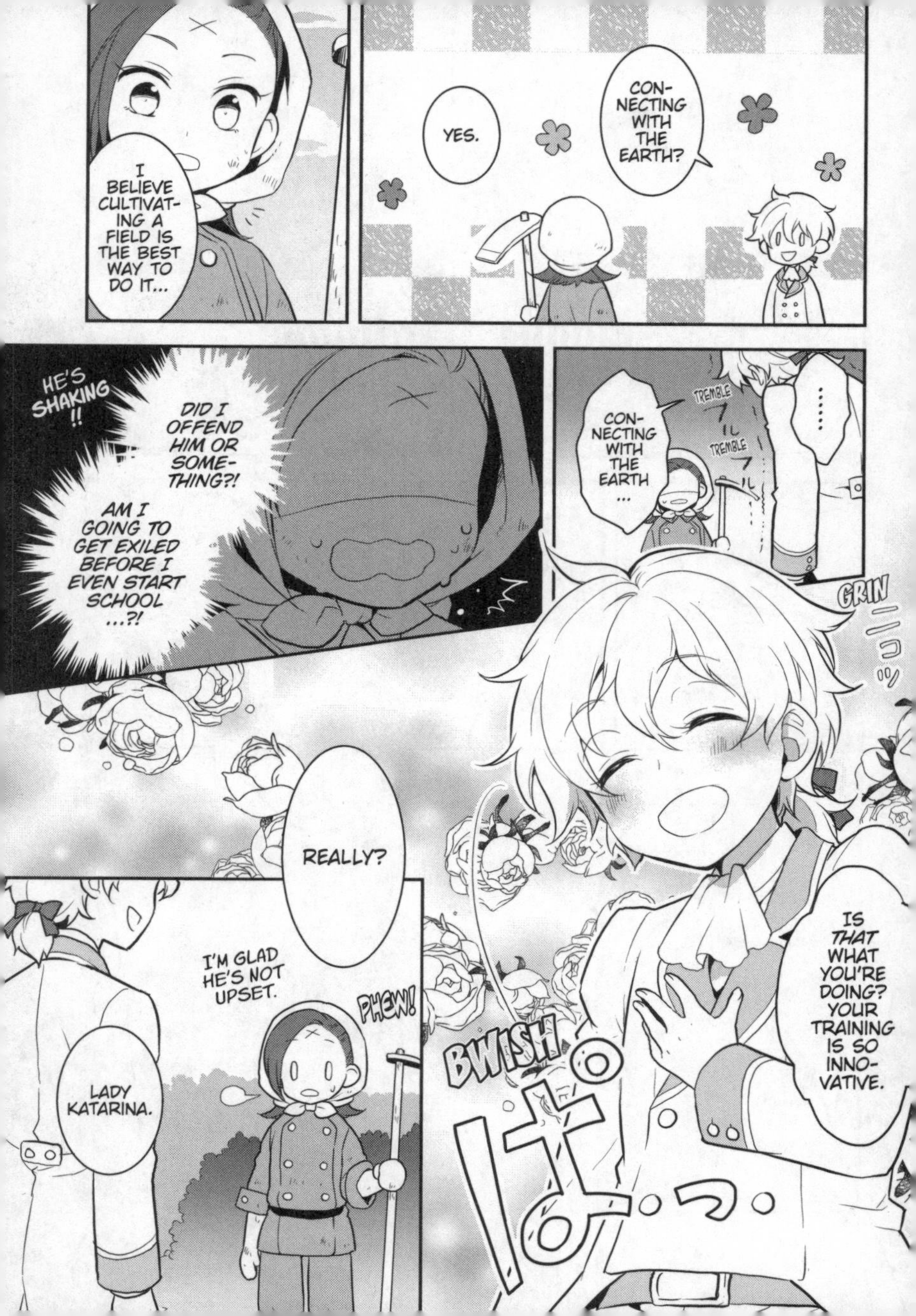
CON-NECTING WITH THE EARTH?
YES.
I BELIEVE CULTIVAT-ING A FIELD IS THE BEST WAY TO DO IT...
......
TREMBLE
TREMBLE
CON-NECTING WITH THE EARTH...
HE'S SHAKING!!
DID I OFFEND HIM OR SOME-THING?!
AM I GOING TO GET EXILED BEFORE I EVEN START SCHOOL...?!
GRIN
IS *THAT* WHAT YOU'RE DOING? YOUR TRAINING IS SO INNO-VATIVE.
BWISH
REALLY?
PHEW!
I'M GLAD HE'S NOT UPSET.
LADY KATARINA.

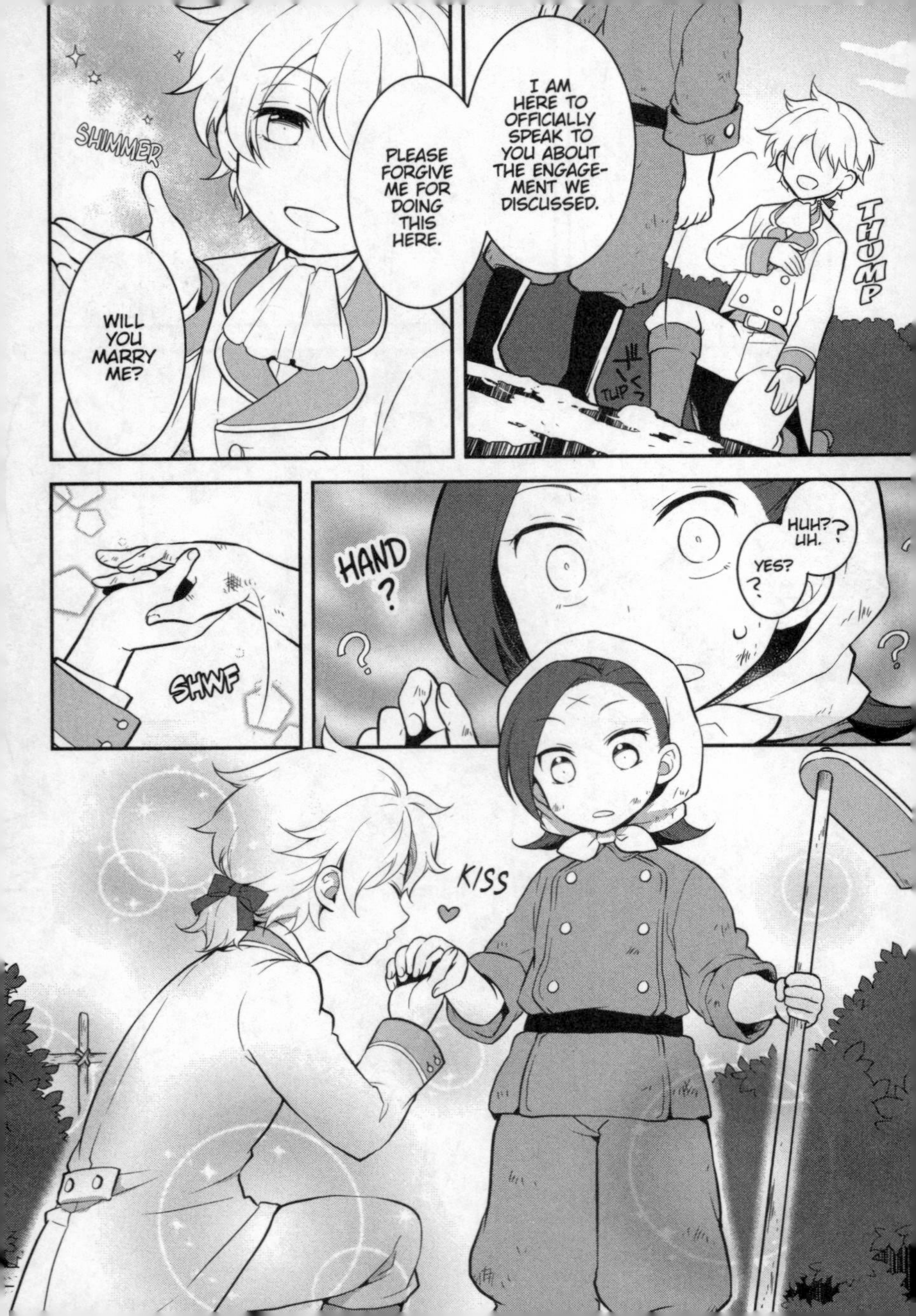
I AM HERE TO OFFICIALLY SPEAK TO YOU ABOUT THE ENGAGEMENT WE DISCUSSED.
THUMP
TUP
PLEASE FORGIVE ME FOR DOING THIS HERE.
SHIMMER
WILL YOU MARRY ME?
HUH? UH.
YES?
HAND?
SHWF
KISS

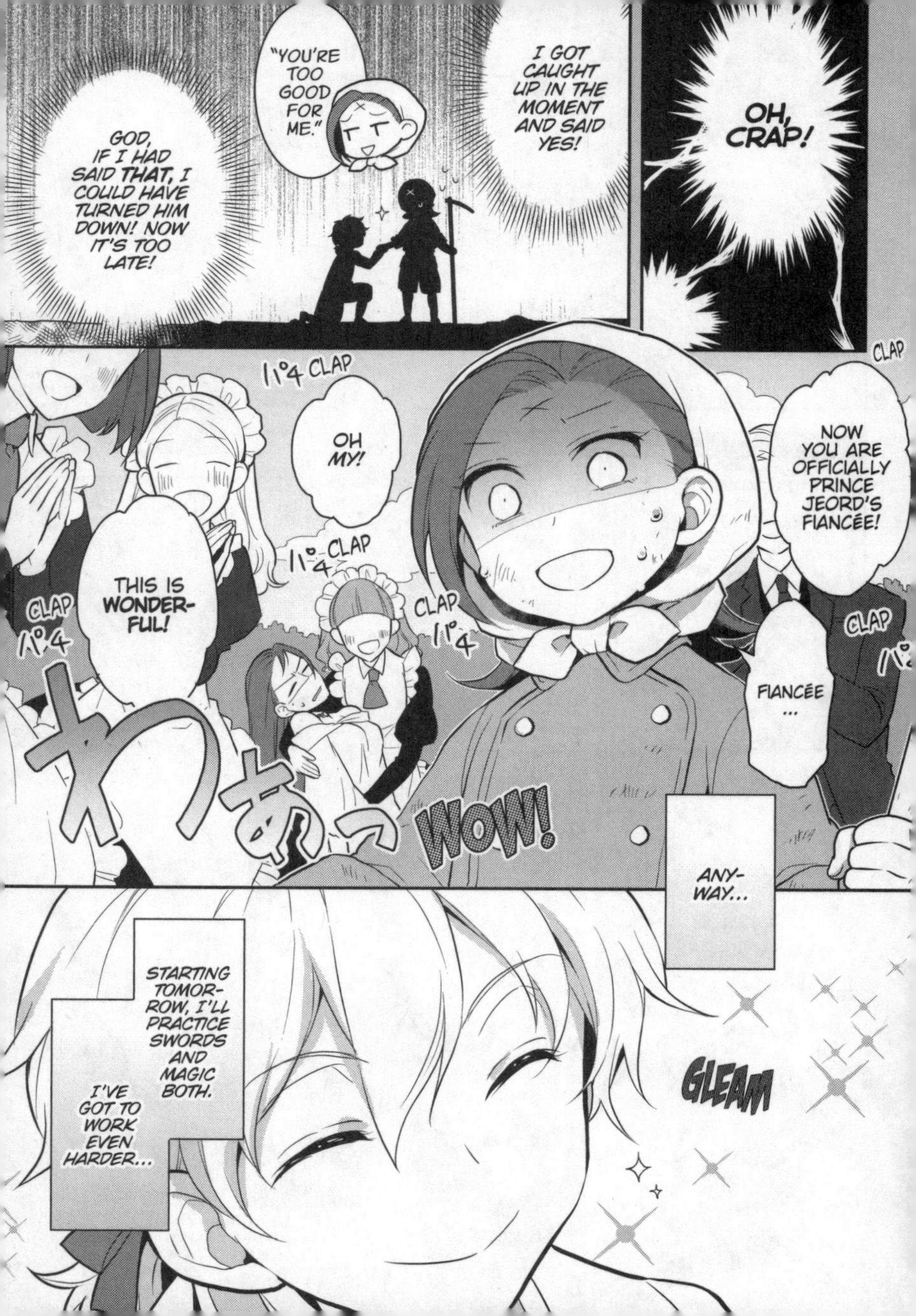
OH, CRAP!
I GOT CAUGHT UP IN THE MOMENT AND SAID YES!
"YOU'RE TOO GOOD FOR ME."
GOD, IF I HAD SAID THAT, I COULD HAVE TURNED HIM DOWN! NOW IT'S TOO LATE!
CLAP
NOW YOU ARE OFFICIALLY PRINCE JEORD'S FIANCÉE!
CLAP
FIANCÉE...
CLAP
OH MY!
CLAP
CLAP
THIS IS WONDERFUL!
CLAP
WOW!
ANYWAY...
GLEAM
STARTING TOMORROW, I'LL PRACTICE SWORDS AND MAGIC BOTH.
I'VE GOT TO WORK EVEN HARDER...

Chapter 2

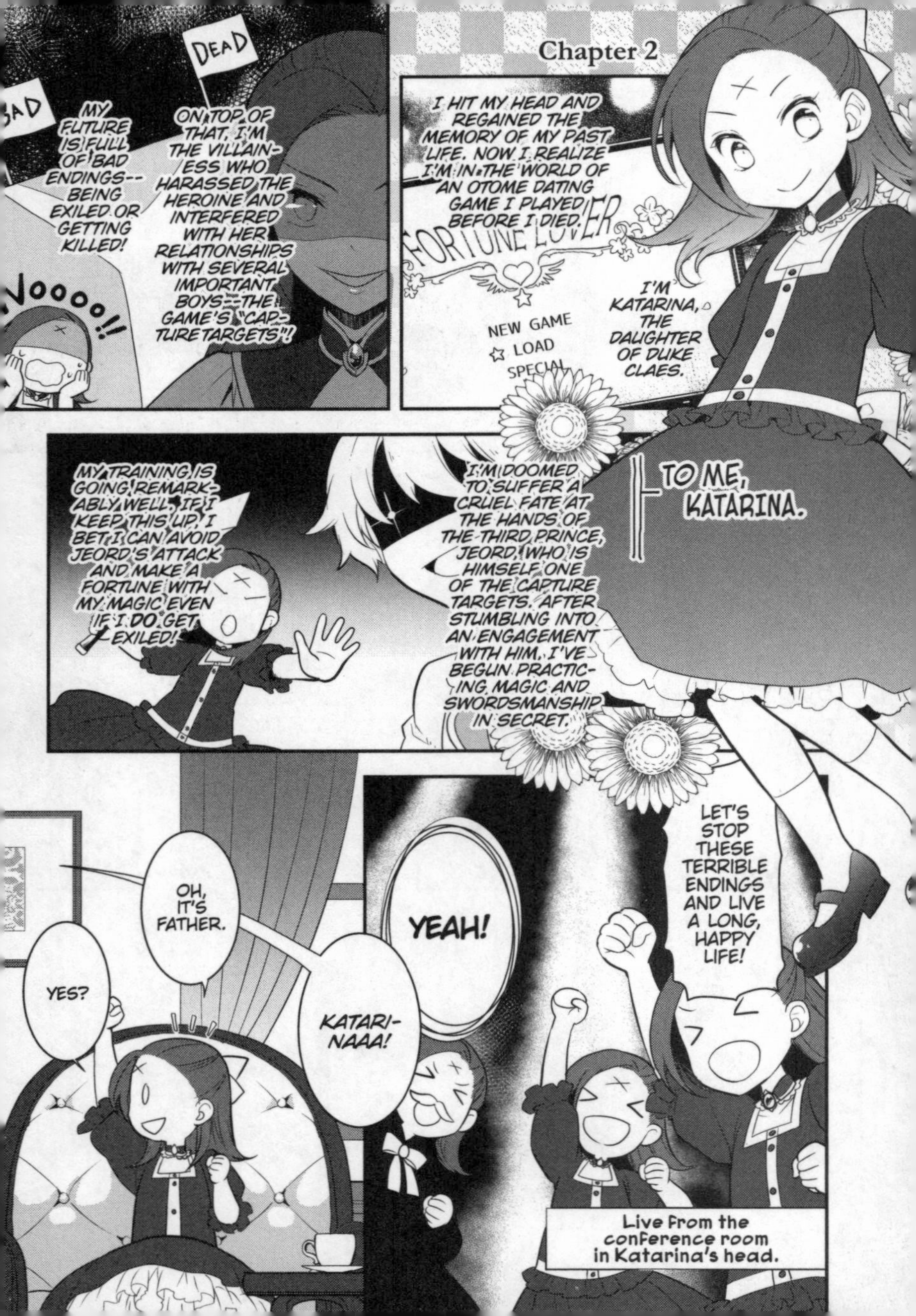
I HIT MY HEAD AND REGAINED THE MEMORY OF MY PAST LIFE. NOW I REALIZE I'M IN THE WORLD OF AN OTOME DATING GAME I PLAYED BEFORE I DIED.
FORTUNE LOVER
NEW GAME
☆ LOAD
SPECIAL
I'M KATARINA, THE DAUGHTER OF DUKE CLAES.
DEAD
ON TOP OF THAT, I'M THE VILLAINESS WHO HARASSED THE HEROINE AND INTERFERED WITH HER RELATIONSHIPS WITH SEVERAL IMPORTANT BOYS--THE GAME'S "CAPTURE TARGETS"!
BAD
MY FUTURE IS FULL OF BAD ENDINGS--BEING EXILED OR GETTING KILLED!
Noooo!!
TO ME, KATARINA.
I'M DOOMED TO SUFFER A CRUEL FATE AT THE HANDS OF THE THIRD PRINCE, JEORD, WHO IS HIMSELF ONE OF THE CAPTURE TARGETS. AFTER STUMBLING INTO AN ENGAGEMENT WITH HIM, I'VE BEGUN PRACTICING MAGIC AND SWORDSMANSHIP IN SECRET.
MY TRAINING IS GOING REMARKABLY WELL. IF I KEEP THIS UP, I BET I CAN AVOID JEORD'S ATTACK AND MAKE A FORTUNE WITH MY MAGIC EVEN IF I DO GET EXILED!
LET'S STOP THESE TERRIBLE ENDINGS AND LIVE A LONG, HAPPY LIFE!
YEAH!
Live from the conference room in Katarina's head.
KATARI-NAAA!
OH, IT'S FATHER.
YES?

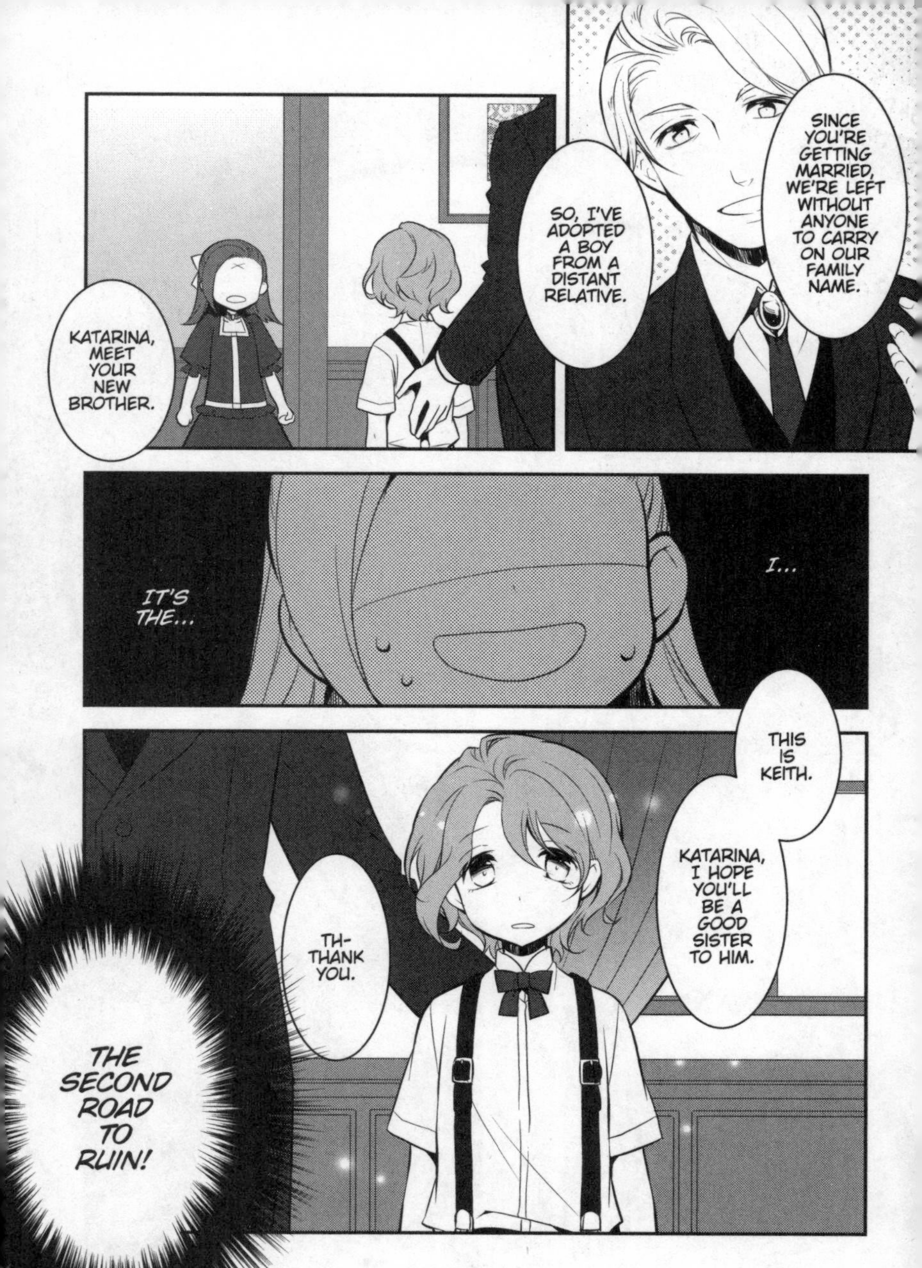
SINCE YOU'RE GETTING MARRIED, WE'RE LEFT WITHOUT ANYONE TO CARRY ON OUR FAMILY NAME.
SO, I'VE ADOPTED A BOY FROM A DISTANT RELATIVE.
KATARINA, MEET YOUR NEW BROTHER.
I...
IT'S THE...
THIS IS KEITH.
KATARINA, I HOPE YOU'LL BE A GOOD SISTER TO HIM.
TH-THANK YOU.
THE SECOND ROAD TO RUIN!

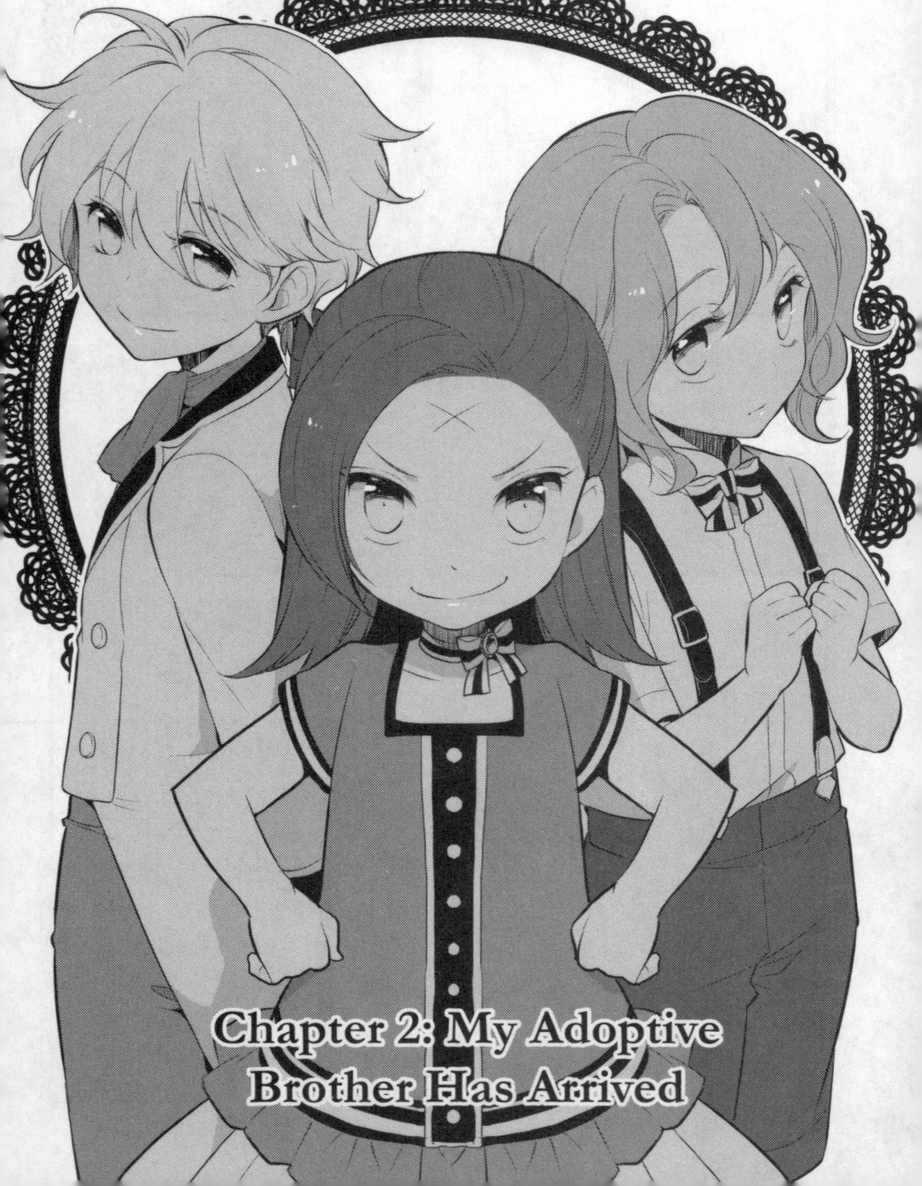

Chapter 2: My Adoptive Brother Has Arrived

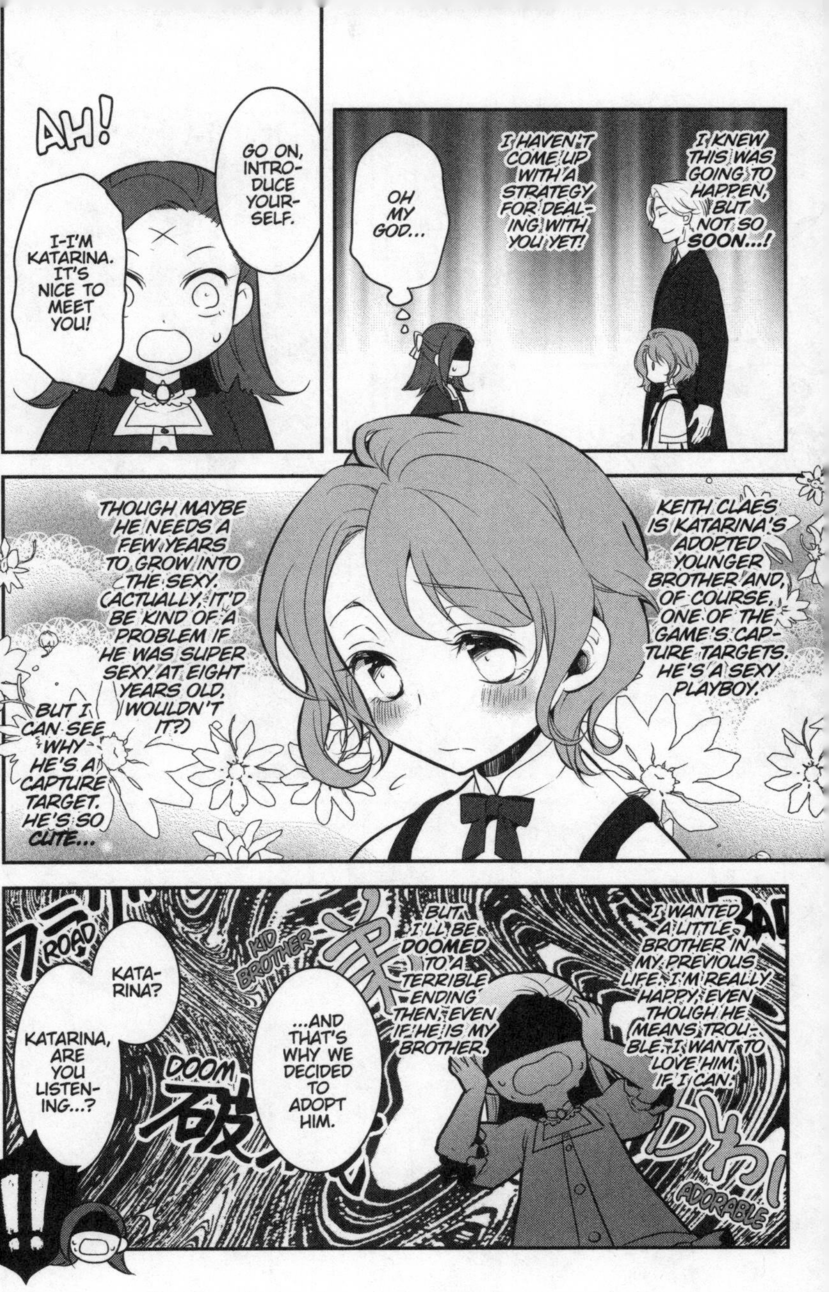
I KNEW THIS WAS GOING TO HAPPEN, BUT NOT SO SOON...!
I HAVEN'T COME UP WITH A STRATEGY FOR DEALING WITH YOU YET!
OH MY GOD...
GO ON, INTRODUCE YOURSELF.
AH!
I-I'M KATARINA. IT'S NICE TO MEET YOU!
KEITH CLAES IS KATARINA'S ADOPTED YOUNGER BROTHER AND, OF COURSE, ONE OF THE GAME'S CAPTURE TARGETS. HE'S A SEXY PLAYBOY.
THOUGH MAYBE HE NEEDS A FEW YEARS TO GROW INTO THE SEXY. (ACTUALLY, IT'D BE KIND OF A PROBLEM IF HE WAS SUPER SEXY AT EIGHT YEARS OLD, WOULDN'T IT?)
BUT I CAN SEE WHY HE'S A CAPTURE TARGET. HE'S SO CUTE...
I WANTED A LITTLE BROTHER IN MY PREVIOUS LIFE. I'M REALLY HAPPY, EVEN THOUGH HE MEANS TROUBLE. I WANT TO LOVE HIM, IF I CAN.
ADORABLE
BUT I'LL BE DOOMED TO A TERRIBLE ENDING THEN, EVEN IF HE IS MY BROTHER.
KID BROTHER
...AND THAT'S WHY WE DECIDED TO ADOPT HIM.
DOOM
ROAD
KATARINA?
KATARINA, ARE YOU LISTENING...?
!!

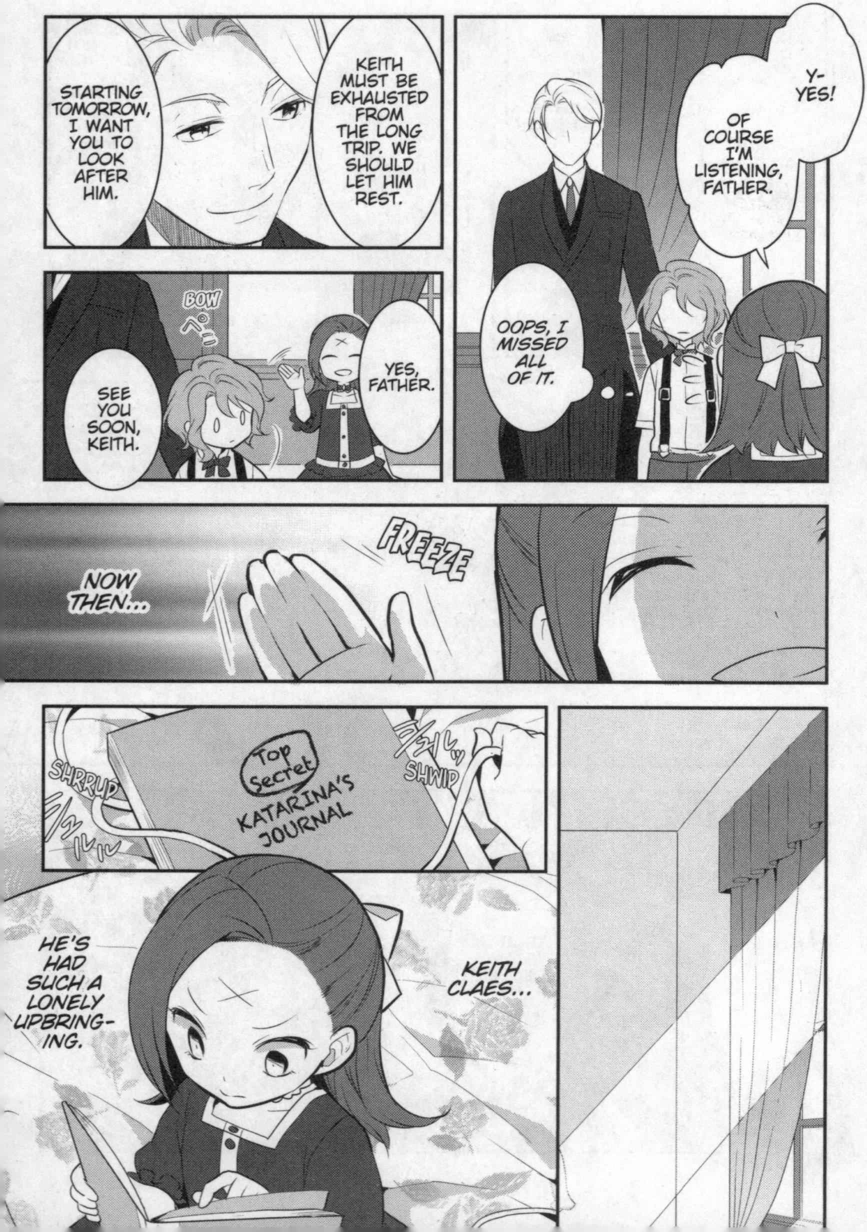
Y-YES!
OF COURSE I'M LISTENING, FATHER.
OOPS, I MISSED ALL OF IT.
KEITH MUST BE EXHAUSTED FROM THE LONG TRIP. WE SHOULD LET HIM REST.
STARTING TOMORROW, I WANT YOU TO LOOK AFTER HIM.
BOW
YES, FATHER.
SEE YOU SOON, KEITH.
FREEZE
NOW THEN...
SHWIP
Top Secret
KATARINA'S JOURNAL
SHRRUP
KEITH CLAES...
HE'S HAD SUCH A LONELY UPBRING-ING.

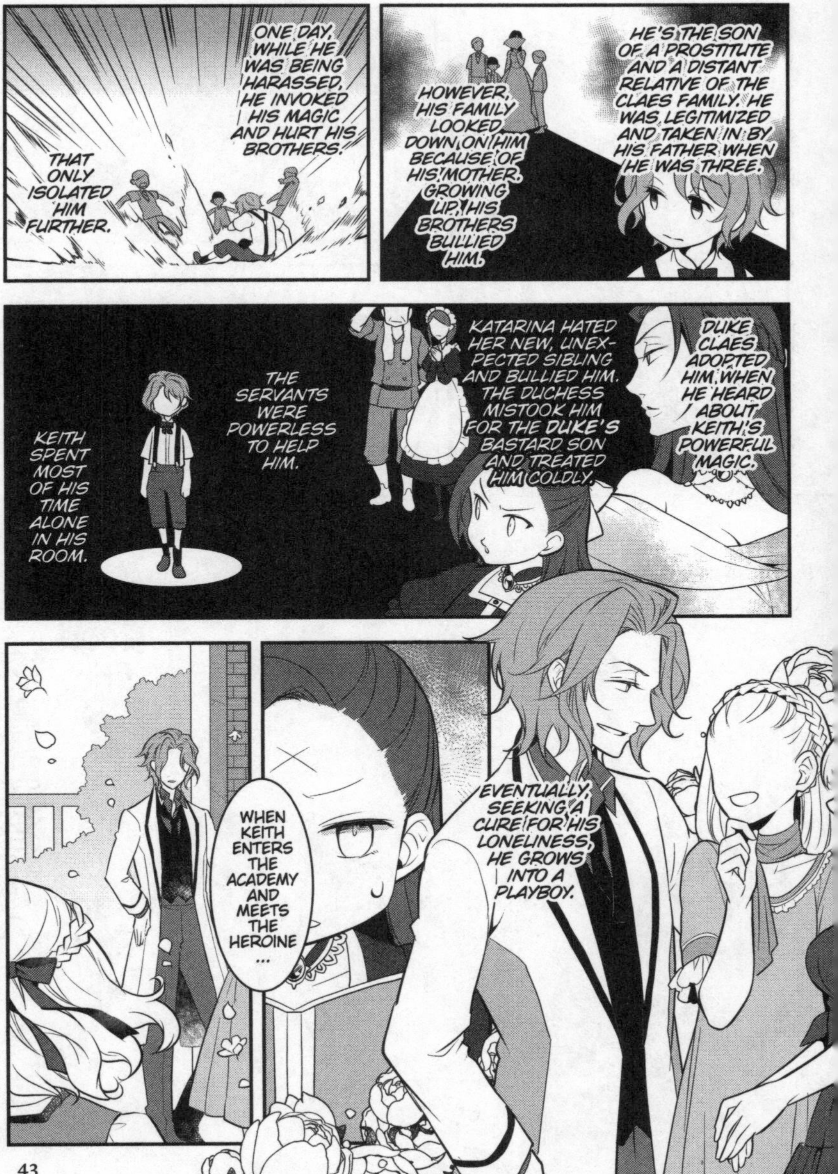
HE'S THE SON OF A PROSTITUTE AND A DISTANT RELATIVE OF THE CLAES FAMILY. HE WAS LEGITIMIZED AND TAKEN IN BY HIS FATHER WHEN HE WAS THREE.
HOWEVER, HIS FAMILY LOOKED DOWN ON HIM BECAUSE OF HIS MOTHER. GROWING UP, HIS BROTHERS BULLIED HIM.
ONE DAY, WHILE HE WAS BEING HARASSED, HE INVOKED HIS MAGIC AND HURT HIS BROTHERS.
THAT ONLY ISOLATED HIM FURTHER.
DUKE CLAES ADOPTED HIM WHEN HE HEARD ABOUT KEITH'S POWERFUL MAGIC.
KATARINA HATED HER NEW, UNEXPECTED SIBLING AND BULLIED HIM. THE DUCHESS MISTOOK HIM FOR THE DUKE'S BASTARD SON AND TREATED HIM COLDLY.
THE SERVANTS WERE POWERLESS TO HELP HIM.
KEITH SPENT MOST OF HIS TIME ALONE IN HIS ROOM.
EVENTUALLY, SEEKING A CURE FOR HIS LONELINESS, HE GROWS INTO A PLAYBOY.
WHEN KEITH ENTERS THE ACADEMY AND MEETS THE HEROINE ...

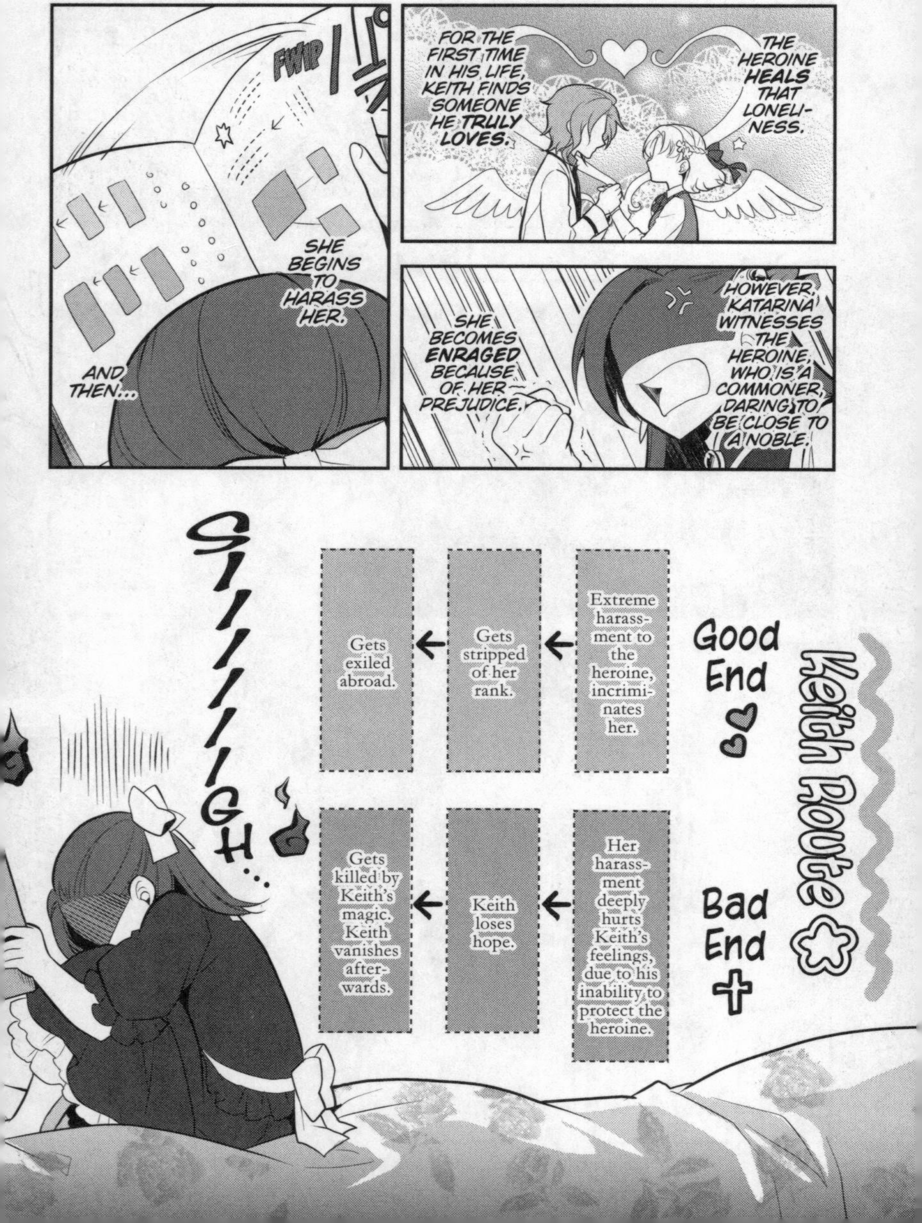
THE HEROINE HEALS THAT LONELI-NESS.
FOR THE FIRST TIME IN HIS LIFE, KEITH FINDS SOMEONE HE TRULY LOVES.
HOWEVER, KATARINA WITNESSES THE HEROINE, WHO IS A COMMONER, DARING TO BE CLOSE TO A NOBLE.
SHE BECOMES ENRAGED BECAUSE OF HER PREJUDICE.
FWIP
SHE BEGINS TO HARASS HER.
AND THEN...
Keith Route
Good End
Extreme harass-ment to the heroine, incrimi-nates her.
Gets stripped of her rank.
Gets exiled abroad.
Bad End
Her harass-ment deeply hurts Keith's feelings, due to his inability to protect the heroine.
Keith loses hope.
Gets killed by Keith's magic. Keith vanishes after-wards.
GIIIIIIIGH...

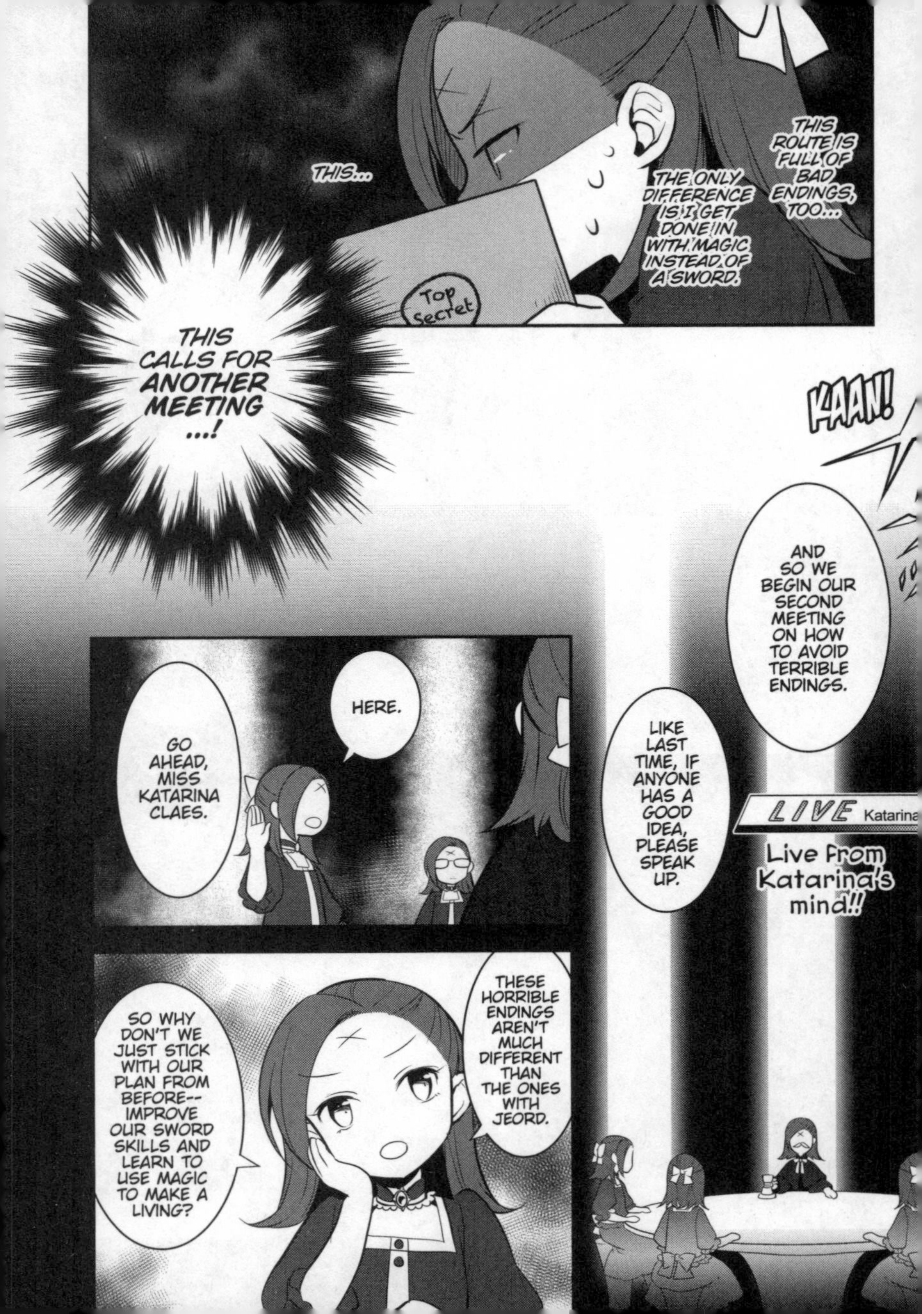

THIS ROUTE IS FULL OF BAD ENDINGS, TOO...
THE ONLY DIFFERENCE IS I GET DONE IN WITH MAGIC INSTEAD OF A SWORD.
THIS...
Top Secret
THIS CALLS FOR ANOTHER MEETING ...!
KAAN!
AND SO WE BEGIN OUR SECOND MEETING ON HOW TO AVOID TERRIBLE ENDINGS.
LIKE LAST TIME, IF ANYONE HAS A GOOD IDEA, PLEASE SPEAK UP.
LIVE Katarina
Live from Katarina's mind!!
HERE.
GO AHEAD, MISS KATARINA CLAES.
THESE HORRIBLE ENDINGS AREN'T MUCH DIFFERENT THAN THE ONES WITH JEORD.
SO WHY DON'T WE JUST STICK WITH OUR PLAN FROM BEFORE-- IMPROVE OUR SWORD SKILLS AND LEARN TO USE MAGIC TO MAKE A LIVING?

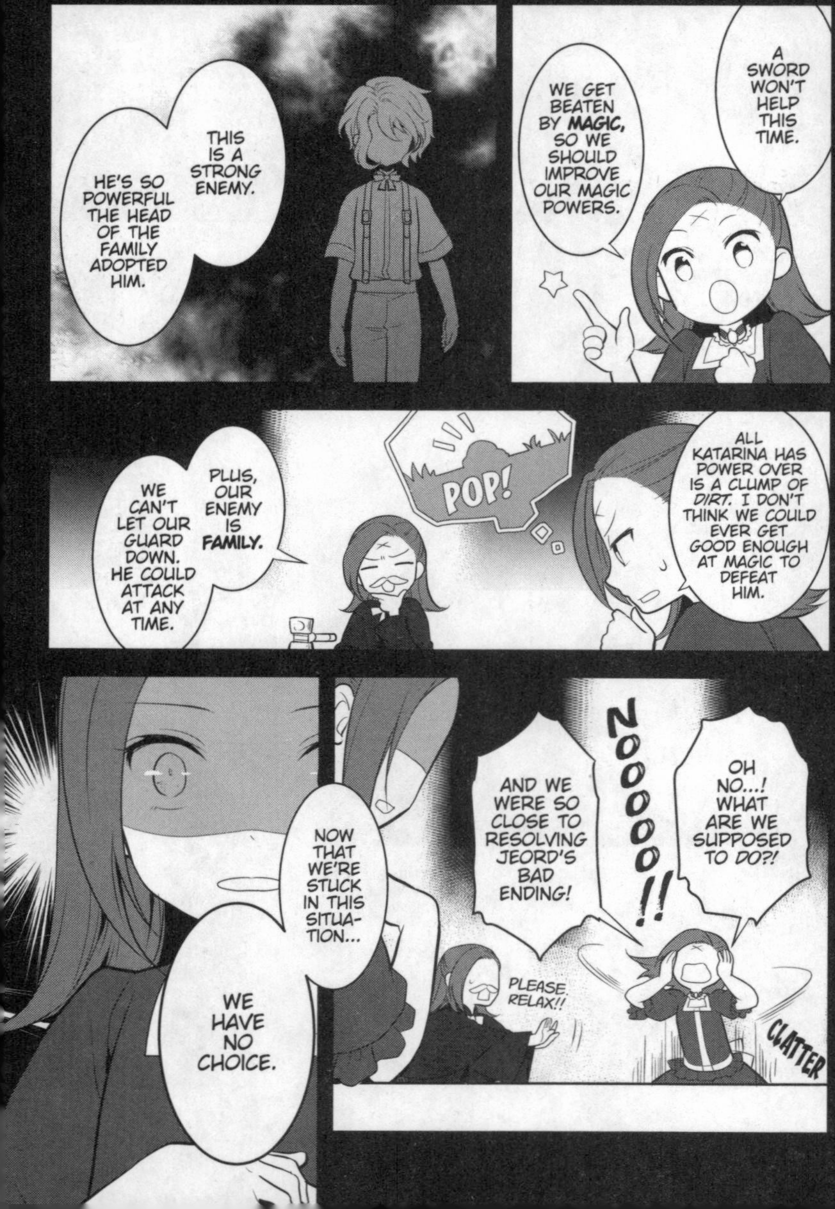
A SWORD WON'T HELP THIS TIME.
WE GET BEATEN BY **MAGIC,** SO WE SHOULD IMPROVE OUR MAGIC POWERS.
THIS IS A STRONG ENEMY.
HE'S SO POWERFUL THE HEAD OF THE FAMILY ADOPTED HIM.
ALL KATARINA HAS POWER OVER IS A CLUMP OF *DIRT.* I DON'T THINK WE COULD EVER GET GOOD ENOUGH AT MAGIC TO DEFEAT HIM.
POP!
PLUS, OUR ENEMY IS **FAMILY.**
WE CAN'T LET OUR GUARD DOWN. HE COULD ATTACK AT ANY TIME.
OH NO...! WHAT ARE WE SUPPOSED TO *DO?!*
NOOOOOO!!
AND WE WERE SO CLOSE TO RESOLVING JEORD'S BAD ENDING!
PLEASE RELAX!!
CLATTER
NOW THAT WE'RE STUCK IN THIS SITUA-TION...
WE HAVE NO CHOICE.

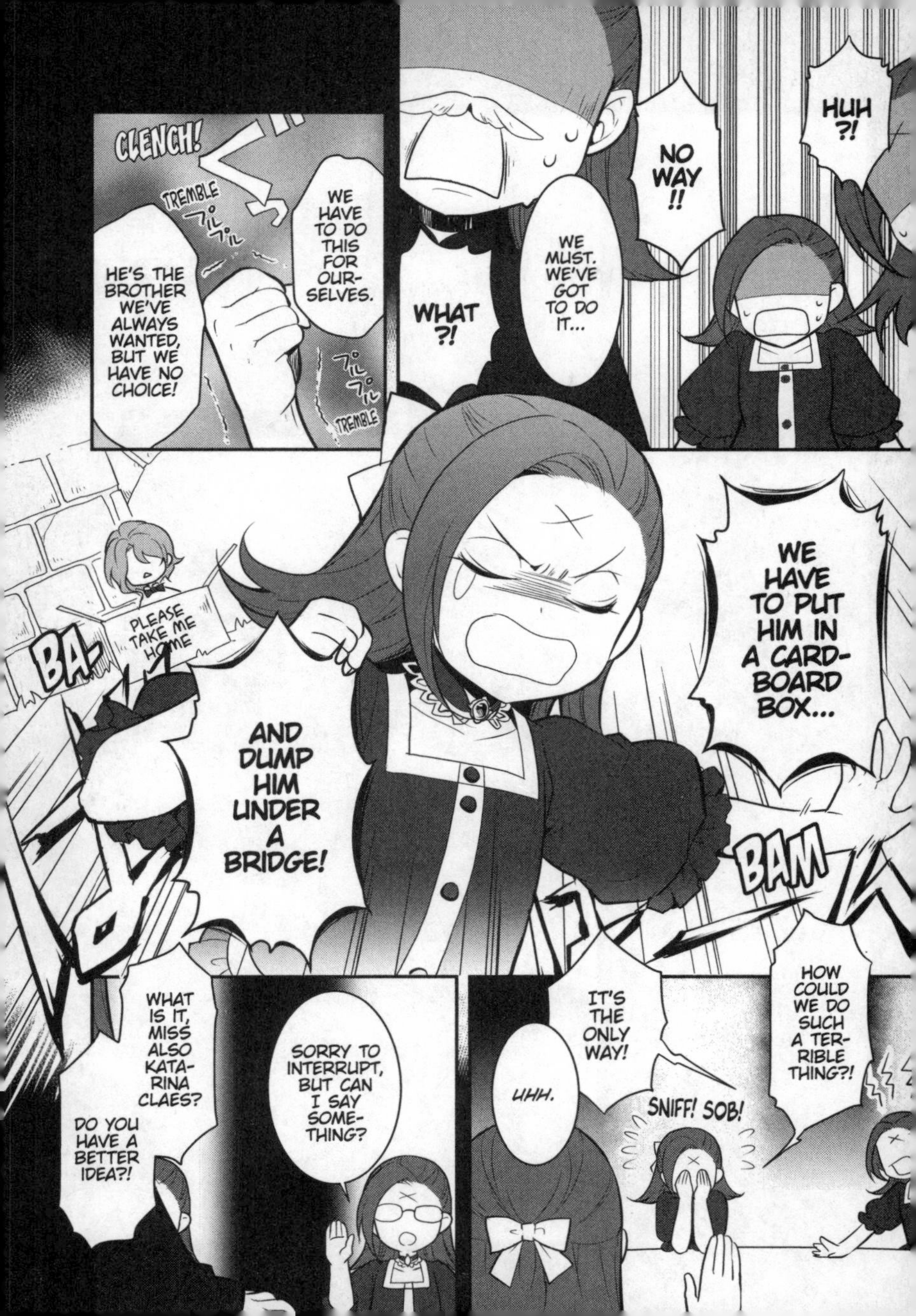
HUH ?!
NO WAY !!
WE MUST. WE'VE GOT TO DO IT...
WHAT ?!
CLENCH!
TREMBLE
WE HAVE TO DO THIS FOR OUR-SELVES.
HE'S THE BROTHER WE'VE ALWAYS WANTED, BUT WE HAVE NO CHOICE!
TREMBLE
WE HAVE TO PUT HIM IN A CARD-BOARD BOX...
AND DUMP HIM UNDER A BRIDGE!
BAM
PLEASE TAKE ME HOME
BA-
HOW COULD WE DO SUCH A TER-RIBLE THING?!
IT'S THE ONLY WAY!
SNIFF! SOB!
UHH.
SORRY TO INTERRUPT, BUT CAN I SAY SOME-THING?
WHAT IS IT, MISS ALSO KATA-RINA CLAES?
DO YOU HAVE A BETTER IDEA?!

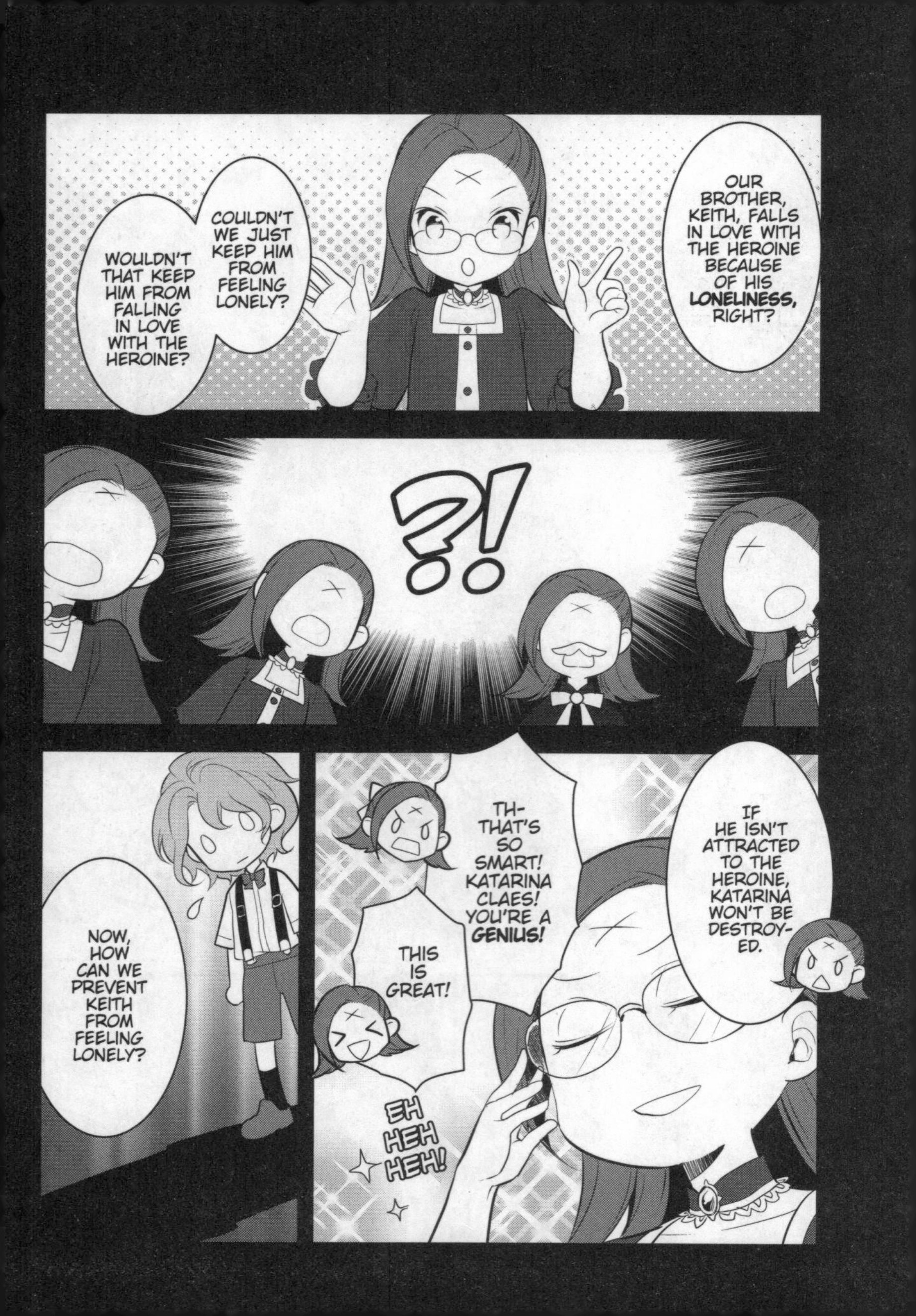
OUR BROTHER, KEITH, FALLS IN LOVE WITH THE HEROINE BECAUSE OF HIS **LONELINESS,** RIGHT?
COULDN'T WE JUST KEEP HIM FROM FEELING LONELY?
WOULDN'T THAT KEEP HIM FROM FALLING IN LOVE WITH THE HEROINE?
?!
IF HE ISN'T ATTRACTED TO THE HEROINE, KATARINA WON'T BE DESTROY-ED.
TH-THAT'S SO SMART! KATARINA CLAES! YOU'RE A **GENIUS!**
THIS IS GREAT!
EH HEH HEH!
NOW, HOW CAN WE PREVENT KEITH FROM FEELING LONELY?

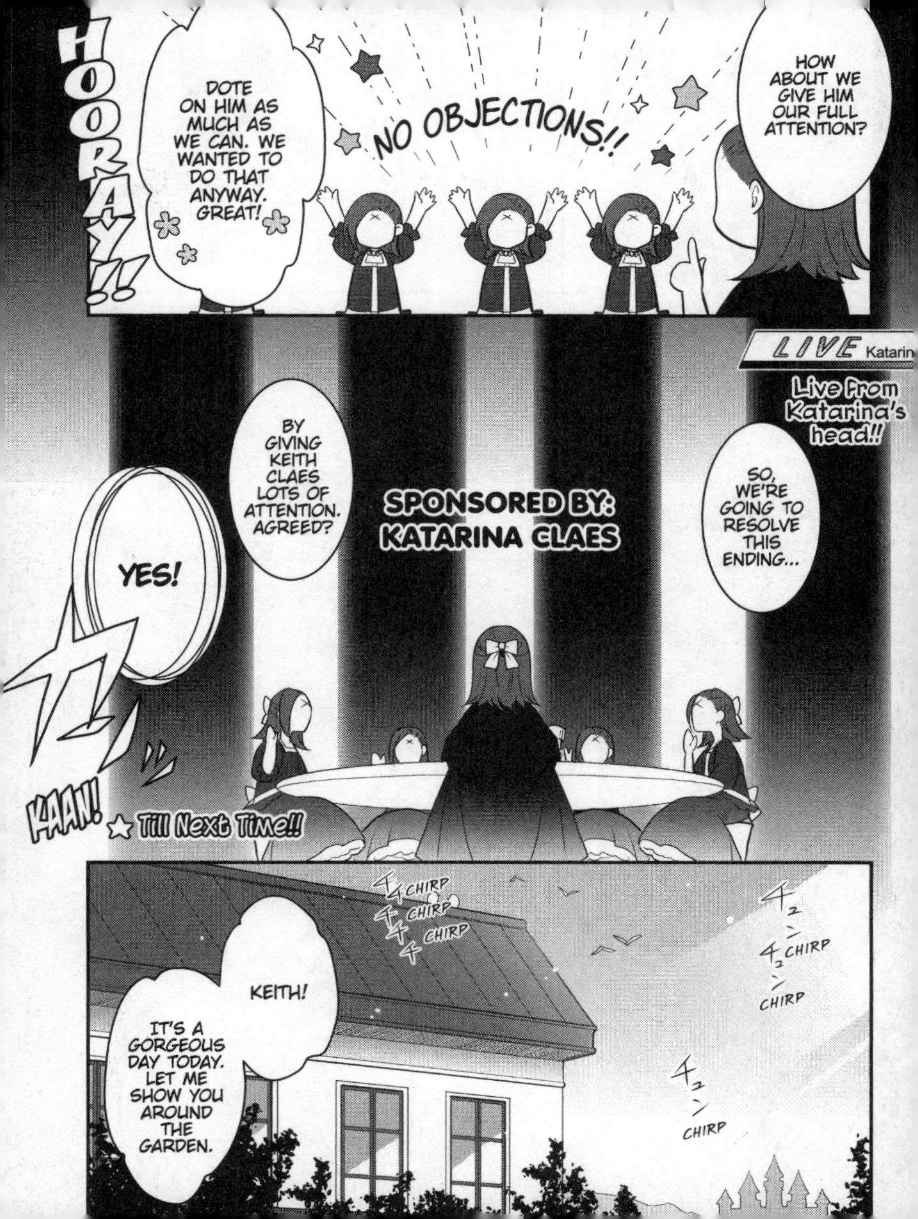
HOW ABOUT WE GIVE HIM OUR FULL ATTENTION?
NO OBJECTIONS!!
DOTE ON HIM AS MUCH AS WE CAN. WE WANTED TO DO THAT ANYWAY. GREAT!
HOORAY!!
LIVE Katarin
Live from Katarina's head!!
SO, WE'RE GOING TO RESOLVE THIS ENDING...
SPONSORED BY: KATARINA CLAES
BY GIVING KEITH CLAES LOTS OF ATTENTION. AGREED?
YES!
KAAN!
☆ Till Next Time!!
CHIRP
CHIRP
CHIRP
CHIRP
CHIRP
CHIRP
KEITH!
IT'S A GORGEOUS DAY TODAY. LET ME SHOW YOU AROUND THE GARDEN.

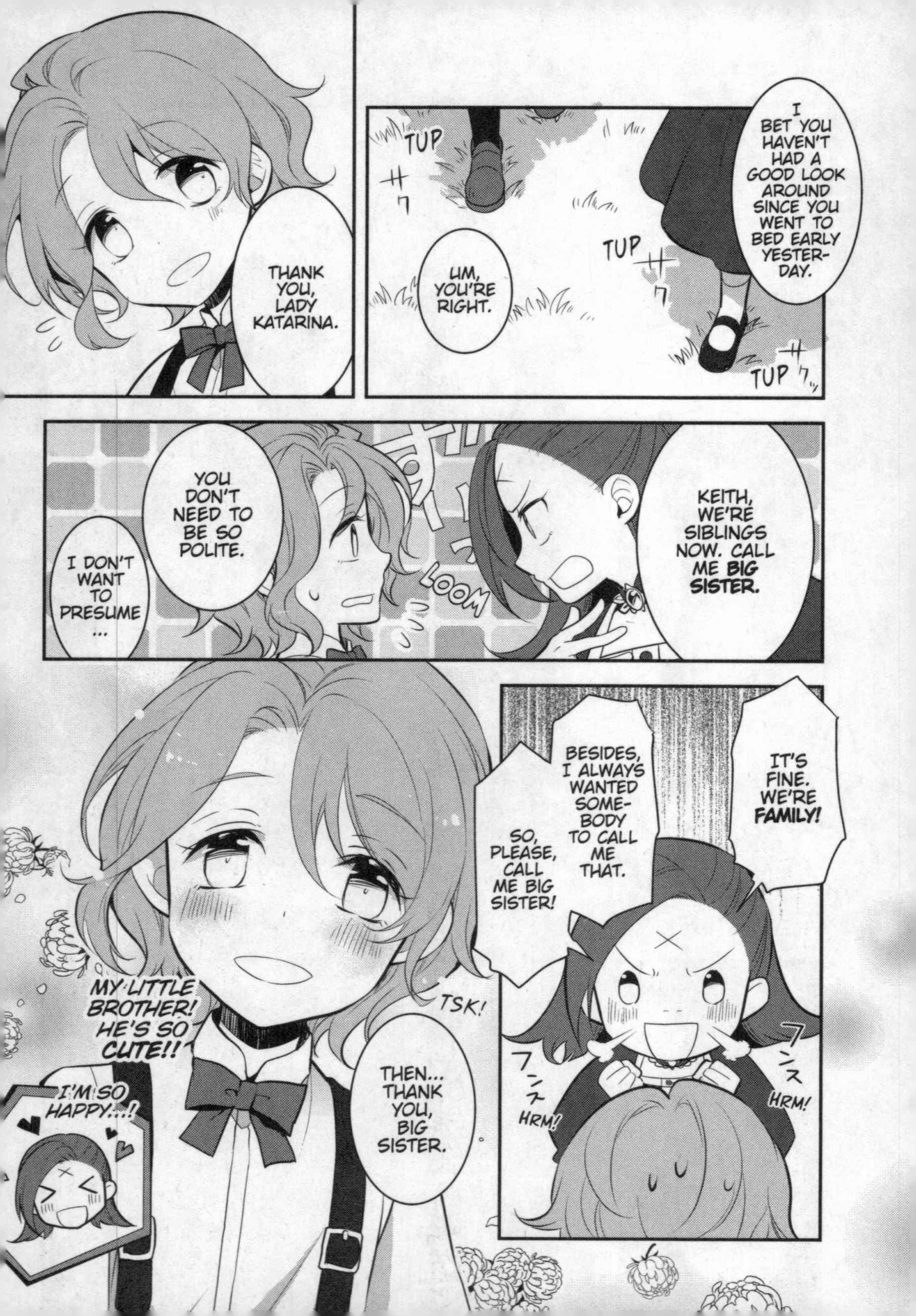
I BET YOU HAVEN'T HAD A GOOD LOOK AROUND SINCE YOU WENT TO BED EARLY YESTER-DAY.
TUP
TUP
UM, YOU'RE RIGHT.
TUP
THANK YOU, LADY KATARINA.
KEITH, WE'RE SIBLINGS NOW. CALL ME **BIG SISTER.**
LOOM
YOU DON'T NEED TO BE SO POLITE.
I DON'T WANT TO PRESUME...
IT'S FINE. WE'RE **FAMILY!**
BESIDES, I ALWAYS WANTED SOME-BODY TO CALL ME THAT.
SO, PLEASE, CALL ME BIG SISTER!
HRM!
HRM!
TSK!
THEN... THANK YOU, BIG SISTER.
MY LITTLE BROTHER! HE'S SO **CUTE!!**
I'M SO HAPPY...!

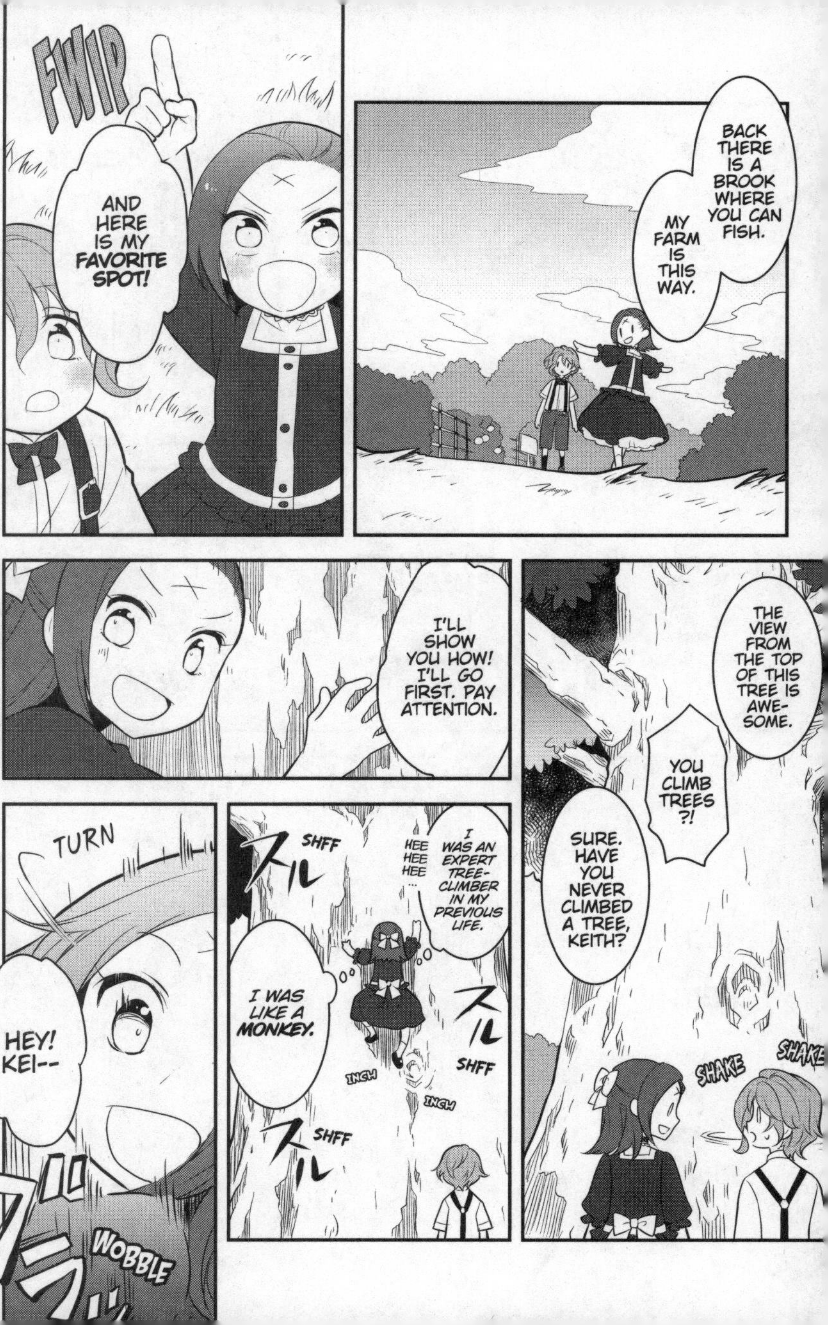
BACK THERE IS A BROOK WHERE YOU CAN FISH.
MY FARM IS THIS WAY.
FWIP
AND HERE IS MY FAVORITE SPOT!
THE VIEW FROM THE TOP OF THIS TREE IS AWE-SOME.
YOU CLIMB TREES?!
SURE. HAVE YOU NEVER CLIMBED A TREE, KEITH?
SHAKE
SHAKE
I'LL SHOW YOU HOW! I'LL GO FIRST. PAY ATTENTION.
I WAS AN EXPERT TREE-CLIMBER IN MY PREVIOUS LIFE.
HEE HEE HEE ...
SHFF
I WAS LIKE A MONKEY.
SHFF
INCH
INCH
SHFF
TURN
HEY! KEI--
WOBBLE

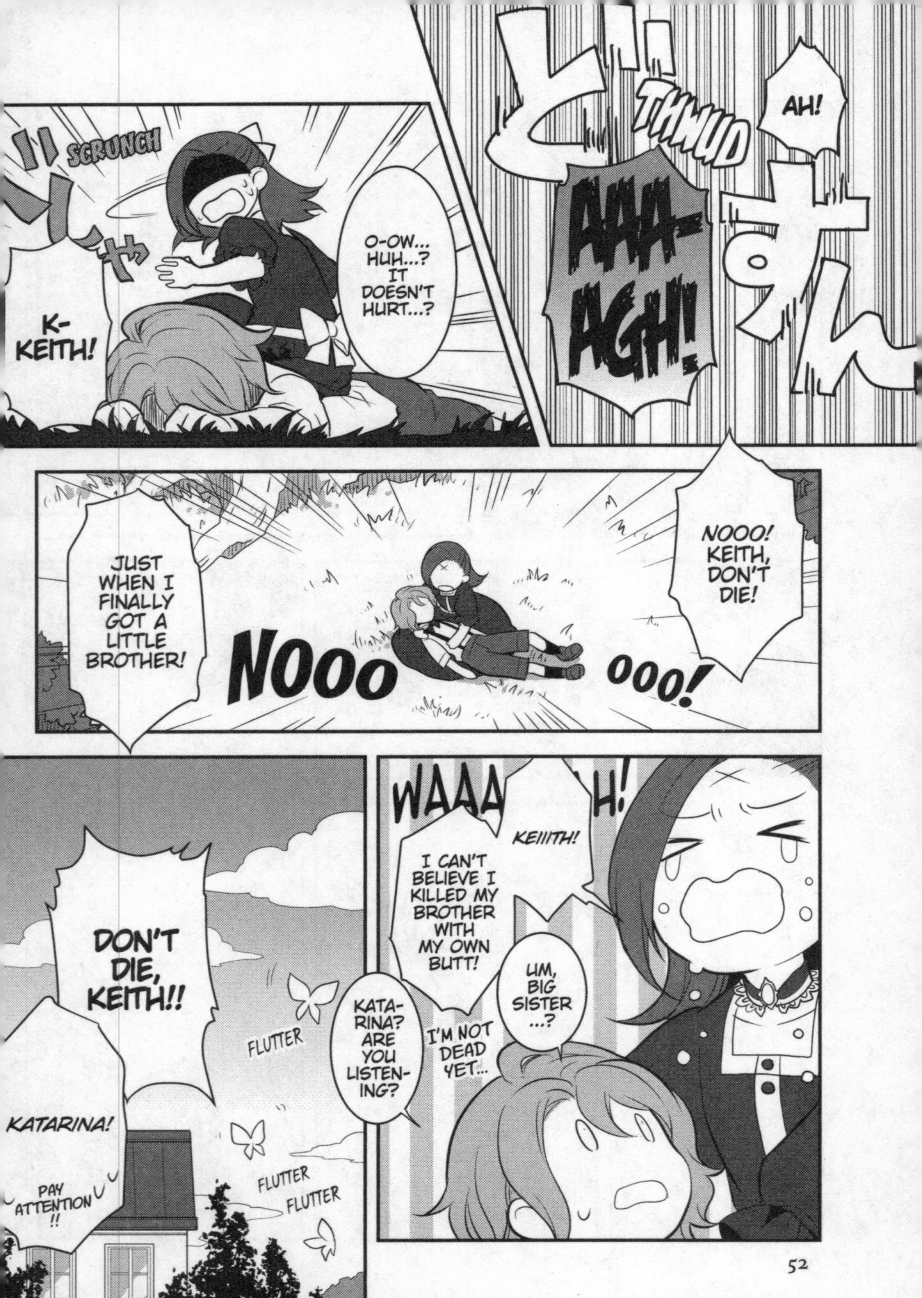
THWUD
AH!
AAA-AGH!
SCRUNCH
O-OW... HUH...? IT DOESN'T HURT...?
K-KEITH!
NOOO! KEITH, DON'T DIE!
JUST WHEN I FINALLY GOT A LITTLE BROTHER!
NOOOOOO!
WAAA...H!
KEIIITH!
I CAN'T BELIEVE I KILLED MY BROTHER WITH MY OWN BUTT!
UM, BIG SISTER ...?
I'M NOT DEAD YET...
KATA-RINA? ARE YOU LISTEN-ING?
DON'T DIE, KEITH!!
FLUTTER
KATARINA!
PAY ATTENTION!!
FLUTTER
FLUTTER

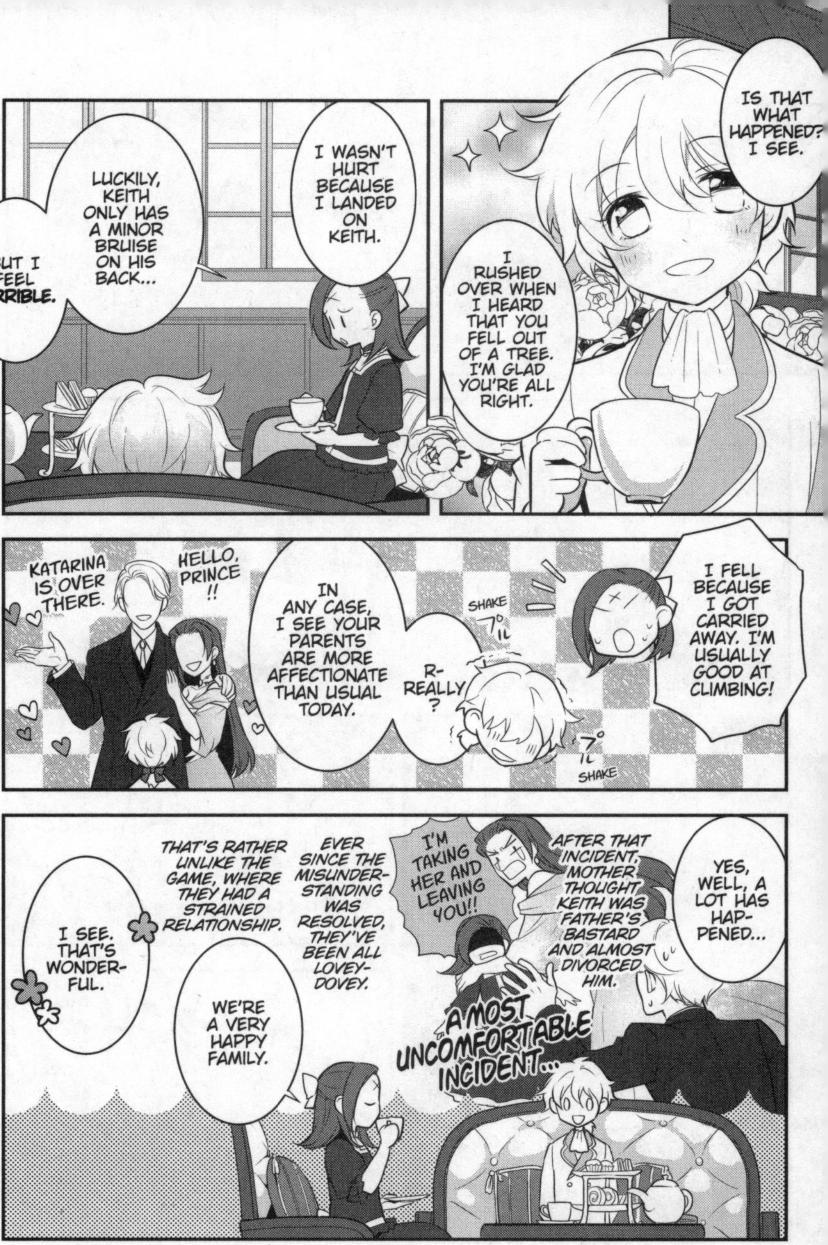
IS THAT WHAT HAPPENED? I SEE.
I RUSHED OVER WHEN I HEARD THAT YOU FELL OUT OF A TREE. I'M GLAD YOU'RE ALL RIGHT.
I WASN'T HURT BECAUSE I LANDED ON KEITH.
LUCKILY, KEITH ONLY HAS A MINOR BRUISE ON HIS BACK...
BUT I FEEL **TERRIBLE.**
I FELL BECAUSE I GOT CARRIED AWAY. I'M USUALLY GOOD AT CLIMBING!
SHAKE
SHAKE
R-REALLY?
IN ANY CASE, I SEE YOUR PARENTS ARE MORE AFFECTIONATE THAN USUAL TODAY.
HELLO, PRINCE!!
KATARINA IS OVER THERE.
YES, WELL, A LOT HAS HAPPENED...
AFTER THAT INCIDENT, MOTHER THOUGHT KEITH WAS FATHER'S BASTARD AND ALMOST DIVORCED HIM.
I'M TAKING HER AND LEAVING YOU!!
A MOST UNCOMFORTABLE INCIDENT...
EVER SINCE THE MISUNDERSTANDING WAS RESOLVED, THEY'VE BEEN ALL LOVEY-DOVEY.
THAT'S RATHER UNLIKE THE GAME, WHERE THEY HAD A STRAINED RELATIONSHIP.
I SEE. THAT'S WONDERFUL.
WE'RE A VERY HAPPY FAMILY.

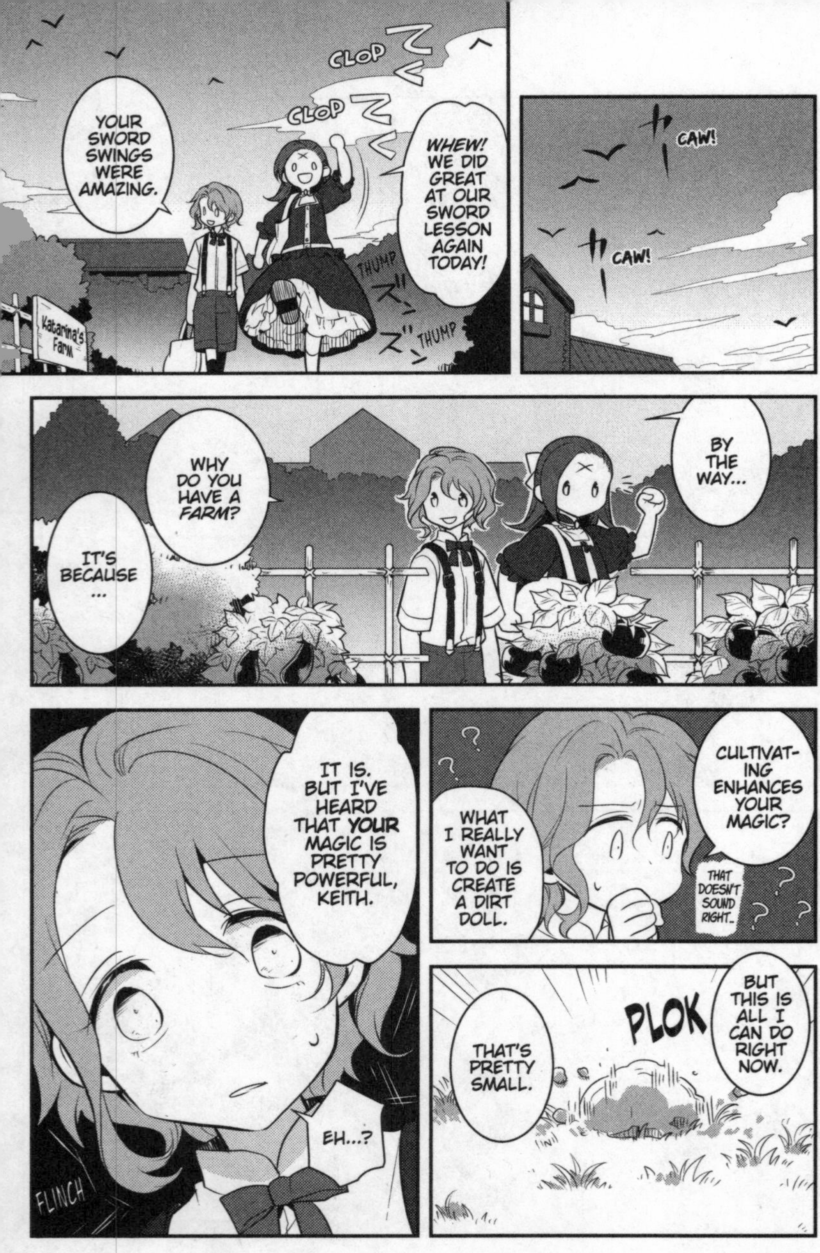
CAW!
CAW!
CLOP
CLOP
WHEW! WE DID GREAT AT OUR SWORD LESSON AGAIN TODAY!
YOUR SWORD SWINGS WERE AMAZING.
THUMP
THUMP
Katarina's Farm
BY THE WAY...
WHY DO YOU HAVE A FARM?
IT'S BECAUSE ...
CULTIVAT-ING ENHANCES YOUR MAGIC?
THAT DOESN'T SOUND RIGHT..
WHAT I REALLY WANT TO DO IS CREATE A DIRT DOLL.
BUT THIS IS ALL I CAN DO RIGHT NOW.
PLOK
THAT'S PRETTY SMALL.
IT IS. BUT I'VE HEARD THAT YOUR MAGIC IS PRETTY POWERFUL, KEITH.
EH...?
FLINCH

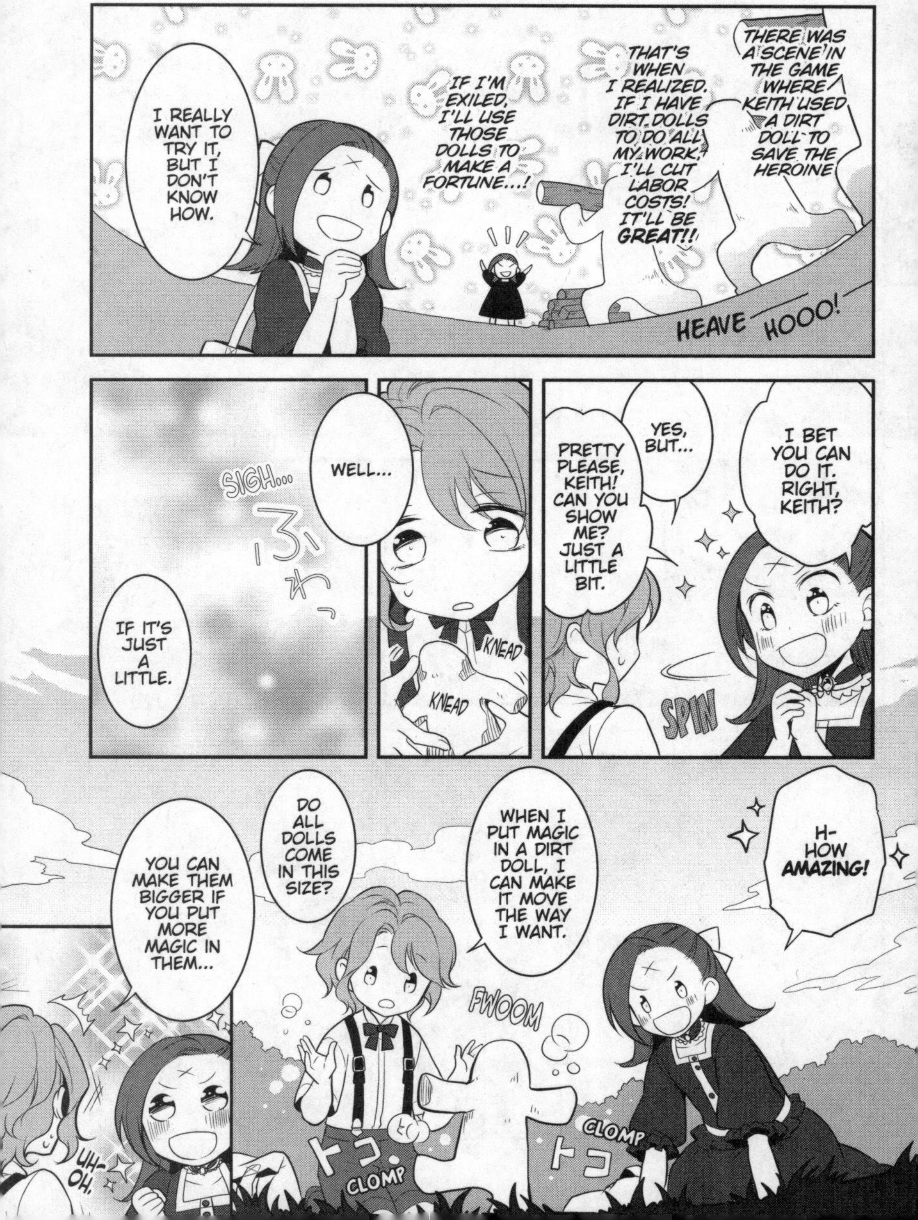
THERE WAS A SCENE IN THE GAME WHERE KEITH USED A DIRT DOLL TO SAVE THE HEROINE
THAT'S WHEN I REALIZED. IF I HAVE DIRT DOLLS TO DO ALL MY WORK, I'LL CUT LABOR COSTS! IT'LL BE GREAT!!
HEAVE HOOO!
IF I'M EXILED, I'LL USE THOSE DOLLS TO MAKE A FORTUNE...!
I REALLY WANT TO TRY IT, BUT I DON'T KNOW HOW.
I BET YOU CAN DO IT. RIGHT, KEITH?
YES, BUT...
PRETTY PLEASE, KEITH! CAN YOU SHOW ME? JUST A LITTLE BIT.
SPIN
WELL...
KNEAD
KNEAD
SIGH...
ふぅ
IF IT'S JUST A LITTLE.
H-HOW AMAZING!
WHEN I PUT MAGIC IN A DIRT DOLL, I CAN MAKE IT MOVE THE WAY I WANT.
DO ALL DOLLS COME IN THIS SIZE?
FWOOM
CLOMP
トコ
CLOMP
トコ
YOU CAN MAKE THEM BIGGER IF YOU PUT MORE MAGIC IN THEM...
UH-OH.

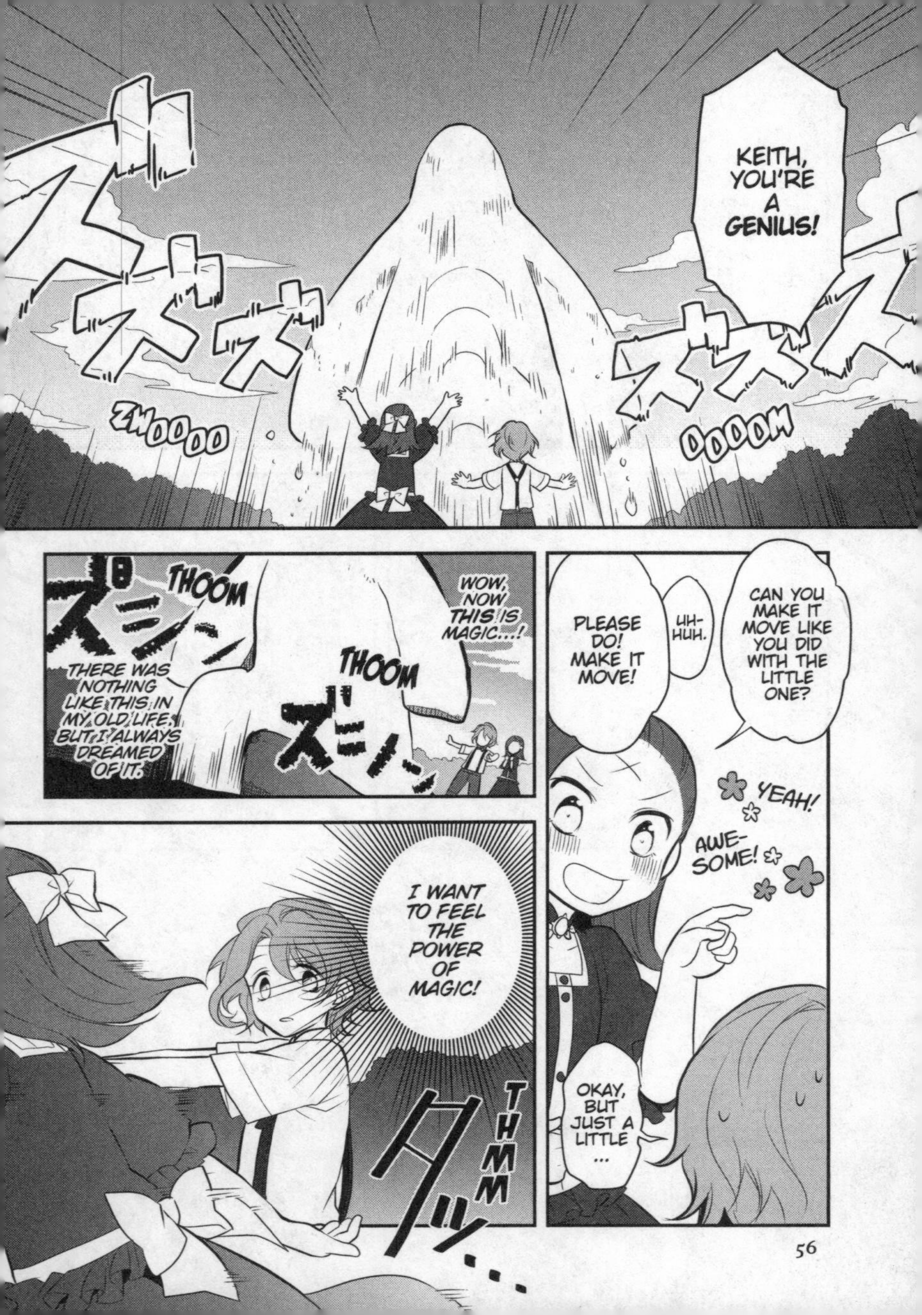
KEITH, YOU'RE A GENIUS!
ZWOOOO
OOOOM
CAN YOU MAKE IT MOVE LIKE YOU DID WITH THE LITTLE ONE?
UH-HUH.
PLEASE DO! MAKE IT MOVE!
YEAH!
AWE-SOME!
OKAY, BUT JUST A LITTLE ...
WOW, NOW THIS IS MAGIC...!
THOOM
THOOM
THERE WAS NOTHING LIKE THIS IN MY OLD LIFE, BUT I ALWAYS DREAMED OF IT.
I WANT TO FEEL THE POWER OF MAGIC!
THMM

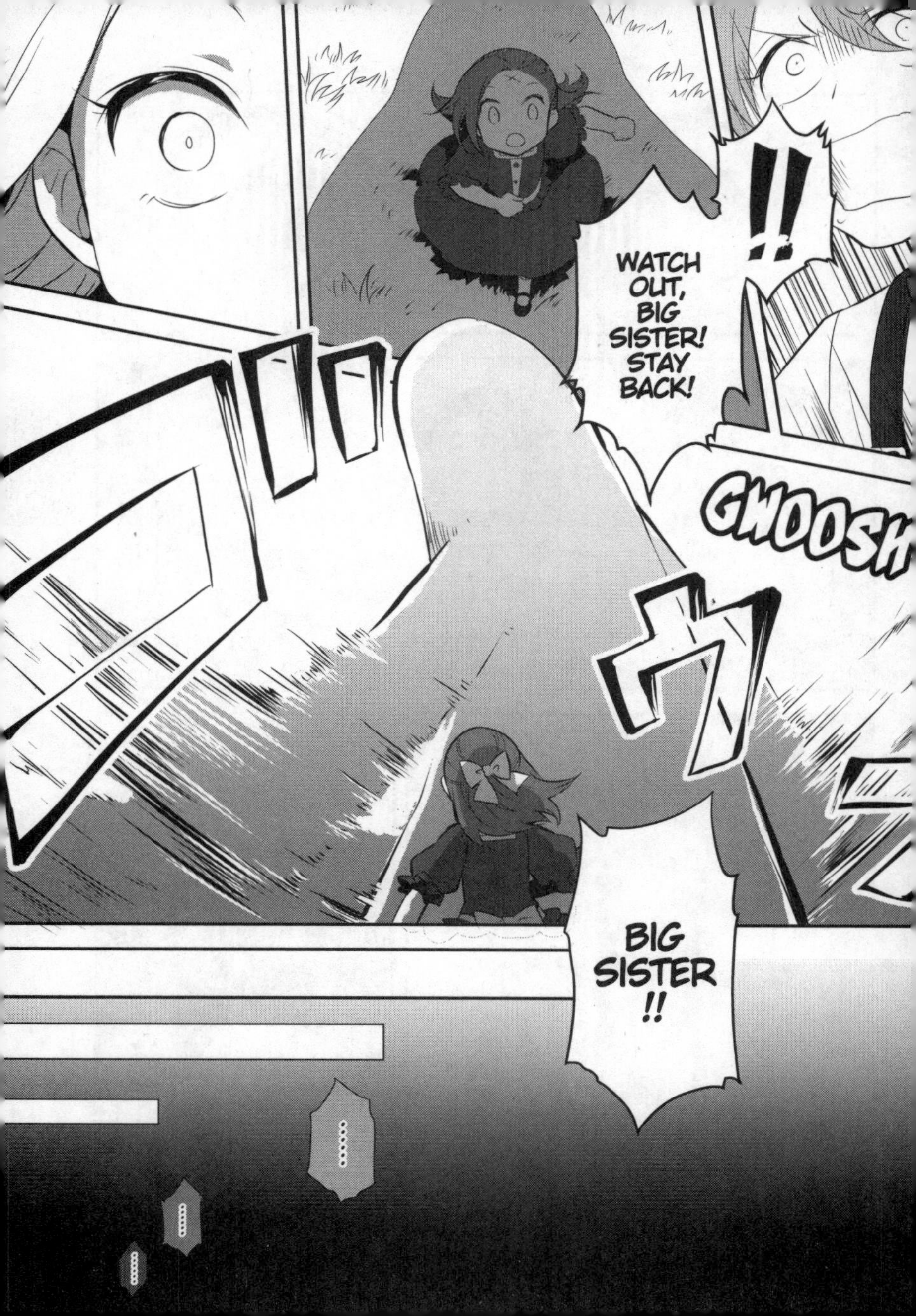
!!
WATCH OUT, BIG SISTER! STAY BACK!
GWOOSH
BIG SISTER!!
......
.....
.....

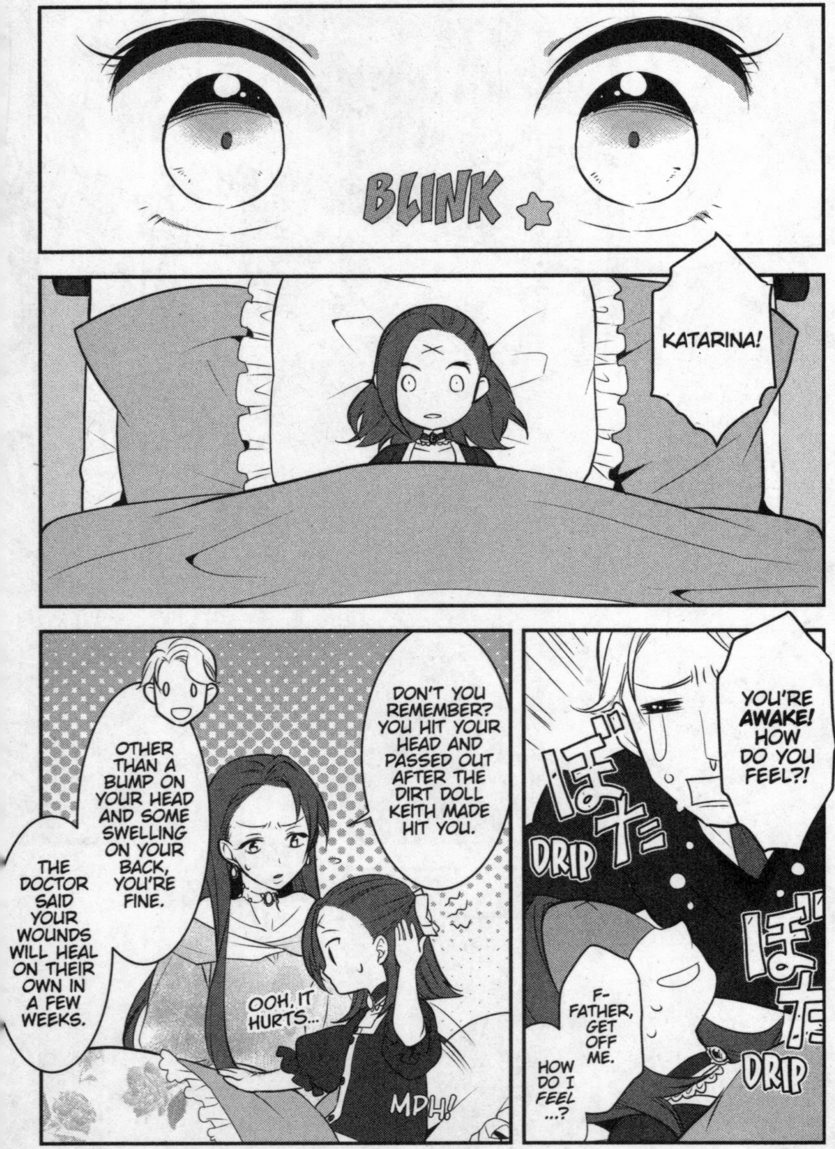
BLINK
KATARINA!
YOU'RE AWAKE! HOW DO YOU FEEL?!
DRIP
DRIP
F-FATHER, GET OFF ME.
HOW DO I FEEL ...?
DON'T YOU REMEMBER? YOU HIT YOUR HEAD AND PASSED OUT AFTER THE DIRT DOLL KEITH MADE HIT YOU.
OTHER THAN A BUMP ON YOUR HEAD AND SOME SWELLING ON YOUR BACK, YOU'RE FINE.
THE DOCTOR SAID YOUR WOUNDS WILL HEAL ON THEIR OWN IN A FEW WEEKS.
OOH, IT HURTS...
MPH!

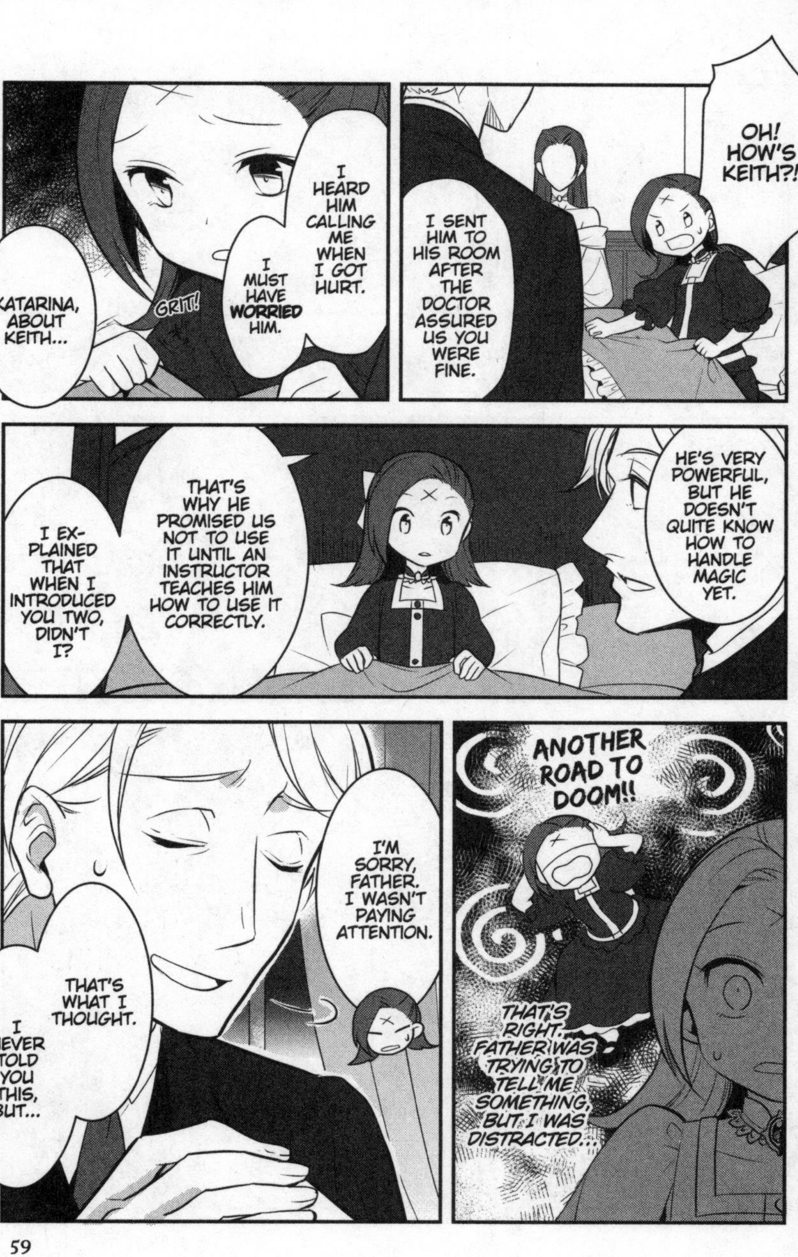
OH! HOW'S KEITH?!
I SENT HIM TO HIS ROOM AFTER THE DOCTOR ASSURED US YOU WERE FINE.
I HEARD HIM CALLING ME WHEN I GOT HURT.
I MUST HAVE WORRIED HIM.
GRIT!
KATARINA, ABOUT KEITH...
HE'S VERY POWERFUL, BUT HE DOESN'T QUITE KNOW HOW TO HANDLE MAGIC YET.
THAT'S WHY HE PROMISED US NOT TO USE IT UNTIL AN INSTRUCTOR TEACHES HIM HOW TO USE IT CORRECTLY.
I EX-PLAINED THAT WHEN I INTRODUCED YOU TWO, DIDN'T I?
ANOTHER ROAD TO DOOM!!
THAT'S RIGHT. FATHER WAS TRYING TO TELL ME SOMETHING, BUT I WAS DISTRACTED...
I'M SORRY, FATHER. I WASN'T PAYING ATTENTION.
THAT'S WHAT I THOUGHT.
I NEVER TOLD YOU THIS, BUT...

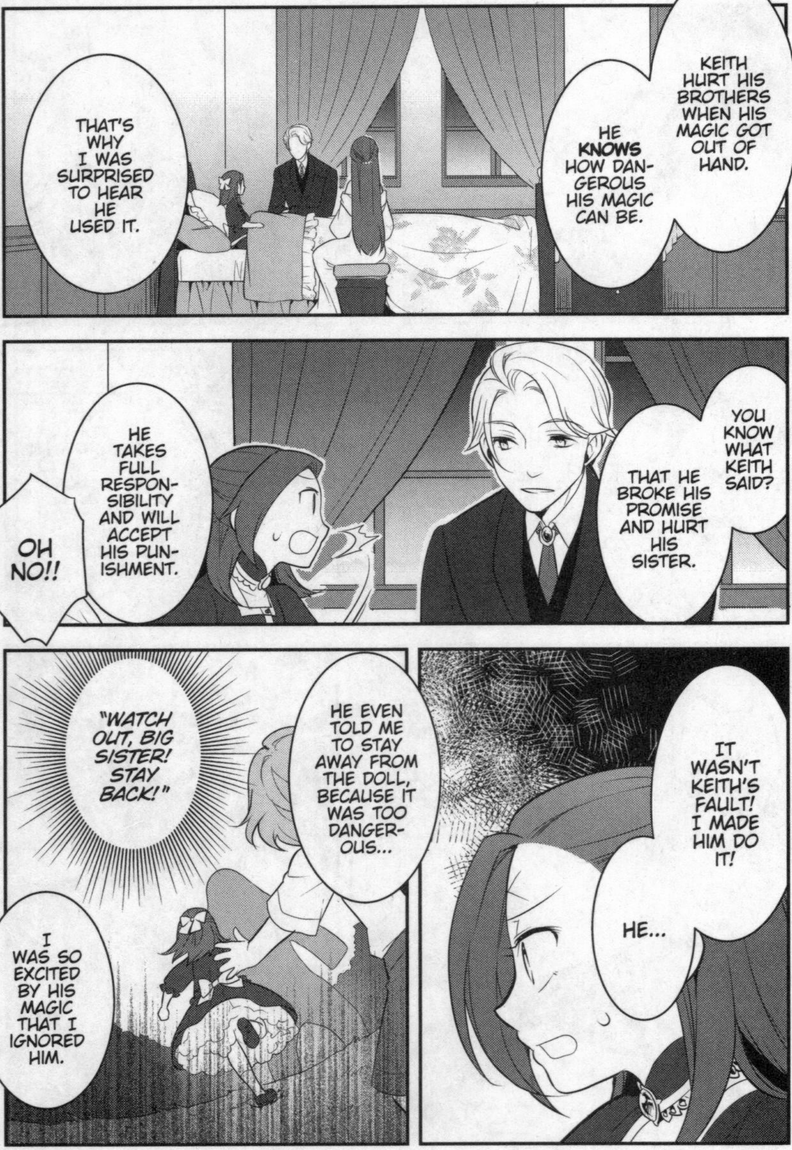
KEITH HURT HIS BROTHERS WHEN HIS MAGIC GOT OUT OF HAND.
HE **KNOWS** HOW DANGEROUS HIS MAGIC CAN BE.
THAT'S WHY I WAS SURPRISED TO HEAR HE USED IT.
YOU KNOW WHAT KEITH SAID?
THAT HE BROKE HIS PROMISE AND HURT HIS SISTER.
HE TAKES FULL RESPONSIBILITY AND WILL ACCEPT HIS PUNISHMENT.
OH NO!!
IT WASN'T KEITH'S FAULT! I MADE HIM DO IT!
HE...
HE EVEN TOLD ME TO STAY AWAY FROM THE DOLL, BECAUSE IT WAS TOO DANGEROUS...
"WATCH OUT, BIG SISTER! STAY BACK!"
I WAS SO EXCITED BY HIS MAGIC THAT I IGNORED HIM.

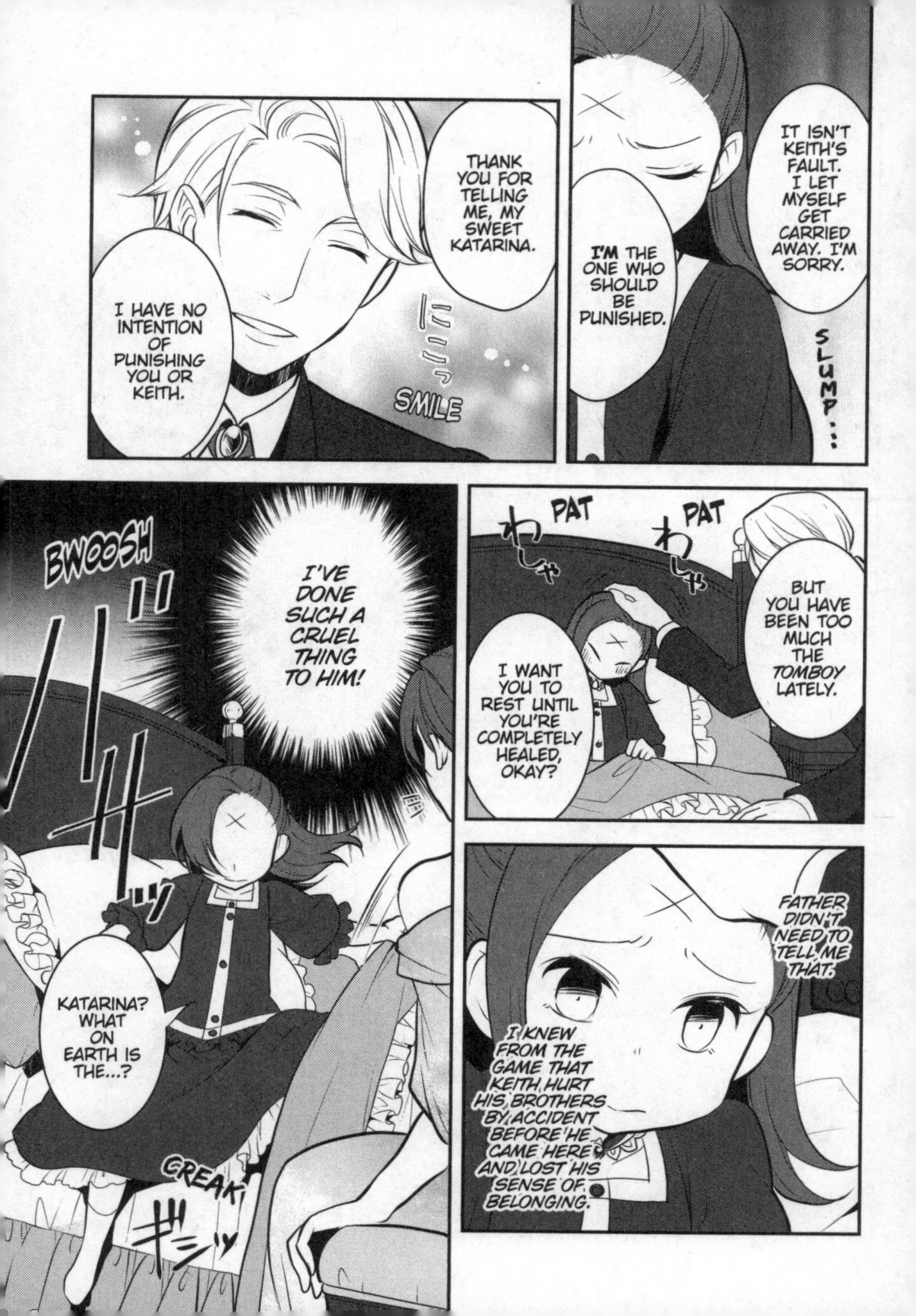
IT ISN'T KEITH'S FAULT. I LET MYSELF GET CARRIED AWAY. I'M SORRY.
I'M THE ONE WHO SHOULD BE PUNISHED.
SLUMP...
THANK YOU FOR TELLING ME, MY SWEET KATARINA.
I HAVE NO INTENTION OF PUNISHING YOU OR KEITH.
SMILE
PAT PAT
BUT YOU HAVE BEEN TOO MUCH THE TOMBOY LATELY.
I WANT YOU TO REST UNTIL YOU'RE COMPLETELY HEALED, OKAY?
FATHER DIDN'T NEED TO TELL ME THAT.
I KNEW FROM THE GAME THAT KEITH HURT HIS BROTHERS BY ACCIDENT BEFORE HE CAME HERE AND LOST HIS SENSE OF BELONGING.
BWOOSH
I'VE DONE SUCH A CRUEL THING TO HIM!
KATARINA? WHAT ON EARTH IS THE...?
CREAK

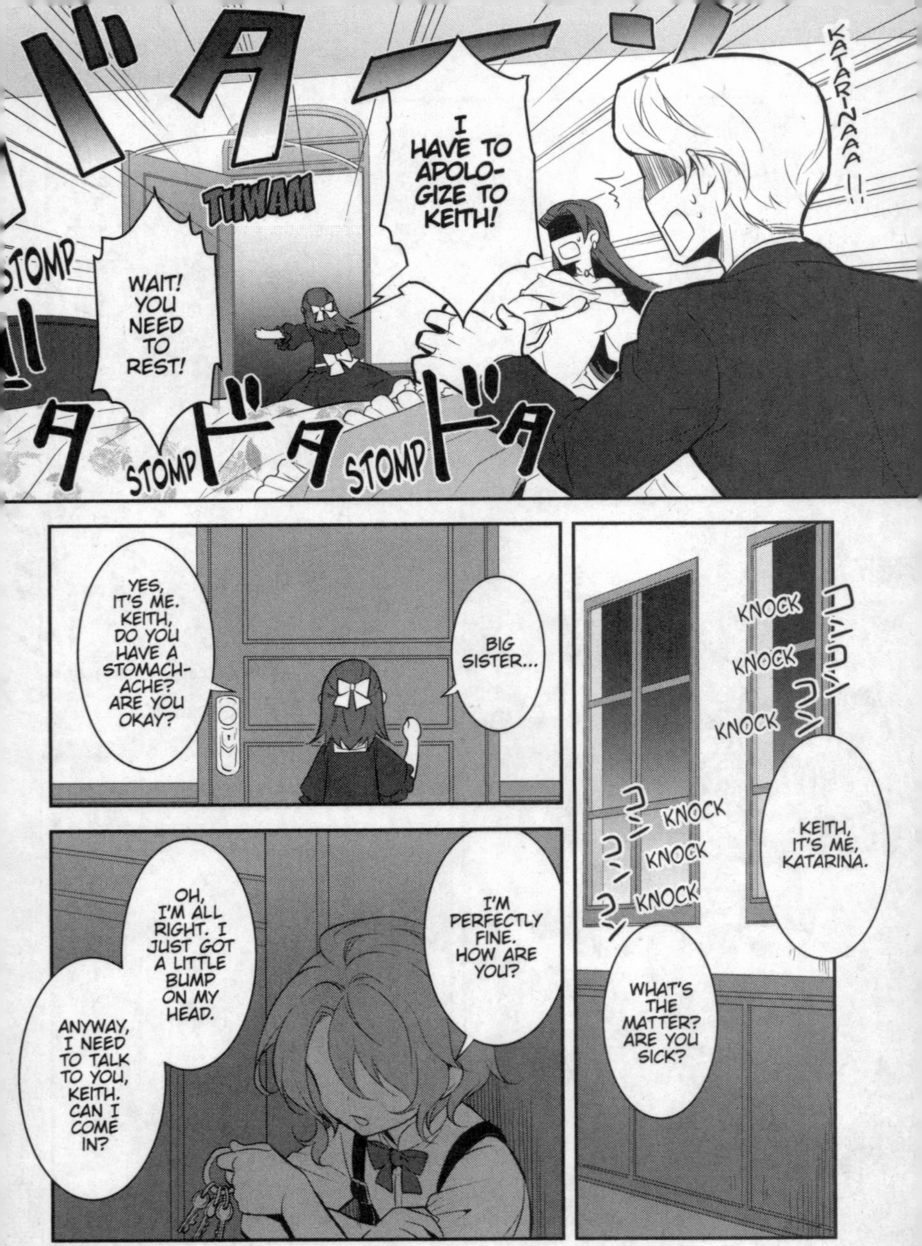

KATARINAAA!!
I HAVE TO APOLOGIZE TO KEITH!
THWAM
WAIT! YOU NEED TO REST!
STOMP
STOMP
STOMP
KNOCK
KNOCK
KNOCK
KEITH, IT'S ME, KATARINA.
KNOCK
KNOCK
KNOCK
WHAT'S THE MATTER? ARE YOU SICK?
BIG SISTER...
YES, IT'S ME. KEITH, DO YOU HAVE A STOMACH-ACHE? ARE YOU OKAY?
I'M PERFECTLY FINE. HOW ARE YOU?
OH, I'M ALL RIGHT. I JUST GOT A LITTLE BUMP ON MY HEAD.
ANYWAY, I NEED TO TALK TO YOU, KEITH. CAN I COME IN?

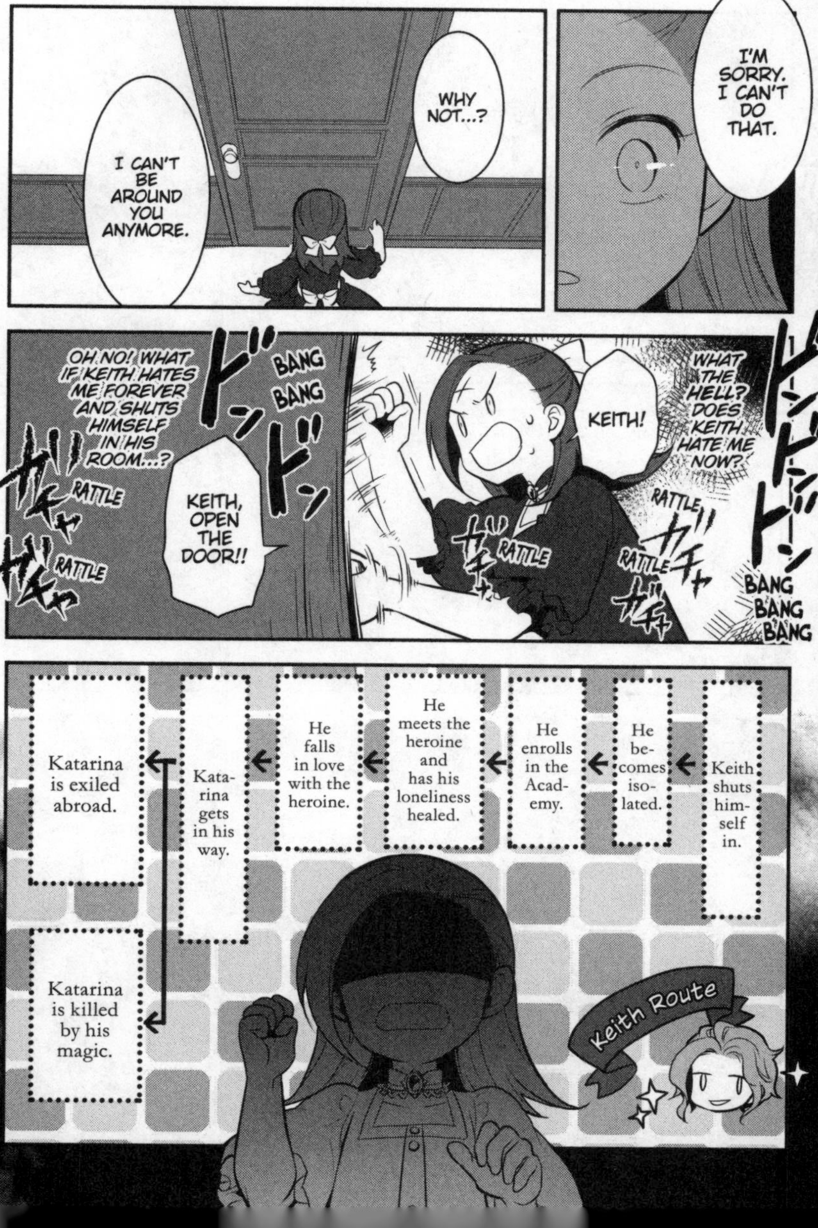
I'M SORRY. I CAN'T DO THAT.
WHY NOT...?
I CAN'T BE AROUND YOU ANYMORE.
WHAT THE HELL? DOES KEITH HATE ME NOW?
BANG BANG BANG
KEITH!
RATTLE
RATTLE
RATTLE
KEITH, OPEN THE DOOR!!
BANG BANG
OH NO! WHAT IF KEITH HATES ME FOREVER AND SHUTS HIMSELF IN HIS ROOM...?
RATTLE
RATTLE
Keith Route
Keith shuts himself in.
He becomes isolated.
He enrolls in the Academy.
He meets the heroine and has his loneliness healed.
He falls in love with the heroine.
Katarina gets in his way.
Katarina is exiled abroad.
Katarina is killed by his magic.

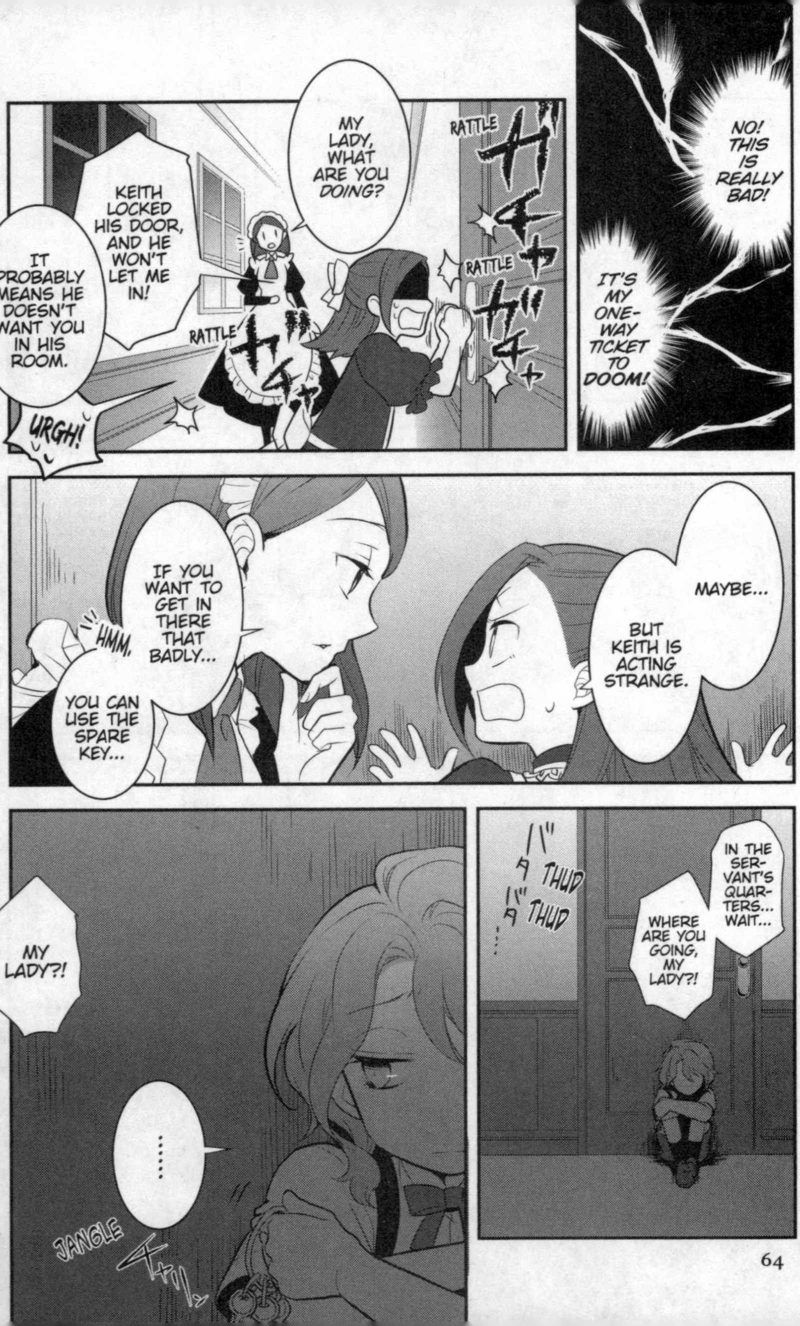
NO! THIS IS REALLY BAD!
IT'S MY ONE-WAY TICKET TO DOOM!
RATTLE
RATTLE
MY LADY, WHAT ARE YOU DOING?
RATTLE
KEITH LOCKED HIS DOOR, AND HE WON'T LET ME IN!
IT PROBABLY MEANS HE DOESN'T WANT YOU IN HIS ROOM.
URGH!
MAYBE...
BUT KEITH IS ACTING STRANGE.
HMM.
IF YOU WANT TO GET IN THERE THAT BADLY...
YOU CAN USE THE SPARE KEY...
IN THE SERVANT'S QUARTERS... WAIT...
WHERE ARE YOU GOING, MY LADY?!
THUD
THUD
MY LADY?!
......
JANGLE

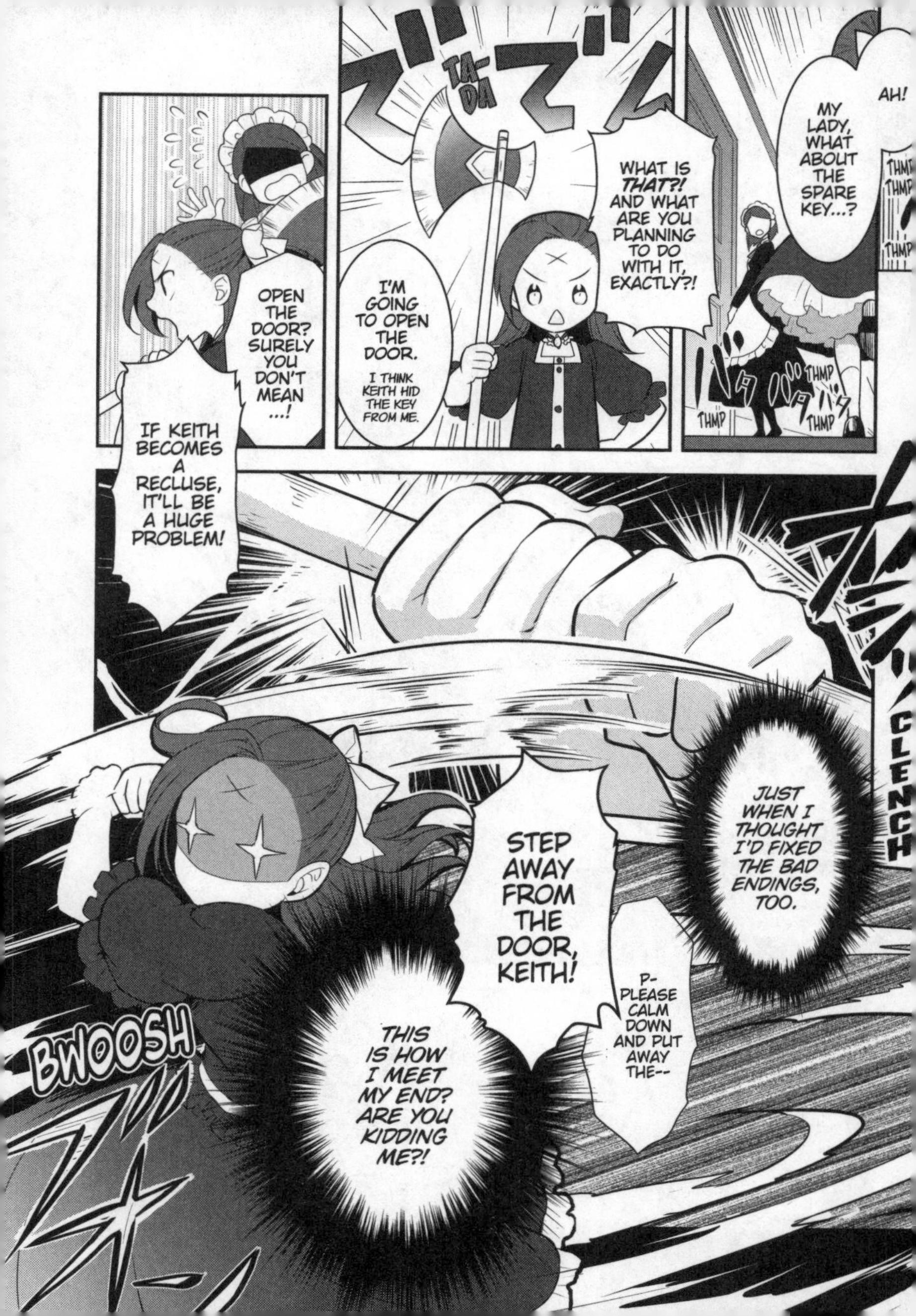
AH!
MY LADY, WHAT ABOUT THE SPARE KEY...?
THMP THMP
THMP
THMP THMP
THMP THMP
TA-DA
WHAT IS THAT?! AND WHAT ARE YOU PLANNING TO DO WITH IT, EXACTLY?!
I'M GOING TO OPEN THE DOOR.
I THINK KEITH HID THE KEY FROM ME.
OPEN THE DOOR? SURELY YOU DON'T MEAN ...!
CLENCH
IF KEITH BECOMES A RECLUSE, IT'LL BE A HUGE PROBLEM!
JUST WHEN I THOUGHT I'D FIXED THE BAD ENDINGS, TOO.
STEP AWAY FROM THE DOOR, KEITH!
P-PLEASE CALM DOWN AND PUT AWAY THE--
THIS IS HOW I MEET MY END? ARE YOU KIDDING ME?!
BWOOSH

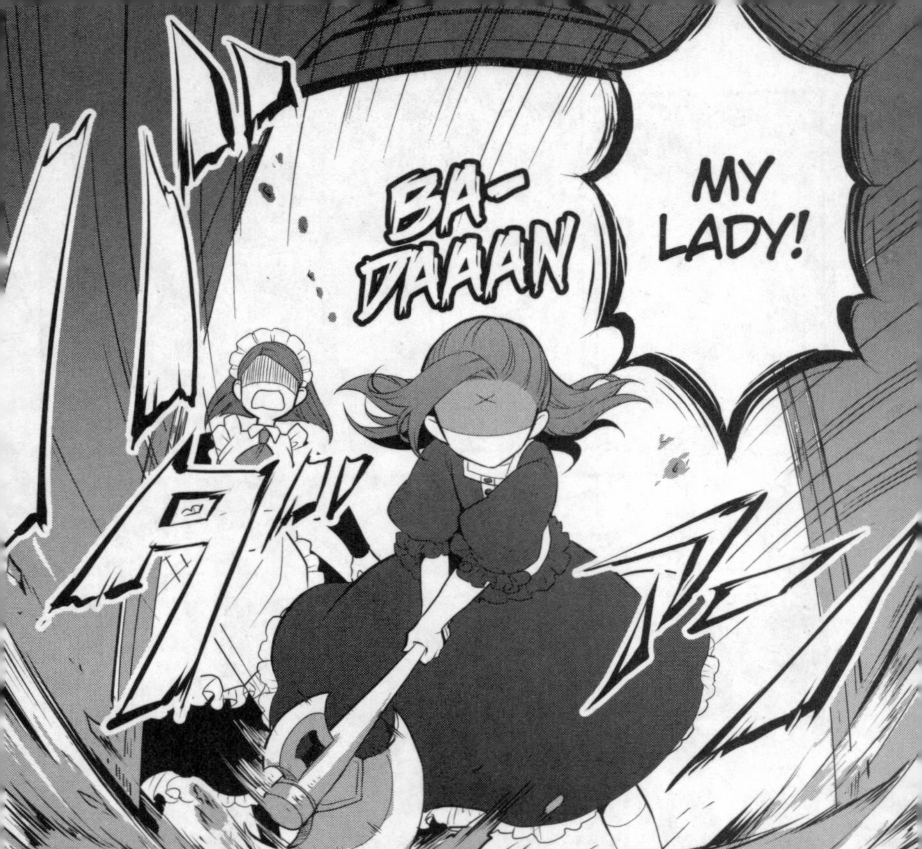
MY LADY!
BA-DAAAN

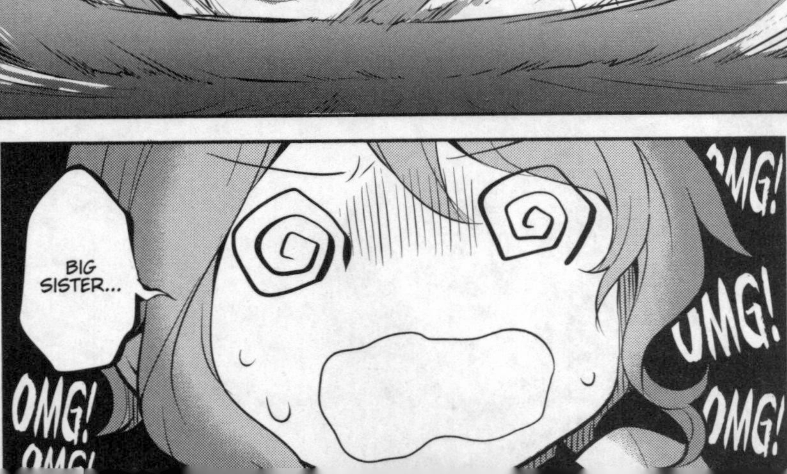
OMG!
OMG!
OMG!
BIG SISTER...
OMG!

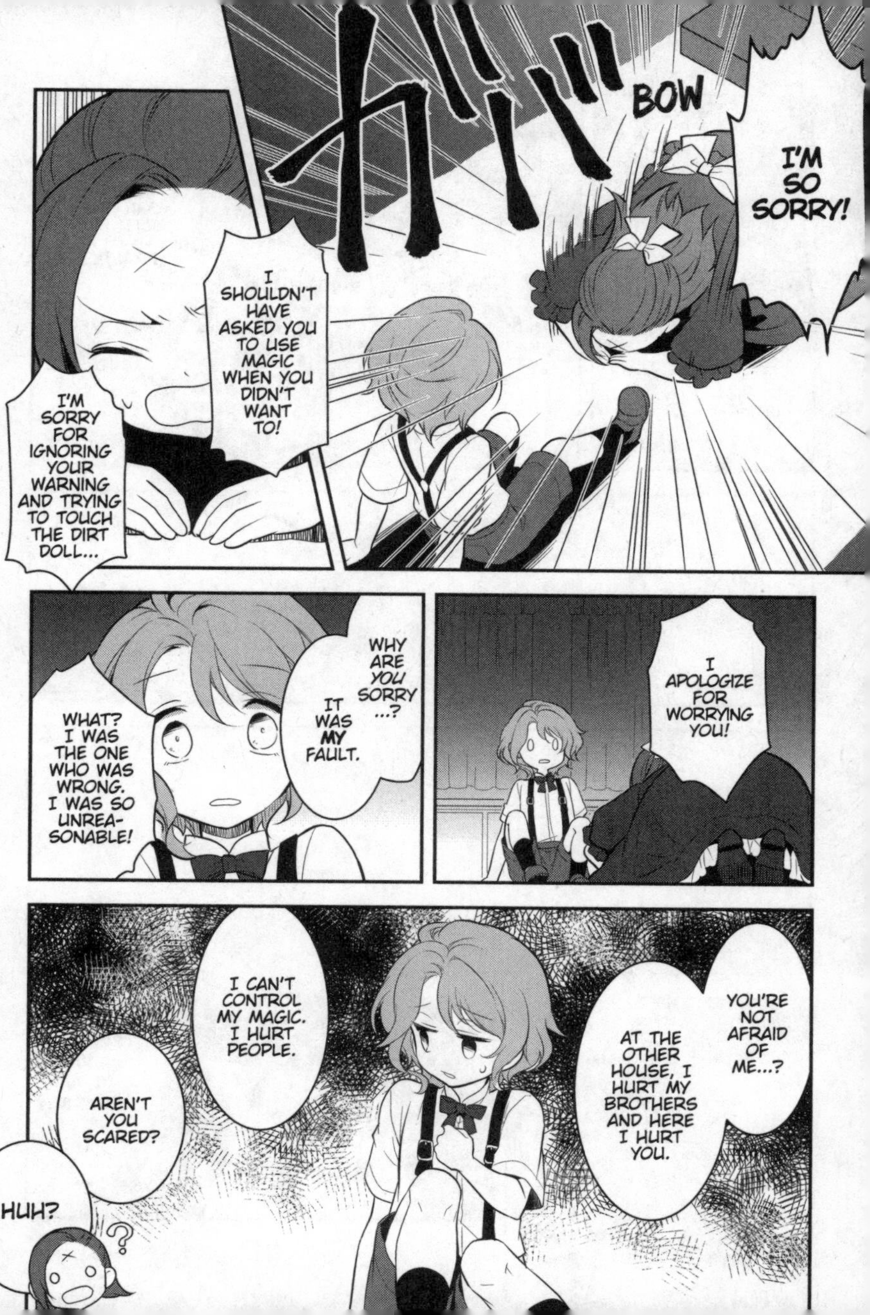
ガバ
BOW
I'M SO SORRY!
I SHOULDN'T HAVE ASKED YOU TO USE MAGIC WHEN YOU DIDN'T WANT TO!
I'M SORRY FOR IGNORING YOUR WARNING AND TRYING TO TOUCH THE DIRT DOLL...
I APOLOGIZE FOR WORRYING YOU!
WHY ARE *YOU* SORRY ...?
IT WAS **MY** FAULT.
WHAT? I WAS THE ONE WHO WAS WRONG. I WAS SO UNREA-SONABLE!
YOU'RE NOT AFRAID OF ME...?
AT THE OTHER HOUSE, I HURT MY BROTHERS AND HERE I HURT YOU.
I CAN'T CONTROL MY MAGIC. I HURT PEOPLE.
AREN'T YOU SCARED?
HUH?

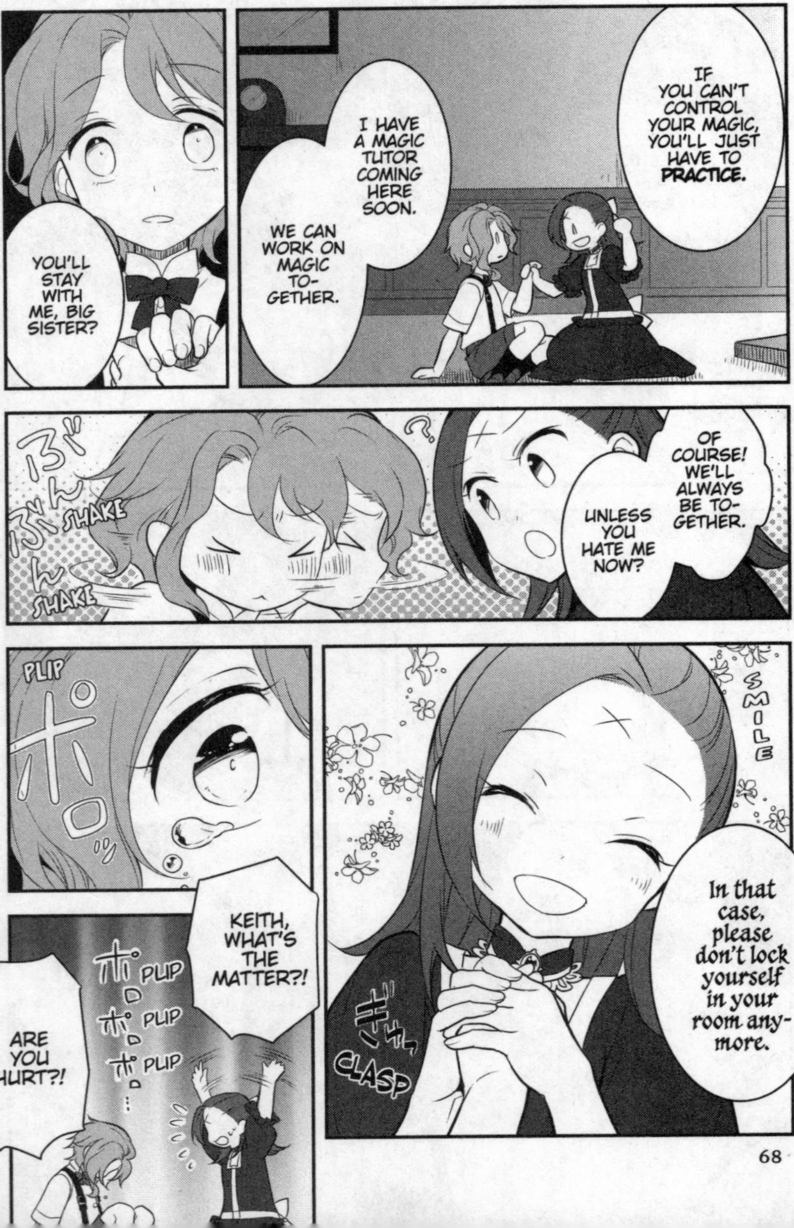
IF YOU CAN'T CONTROL YOUR MAGIC, YOU'LL JUST HAVE TO **PRACTICE.**
I HAVE A MAGIC TUTOR COMING HERE SOON.
WE CAN WORK ON MAGIC TO-GETHER.
YOU'LL STAY WITH ME, BIG SISTER?
OF COURSE! WE'LL ALWAYS BE TO-GETHER.
UNLESS YOU HATE ME NOW?
?
ぶんぶん
SHAKE
SHAKE
SMILE
In that case, please don't lock yourself in your room any-more.
ぎゅっ
CLASP
ポロッ
PLIP
KEITH, WHAT'S THE MATTER?!
ポロ
PLIP
ポロ
PLIP
ポロ
PLIP
ARE YOU HURT?!

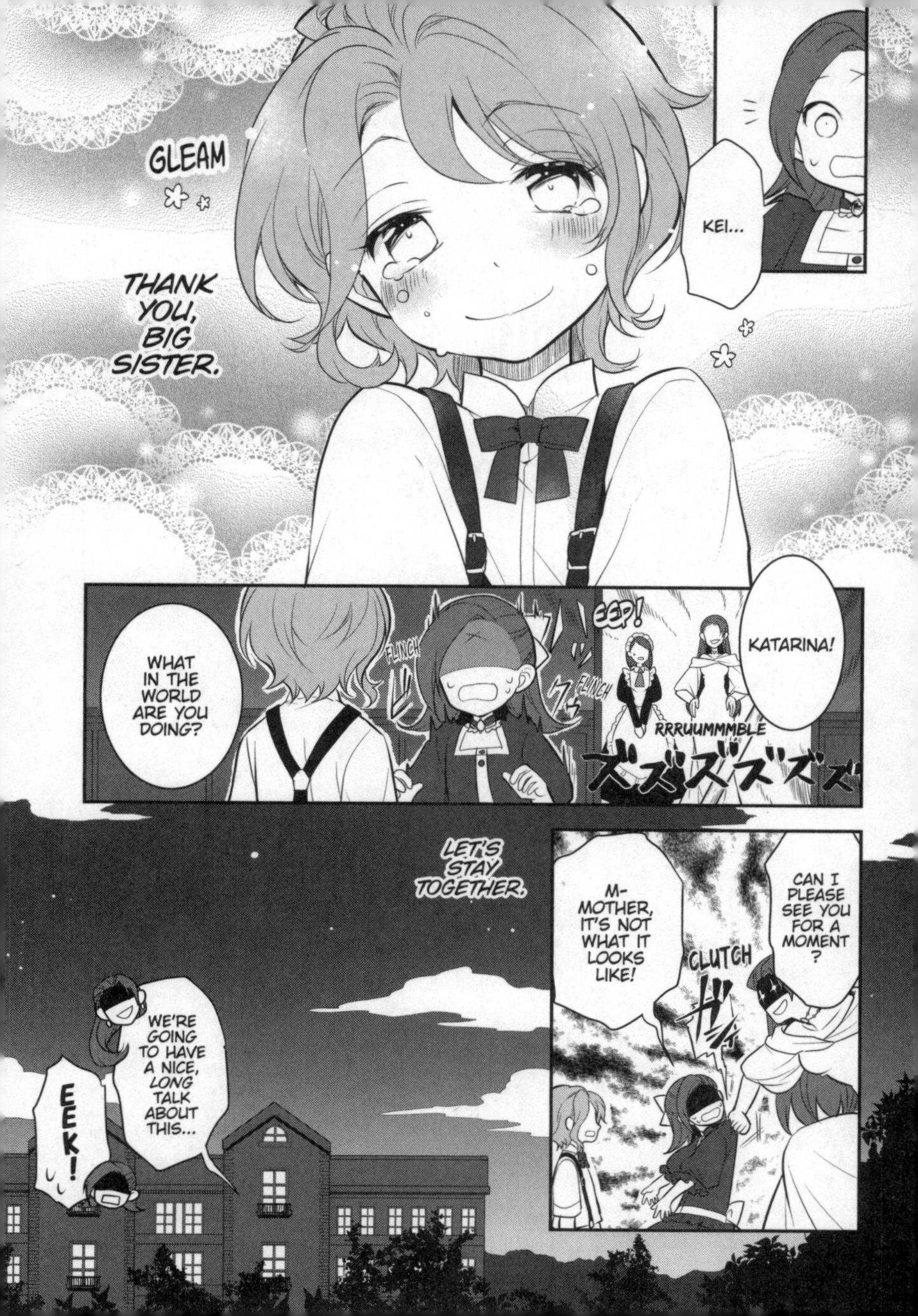
KEI...
GLEAM
THANK YOU, BIG SISTER.
KATARINA!
EEP!
RRRUUMMMBLE
ズズズズズズ
FLINCH
FLINCH
WHAT IN THE WORLD ARE YOU DOING?
CAN I PLEASE SEE YOU FOR A MOMENT?
CLUTCH
M-MOTHER, IT'S NOT WHAT IT LOOKS LIKE!
LET'S STAY TOGETHER.
WE'RE GOING TO HAVE A NICE, LONG TALK ABOUT THIS...
EEK!

My Next Life
as a VILLAINESS:
ALL ROUTES
LEAD TO DOOM!

Chapter 3

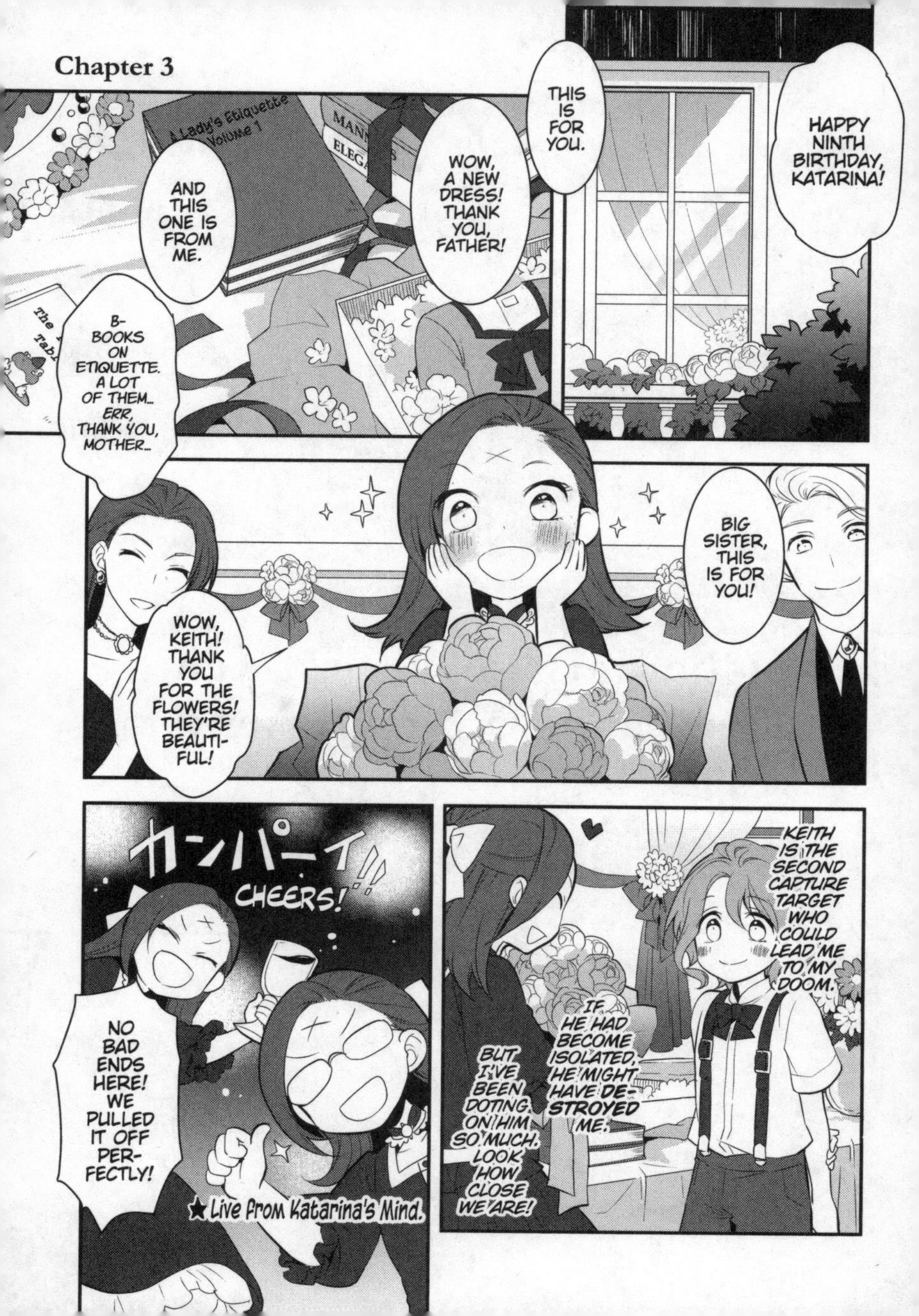
HAPPY NINTH BIRTHDAY, KATARINA!
THIS IS FOR YOU.
WOW, A NEW DRESS! THANK YOU, FATHER!
A Lady's Etiquette Volume 1
AND THIS ONE IS FROM ME.
B-BOOKS ON ETIQUETTE. A LOT OF THEM... ERR, THANK YOU, MOTHER...
BIG SISTER, THIS IS FOR YOU!
WOW, KEITH! THANK YOU FOR THE FLOWERS! THEY'RE BEAUTIFUL!
KEITH IS THE SECOND CAPTURE TARGET WHO COULD LEAD ME TO MY DOOM.
IF HE HAD BECOME ISOLATED, HE MIGHT HAVE DESTROYED ME.
BUT I'VE BEEN DOTING ON HIM SO MUCH. LOOK HOW CLOSE WE ARE!
カンパーイ!!!
CHEERS!
NO BAD ENDS HERE! WE PULLED IT OFF PERFECTLY!
★ Live from Katarina's Mind.

Chapter 3: My First Tea Party and a New Friend

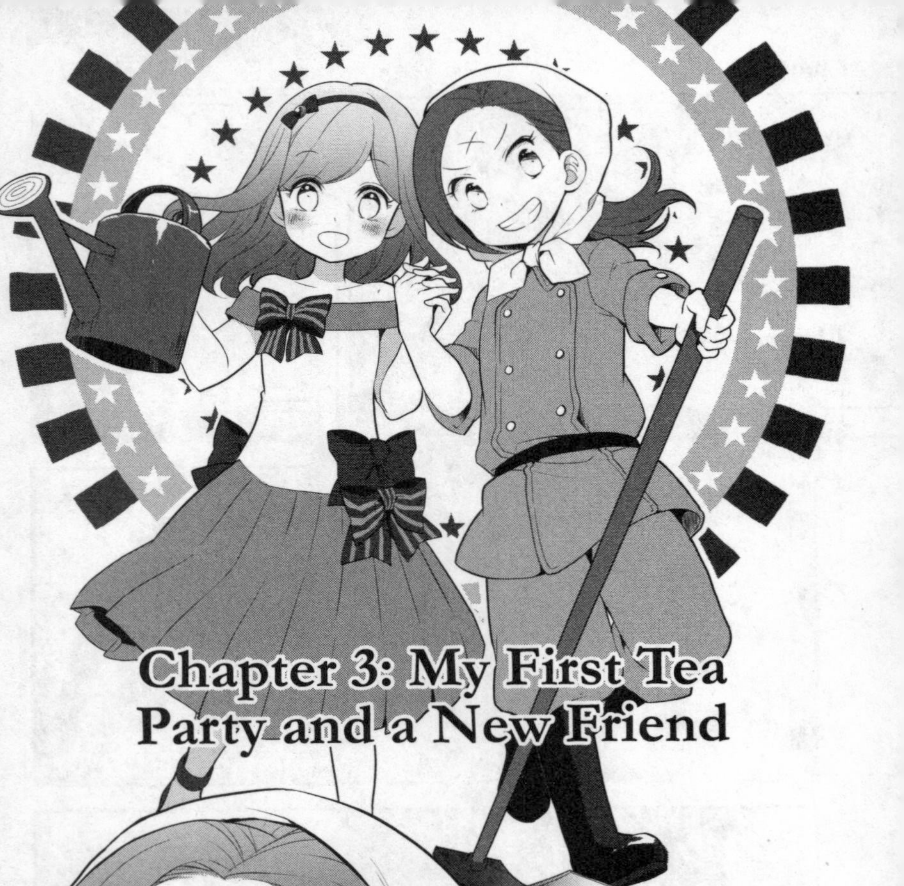

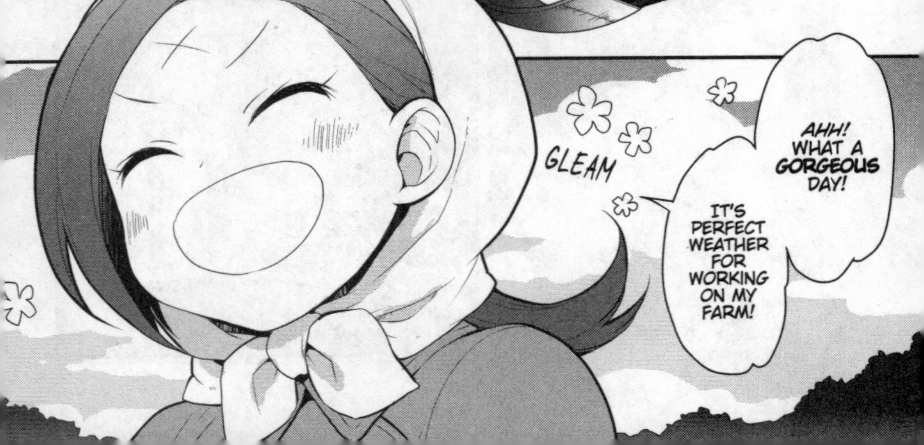
AHH! WHAT A GORGEOUS DAY!
IT'S PERFECT WEATHER FOR WORKING ON MY FARM!
GLEAM

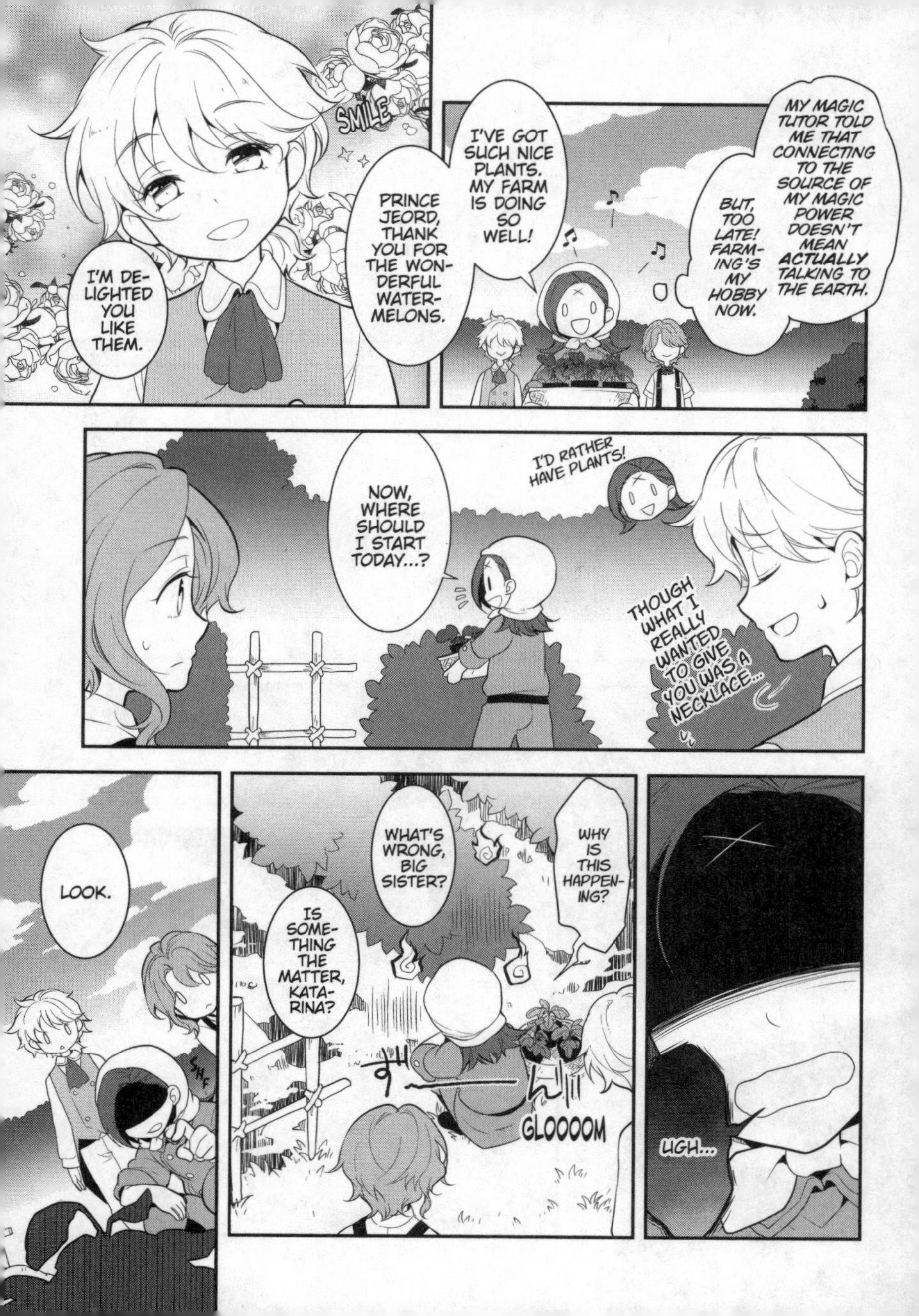
MY MAGIC TUTOR TOLD ME THAT CONNECTING TO THE SOURCE OF MY MAGIC POWER DOESN'T MEAN ACTUALLY TALKING TO THE EARTH.
BUT, TOO LATE! FARMING'S MY HOBBY NOW.
I'VE GOT SUCH NICE PLANTS. MY FARM IS DOING SO WELL!
SMILE
PRINCE JEORD, THANK YOU FOR THE WONDERFUL WATERMELONS.
I'M DELIGHTED YOU LIKE THEM.
THOUGH WHAT I REALLY WANTED TO GIVE YOU WAS A NECKLACE...
I'D RATHER HAVE PLANTS!
NOW, WHERE SHOULD I START TODAY...?
UGH...
WHY IS THIS HAPPENING?
WHAT'S WRONG, BIG SISTER?
IS SOMETHING THE MATTER, KATARINA?
GLOOOOM
LOOK.

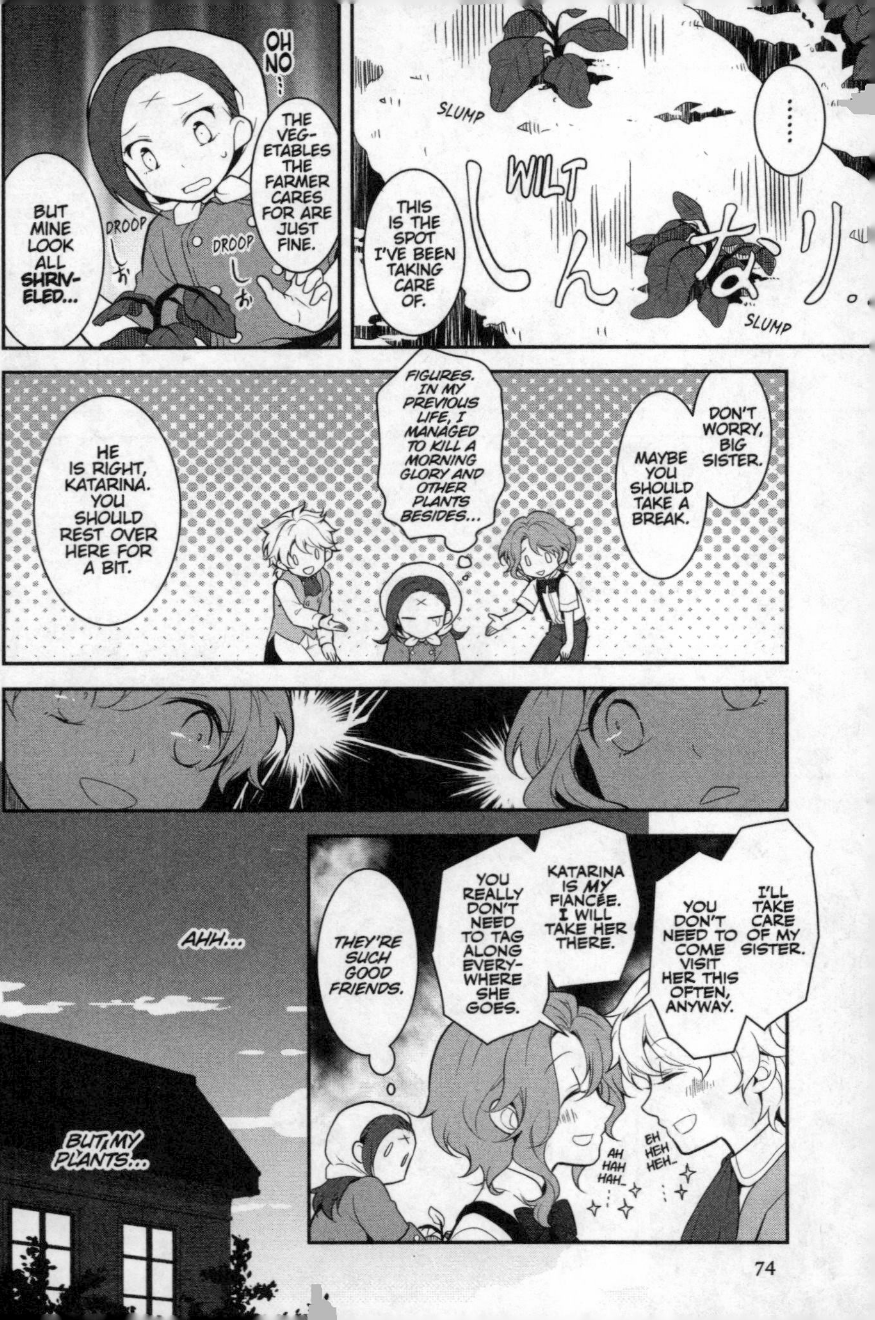
SLUMP
......
WILT
しんなり。
SLUMP
THIS IS THE SPOT I'VE BEEN TAKING CARE OF.
OH NO...
THE VEGETABLES THE FARMER CARES FOR ARE JUST FINE.
DROOP しお
DROOP しお
BUT MINE LOOK ALL SHRIVELED...
DON'T WORRY, BIG SISTER.
MAYBE YOU SHOULD TAKE A BREAK.
FIGURES. IN MY PREVIOUS LIFE, I MANAGED TO KILL A MORNING GLORY AND OTHER PLANTS BESIDES...
HE IS RIGHT, KATARINA. YOU SHOULD REST OVER HERE FOR A BIT.
I'LL TAKE CARE OF MY SISTER.
YOU DON'T NEED TO COME VISIT HER THIS OFTEN, ANYWAY.
KATARINA IS MY FIANCÉE. I WILL TAKE HER THERE.
YOU REALLY DON'T NEED TO TAG ALONG EVERYWHERE SHE GOES.
EH HEH HEH...
AH HAH HAH...
THEY'RE SUCH GOOD FRIENDS.
AHH...
BUT, MY PLANTS...

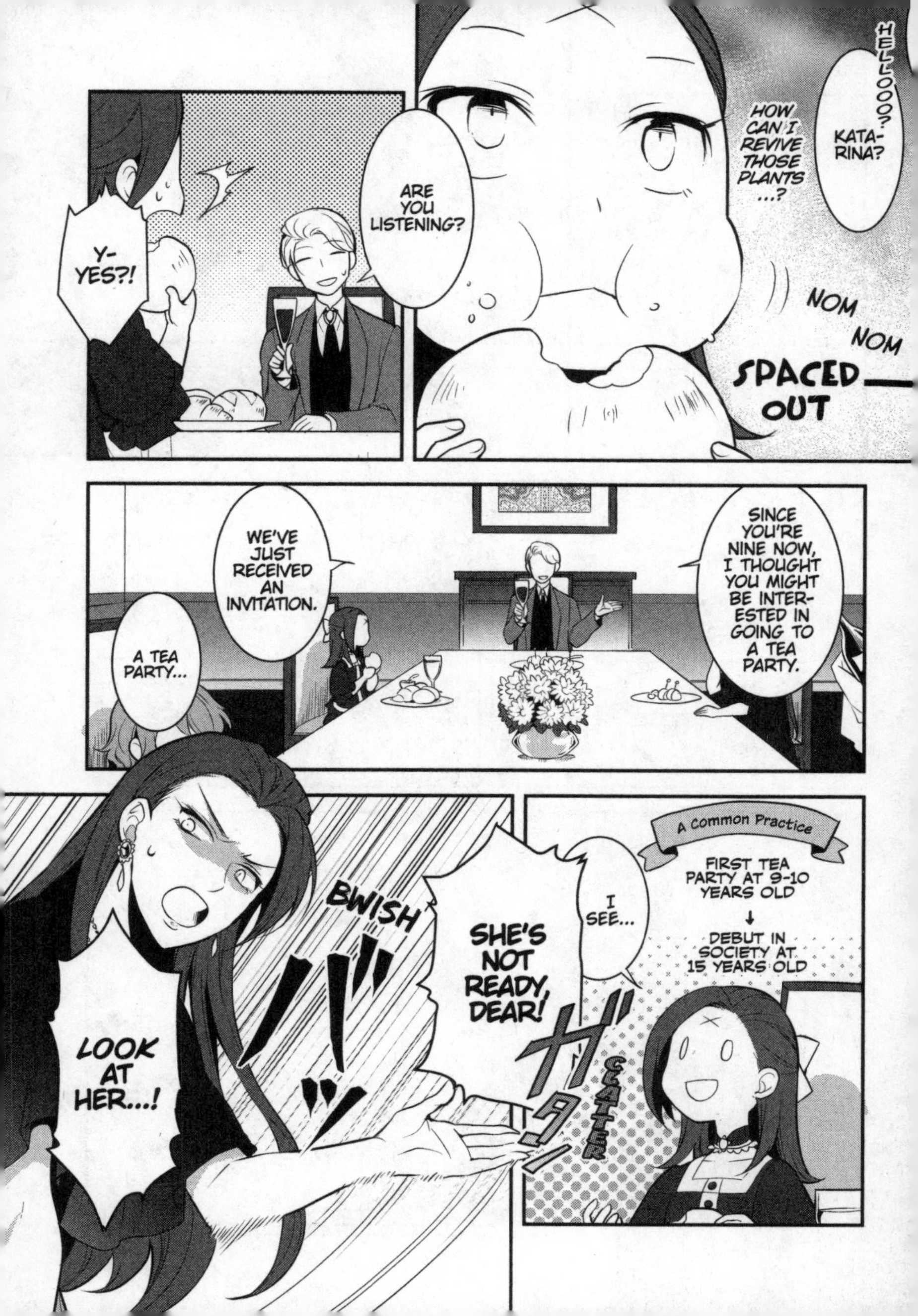
HELLOOOO? KATA-RINA?
HOW CAN I REVIVE THOSE PLANTS...?
NOM NOM
SPACED OUT
ARE YOU LISTENING?
Y-YES?!
SINCE YOU'RE NINE NOW, I THOUGHT YOU MIGHT BE INTER-ESTED IN GOING TO A TEA PARTY.
WE'VE JUST RECEIVED AN INVITATION.
A TEA PARTY...
A Common Practice
FIRST TEA PARTY AT 9-10 YEARS OLD
↓
DEBUT IN SOCIETY AT 15 YEARS OLD
I SEE...
CLATTER
SHE'S NOT READY, DEAR!
BWISH
LOOK AT HER...!

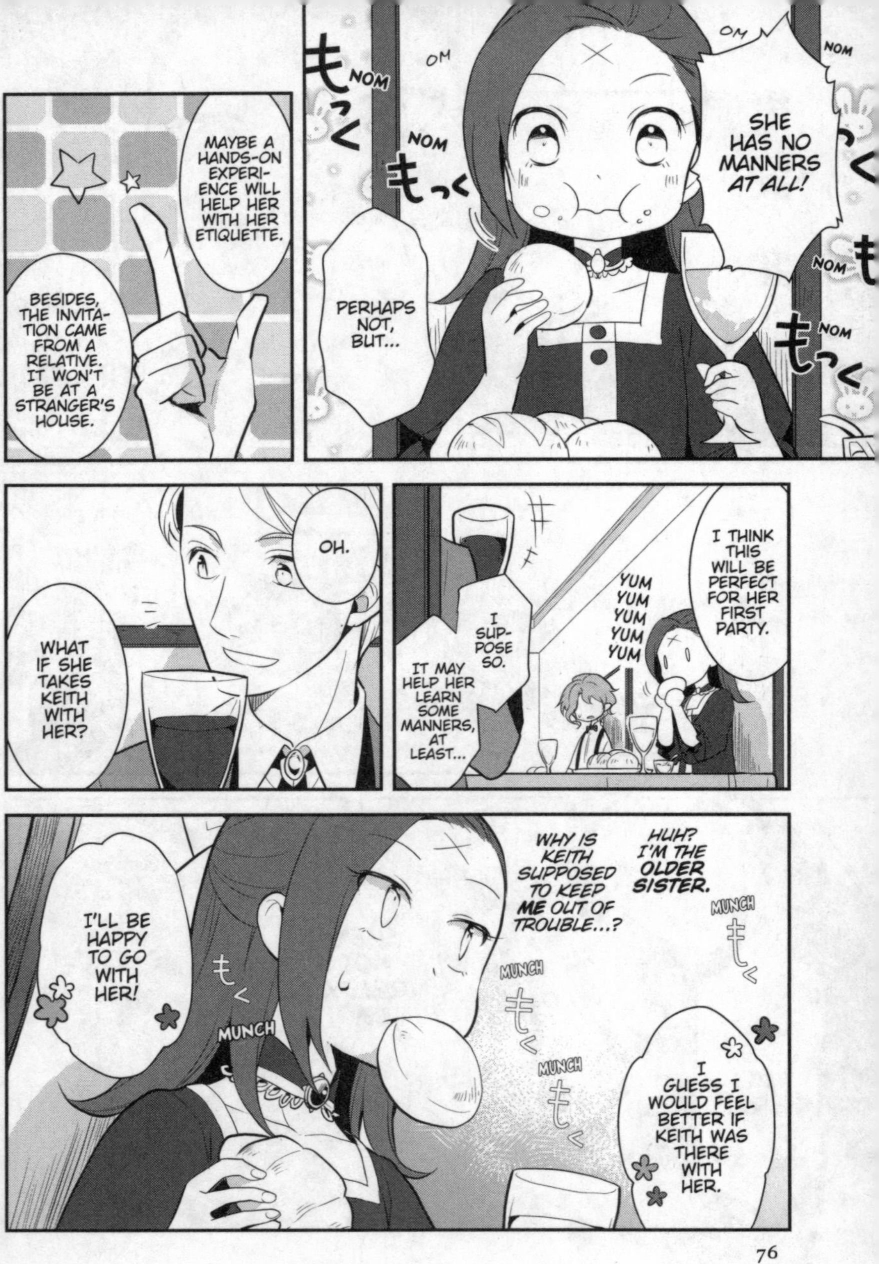
OM NOM
もっく
NOM
SHE HAS NO MANNERS AT ALL!
OM NOM
もっく
NOM
もっく
NOM
もっく
NOM
もっく
PERHAPS NOT, BUT...
MAYBE A HANDS-ON EXPERIENCE WILL HELP HER WITH HER ETIQUETTE.
BESIDES, THE INVITATION CAME FROM A RELATIVE. IT WON'T BE AT A STRANGER'S HOUSE.
I THINK THIS WILL BE PERFECT FOR HER FIRST PARTY.
YUM YUM YUM YUM YUM YUM
I SUPPOSE SO.
IT MAY HELP HER LEARN SOME MANNERS, AT LEAST...
OH.
WHAT IF SHE TAKES KEITH WITH HER?
HUH? I'M THE OLDER SISTER.
WHY IS KEITH SUPPOSED TO KEEP ME OUT OF TROUBLE...?
MUNCH もく
MUNCH もく
MUNCH もく
MUNCH もく
I GUESS I WOULD FEEL BETTER IF KEITH WAS THERE WITH HER.
I'LL BE HAPPY TO GO WITH HER!

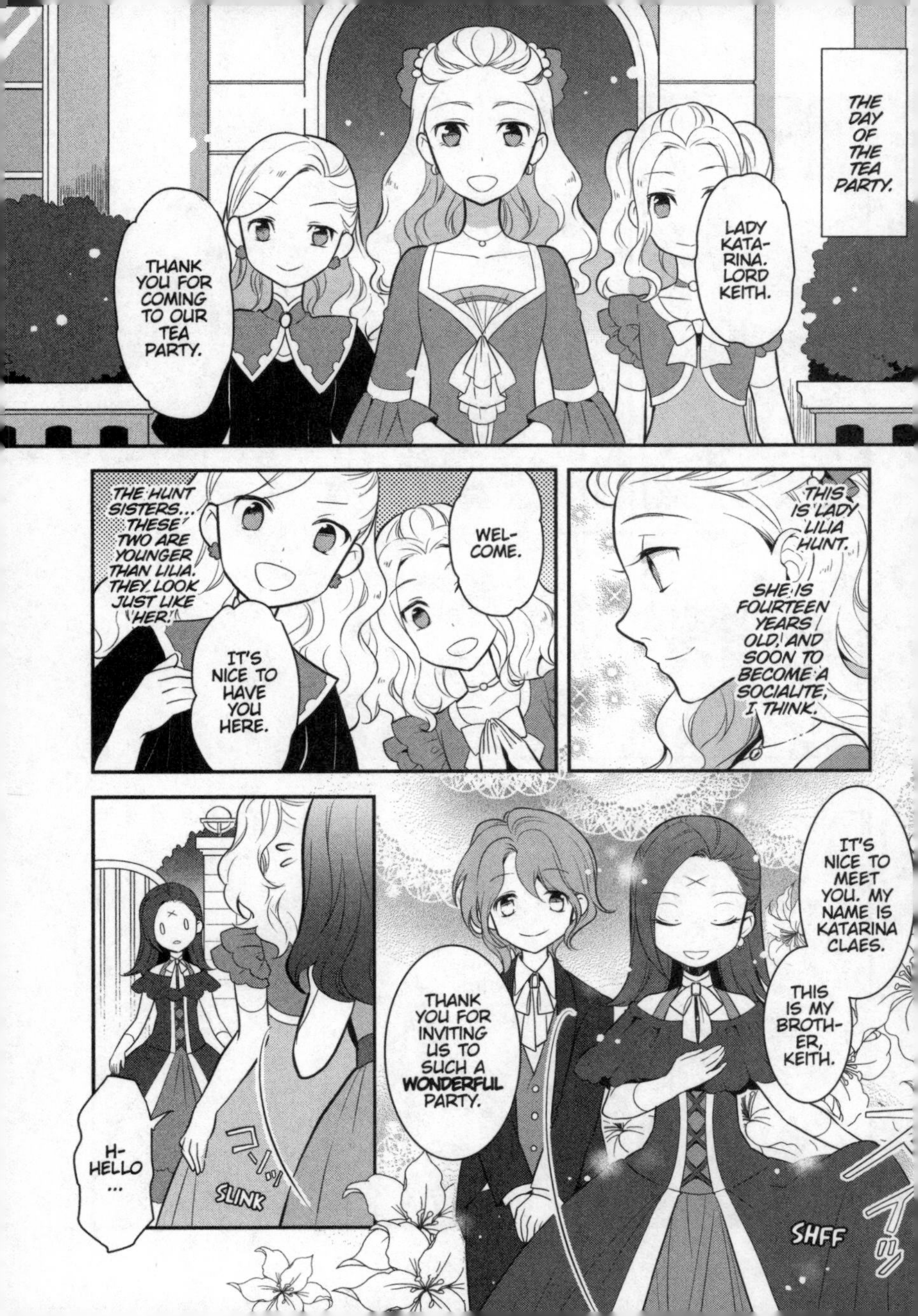
THE DAY OF THE TEA PARTY.
LADY KATARINA. LORD KEITH.
THANK YOU FOR COMING TO OUR TEA PARTY.
THIS IS LADY LILIA HUNT.
SHE IS FOURTEEN YEARS OLD, AND SOON TO BECOME A SOCIALITE, I THINK.
WELCOME.
THE HUNT SISTERS... THESE TWO ARE YOUNGER THAN LILIA. THEY LOOK JUST LIKE HER!
IT'S NICE TO HAVE YOU HERE.
IT'S NICE TO MEET YOU. MY NAME IS KATARINA CLAES.
THIS IS MY BROTHER, KEITH.
THANK YOU FOR INVITING US TO SUCH A **WONDERFUL** PARTY.
SHFF
SLINK
H-HELLO...

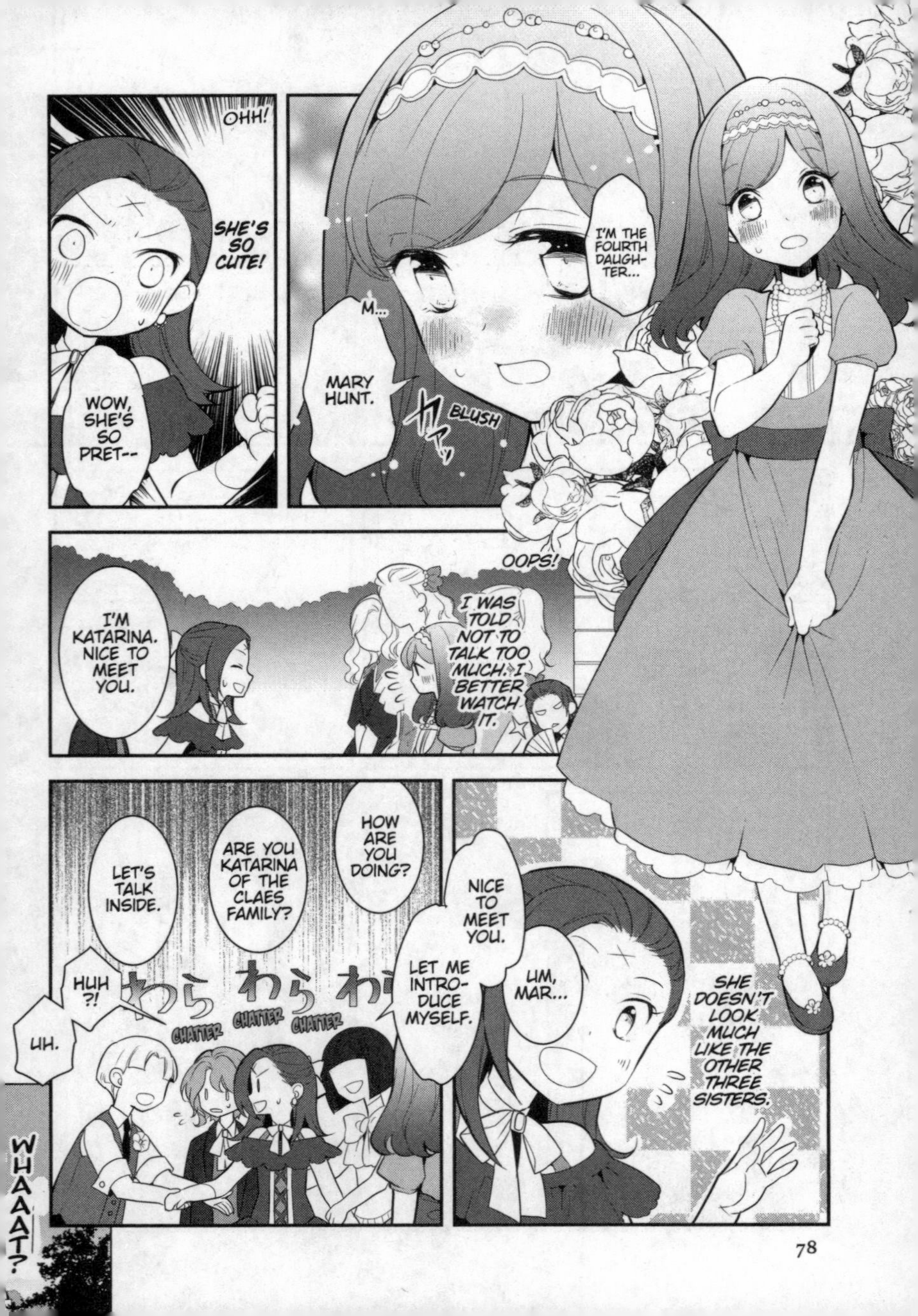
I'M THE FOURTH DAUGHTER...
M...
MARY HUNT.
BLUSH
OHH!
SHE'S SO CUTE!
WOW, SHE'S SO PRET--
OOPS!
I WAS TOLD NOT TO TALK TOO MUCH. I BETTER WATCH IT.
I'M KATARINA. NICE TO MEET YOU.
SHE DOESN'T LOOK MUCH LIKE THE OTHER THREE SISTERS.
UM, MAR...
NICE TO MEET YOU.
HOW ARE YOU DOING?
LET ME INTRODUCE MYSELF.
ARE YOU KATARINA OF THE CLAES FAMILY?
LET'S TALK INSIDE.
CHATTER CHATTER CHATTER
HUH?!
UH.
WHAAAT?

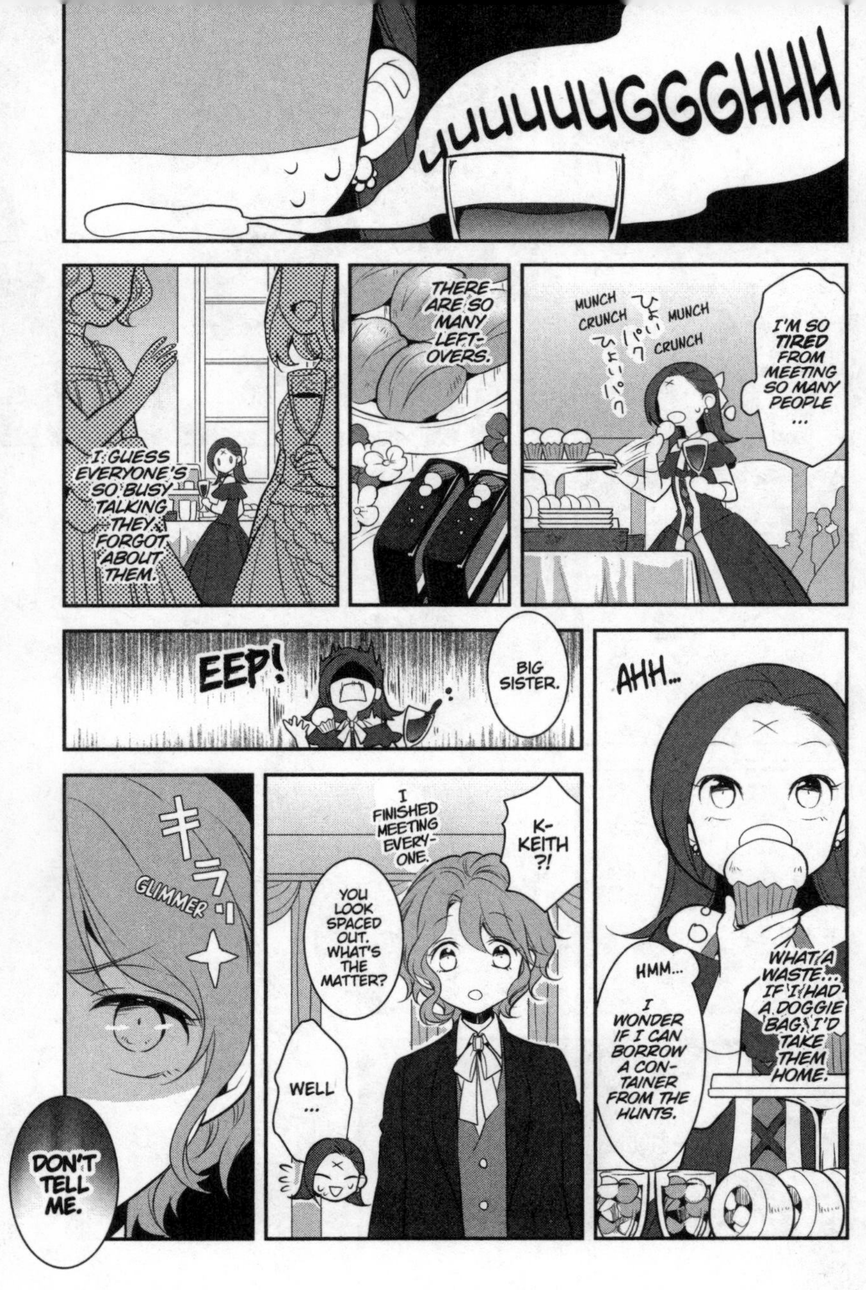
UUUUUUGGGHHH
MUNCH
CRUNCH
ひょいパク
ひょいパク
MUNCH
CRUNCH
I'M SO TIRED FROM MEETING SO MANY PEOPLE...
THERE ARE SO MANY LEFT-OVERS.
I GUESS EVERYONE'S SO BUSY TALKING THEY FORGOT ABOUT THEM.
AHH...
WHAT A WASTE... IF I HAD A DOGGIE BAG, I'D TAKE THEM HOME.
HMM...
I WONDER IF I CAN BORROW A CON-TAINER FROM THE HUNTS.
BIG SISTER.
EEP!
I FINISHED MEETING EVERY-ONE.
K-KEITH?!
YOU LOOK SPACED OUT. WHAT'S THE MATTER?
WELL...
キラッ
GLIMMER
DON'T TELL ME.

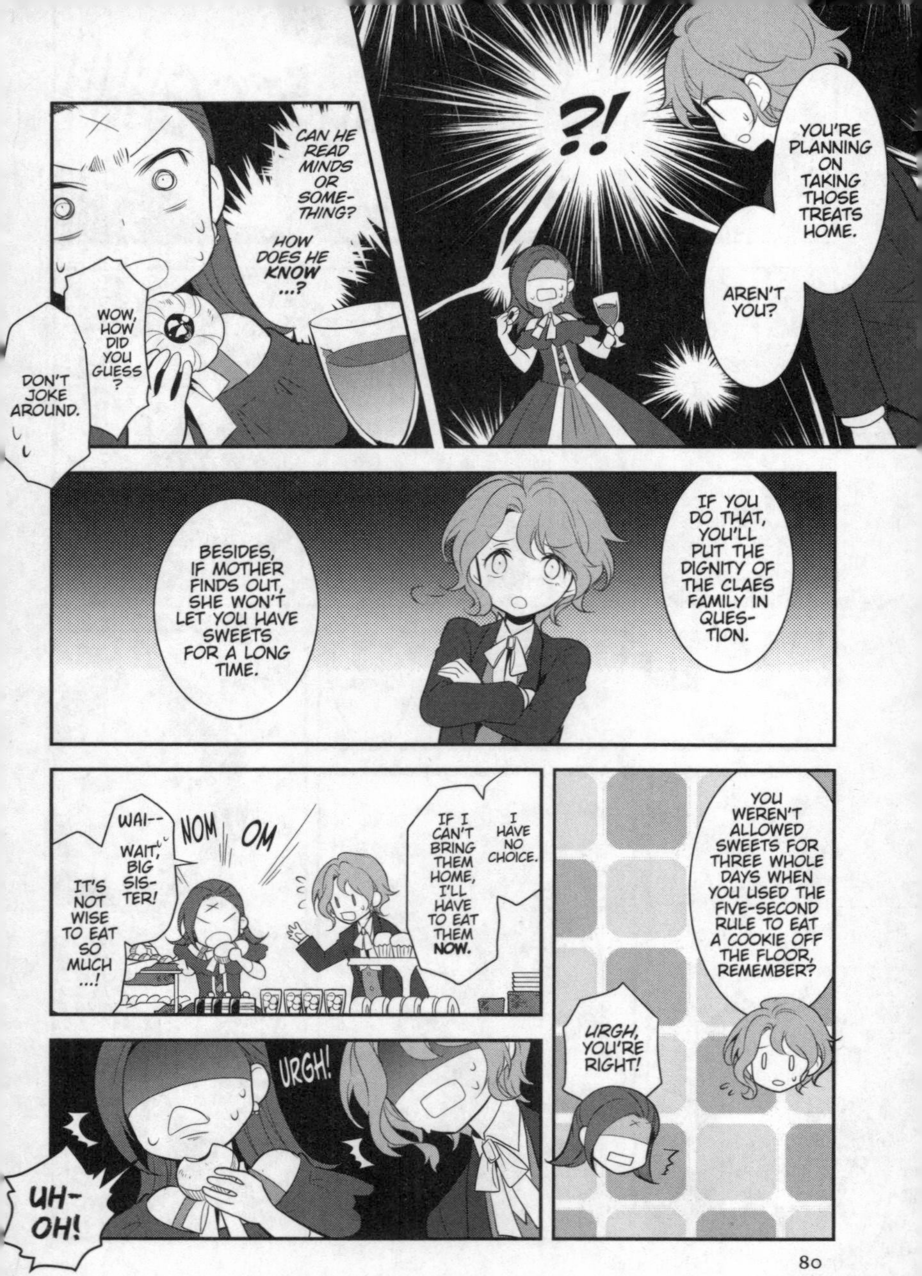
?!
YOU'RE PLANNING ON TAKING THOSE TREATS HOME.
AREN'T YOU?
CAN HE READ MINDS OR SOME-THING?
HOW DOES HE KNOW ...?
WOW, HOW DID YOU GUESS?
DON'T JOKE AROUND.
IF YOU DO THAT, YOU'LL PUT THE DIGNITY OF THE CLAES FAMILY IN QUES-TION.
BESIDES, IF MOTHER FINDS OUT, SHE WON'T LET YOU HAVE SWEETS FOR A LONG TIME.
YOU WEREN'T ALLOWED SWEETS FOR THREE WHOLE DAYS WHEN YOU USED THE FIVE-SECOND RULE TO EAT A COOKIE OFF THE FLOOR, REMEMBER?
URGH, YOU'RE RIGHT!
I HAVE NO CHOICE.
IF I CAN'T BRING THEM HOME, I'LL HAVE TO EAT THEM NOW.
NOM
OM
WAI--
WAIT, BIG SIS-TER!
IT'S NOT WISE TO EAT SO MUCH ...!
URGH!
UH-OH!

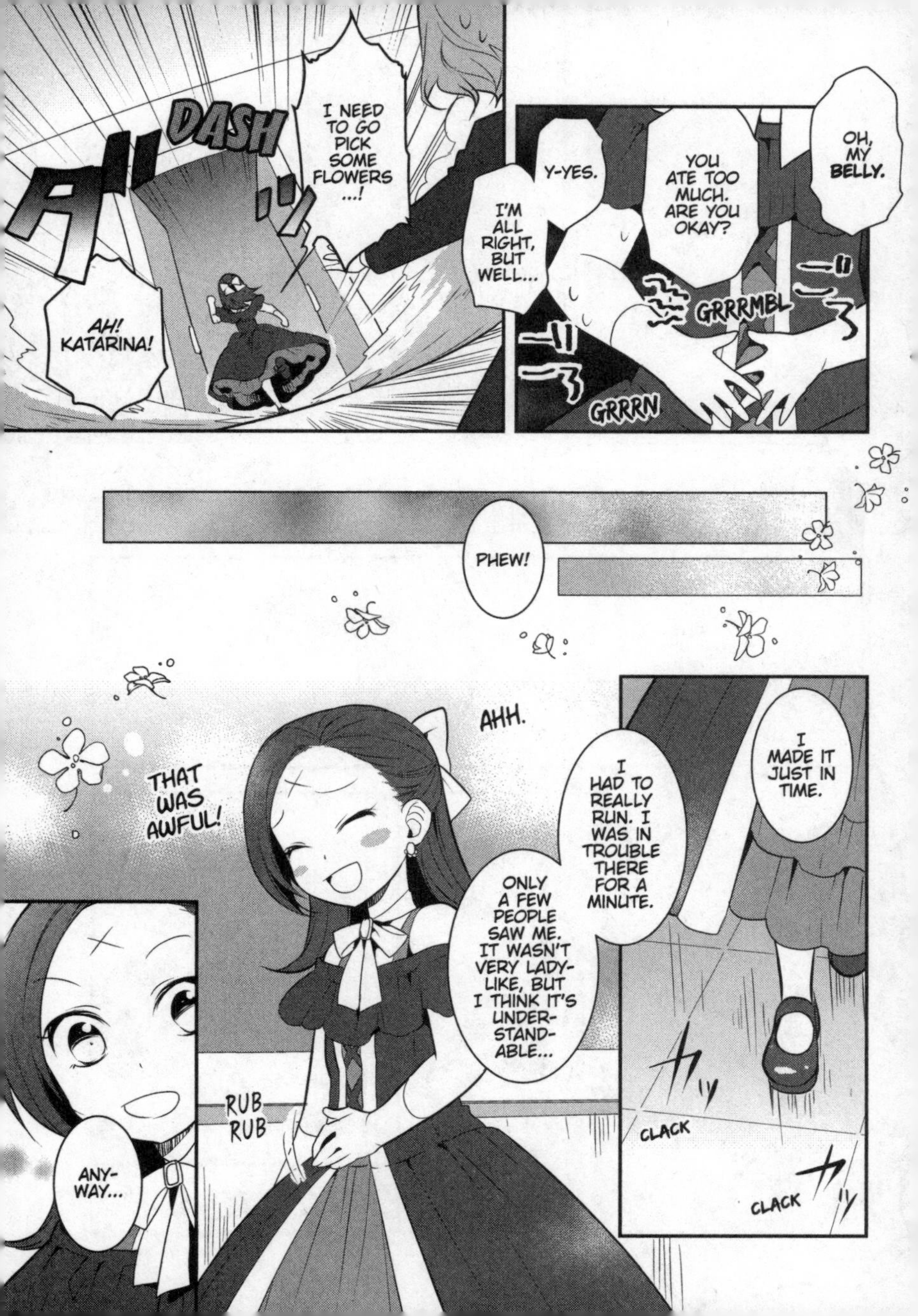
OH, MY BELLY.
YOU ATE TOO MUCH. ARE YOU OKAY?
Y-YES.
I'M ALL RIGHT, BUT WELL...
GRRRMBL
GRRRN
I NEED TO GO PICK SOME FLOWERS ...!
DASH
AH! KATARINA!
PHEW!
I MADE IT JUST IN TIME.
CLACK
CLACK
I HAD TO REALLY RUN. I WAS IN TROUBLE THERE FOR A MINUTE.
ONLY A FEW PEOPLE SAW ME. IT WASN'T VERY LADY-LIKE, BUT I THINK IT'S UNDER-STAND-ABLE...
AHH.
THAT WAS AWFUL!
RUB RUB
ANY-WAY...

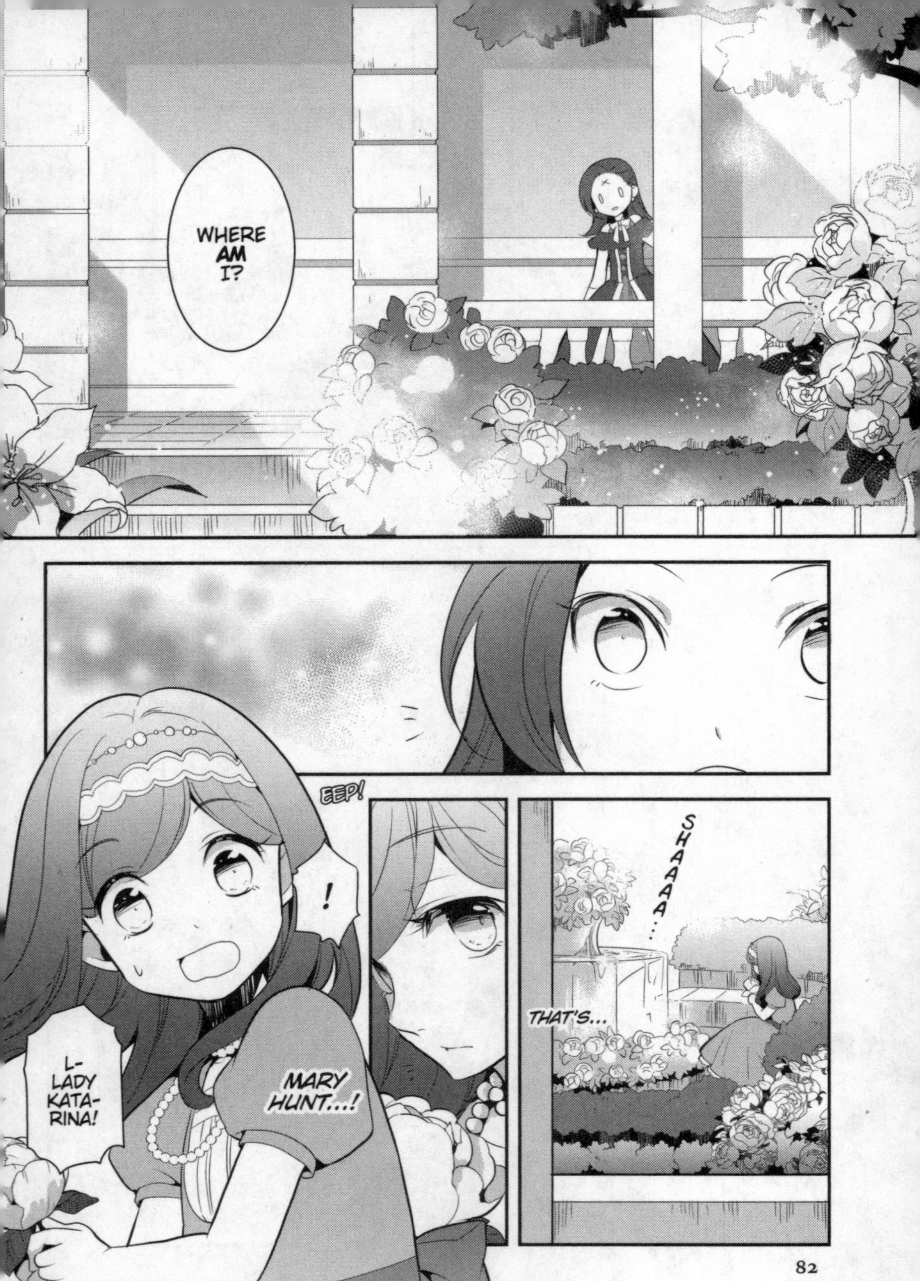
WHERE AM I?
SHAAAAA...
THAT'S...
MARY HUNT...!
EEP!
!
L-LADY KATA-RINA!

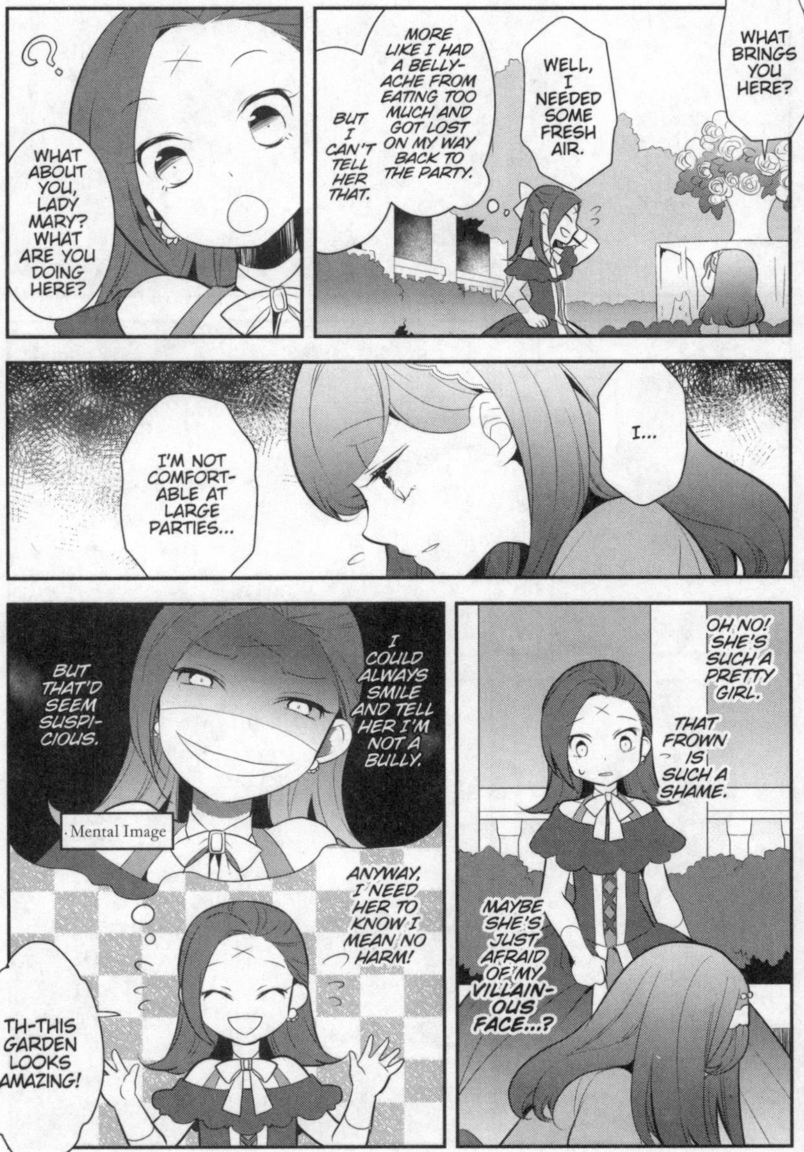
WHAT BRINGS YOU HERE?
WELL, I NEEDED SOME FRESH AIR.
MORE LIKE I HAD A BELLY-ACHE FROM EATING TOO MUCH AND GOT LOST ON MY WAY BACK TO THE PARTY.
BUT I CAN'T TELL HER THAT.
?
WHAT ABOUT YOU, LADY MARY? WHAT ARE YOU DOING HERE?
I...
I'M NOT COMFORTABLE AT LARGE PARTIES...
OH NO! SHE'S SUCH A PRETTY GIRL.
THAT FROWN IS SUCH A SHAME.
MAYBE SHE'S JUST AFRAID OF MY VILLAINOUS FACE...?
I COULD ALWAYS SMILE AND TELL HER I'M NOT A BULLY.
BUT THAT'D SEEM SUSPICIOUS.
Mental Image
ANYWAY, I NEED HER TO KNOW I MEAN NO HARM!
TH-THIS GARDEN LOOKS AMAZING!

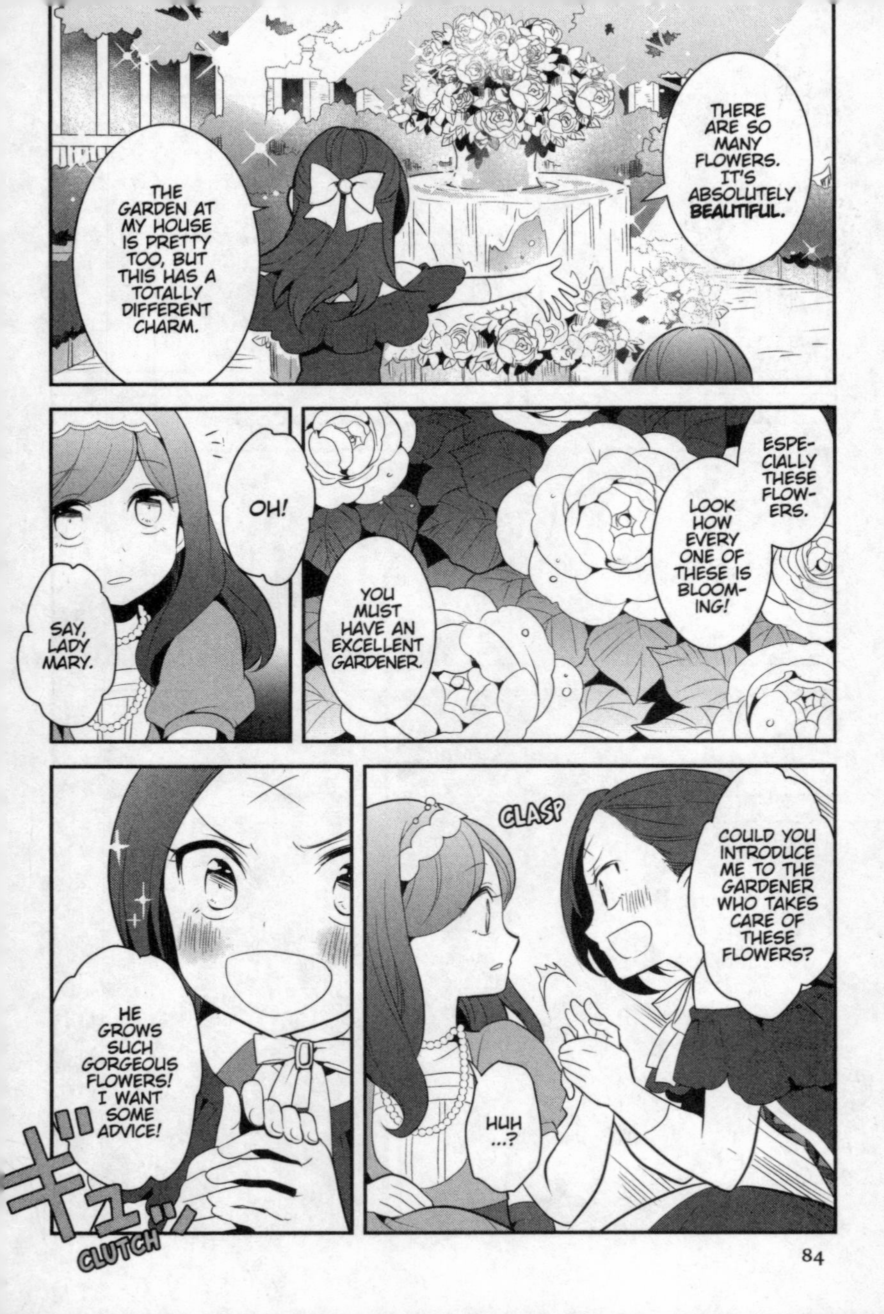
THERE ARE SO MANY FLOWERS. IT'S ABSOLUTELY BEAUTIFUL.
THE GARDEN AT MY HOUSE IS PRETTY TOO, BUT THIS HAS A TOTALLY DIFFERENT CHARM.
ESPE-CIALLY THESE FLOW-ERS.
LOOK HOW EVERY ONE OF THESE IS BLOOM-ING!
YOU MUST HAVE AN EXCELLENT GARDENER.
OH!
SAY, LADY MARY.
CLASP
COULD YOU INTRODUCE ME TO THE GARDENER WHO TAKES CARE OF THESE FLOWERS?
HUH ...?
HE GROWS SUCH GORGEOUS FLOWERS! I WANT SOME ADVICE!
ギュッ
CLUTCH

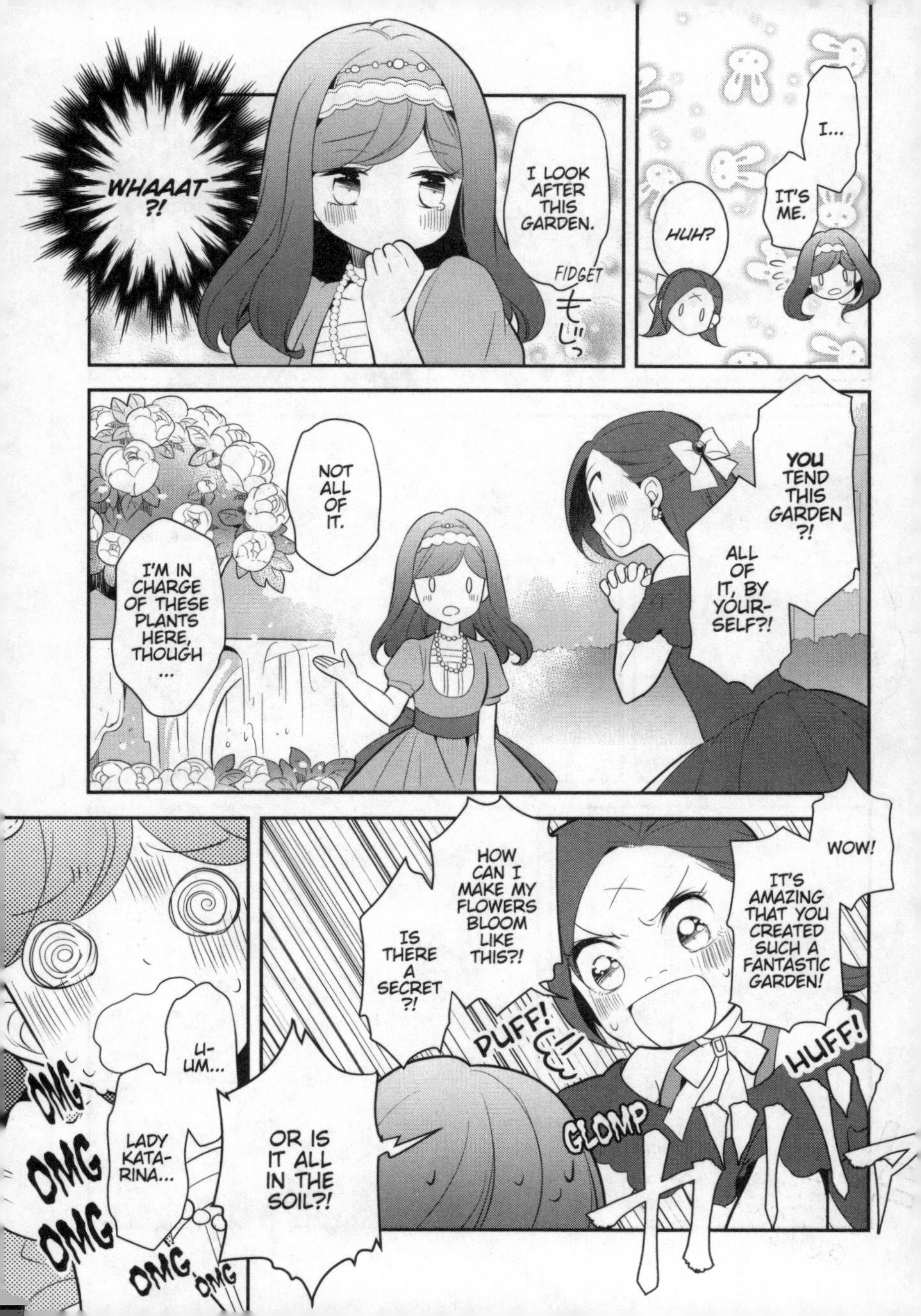
I...
IT'S ME.
HUH?
I LOOK AFTER THIS GARDEN.
FIDGET
もじっ
WHAAAT ?!
YOU TEND THIS GARDEN ?!
ALL OF IT, BY YOUR-SELF?!
NOT ALL OF IT.
I'M IN CHARGE OF THESE PLANTS HERE, THOUGH ...
WOW!
IT'S AMAZING THAT YOU CREATED SUCH A FANTASTIC GARDEN!
HUFF!
HOW CAN I MAKE MY FLOWERS BLOOM LIKE THIS?!
PUFF!
IS THERE A SECRET ?!
OR IS IT ALL IN THE SOIL?!
GLOMP
U-UM...
LADY KATA-RINA...
OMG
OMG
OMG
OMG
OMG

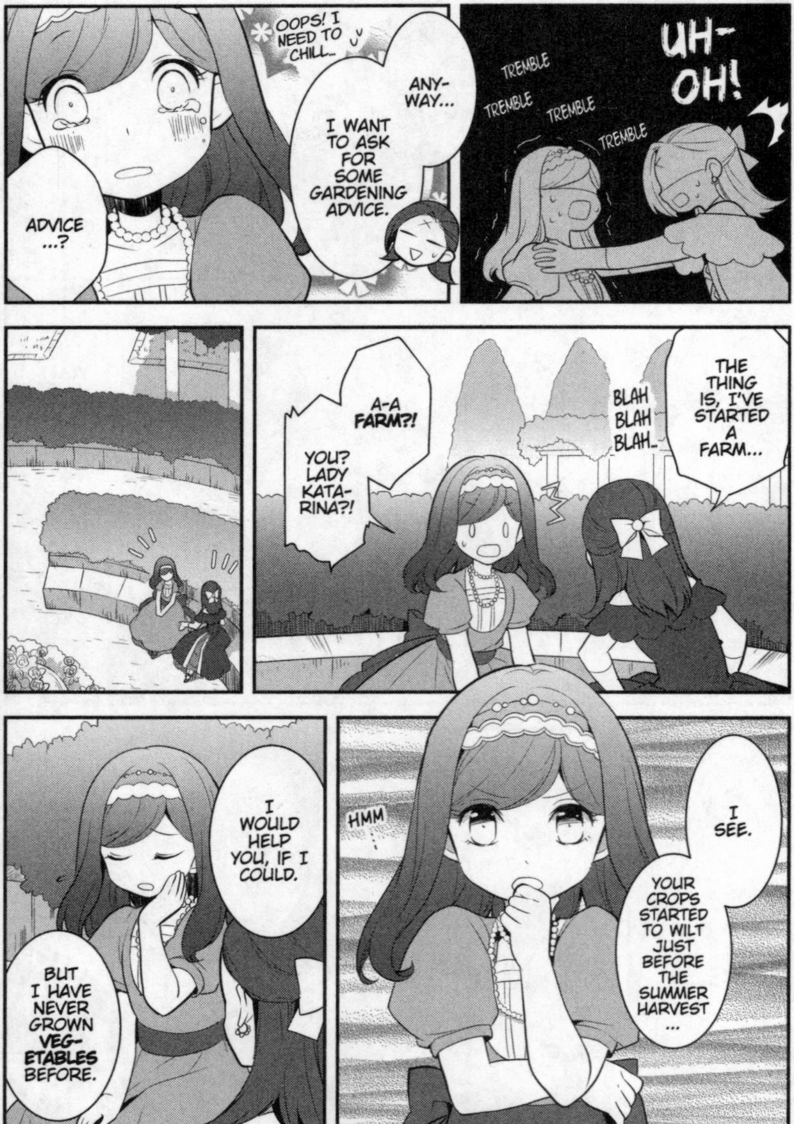
UH-OH!
TREMBLE
TREMBLE
TREMBLE
TREMBLE
OOPS! I NEED TO CHILL...
ANY-WAY...
I WANT TO ASK FOR SOME GARDENING ADVICE.
ADVICE ...?
THE THING IS, I'VE STARTED A FARM...
BLAH BLAH BLAH...
A-A **FARM?!**
YOU? LADY KATA-RINA?!
I SEE.
HMM ...
YOUR CROPS STARTED TO WILT JUST BEFORE THE SUMMER HARVEST ...
I WOULD HELP YOU, IF I COULD.
BUT I HAVE NEVER GROWN **VEG-ETABLES** BEFORE.

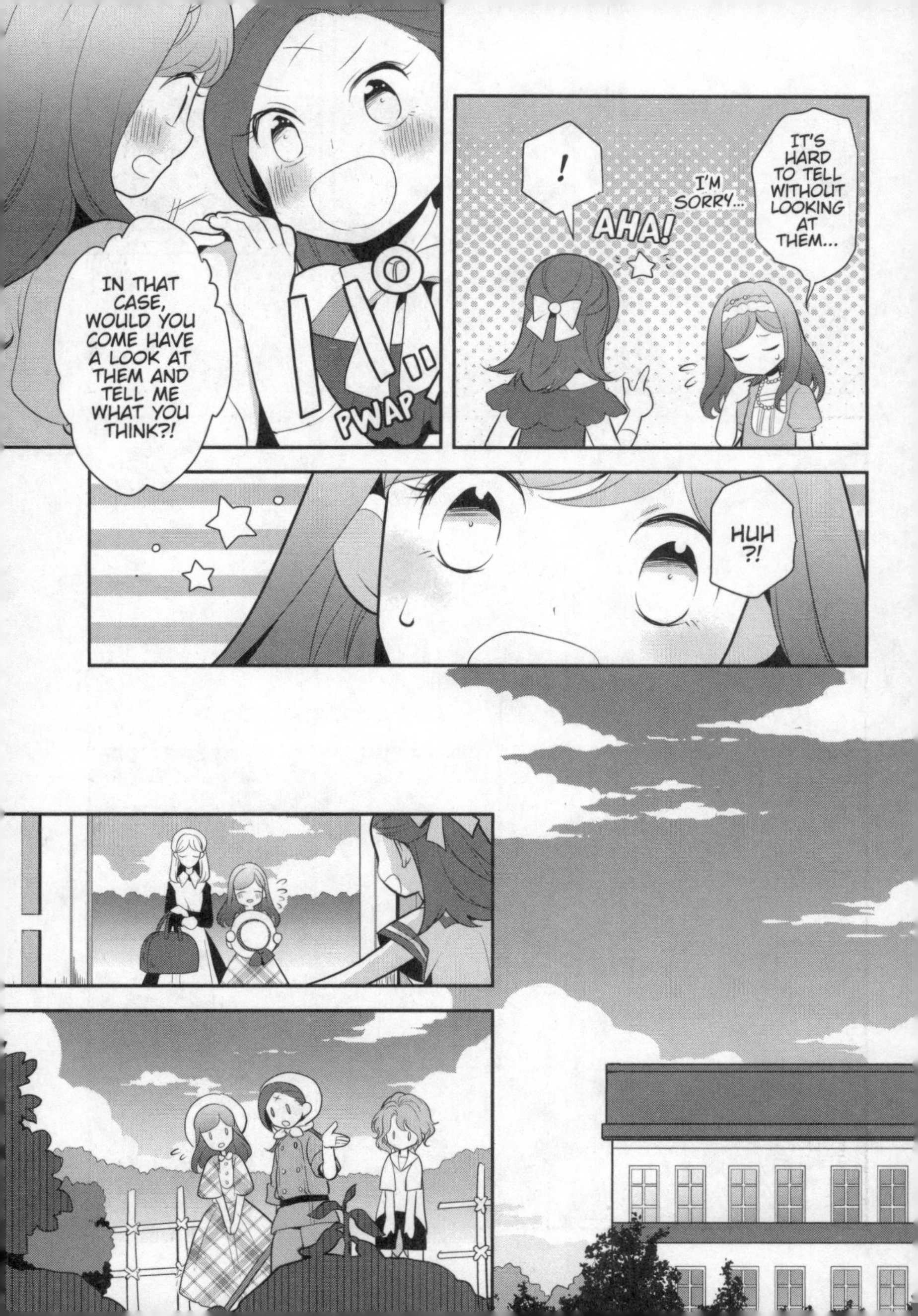
IT'S HARD TO TELL WITHOUT LOOKING AT THEM...
I'M SORRY...
!
AHA!
IN THAT CASE, WOULD YOU COME HAVE A LOOK AT THEM AND TELL ME WHAT YOU THINK?!
PWAP
HUH?!

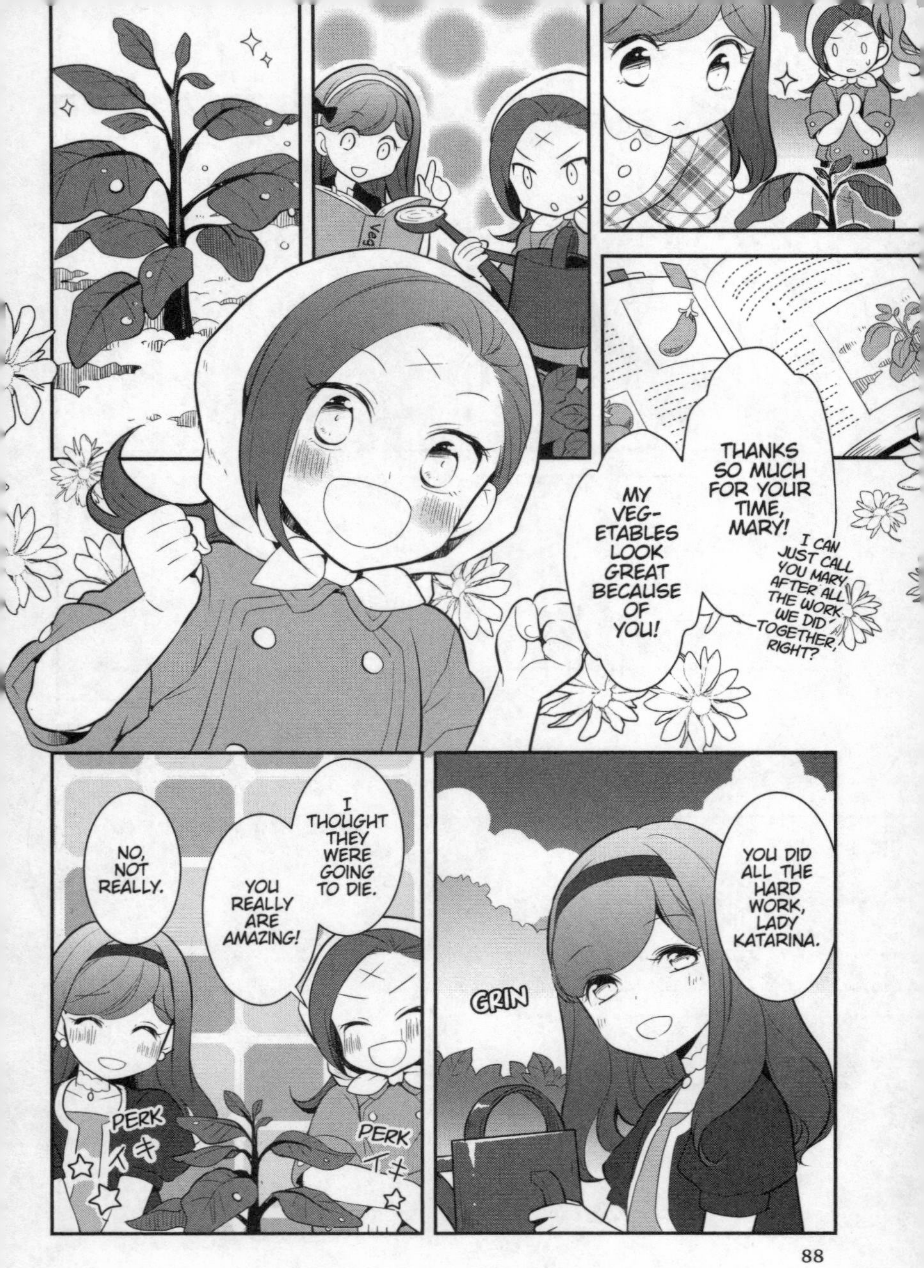
Veg
THANKS SO MUCH FOR YOUR TIME, MARY!
I CAN JUST CALL YOU MARY, AFTER ALL THE WORK WE DID TOGETHER, RIGHT?
MY VEG-ETABLES LOOK GREAT BECAUSE OF YOU!
YOU DID ALL THE HARD WORK, LADY KATARINA.
GRIN
I THOUGHT THEY WERE GOING TO DIE.
YOU REALLY ARE AMAZING!
NO, NOT REALLY.
PERK
イキ
PERK
イキ

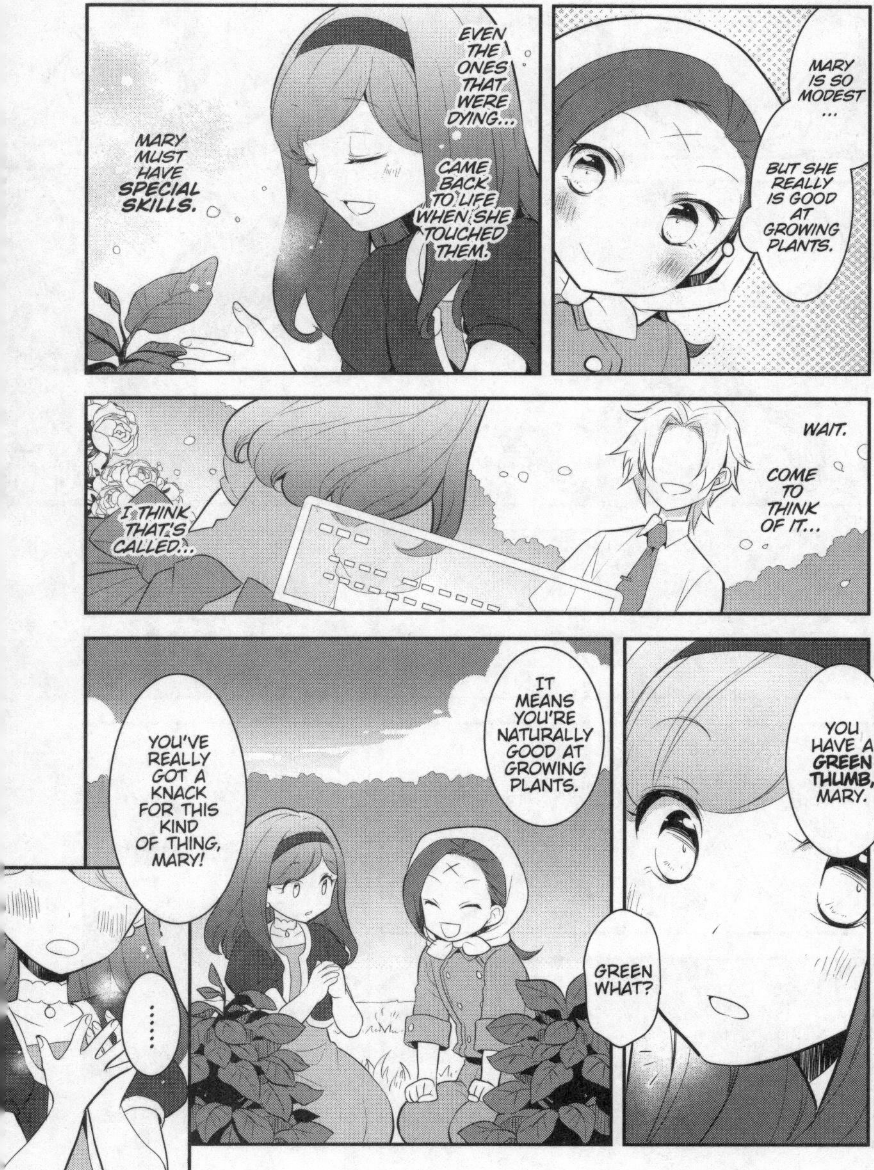

MARY IS SO MODEST ...
BUT SHE REALLY IS GOOD AT GROWING PLANTS.
EVEN THE ONES THAT WERE DYING...
CAME BACK TO LIFE WHEN SHE TOUCHED THEM.
MARY MUST HAVE SPECIAL SKILLS.
WAIT.
COME TO THINK OF IT...
I THINK THAT'S CALLED...
YOU HAVE A GREEN THUMB, MARY.
GREEN WHAT?
IT MEANS YOU'RE NATURALLY GOOD AT GROWING PLANTS.
YOU'VE REALLY GOT A KNACK FOR THIS KIND OF THING, MARY!
......

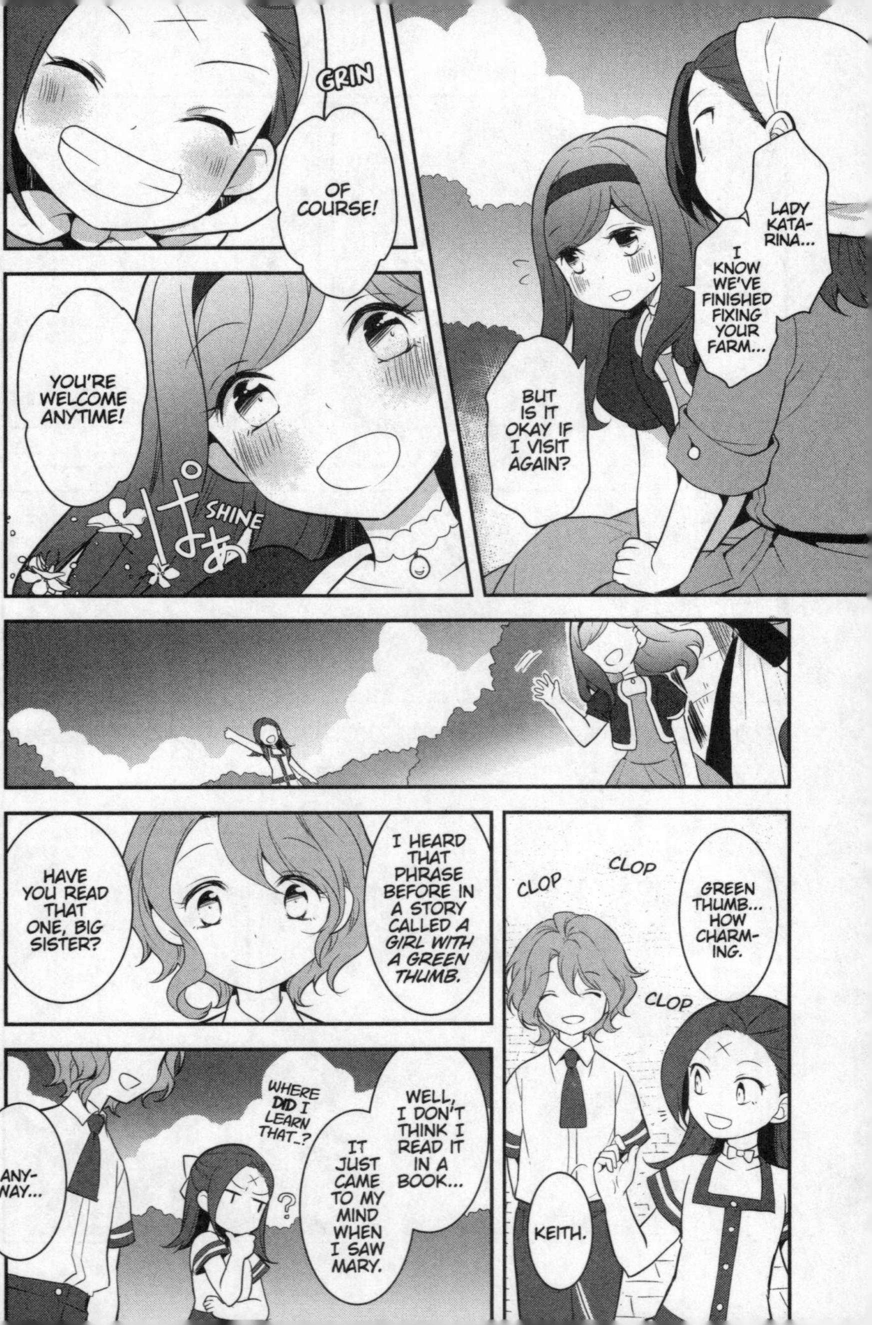
LADY KATA-RINA...
I KNOW WE'VE FINISHED FIXING YOUR FARM...
BUT IS IT OKAY IF I VISIT AGAIN?
GRIN
OF COURSE!
YOU'RE WELCOME ANYTIME!
ぱあ
SHINE
CLOP
CLOP
GREEN THUMB... HOW CHARM-ING.
CLOP
KEITH.
I HEARD THAT PHRASE BEFORE IN A STORY CALLED *A GIRL WITH A GREEN THUMB.*
HAVE YOU READ THAT ONE, BIG SISTER?
WELL, I DON'T THINK I READ IT IN A BOOK...
IT JUST CAME TO MY MIND WHEN I SAW MARY.
WHERE **DID** I LEARN THAT..?
?
ANY-WAY...

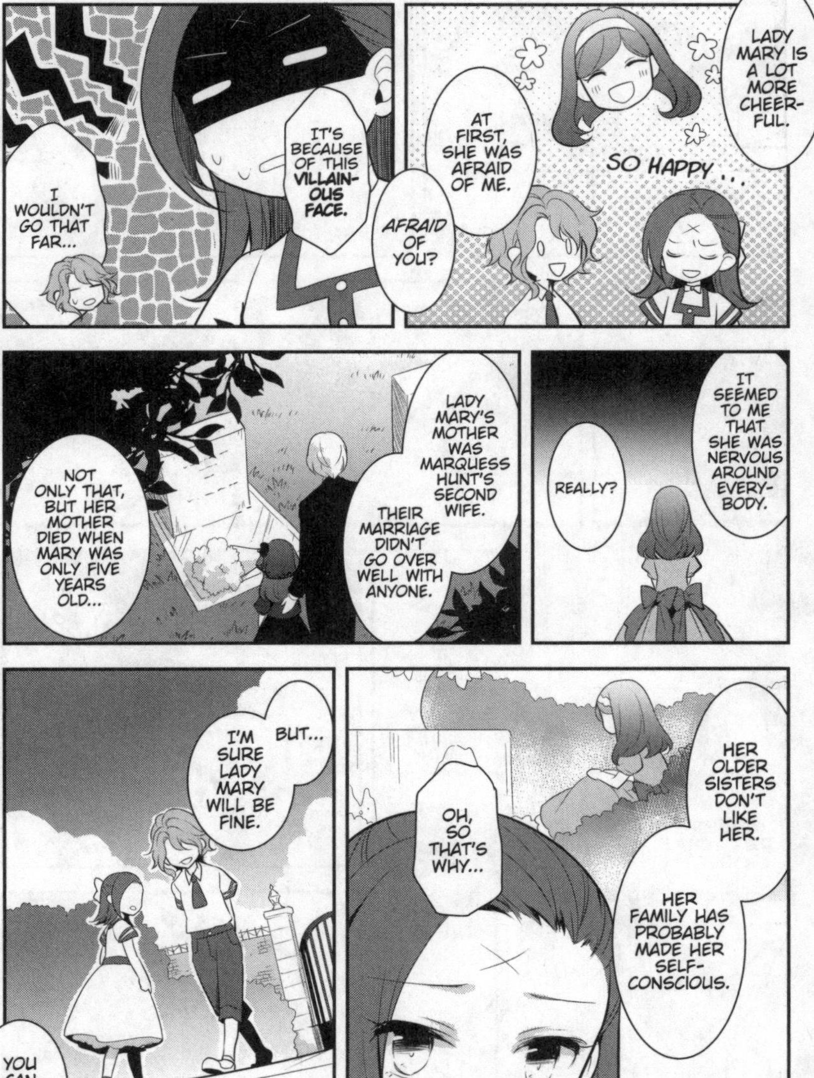

LADY MARY IS A LOT MORE CHEERFUL.
SO HAPPY...
AT FIRST, SHE WAS AFRAID OF ME.
AFRAID OF YOU?
IT'S BECAUSE OF THIS VILLAINOUS FACE.
I WOULDN'T GO THAT FAR...
IT SEEMED TO ME THAT SHE WAS NERVOUS AROUND EVERYBODY.
REALLY?
LADY MARY'S MOTHER WAS MARQUESS HUNT'S SECOND WIFE.
THEIR MARRIAGE DIDN'T GO OVER WELL WITH ANYONE.
NOT ONLY THAT, BUT HER MOTHER DIED WHEN MARY WAS ONLY FIVE YEARS OLD...
HER OLDER SISTERS DON'T LIKE HER.
OH, SO THAT'S WHY...
HER FAMILY HAS PROBABLY MADE HER SELF-CONSCIOUS.
BUT...
I'M SURE LADY MARY WILL BE FINE.
YOU CAN TELL, KEITH?

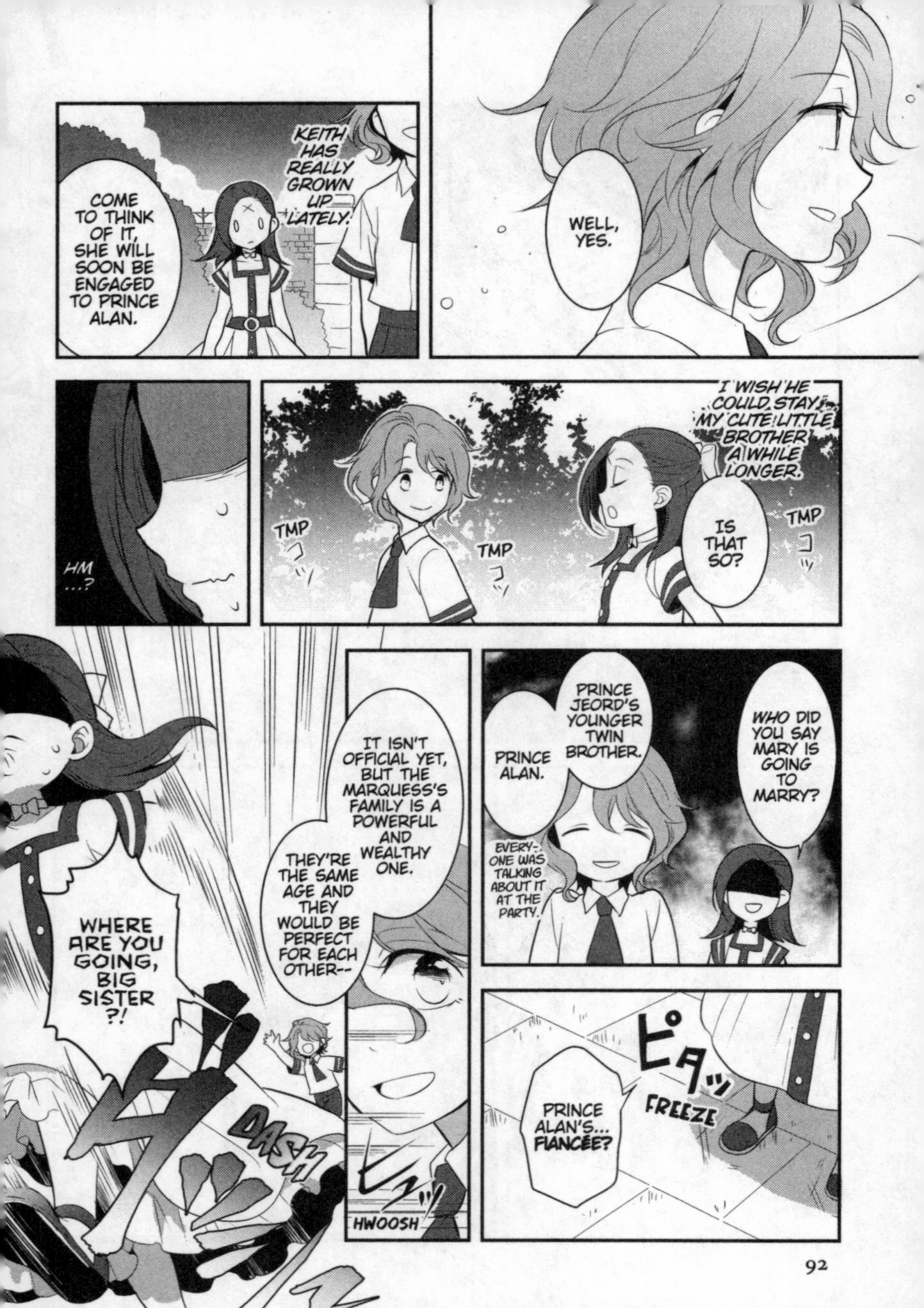
WELL, YES.
KEITH HAS REALLY GROWN UP LATELY.
COME TO THINK OF IT, SHE WILL SOON BE ENGAGED TO PRINCE ALAN.
I WISH HE COULD STAY MY CUTE LITTLE BROTHER A WHILE LONGER.
TMP
IS THAT SO?
TMP
TMP
HM...?
WHO DID YOU SAY MARY IS GOING TO MARRY?
PRINCE JEORD'S YOUNGER TWIN BROTHER.
PRINCE ALAN.
EVERY-ONE WAS TALKING ABOUT IT AT THE PARTY.
ピタッ
FREEZE
PRINCE ALAN'S... FIANCÉE?
IT ISN'T OFFICIAL YET, BUT THE MARQUESS'S FAMILY IS A POWERFUL AND WEALTHY ONE.
THEY'RE THE SAME AGE AND THEY WOULD BE PERFECT FOR EACH OTHER--
ヒュッ
HWOOSH
WHERE ARE YOU GOING, BIG SISTER?!
DASH

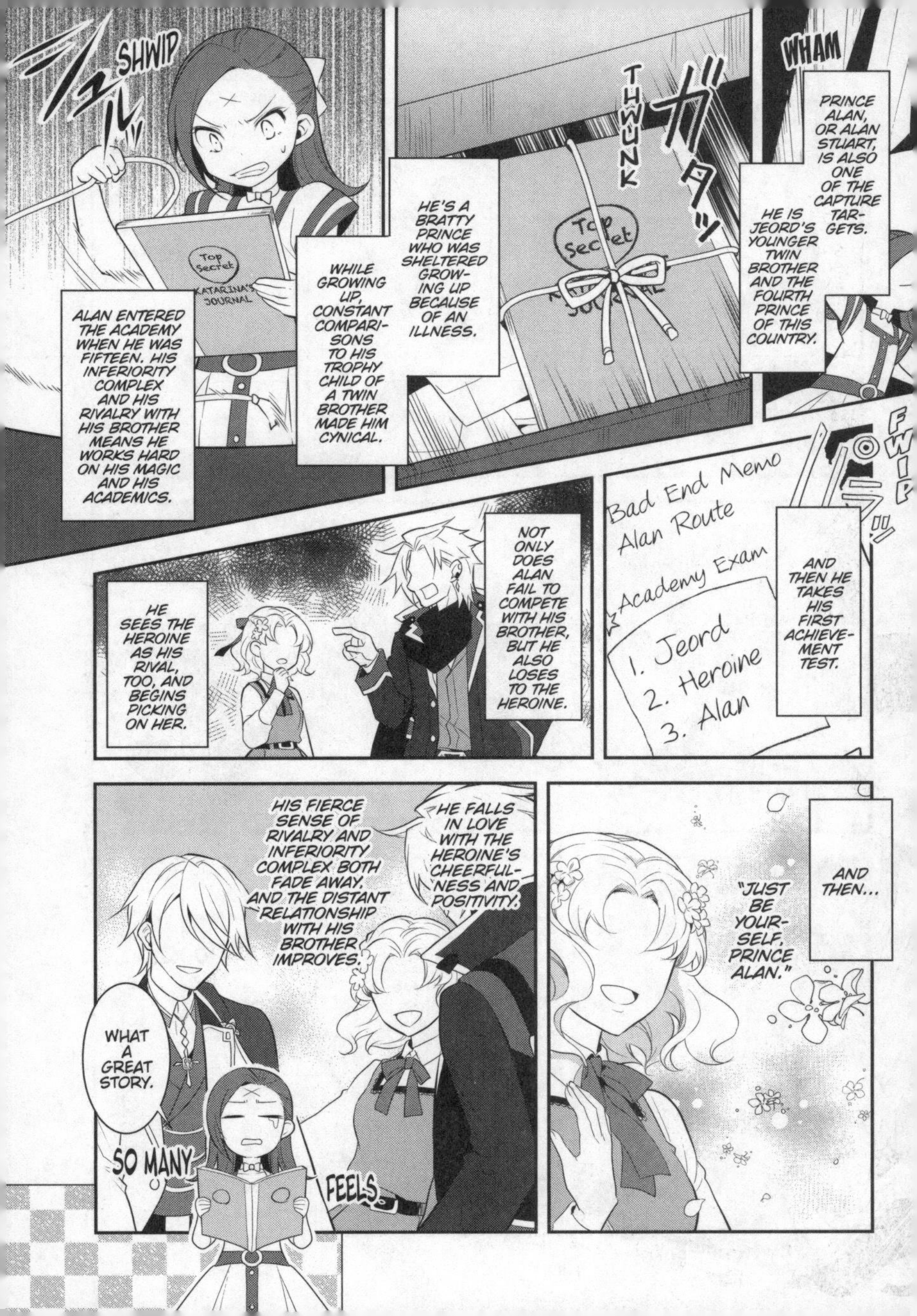
WHAM
PRINCE ALAN, OR ALAN STUART, IS ALSO ONE OF THE CAPTURE TARGETS.
HE IS JEORD'S YOUNGER TWIN BROTHER AND THE FOURTH PRINCE OF THIS COUNTRY.
THWUNK
Top Secret
HE'S A BRATTY PRINCE WHO WAS SHELTERED GROWING UP BECAUSE OF AN ILLNESS.
WHILE GROWING UP, CONSTANT COMPARISONS TO HIS TROPHY CHILD OF A TWIN BROTHER MADE HIM CYNICAL.
SHWIP
Top Secret
KATARINA'S JOURNAL
ALAN ENTERED THE ACADEMY WHEN HE WAS FIFTEEN. HIS INFERIORITY COMPLEX AND HIS RIVALRY WITH HIS BROTHER MEANS HE WORKS HARD ON HIS MAGIC AND HIS ACADEMICS.
FWIP
Bad End Memo
Alan Route
Academy Exam
1. Jeord
2. Heroine
3. Alan
AND THEN HE TAKES HIS FIRST ACHIEVEMENT TEST.
NOT ONLY DOES ALAN FAIL TO COMPETE WITH HIS BROTHER, BUT HE ALSO LOSES TO THE HEROINE.
HE SEES THE HEROINE AS HIS RIVAL, TOO, AND BEGINS PICKING ON HER.
AND THEN...
"JUST BE YOURSELF, PRINCE ALAN."
HE FALLS IN LOVE WITH THE HEROINE'S CHEERFULNESS AND POSITIVITY.
HIS FIERCE SENSE OF RIVALRY AND INFERIORITY COMPLEX BOTH FADE AWAY, AND THE DISTANT RELATIONSHIP WITH HIS BROTHER IMPROVES.
WHAT A GREAT STORY.
SO MANY FEELS.

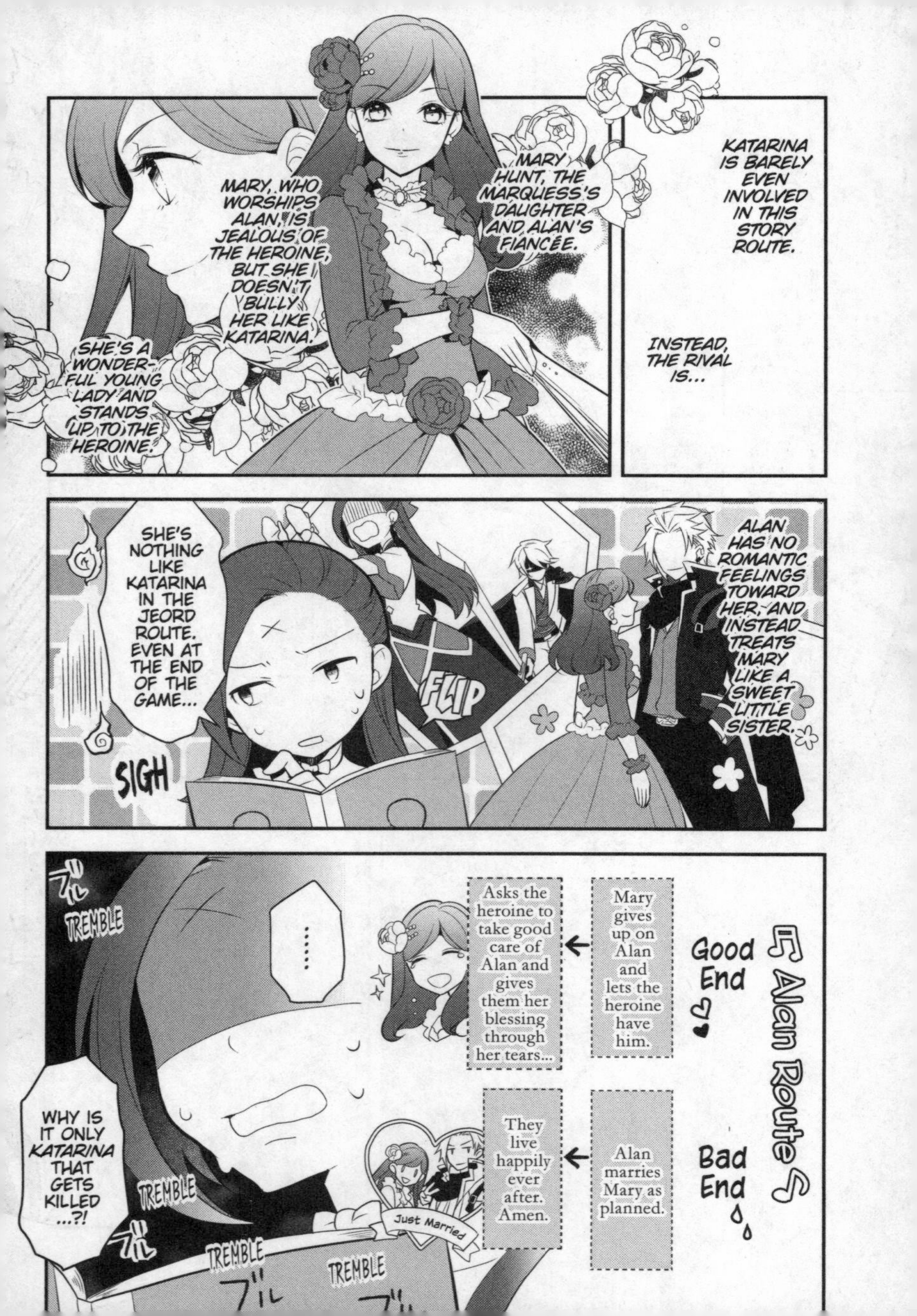

KATARINA IS BARELY EVEN INVOLVED IN THIS STORY ROUTE.
INSTEAD, THE RIVAL IS...
MARY HUNT, THE MARQUESS'S DAUGHTER AND ALAN'S FIANCÉE.
MARY, WHO WORSHIPS ALAN, IS JEALOUS OF THE HEROINE, BUT SHE DOESN'T BULLY HER LIKE KATARINA.
SHE'S A WONDERFUL YOUNG LADY AND STANDS UP TO THE HEROINE.
ALAN HAS NO ROMANTIC FEELINGS TOWARD HER, AND INSTEAD TREATS MARY LIKE A SWEET LITTLE SISTER.
FLIP
SHE'S NOTHING LIKE KATARINA IN THE JEORD ROUTE. EVEN AT THE END OF THE GAME...
SIGH
♫ Alan Route ♫
Good End ♥
Mary gives up on Alan and lets the heroine have him.
Asks the heroine to take good care of Alan and gives them her blessing through her tears...
Bad End
Alan marries Mary as planned.
They live happily ever after. Amen.
Just Married
……
ブル
TREMBLE
WHY IS IT ONLY KATARINA THAT GETS KILLED ...?!
TREMBLE
ブル
TREMBLE
TREMBLE
ブル
ブル

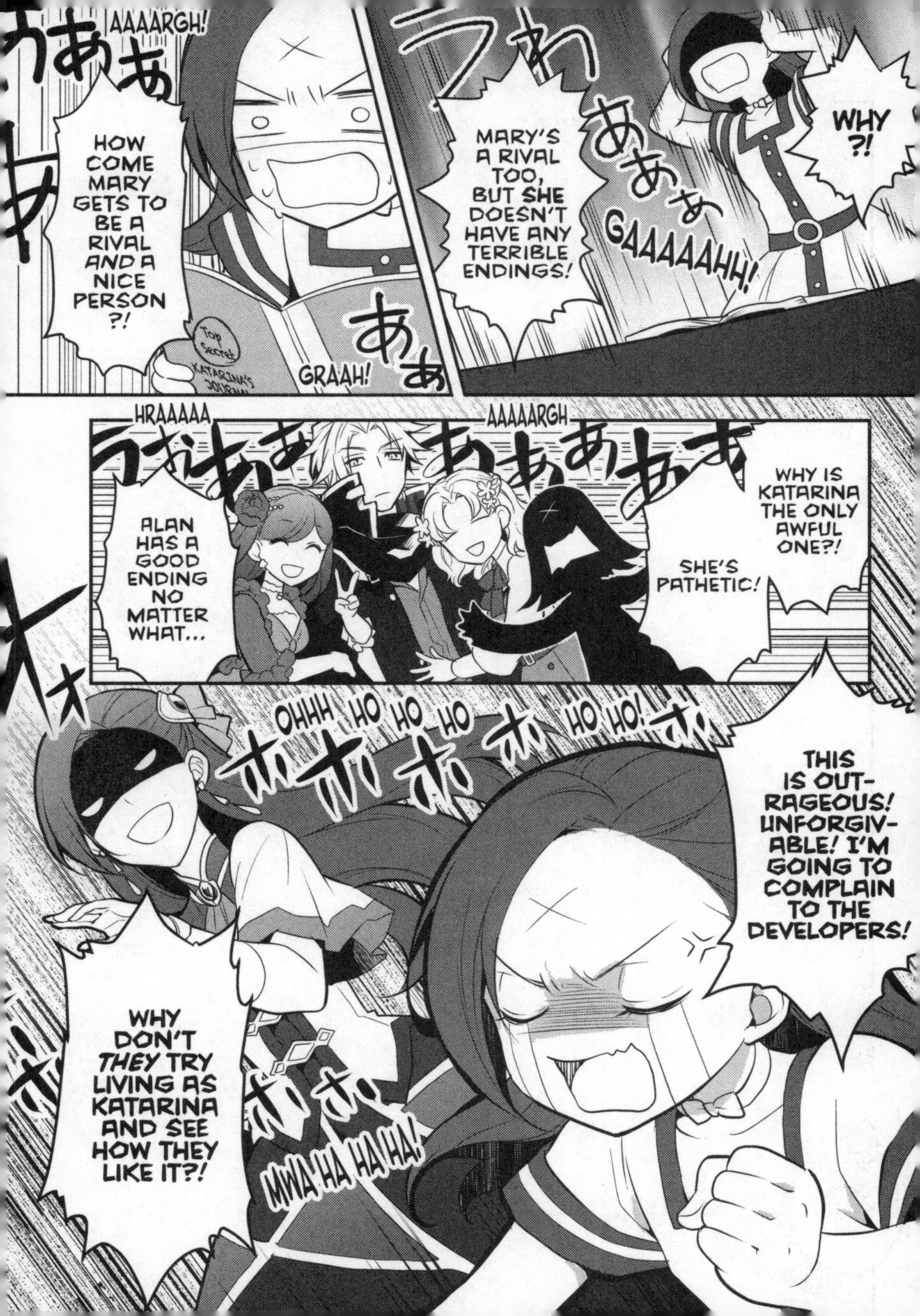
WHY ?!
MARY'S A RIVAL TOO, BUT SHE DOESN'T HAVE ANY TERRIBLE ENDINGS!
GAAAAAAHH!
AAAARGH!
HOW COME MARY GETS TO BE A RIVAL AND A NICE PERSON ?!
Top Secret
KATARINA'S
GRAAH!
HRAAAAA
AAAAARGH
WHY IS KATARINA THE ONLY AWFUL ONE?!
SHE'S PATHETIC!
ALAN HAS A GOOD ENDING NO MATTER WHAT...
OHHH HO HO HO HO HO!
THIS IS OUTRAGEOUS! UNFORGIVABLE! I'M GOING TO COMPLAIN TO THE DEVELOPERS!
WHY DON'T *THEY* TRY LIVING AS KATARINA AND SEE HOW THEY LIKE IT?!
MWA HA HA HA!

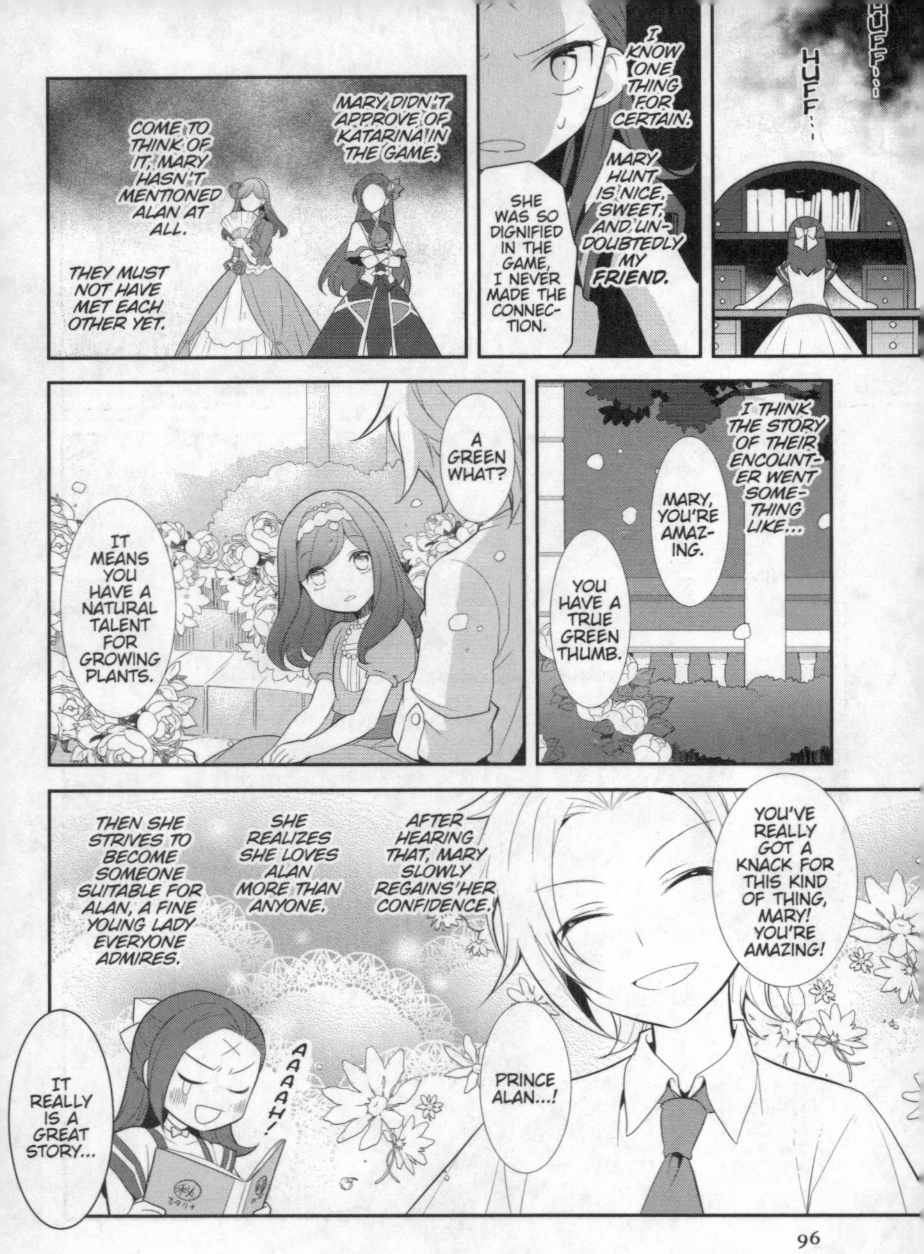
HUFF... HUFF...
I KNOW ONE THING FOR CERTAIN.
MARY HUNT IS NICE, SWEET, AND UN-DOUBTEDLY MY FRIEND.
SHE WAS SO DIGNIFIED IN THE GAME, I NEVER MADE THE CONNEC-TION.
MARY DIDN'T APPROVE OF KATARINA IN THE GAME.
COME TO THINK OF IT, MARY HASN'T MENTIONED ALAN AT ALL.
THEY MUST NOT HAVE MET EACH OTHER YET.
I THINK THE STORY OF THEIR ENCOUNT-ER WENT SOME-THING LIKE...
MARY, YOU'RE AMAZ-ING.
YOU HAVE A TRUE GREEN THUMB.
A GREEN WHAT?
IT MEANS YOU HAVE A NATURAL TALENT FOR GROWING PLANTS.
YOU'VE REALLY GOT A KNACK FOR THIS KIND OF THING, MARY! YOU'RE AMAZING!
PRINCE ALAN...!
AFTER HEARING THAT, MARY SLOWLY REGAINS HER CONFIDENCE.
SHE REALIZES SHE LOVES ALAN MORE THAN ANYONE.
THEN SHE STRIVES TO BECOME SOMEONE SUITABLE FOR ALAN, A FINE YOUNG LADY EVERYONE ADMIRES.
AAAAAH!
IT REALLY IS A GREAT STORY...

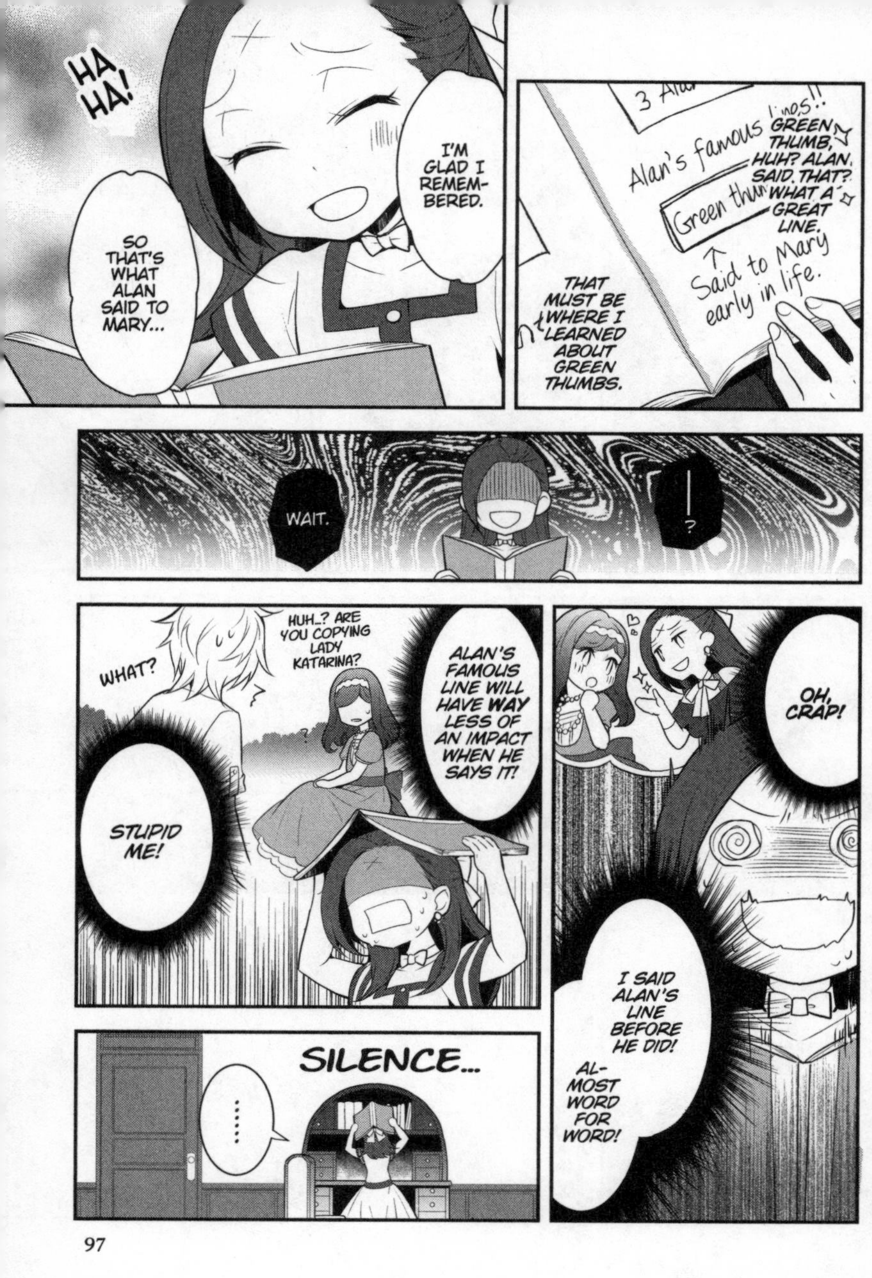
Alan's famous lines!!
Said to Mary early in life.
GREEN THUMB, HUH? ALAN SAID THAT? WHAT A GREAT LINE.
THAT MUST BE WHERE I LEARNED ABOUT GREEN THUMBS.
I'M GLAD I REMEMBERED.
HA HA!
SO THAT'S WHAT ALAN SAID TO MARY...
—?
WAIT.
OH, CRAP!
I SAID ALAN'S LINE BEFORE HE DID!
AL-MOST WORD FOR WORD!
ALAN'S FAMOUS LINE WILL HAVE WAY LESS OF AN IMPACT WHEN HE SAYS IT!
HUH...? ARE YOU COPYING LADY KATARINA?
WHAT?
STUPID ME!
SILENCE...
......

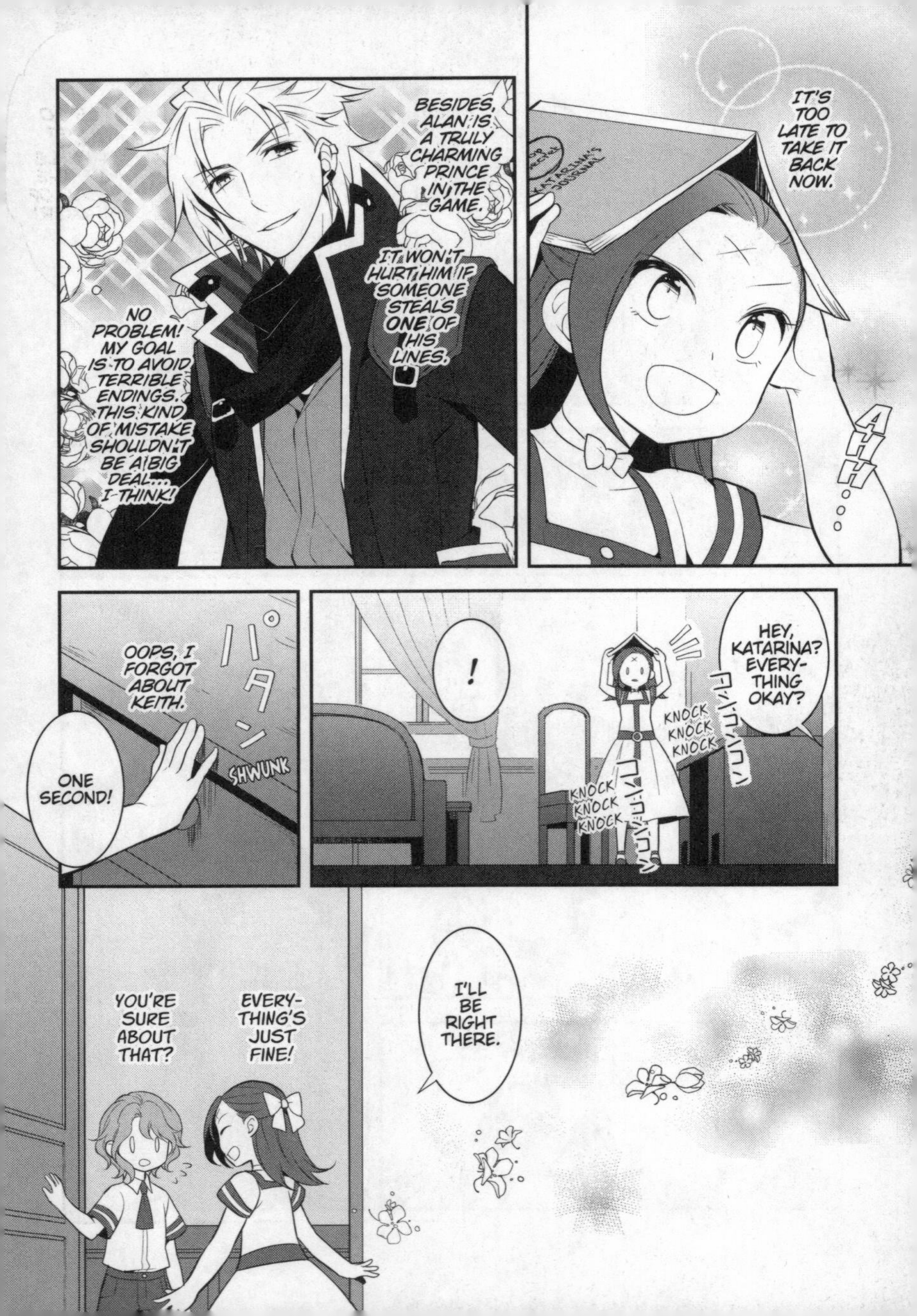
IT'S TOO LATE TO TAKE IT BACK NOW.
AHH...
KATARINA'S JOURNAL
BESIDES, ALAN IS A TRULY CHARMING PRINCE IN THE GAME.
IT WON'T HURT HIM IF SOMEONE STEALS ONE OF HIS LINES.
NO PROBLEM! MY GOAL IS TO AVOID TERRIBLE ENDINGS. THIS KIND OF MISTAKE SHOULDN'T BE A BIG DEAL... I THINK!
HEY, KATARINA? EVERYTHING OKAY?
KNOCK KNOCK KNOCK
KNOCK KNOCK KNOCK
!
OOPS, I FORGOT ABOUT KEITH.
パタン
SHWUNK
ONE SECOND!
I'LL BE RIGHT THERE.
EVERYTHING'S JUST FINE!
YOU'RE SURE ABOUT THAT?

Chapter 4

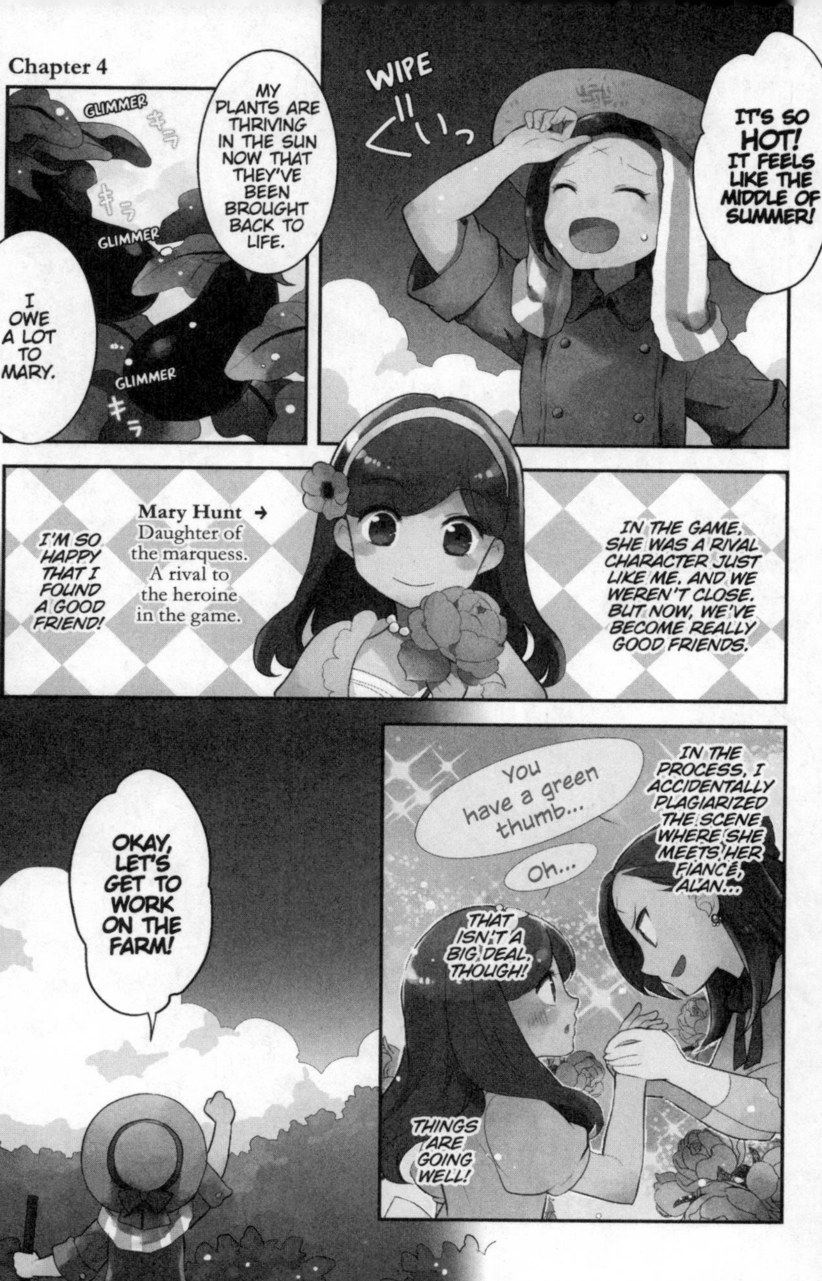
WIPE
IT'S SO HOT! IT FEELS LIKE THE MIDDLE OF SUMMER!
MY PLANTS ARE THRIVING IN THE SUN NOW THAT THEY'VE BEEN BROUGHT BACK TO LIFE.
GLIMMER
GLIMMER
I OWE A LOT TO MARY.
GLIMMER
IN THE GAME, SHE WAS A RIVAL CHARACTER JUST LIKE ME, AND WE WEREN'T CLOSE. BUT NOW, WE'VE BECOME REALLY GOOD FRIENDS.
Mary Hunt → Daughter of the marquess. A rival to the heroine in the game.
I'M SO HAPPY THAT I FOUND A GOOD FRIEND!
IN THE PROCESS, I ACCIDENTALLY PLAGIARIZED THE SCENE WHERE SHE MEETS HER FIANCÉ, ALAN...
You have a green thumb...
Oh...
THAT ISN'T A BIG DEAL, THOUGH!
THINGS ARE GOING WELL!
OKAY, LET'S GET TO WORK ON THE FARM!

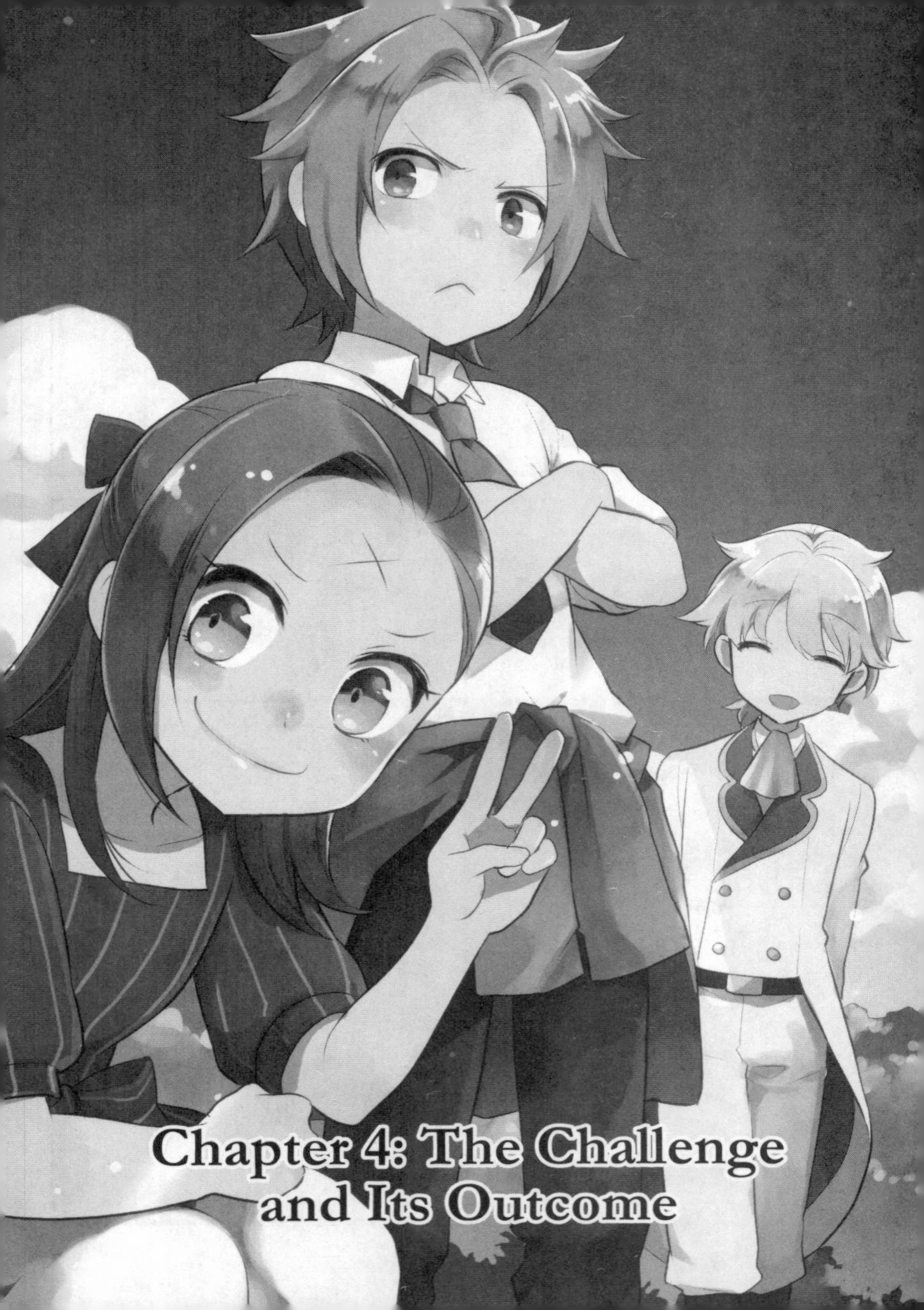

Chapter 4: The Challenge and Its Outcome

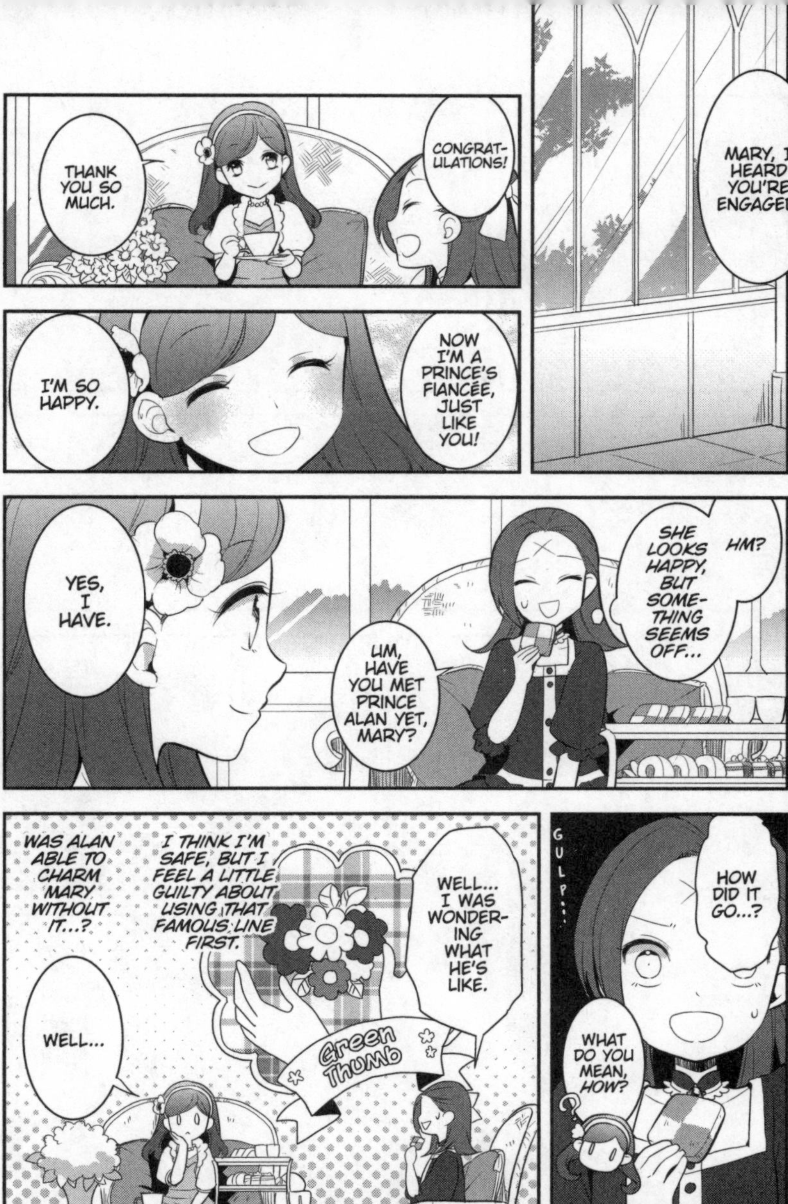
MARY, I HEARD YOU'RE ENGAGED.
CONGRAT-ULATIONS!
THANK YOU SO MUCH.
NOW I'M A PRINCE'S FIANCÉE, JUST LIKE YOU!
I'M SO HAPPY.
HM?
SHE LOOKS HAPPY, BUT SOME-THING SEEMS OFF...
UM, HAVE YOU MET PRINCE ALAN YET, MARY?
YES, I HAVE.
GULP...
HOW DID IT GO...?
WHAT DO YOU MEAN, HOW?
WELL... I WAS WONDER-ING WHAT HE'S LIKE.
I THINK I'M SAFE, BUT I FEEL A LITTLE GUILTY ABOUT USING THAT FAMOUS LINE FIRST.
WAS ALAN ABLE TO CHARM MARY WITHOUT IT...?
Green Thumb
WELL...

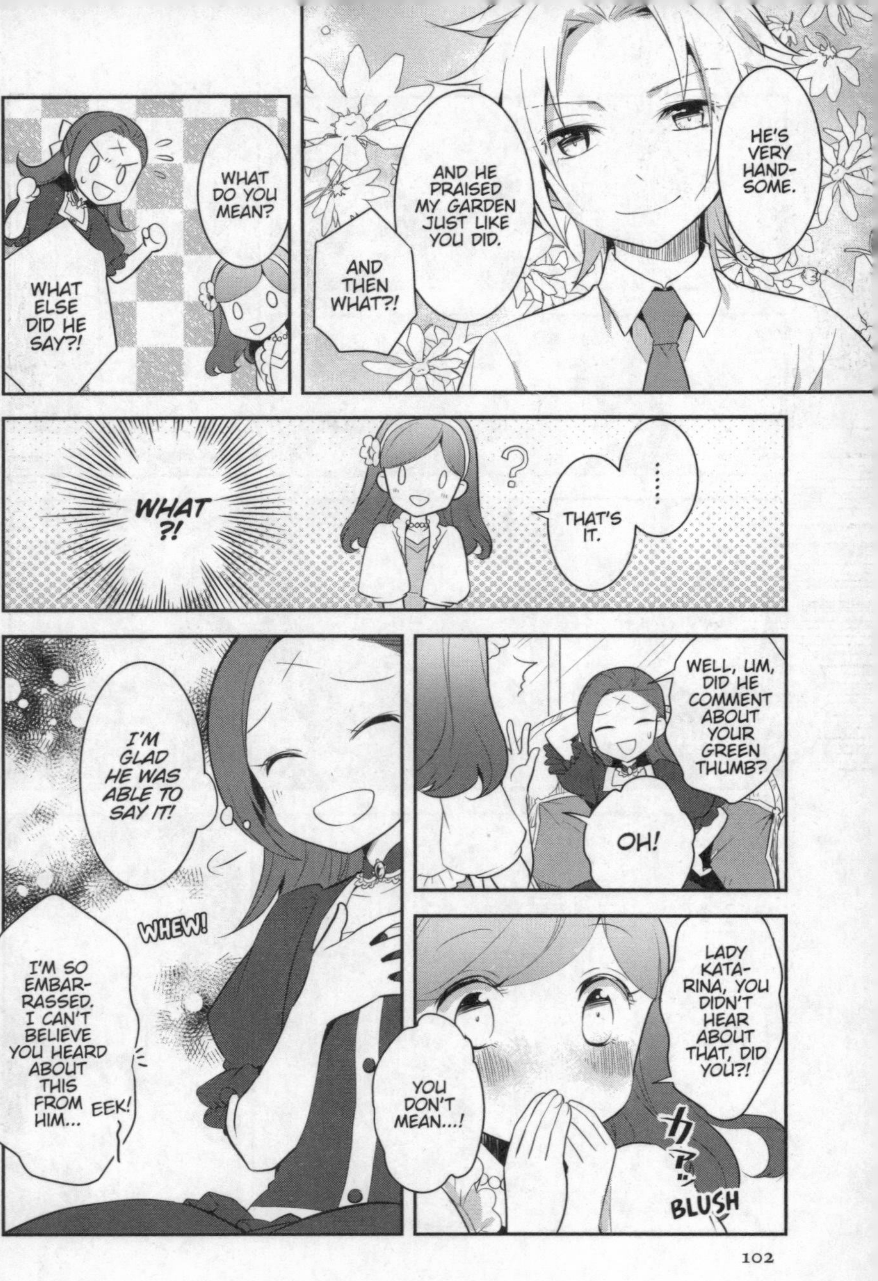
HE'S VERY HAND-SOME.
AND HE PRAISED MY GARDEN JUST LIKE YOU DID.
AND THEN WHAT?!
WHAT DO YOU MEAN?
WHAT ELSE DID HE SAY?!
......
THAT'S IT.
?
WHAT ?!
WELL, UM, DID HE COMMENT ABOUT YOUR GREEN THUMB?
OH!
LADY KATA-RINA, YOU DIDN'T HEAR ABOUT THAT, DID YOU?!
カアッ
BLUSH
YOU DON'T MEAN...!
I'M GLAD HE WAS ABLE TO SAY IT!
WHEW!
I'M SO EMBAR-RASSED. I CAN'T BELIEVE YOU HEARD ABOUT THIS FROM HIM...
EEK!

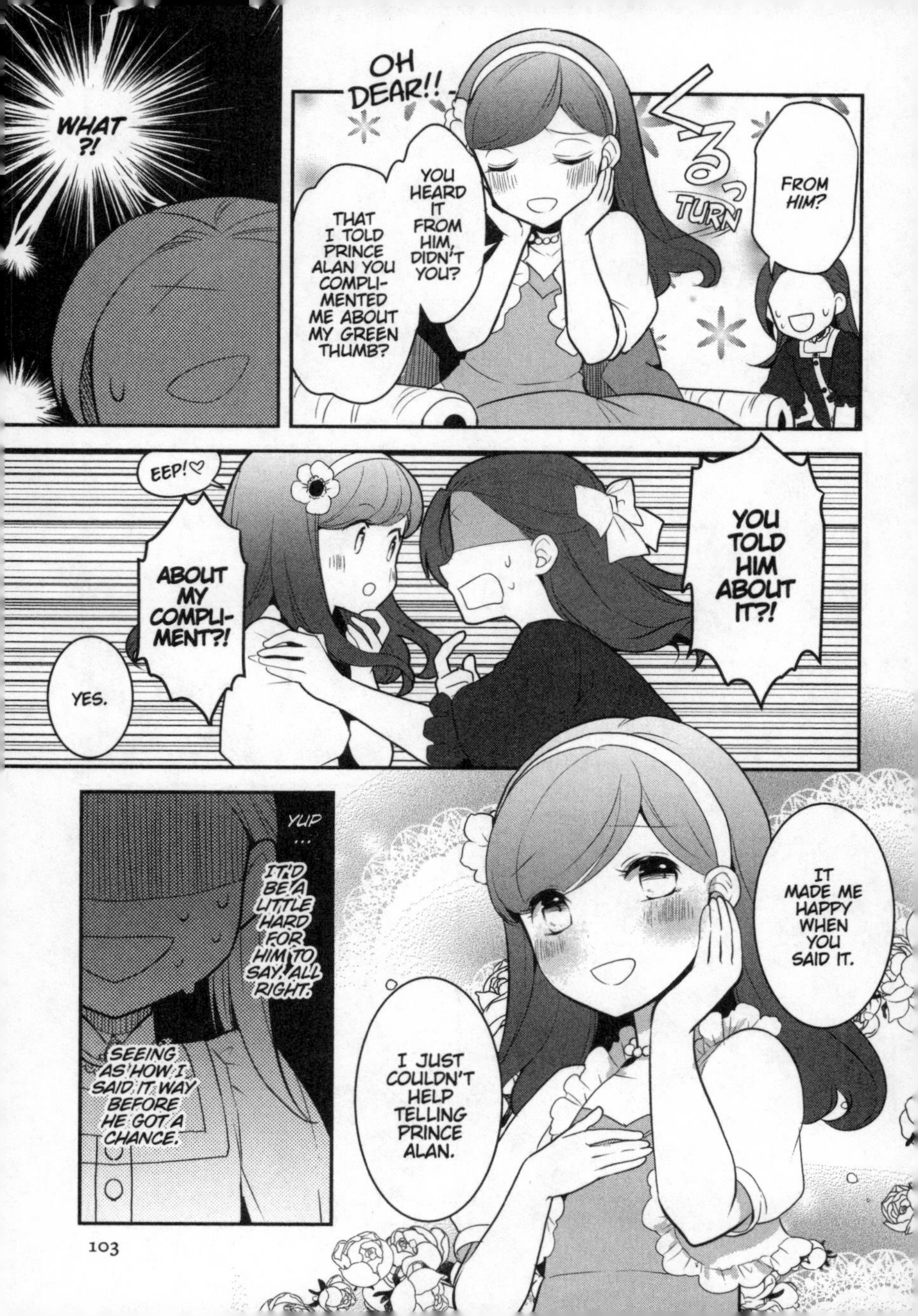
FROM HIM?
OH DEAR!!
くるっ TURN
YOU HEARD IT FROM HIM, DIDN'T YOU?
THAT I TOLD PRINCE ALAN YOU COMPLIMENTED ME ABOUT MY GREEN THUMB?
WHAT?!
YOU TOLD HIM ABOUT IT?!
EEP!♡
ABOUT MY COMPLIMENT?!
YES.
IT MADE ME HAPPY WHEN YOU SAID IT.
I JUST COULDN'T HELP TELLING PRINCE ALAN.
YUP...
IT'D BE A LITTLE HARD FOR HIM TO SAY, ALL RIGHT.
SEEING AS HOW I SAID IT WAY BEFORE HE GOT A CHANCE.

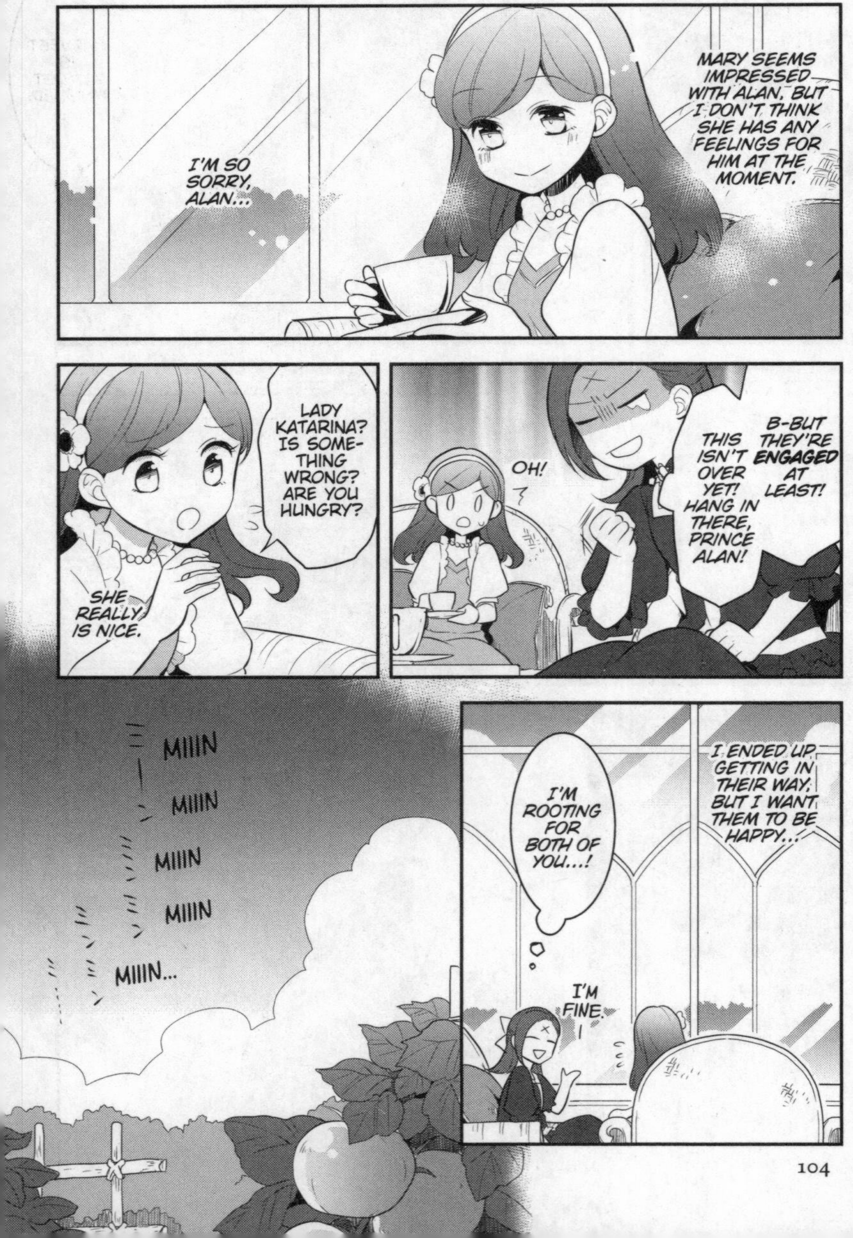
MARY SEEMS IMPRESSED WITH ALAN, BUT I DON'T THINK SHE HAS ANY FEELINGS FOR HIM AT THE MOMENT.
I'M SO SORRY, ALAN...
B-BUT THEY'RE ENGAGED AT LEAST!
THIS ISN'T OVER YET! HANG IN THERE, PRINCE ALAN!
OH!
LADY KATARINA? IS SOME-THING WRONG? ARE YOU HUNGRY?
SHE REALLY IS NICE.
I ENDED UP GETTING IN THEIR WAY, BUT I WANT THEM TO BE HAPPY...
I'M ROOTING FOR BOTH OF YOU...!
I'M FINE.
MIIIN
MIIIN
MIIIN
MIIIN
MIIIN...

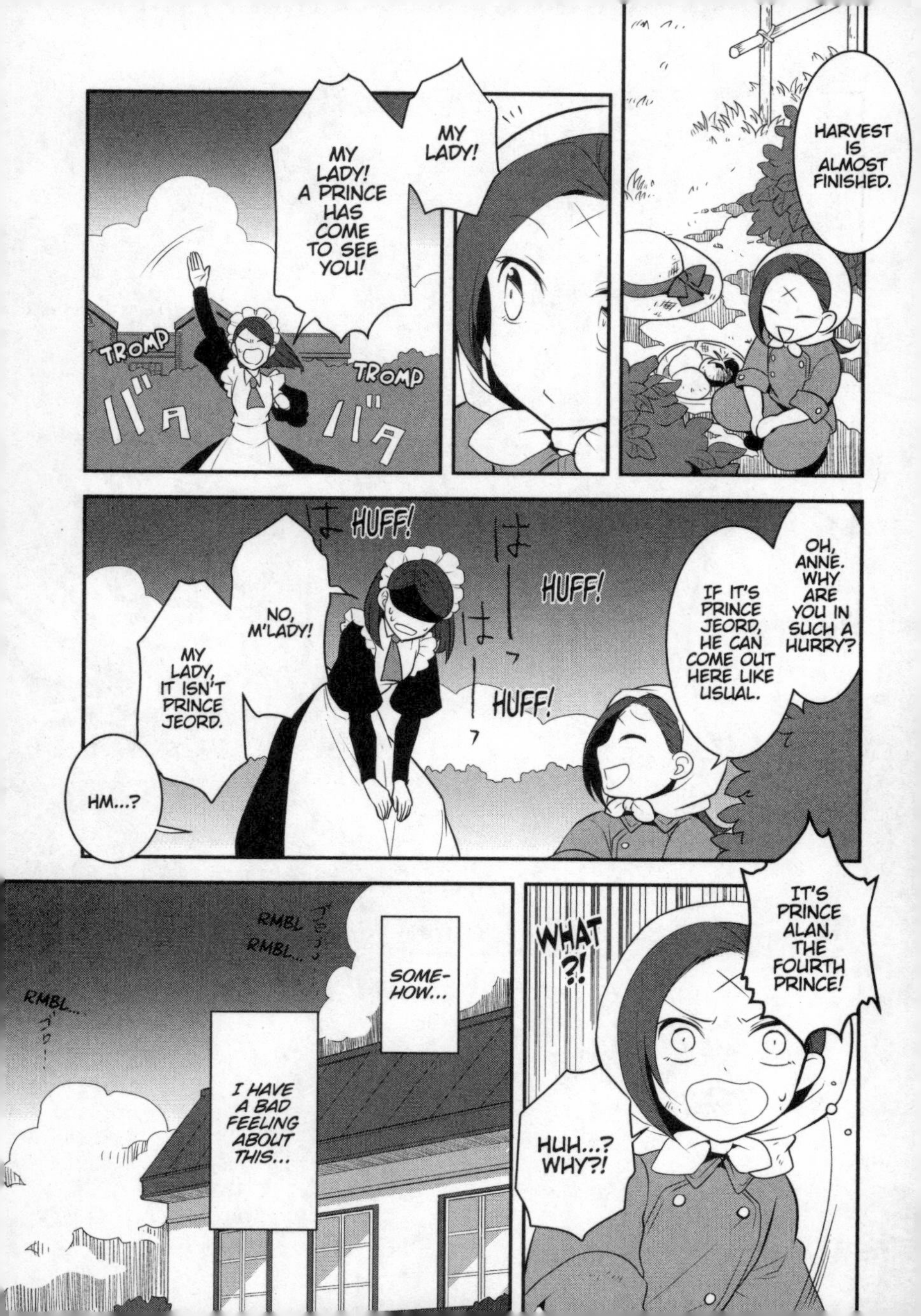
HARVEST IS ALMOST FINISHED.
MY LADY!
MY LADY! A PRINCE HAS COME TO SEE YOU!
TROMP
TROMP
バタ
バタ
OH, ANNE. WHY ARE YOU IN SUCH A HURRY?
IF IT'S PRINCE JEORD, HE CAN COME OUT HERE LIKE USUAL.
HUFF!
HUFF!
HUFF!
NO, M'LADY!
MY LADY, IT ISN'T PRINCE JEORD.
HM...?
IT'S PRINCE ALAN, THE FOURTH PRINCE!
WHAT?!
HUH...? WHY?!
RMBL
RMBL...
SOME-HOW...
RMBL...
I HAVE A BAD FEELING ABOUT THIS...

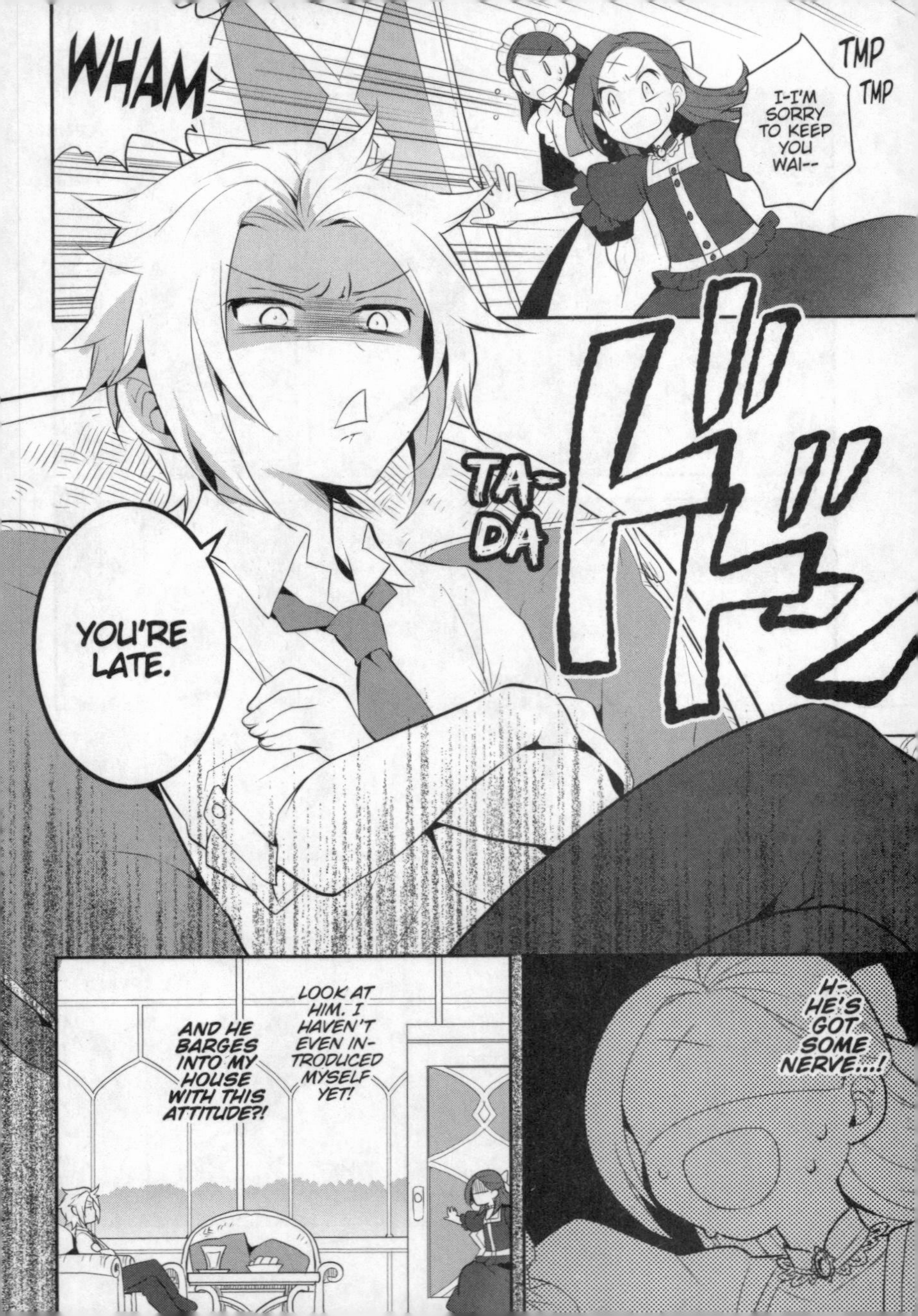
TMP TMP
I-I'M SORRY TO KEEP YOU WAI--
WHAM
TA-DA
YOU'RE LATE.
H-HE'S GOT SOME NERVE...!
LOOK AT HIM. I HAVEN'T EVEN INTRODUCED MYSELF YET!
AND HE BARGES INTO MY HOUSE WITH THIS ATTITUDE?!

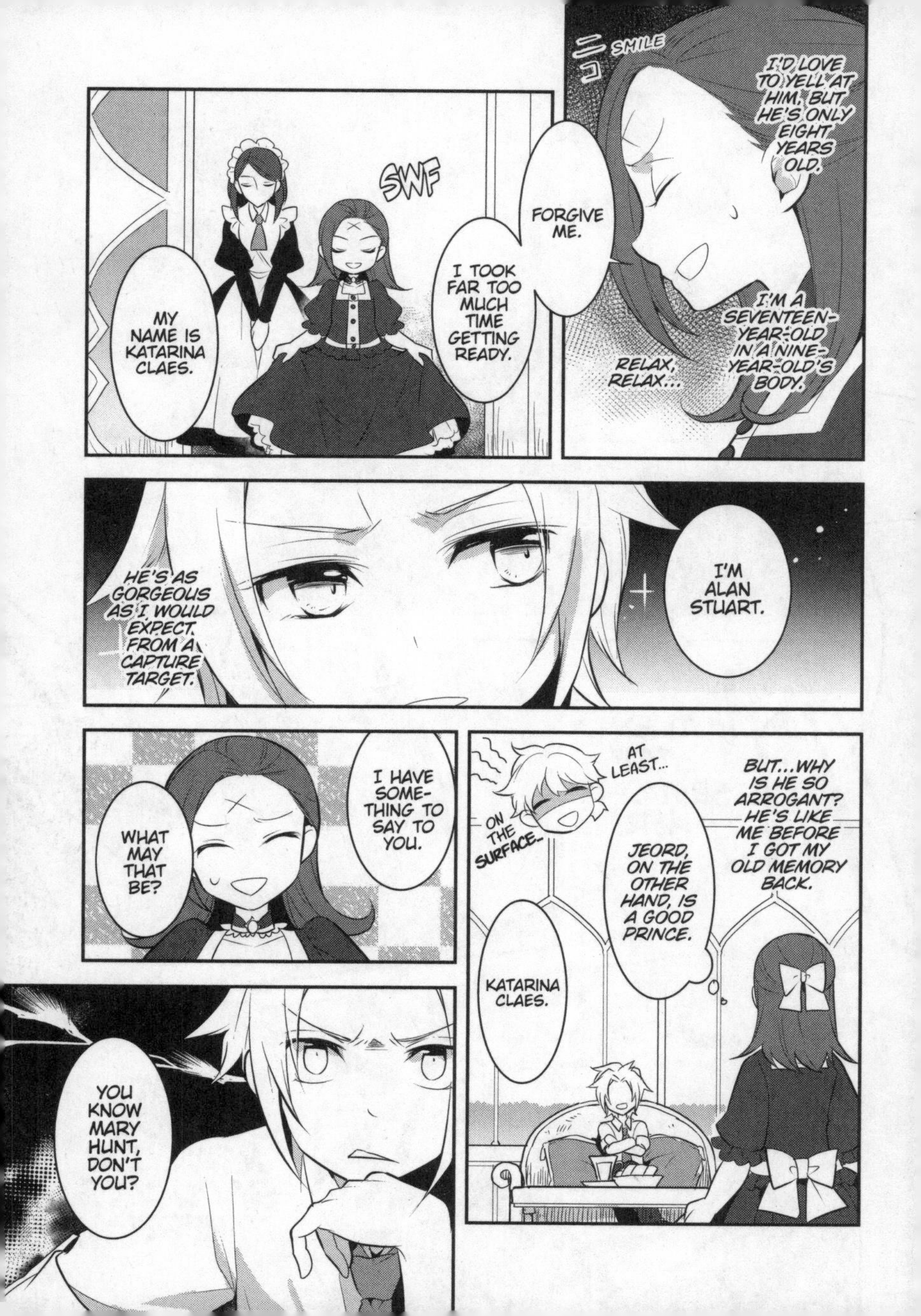
ニコ SMILE
I'D LOVE TO YELL AT HIM. BUT HE'S ONLY EIGHT YEARS OLD.
I'M A SEVENTEEN-YEAR-OLD IN A NINE-YEAR-OLD'S BODY.
RELAX, RELAX...
FORGIVE ME.
I TOOK FAR TOO MUCH TIME GETTING READY.
SWF
MY NAME IS KATARINA CLAES.
I'M ALAN STUART.
HE'S AS GORGEOUS AS I WOULD EXPECT FROM A CAPTURE TARGET.
BUT...WHY IS HE SO ARROGANT? HE'S LIKE ME BEFORE I GOT MY OLD MEMORY BACK.
AT LEAST...
ON THE SURFACE...
JEORD, ON THE OTHER HAND, IS A GOOD PRINCE.
KATARINA CLAES.
I HAVE SOMETHING TO SAY TO YOU.
WHAT MAY THAT BE?
YOU KNOW MARY HUNT, DON'T YOU?

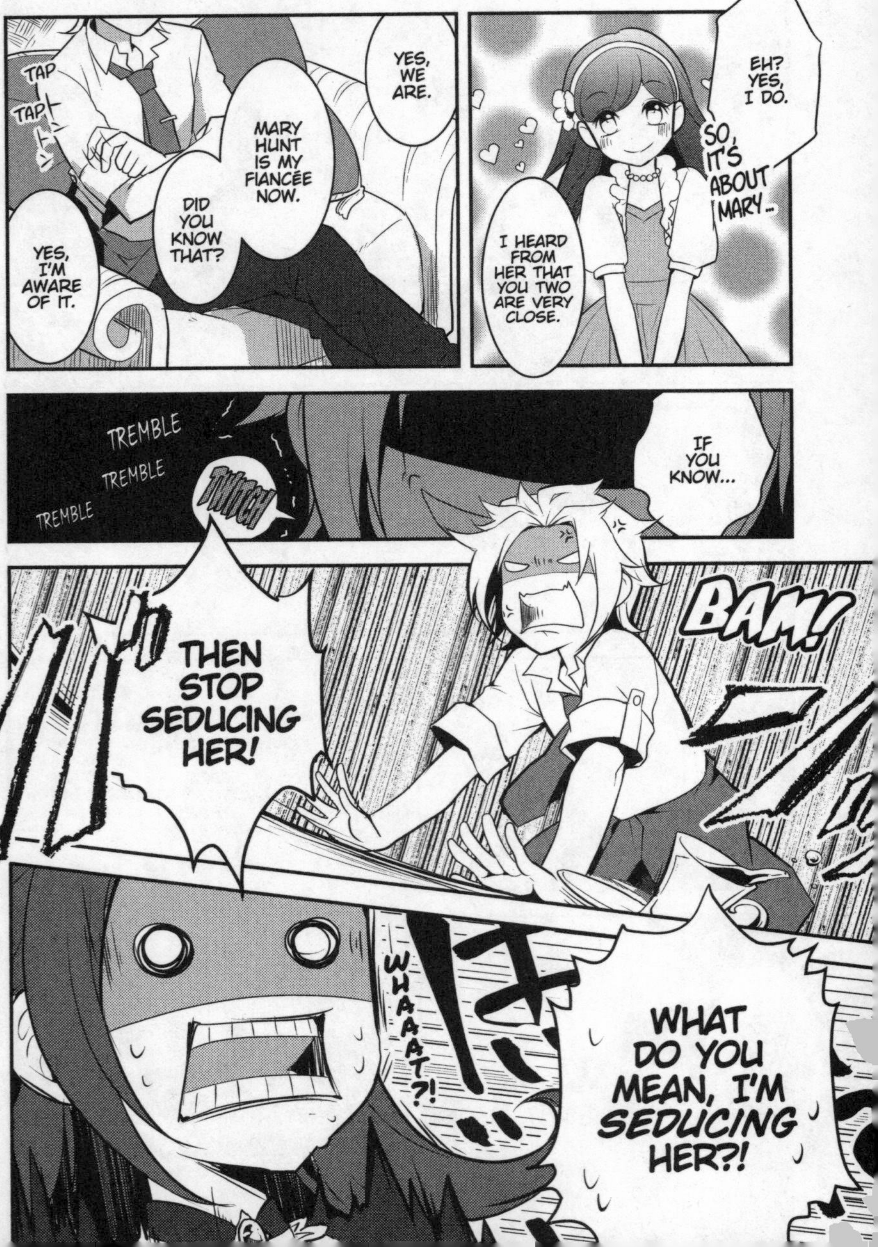
EH? YES, I DO.
SO, IT'S ABOUT MARY...
I HEARD FROM HER THAT YOU TWO ARE VERY CLOSE.
YES, WE ARE.
MARY HUNT IS MY FIANCÉE NOW.
DID YOU KNOW THAT?
TAP TAP
YES, I'M AWARE OF IT.
IF YOU KNOW...
TREMBLE TREMBLE TREMBLE
TWITCH
BAM!
THEN STOP SEDUCING HER!
WHAT DO YOU MEAN, I'M SEDUCING HER?!
WHAAAAT?!

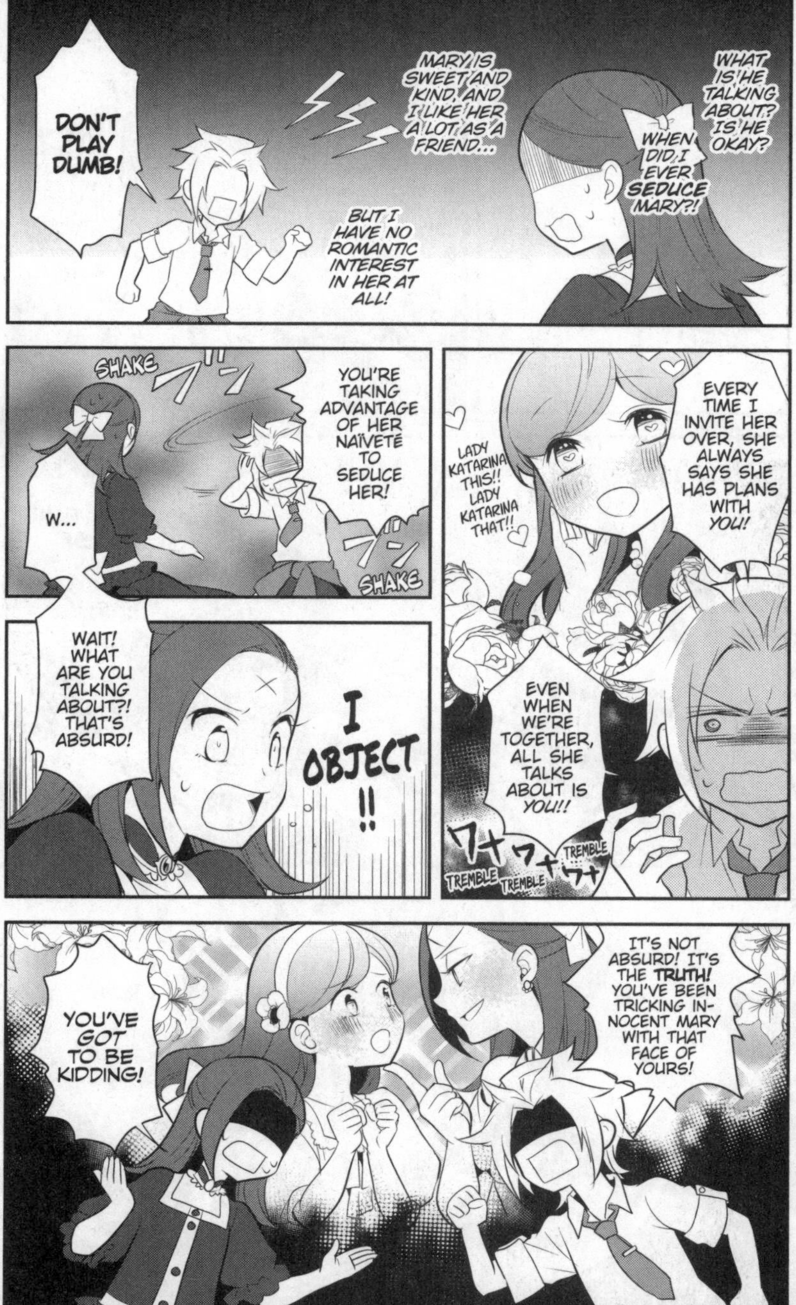
WHAT IS HE TALKING ABOUT? IS HE OKAY?
WHEN DID I EVER SEDUCE MARY?!
MARY IS SWEET AND KIND, AND I LIKE HER A LOT AS A FRIEND...
BUT I HAVE NO ROMANTIC INTEREST IN HER AT ALL!
DON'T PLAY DUMB!
EVERY TIME I INVITE HER OVER, SHE ALWAYS SAYS SHE HAS PLANS WITH YOU!
LADY KATARINA THIS!! LADY KATARINA THAT!!
EVEN WHEN WE'RE TOGETHER, ALL SHE TALKS ABOUT IS YOU!!
TREMBLE
TREMBLE
TREMBLE
SHAKE
YOU'RE TAKING ADVANTAGE OF HER NAÏVETÉ TO SEDUCE HER!
SHAKE
W...
I OBJECT!!
WAIT! WHAT ARE YOU TALKING ABOUT?! THAT'S ABSURD!
IT'S NOT ABSURD! IT'S THE TRUTH! YOU'VE BEEN TRICKING IN-NOCENT MARY WITH THAT FACE OF YOURS!
YOU'VE GOT TO BE KIDDING!

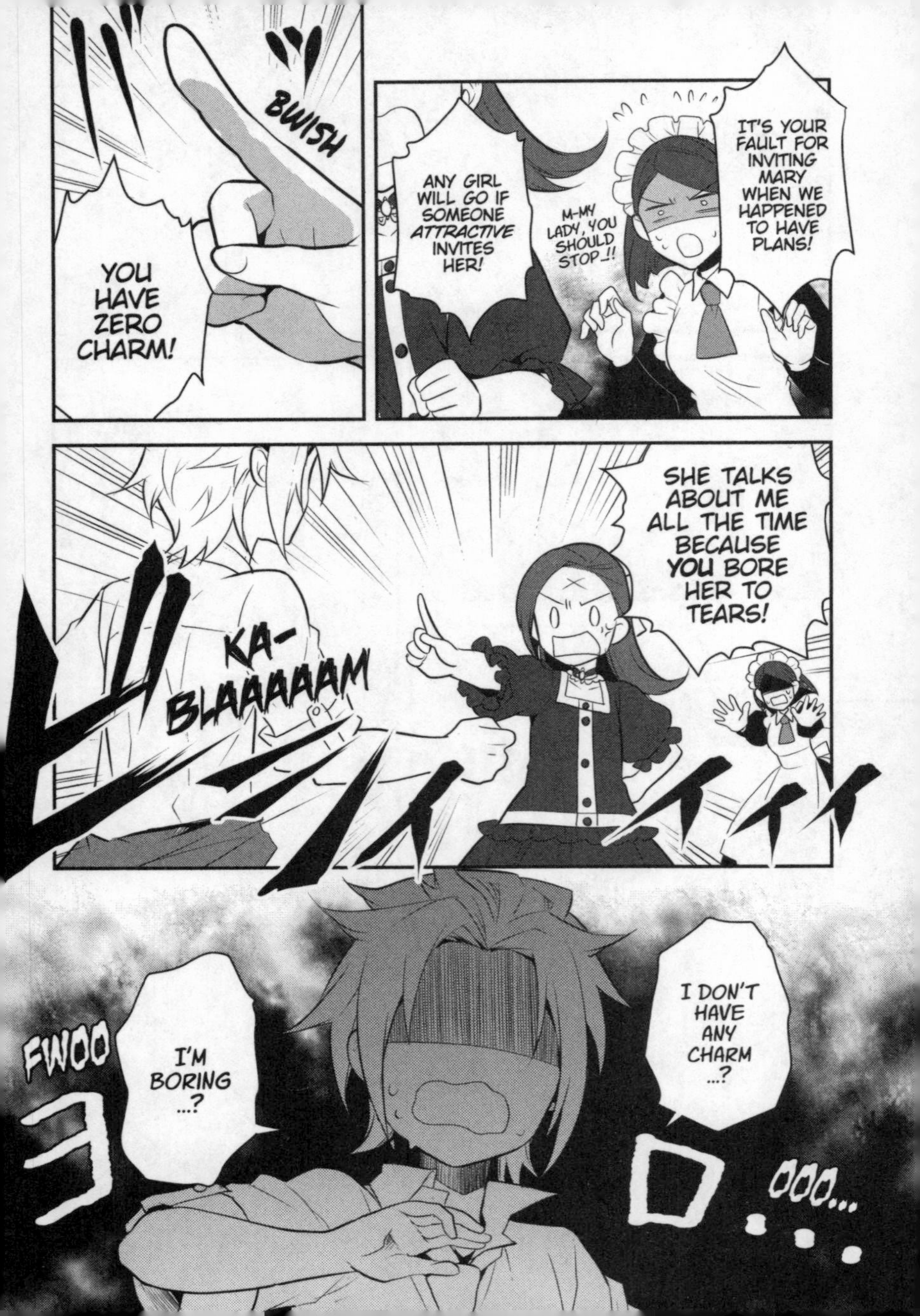
IT'S YOUR FAULT FOR INVITING MARY WHEN WE HAPPENED TO HAVE PLANS!
M-MY LADY, YOU SHOULD STOP..!!
ANY GIRL WILL GO IF SOMEONE *ATTRACTIVE* INVITES HER!
BWISH
YOU HAVE ZERO CHARM!
SHE TALKS ABOUT ME ALL THE TIME BECAUSE **YOU** BORE HER TO TEARS!
KA-BLAAAAAM
I DON'T HAVE ANY CHARM ...?
OOO...
I'M BORING ...?
FWOO

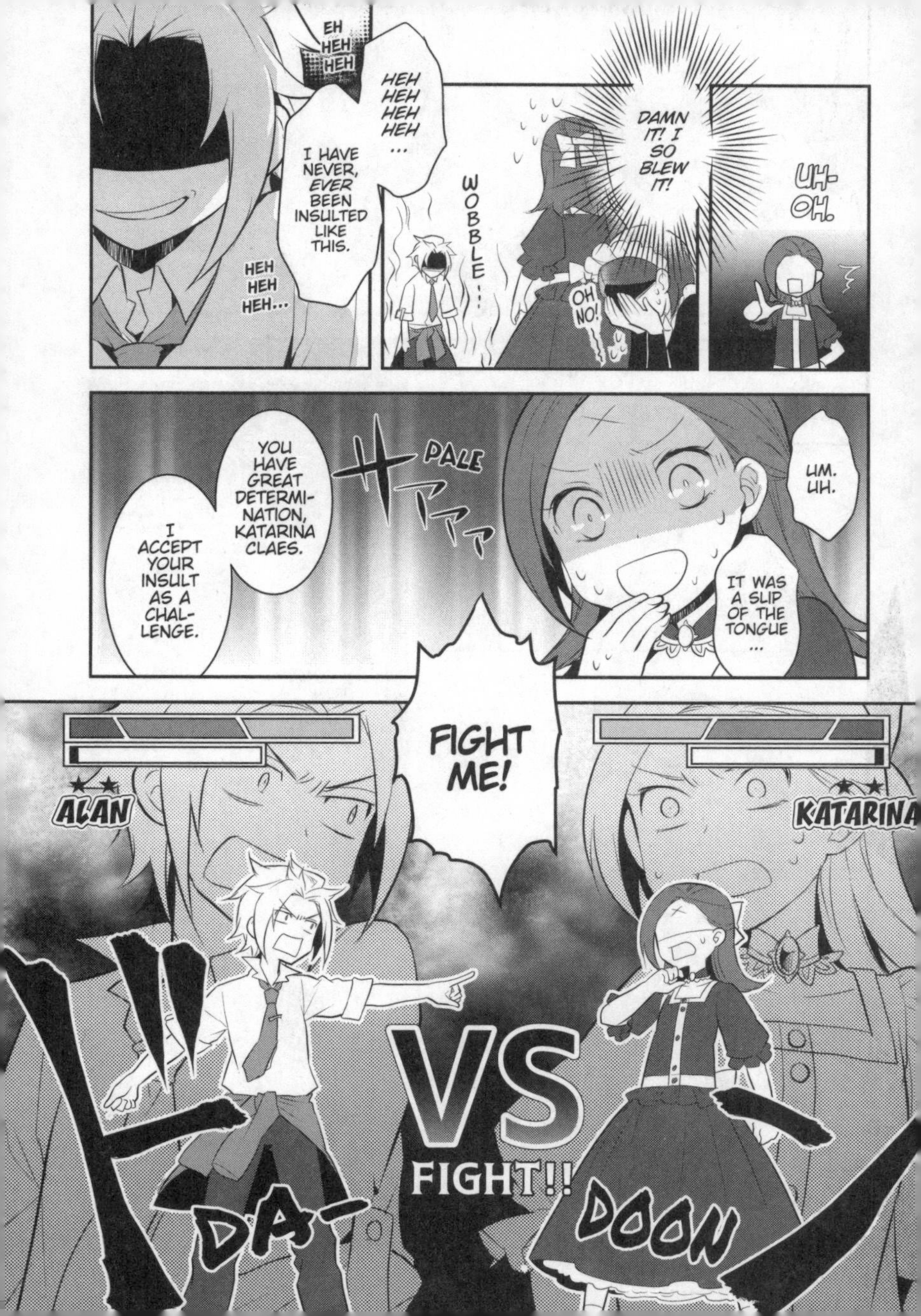
UH-OH.
DAMN IT! I SO BLEW IT!
WOBBLE...
OH NO!
EH HEH HEH
HEH HEH HEH HEH ...
I HAVE NEVER, *EVER* BEEN INSULTED LIKE THIS.
HEH HEH HEH...
UM. UH.
IT WAS A SLIP OF THE TONGUE ...
PALE
YOU HAVE GREAT DETERMINATION, KATARINA CLAES.
I ACCEPT YOUR INSULT AS A CHALLENGE.
FIGHT ME!
KATARINA
ALAN
VS
FIGHT!!
DA-
DOON

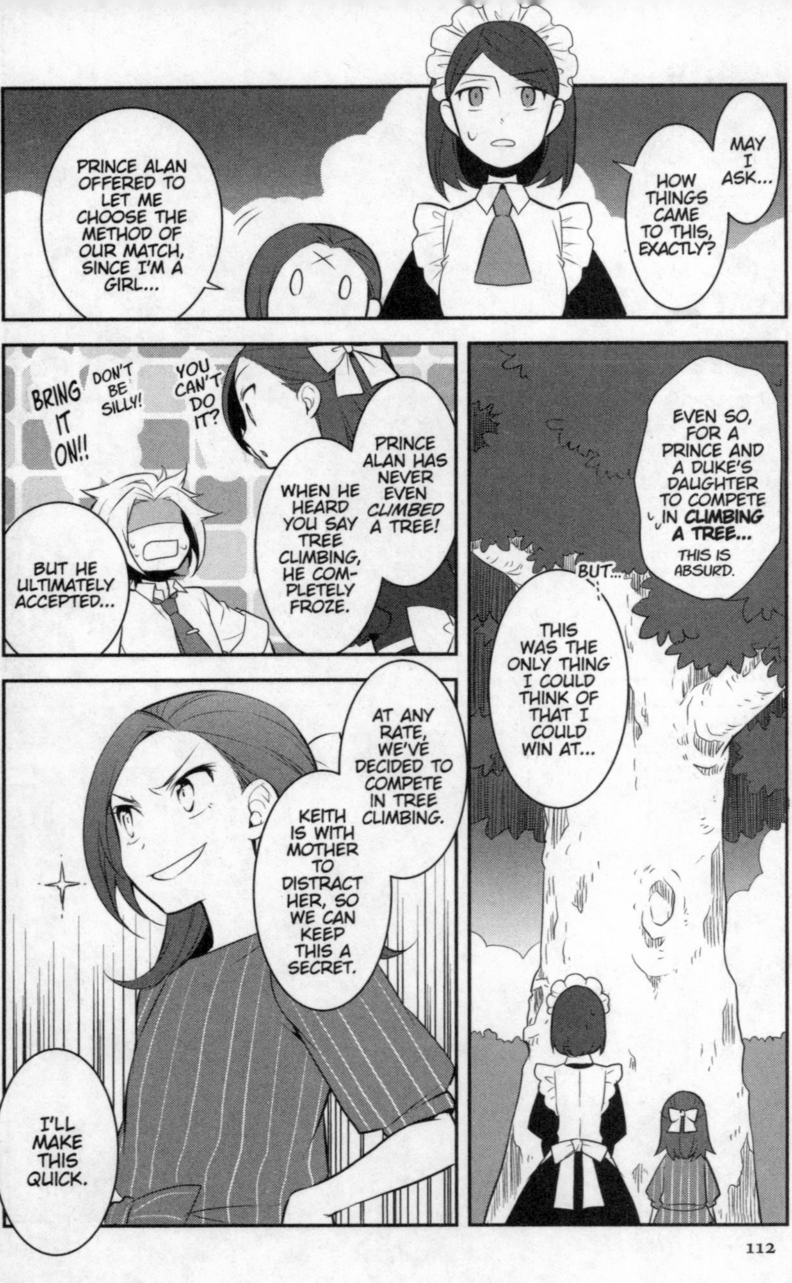
MAY I ASK... HOW THINGS CAME TO THIS, EXACTLY?
PRINCE ALAN OFFERED TO LET ME CHOOSE THE METHOD OF OUR MATCH, SINCE I'M A GIRL...
EVEN SO, FOR A PRINCE AND A DUKE'S DAUGHTER TO COMPETE IN **CLIMBING A TREE...** THIS IS ABSURD.
BUT...
THIS WAS THE ONLY THING I COULD THINK OF THAT I COULD WIN AT...
YOU CAN'T DO IT?
DON'T BE SILLY!
BRING IT ON!!
PRINCE ALAN HAS NEVER EVEN *CLIMBED* A TREE!
WHEN HE HEARD YOU SAY TREE CLIMBING, HE COMPLETELY FROZE.
BUT HE ULTIMATELY ACCEPTED...
AT ANY RATE, WE'VE DECIDED TO COMPETE IN TREE CLIMBING.
KEITH IS WITH MOTHER TO DISTRACT HER, SO WE CAN KEEP THIS A SECRET.
I'LL MAKE THIS QUICK.

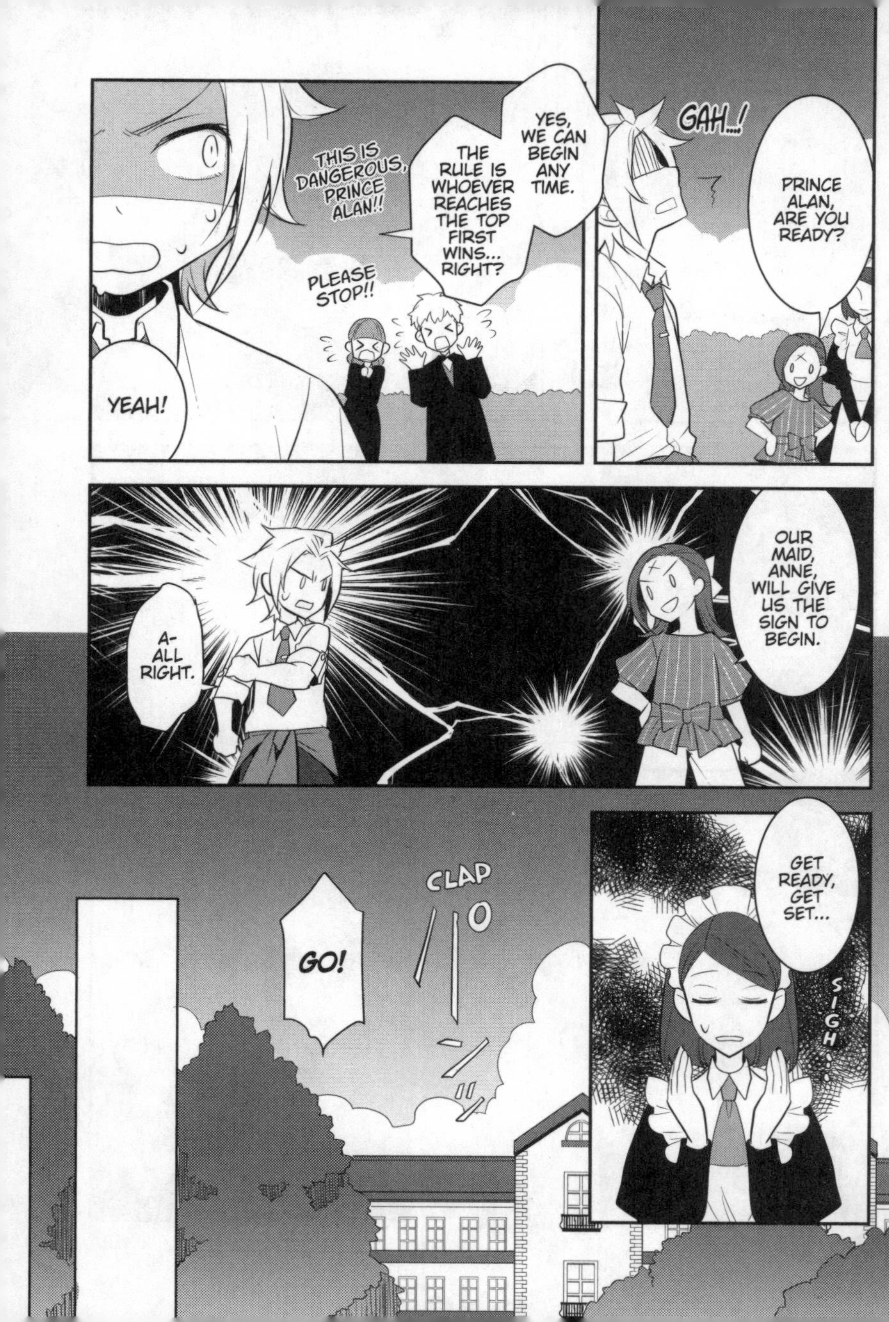
PRINCE ALAN, ARE YOU READY?
GAH...!
YES, WE CAN BEGIN ANY TIME.
THE RULE IS WHOEVER REACHES THE TOP FIRST WINS... RIGHT?
THIS IS DANGEROUS, PRINCE ALAN!!
PLEASE STOP!!
YEAH!
OUR MAID, ANNE, WILL GIVE US THE SIGN TO BEGIN.
A-ALL RIGHT.
GET READY, GET SET...
SIGH...
CLAP
GO!

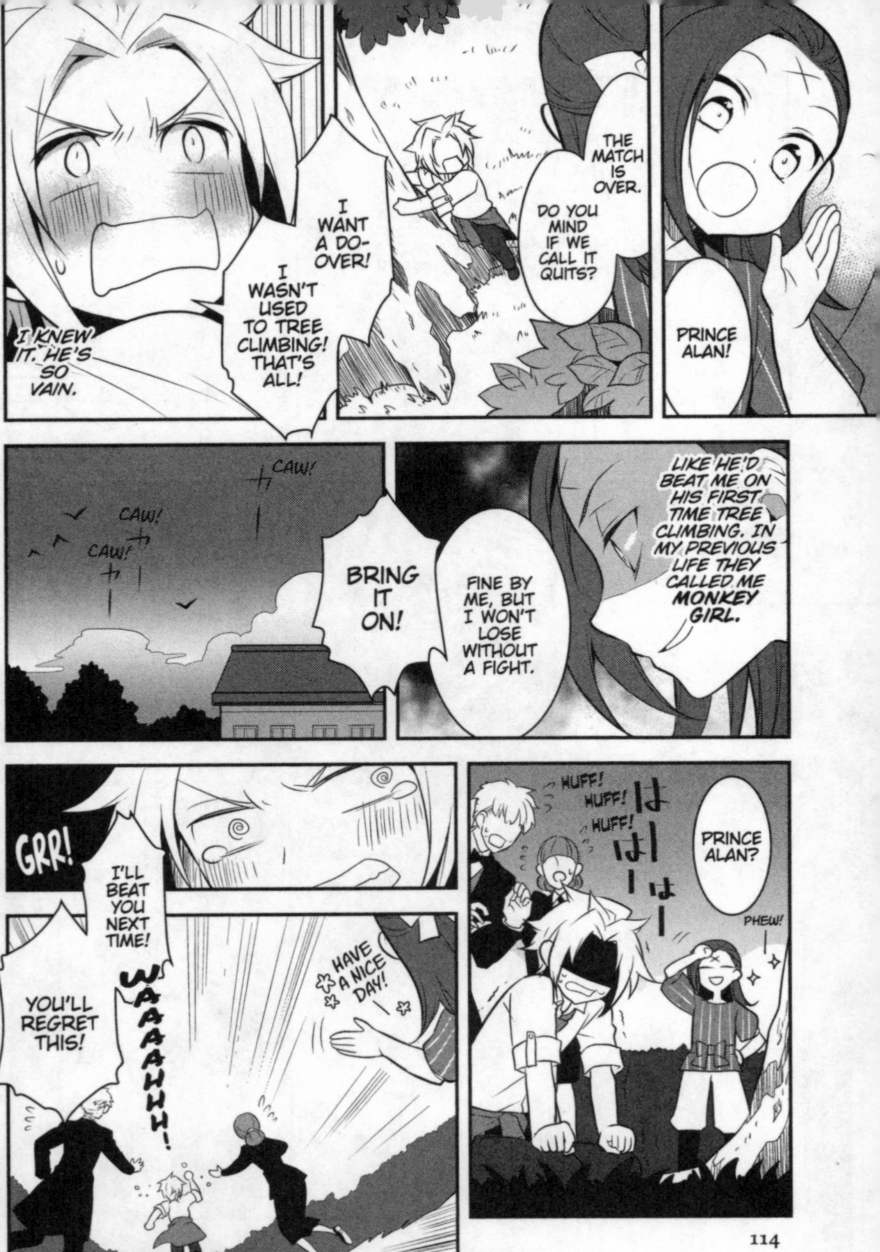
PRINCE ALAN!
THE MATCH IS OVER.
DO YOU MIND IF WE CALL IT QUITS?
I WANT A DO-OVER!
I WASN'T USED TO TREE CLIMBING! THAT'S ALL!
I KNEW IT. HE'S SO VAIN.
LIKE HE'D BEAT ME ON HIS FIRST TIME TREE CLIMBING. IN MY PREVIOUS LIFE THEY CALLED ME MONKEY GIRL.
FINE BY ME, BUT I WON'T LOSE WITHOUT A FIGHT.
BRING IT ON!
CAW!
CAW!
CAW!
HUFF!
HUFF!
HUFF!
はーはー
PRINCE ALAN?
PHEW!
GRR!
I'LL BEAT YOU NEXT TIME!
HAVE A NICE DAY!
WAAAAAHHH!
YOU'LL REGRET THIS!

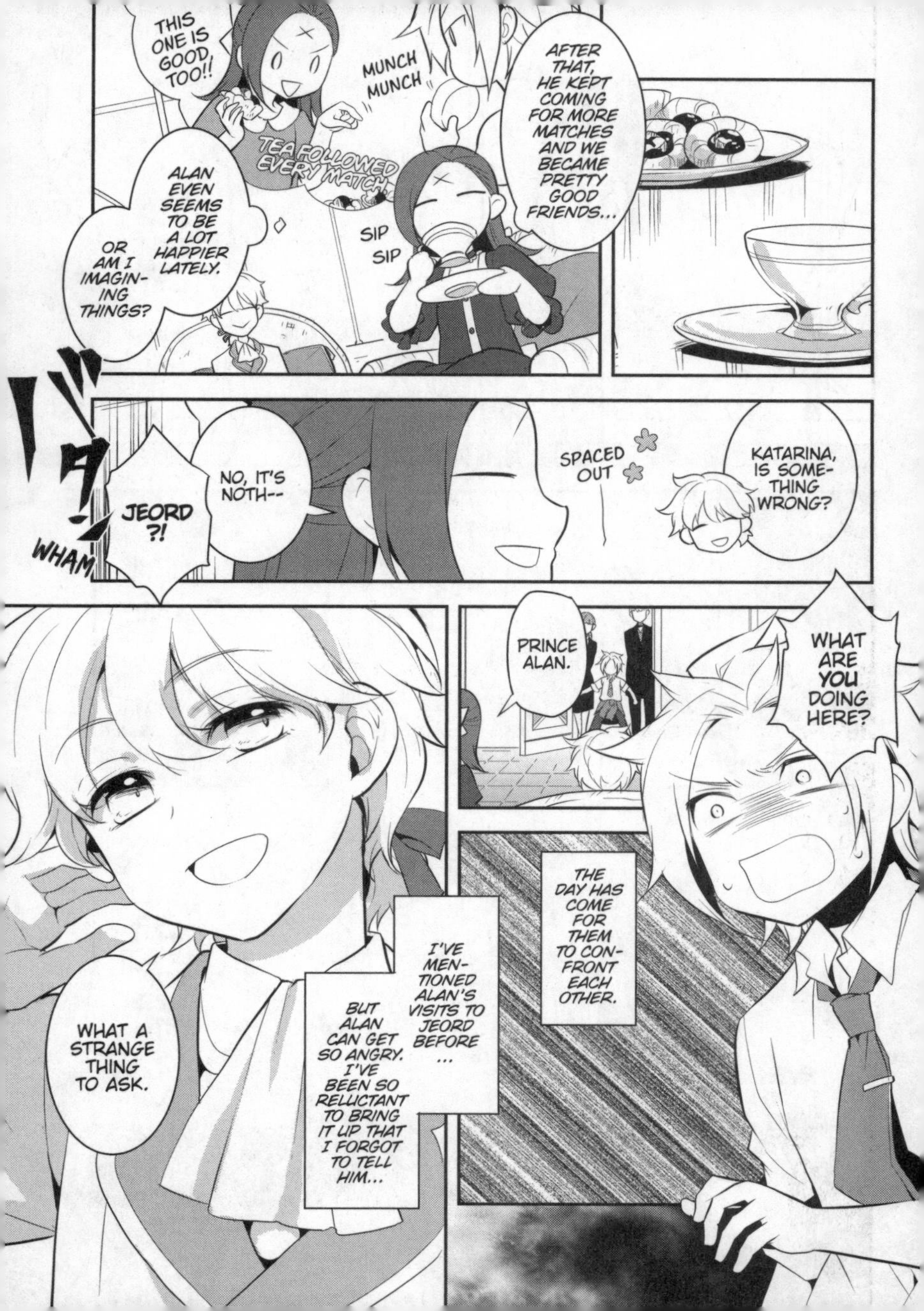
AFTER THAT, HE KEPT COMING FOR MORE MATCHES AND WE BECAME PRETTY GOOD FRIENDS...
THIS ONE IS GOOD TOO!!
MUNCH MUNCH
TEA FOLLOWED EVERY MATCH
SIP SIP
ALAN EVEN SEEMS TO BE A LOT HAPPIER LATELY.
OR AM I IMAGINING THINGS?
KATARINA, IS SOMETHING WRONG?
SPACED OUT
NO, IT'S NOTH--
JEORD ?!
WHAM
WHAT ARE YOU DOING HERE?
PRINCE ALAN.
THE DAY HAS COME FOR THEM TO CONFRONT EACH OTHER.
I'VE MENTIONED ALAN'S VISITS TO JEORD BEFORE ...
BUT ALAN CAN GET SO ANGRY. I'VE BEEN SO RELUCTANT TO BRING IT UP THAT I FORGOT TO TELL HIM...
WHAT A STRANGE THING TO ASK.

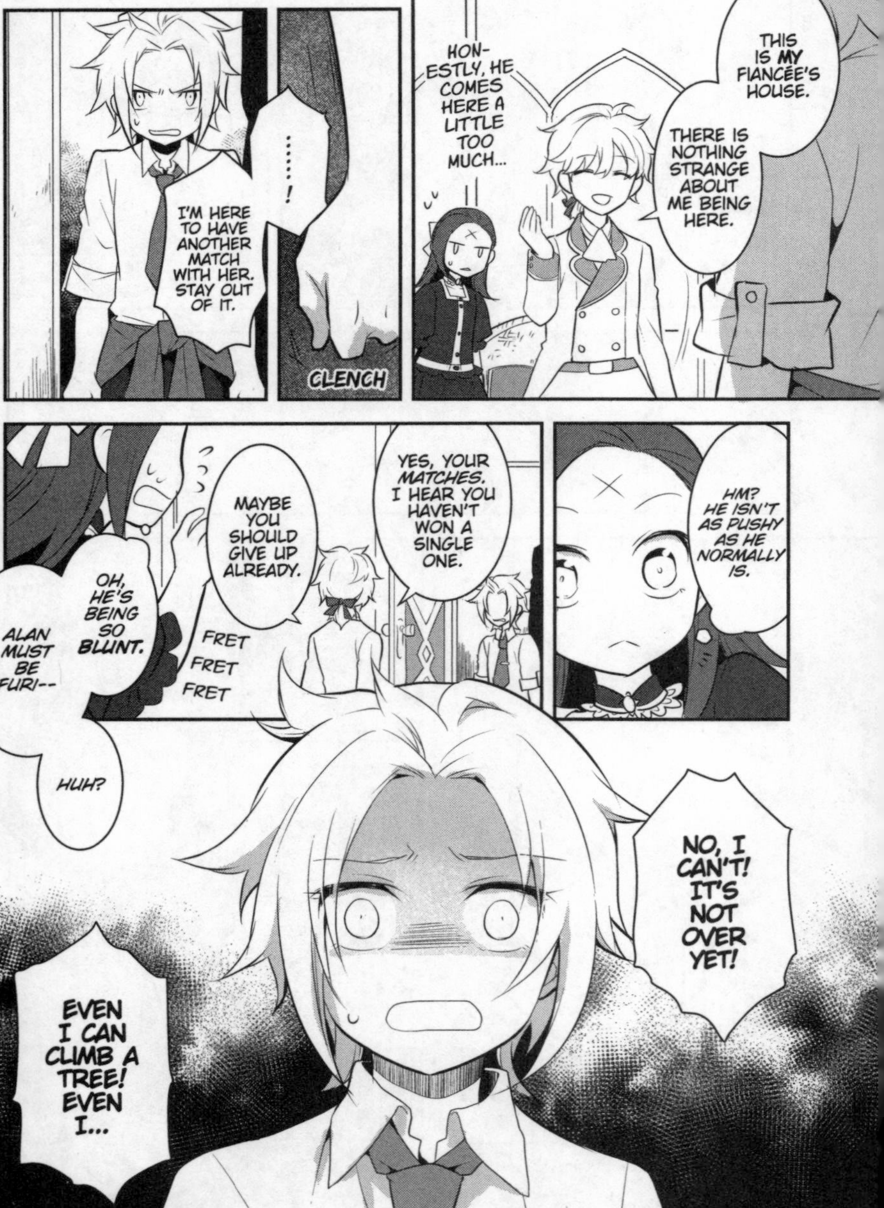
THIS IS MY FIANCÉE'S HOUSE.
THERE IS NOTHING STRANGE ABOUT ME BEING HERE.
HON-ESTLY, HE COMES HERE A LITTLE TOO MUCH...
......!
CLENCH
I'M HERE TO HAVE ANOTHER MATCH WITH HER. STAY OUT OF IT.
HM? HE ISN'T AS PUSHY AS HE NORMALLY IS.
YES, YOUR MATCHES. I HEAR YOU HAVEN'T WON A SINGLE ONE.
MAYBE YOU SHOULD GIVE UP ALREADY.
FRET FRET FRET
OH, HE'S BEING SO BLUNT.
ALAN MUST BE FURI--
HUH?
NO, I CAN'T! IT'S NOT OVER YET!
EVEN I CAN CLIMB A TREE! EVEN I...

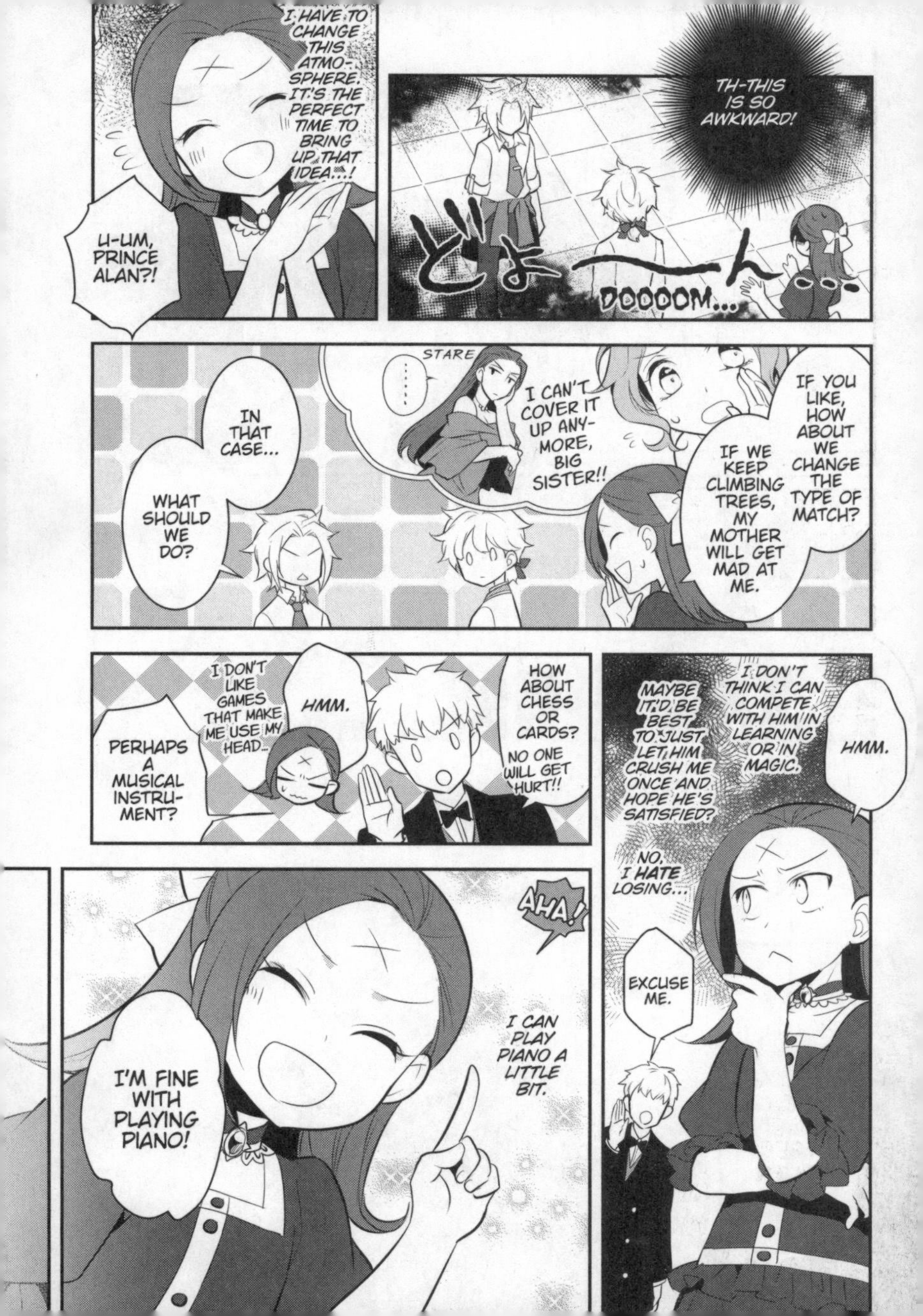
TH-THIS IS SO AWKWARD!
どよーーん
DOOOOM...
I HAVE TO CHANGE THIS ATMOSPHERE. IT'S THE PERFECT TIME TO BRING UP THAT IDEA...!
U-UM, PRINCE ALAN?!
IF YOU LIKE, HOW ABOUT WE CHANGE THE TYPE OF MATCH?
IF WE KEEP CLIMBING TREES, MY MOTHER WILL GET MAD AT ME.
STARE
......
I CAN'T COVER IT UP ANY-MORE, BIG SISTER!!
IN THAT CASE...
WHAT SHOULD WE DO?
HMM.
I DON'T THINK I CAN COMPETE WITH HIM IN LEARNING OR IN MAGIC.
MAYBE IT'D BE BEST TO JUST LET HIM CRUSH ME ONCE AND HOPE HE'S SATISFIED?
NO. I HATE LOSING...
EXCUSE ME.
HOW ABOUT CHESS OR CARDS?
NO ONE WILL GET HURT!!
HMM.
I DON'T LIKE GAMES THAT MAKE ME USE MY HEAD...
PERHAPS A MUSICAL INSTRU-MENT?
AHA!
I CAN PLAY PIANO A LITTLE BIT.
I'M FINE WITH PLAYING PIANO!

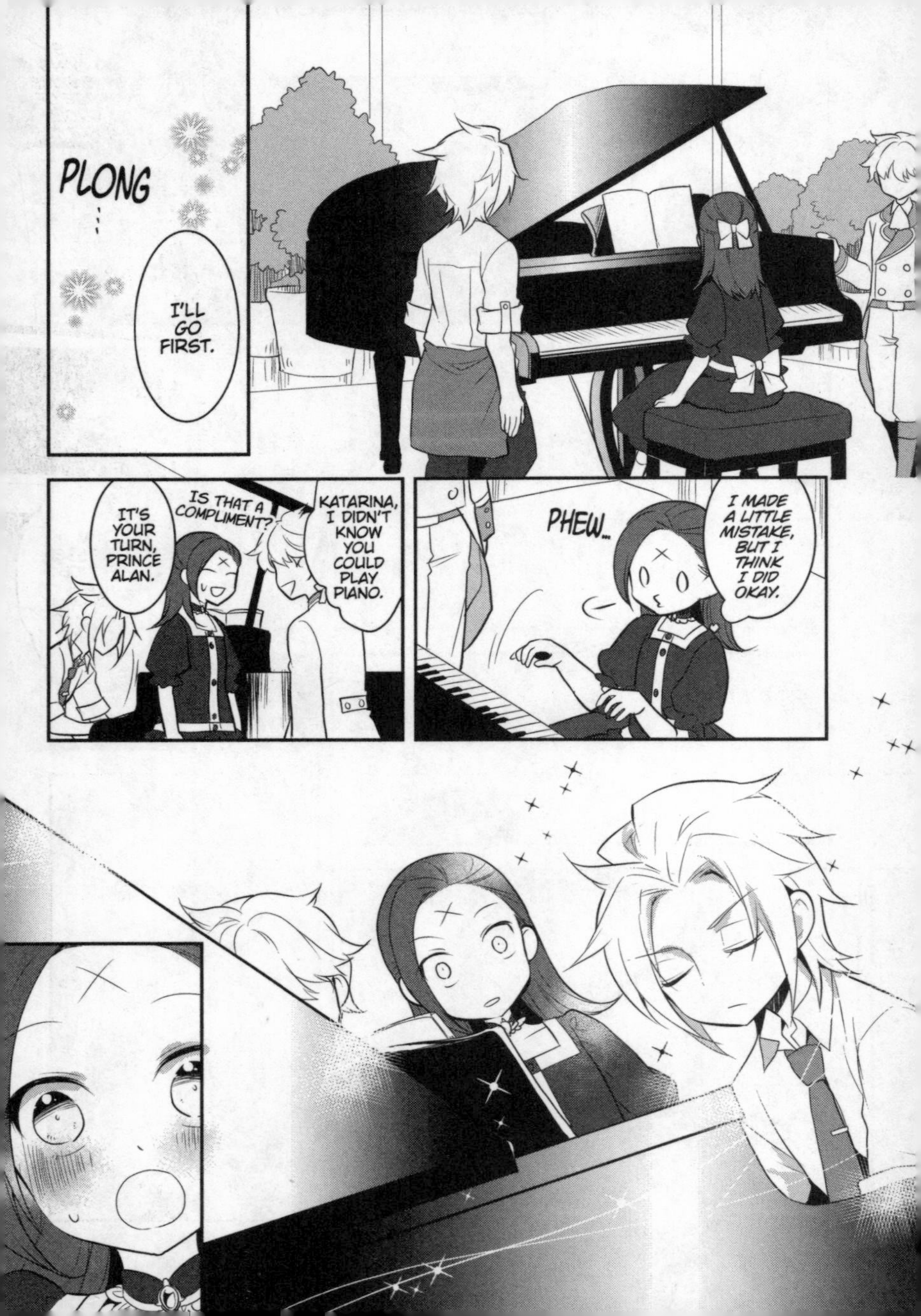
PLONG
...
I'LL GO FIRST.
PHEW...
I MADE A LITTLE MISTAKE, BUT I THINK I DID OKAY.
KATARINA, I DIDN'T KNOW YOU COULD PLAY PIANO.
IS THAT A COMPLIMENT?
IT'S YOUR TURN, PRINCE ALAN.

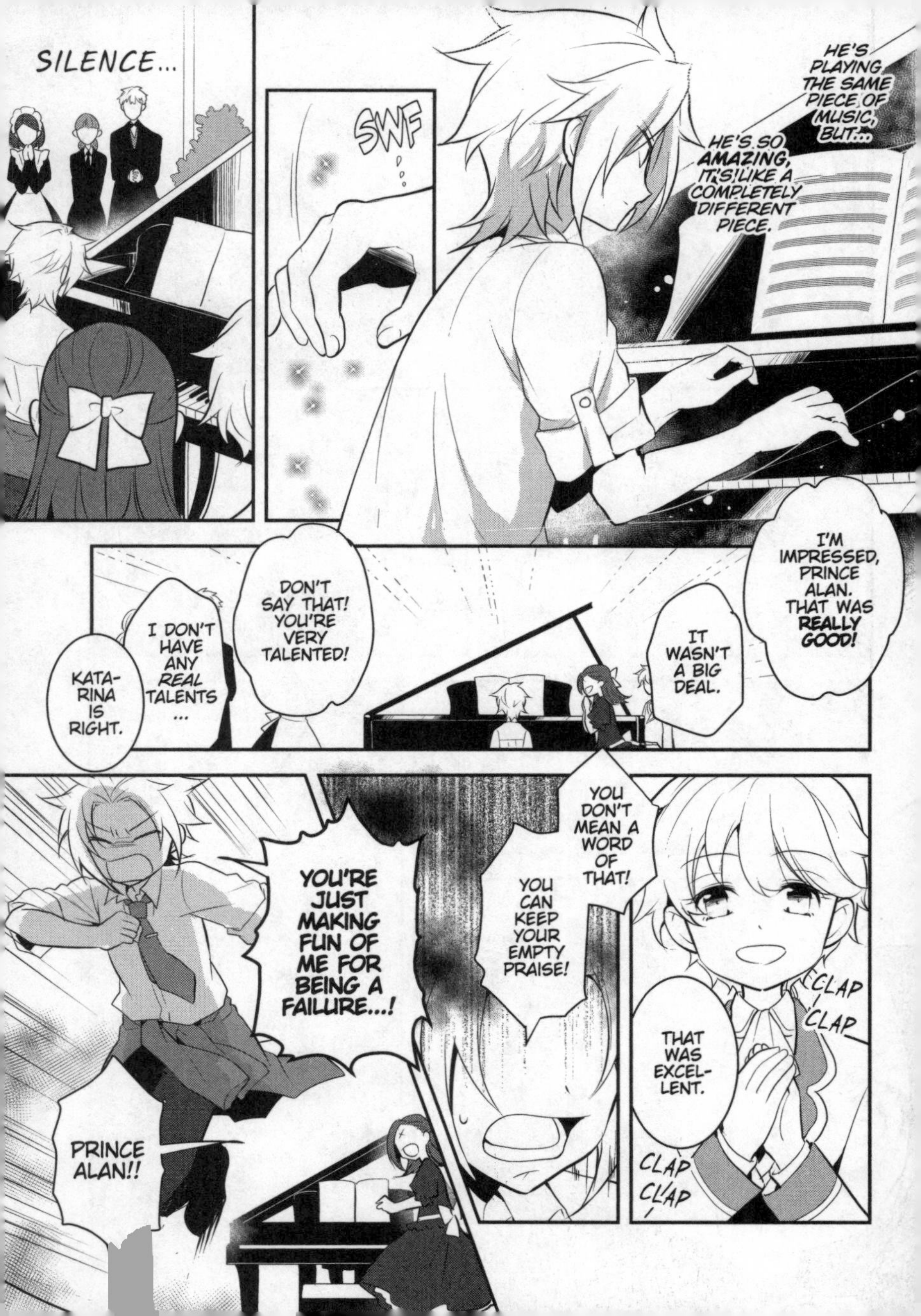
HE'S PLAYING THE SAME PIECE OF MUSIC, BUT...
HE'S SO AMAZING, IT'S LIKE A COMPLETELY DIFFERENT PIECE.
SWF
SILENCE...
I'M IMPRESSED, PRINCE ALAN. THAT WAS REALLY GOOD!
IT WASN'T A BIG DEAL.
DON'T SAY THAT! YOU'RE VERY TALENTED!
I DON'T HAVE ANY REAL TALENTS...
KATARINA IS RIGHT.
CLAP CLAP
THAT WAS EXCELLENT.
CLAP CLAP
YOU DON'T MEAN A WORD OF THAT!
YOU CAN KEEP YOUR EMPTY PRAISE!
YOU'RE JUST MAKING FUN OF ME FOR BEING A FAILURE...!
PRINCE ALAN!!

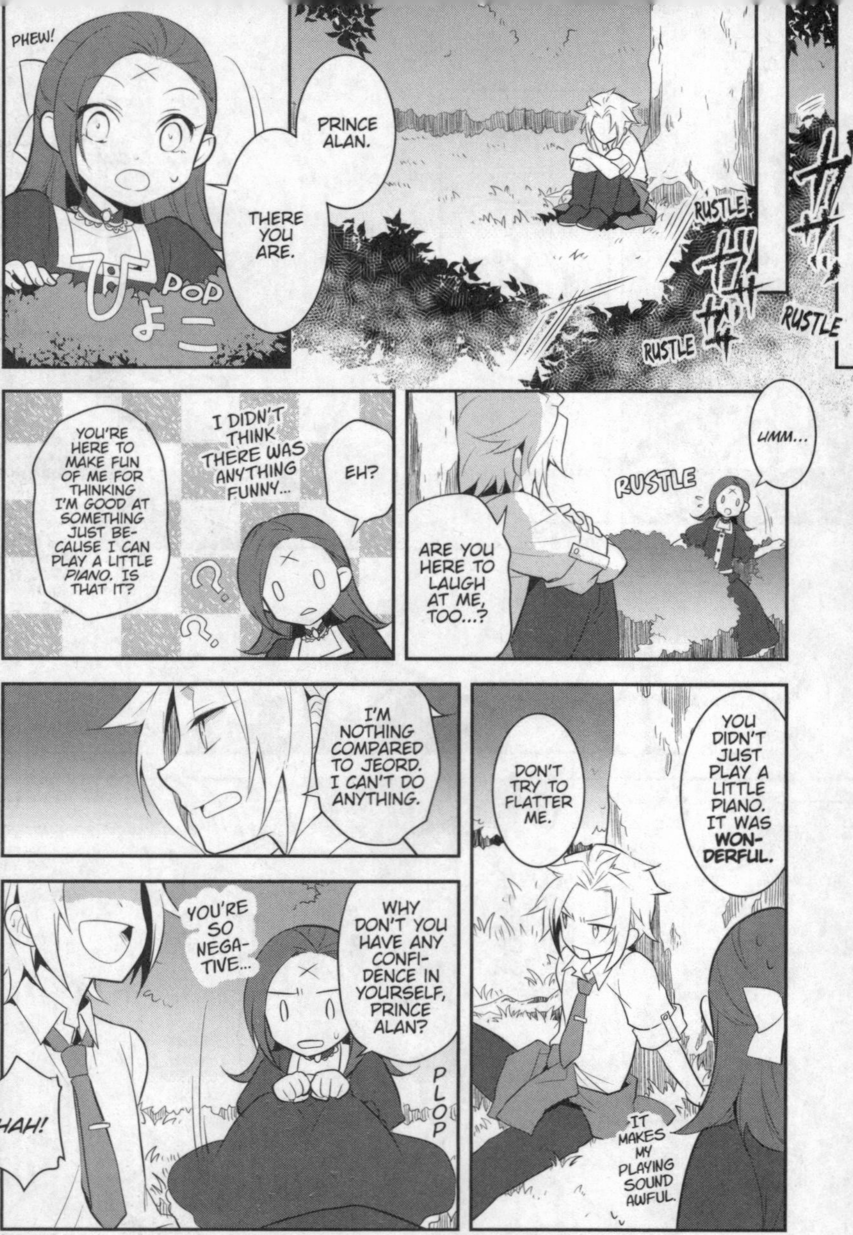
RUSTLE
RUSTLE
RUSTLE
PHEW!
PRINCE ALAN.
THERE YOU ARE.
POP
UMM...
RUSTLE
ARE YOU HERE TO LAUGH AT ME, TOO...?
EH?
I DIDN'T THINK THERE WAS ANYTHING FUNNY...
YOU'RE HERE TO MAKE FUN OF ME FOR THINKING I'M GOOD AT SOMETHING JUST BE-CAUSE I CAN PLAY A LITTLE *PIANO*. IS THAT IT?
YOU DIDN'T JUST PLAY A LITTLE PIANO. IT WAS **WON-DERFUL.**
DON'T TRY TO FLATTER ME.
IT MAKES MY PLAYING SOUND AWFUL.
I'M NOTHING COMPARED TO JEORD. I CAN'T DO ANYTHING.
WHY DON'T YOU HAVE ANY CONFI-DENCE IN YOURSELF, PRINCE ALAN?
YOU'RE SO NEGA-TIVE...
PLOP
HAH!

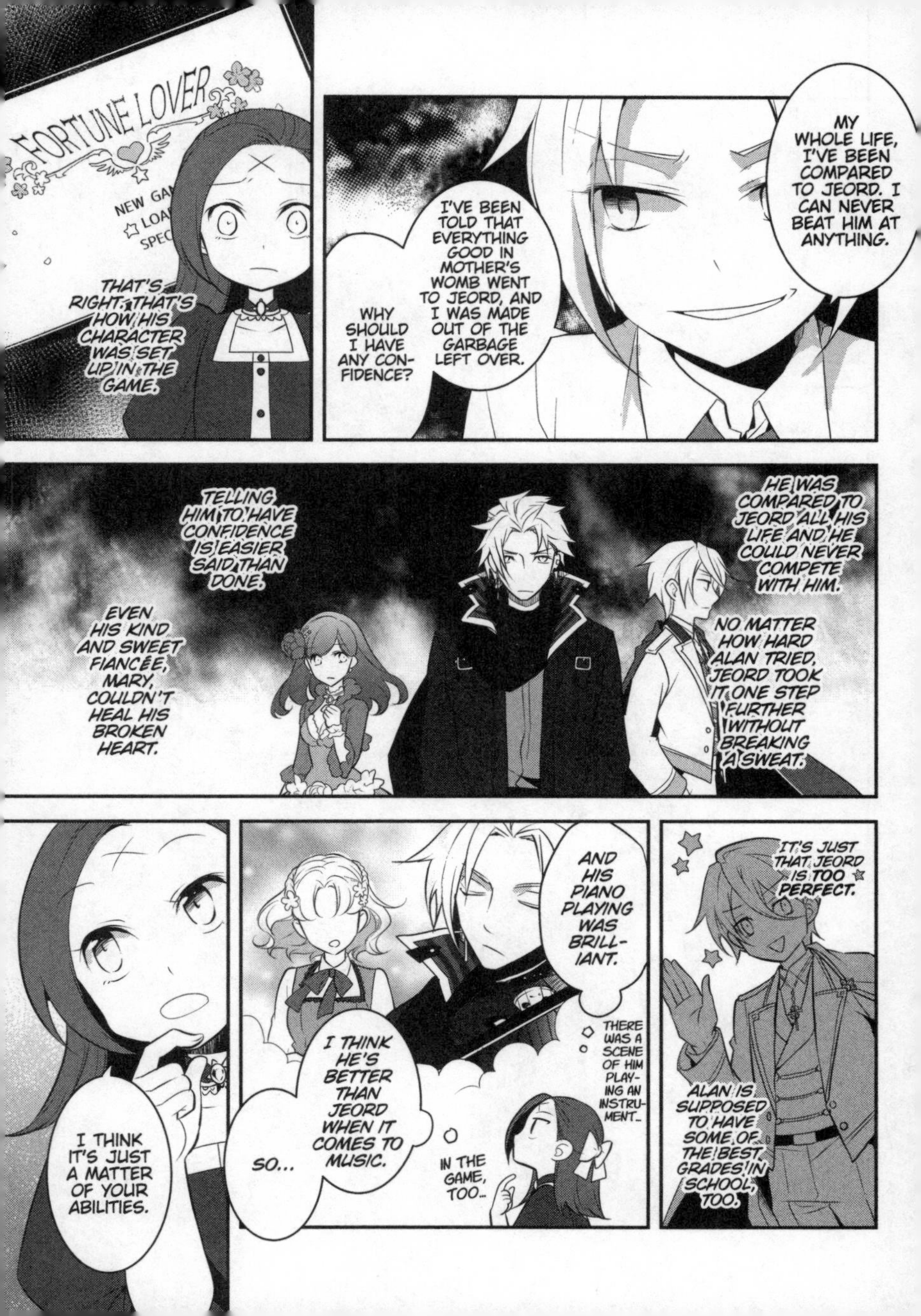
MY WHOLE LIFE, I'VE BEEN COMPARED TO JEORD. I CAN NEVER BEAT HIM AT ANYTHING.
I'VE BEEN TOLD THAT EVERYTHING GOOD IN MOTHER'S WOMB WENT TO JEORD, AND I WAS MADE OUT OF THE GARBAGE LEFT OVER.
WHY SHOULD I HAVE ANY CONFIDENCE?
FORTUNE LOVER
THAT'S RIGHT. THAT'S HOW HIS CHARACTER WAS SET UP IN THE GAME.
HE WAS COMPARED TO JEORD ALL HIS LIFE AND HE COULD NEVER COMPETE WITH HIM.
NO MATTER HOW HARD ALAN TRIED, JEORD TOOK IT ONE STEP FURTHER WITHOUT BREAKING A SWEAT.
TELLING HIM TO HAVE CONFIDENCE IS EASIER SAID THAN DONE.
EVEN HIS KIND AND SWEET FIANCÉE, MARY, COULDN'T HEAL HIS BROKEN HEART.
IT'S JUST THAT JEORD IS TOO PERFECT.
ALAN IS SUPPOSED TO HAVE SOME OF THE BEST GRADES IN SCHOOL, TOO.
AND HIS PIANO PLAYING WAS BRILLIANT.
THERE WAS A SCENE OF HIM PLAYING AN INSTRUMENT...
IN THE GAME, TOO...
I THINK HE'S BETTER THAN JEORD WHEN IT COMES TO MUSIC.
SO...
I THINK IT'S JUST A MATTER OF YOUR ABILITIES.

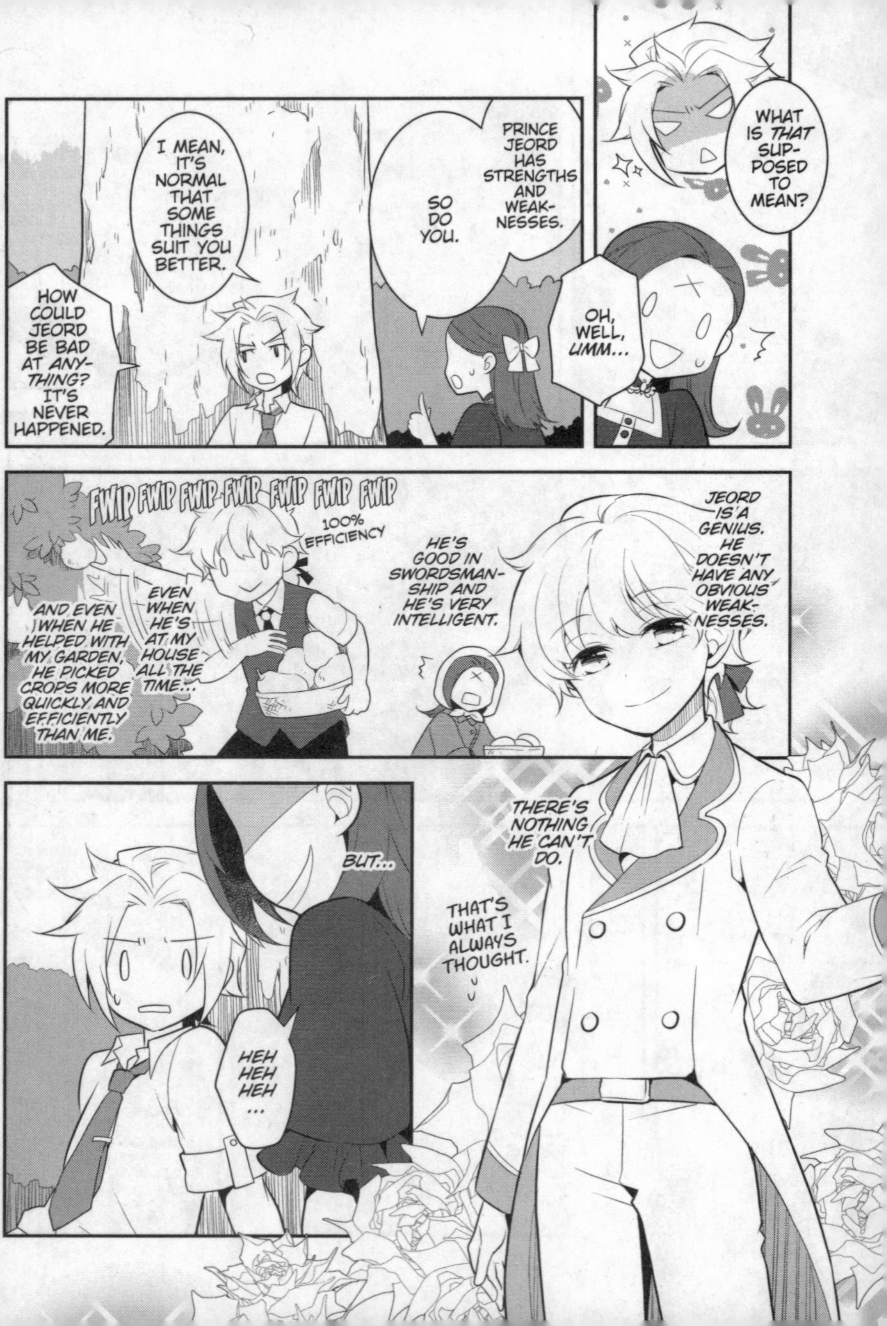
WHAT IS THAT SUPPOSED TO MEAN?
OH, WELL, UMM...
PRINCE JEORD HAS STRENGTHS AND WEAKNESSES.
SO DO YOU.
I MEAN, IT'S NORMAL THAT SOME THINGS SUIT YOU BETTER.
HOW COULD JEORD BE BAD AT ANYTHING? IT'S NEVER HAPPENED.
JEORD IS A GENIUS. HE DOESN'T HAVE ANY OBVIOUS WEAKNESSES.
HE'S GOOD IN SWORDSMANSHIP AND HE'S VERY INTELLIGENT.
100% EFFICIENCY
FWIP FWIP FWIP FWIP FWIP FWIP FWIP
EVEN WHEN HE'S AT MY HOUSE ALL THE TIME...
AND EVEN WHEN HE HELPED WITH MY GARDEN, HE PICKED CROPS MORE QUICKLY AND EFFICIENTLY THAN ME.
THERE'S NOTHING HE CAN'T DO.
THAT'S WHAT I ALWAYS THOUGHT.
BUT...
HEH HEH HEH ...

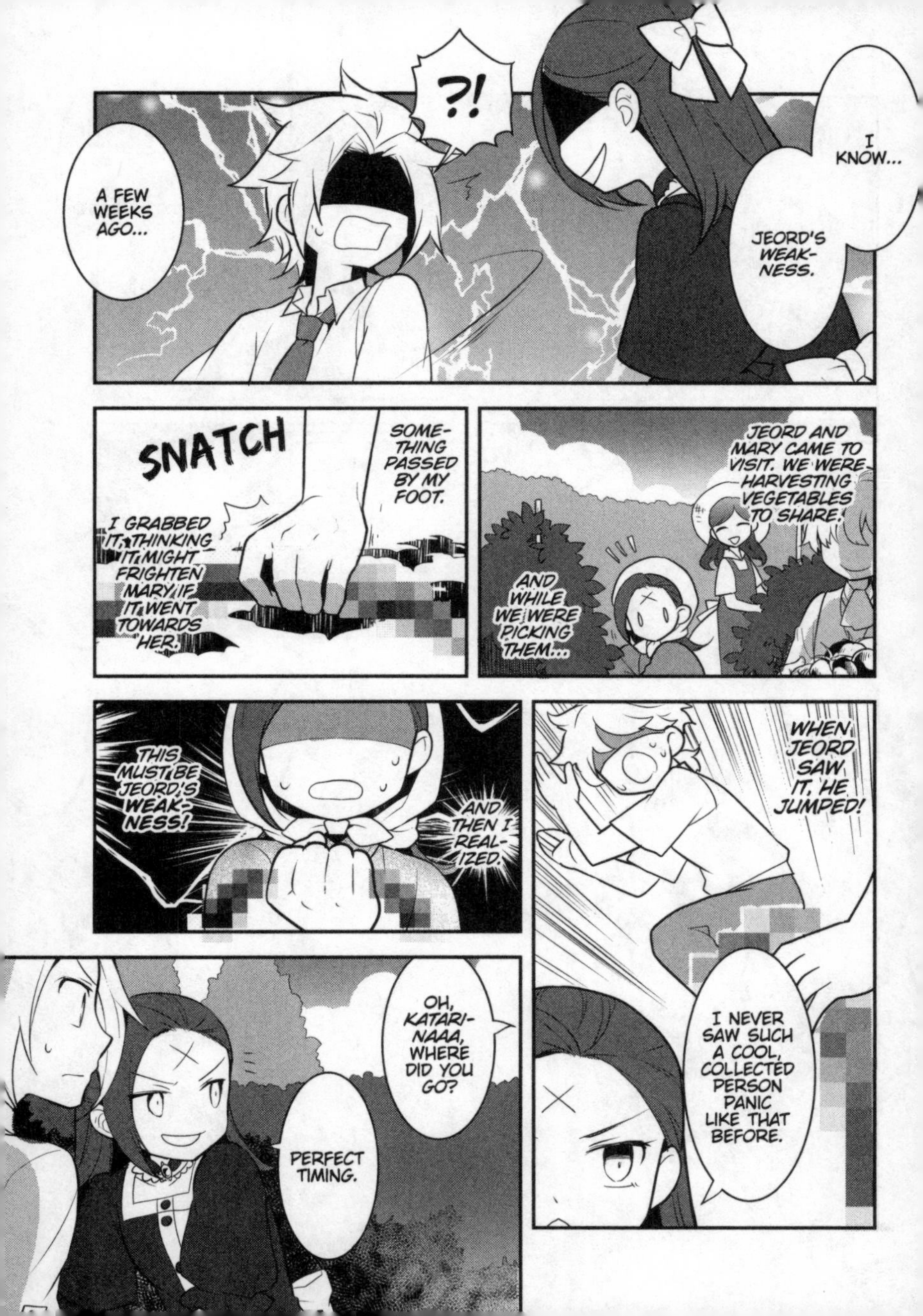
I KNOW...
JEORD'S WEAK-NESS.
?!
A FEW WEEKS AGO...
JEORD AND MARY CAME TO VISIT. WE WERE HARVESTING VEGETABLES TO SHARE.
AND WHILE WE WERE PICKING THEM...
SNATCH
SOME-THING PASSED BY MY FOOT.
I GRABBED IT, THINKING IT MIGHT FRIGHTEN MARY IF IT WENT TOWARDS HER.
WHEN JEORD SAW IT, HE JUMPED!
I NEVER SAW SUCH A COOL, COLLECTED PERSON PANIC LIKE THAT BEFORE.
AND THEN I REAL-IZED.
THIS MUST BE JEORD'S WEAK-NESS!
OH, KATARI-NAAA, WHERE DID YOU GO?
PERFECT TIMING.

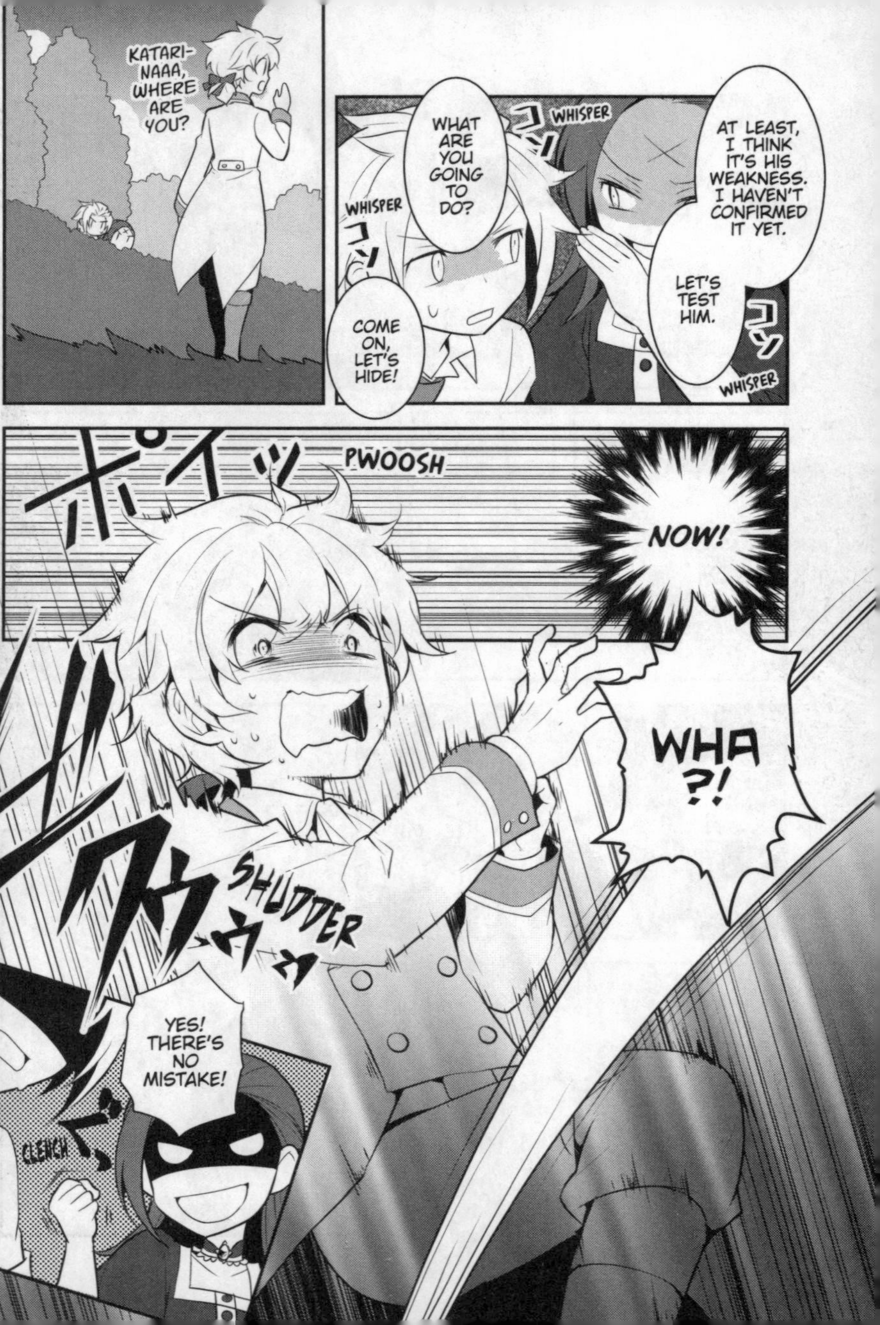
WHISPER
AT LEAST, I THINK IT'S HIS WEAKNESS. I HAVEN'T CONFIRMED IT YET.
WHAT ARE YOU GOING TO DO?
WHISPER
LET'S TEST HIM.
WHISPER
WHISPER
COME ON, LET'S HIDE!
KATARI-NAAA, WHERE ARE YOU?
NOW!
PWOOSH
WHA ?!
SHUDDER
YES! THERE'S NO MISTAKE!
CLENCH

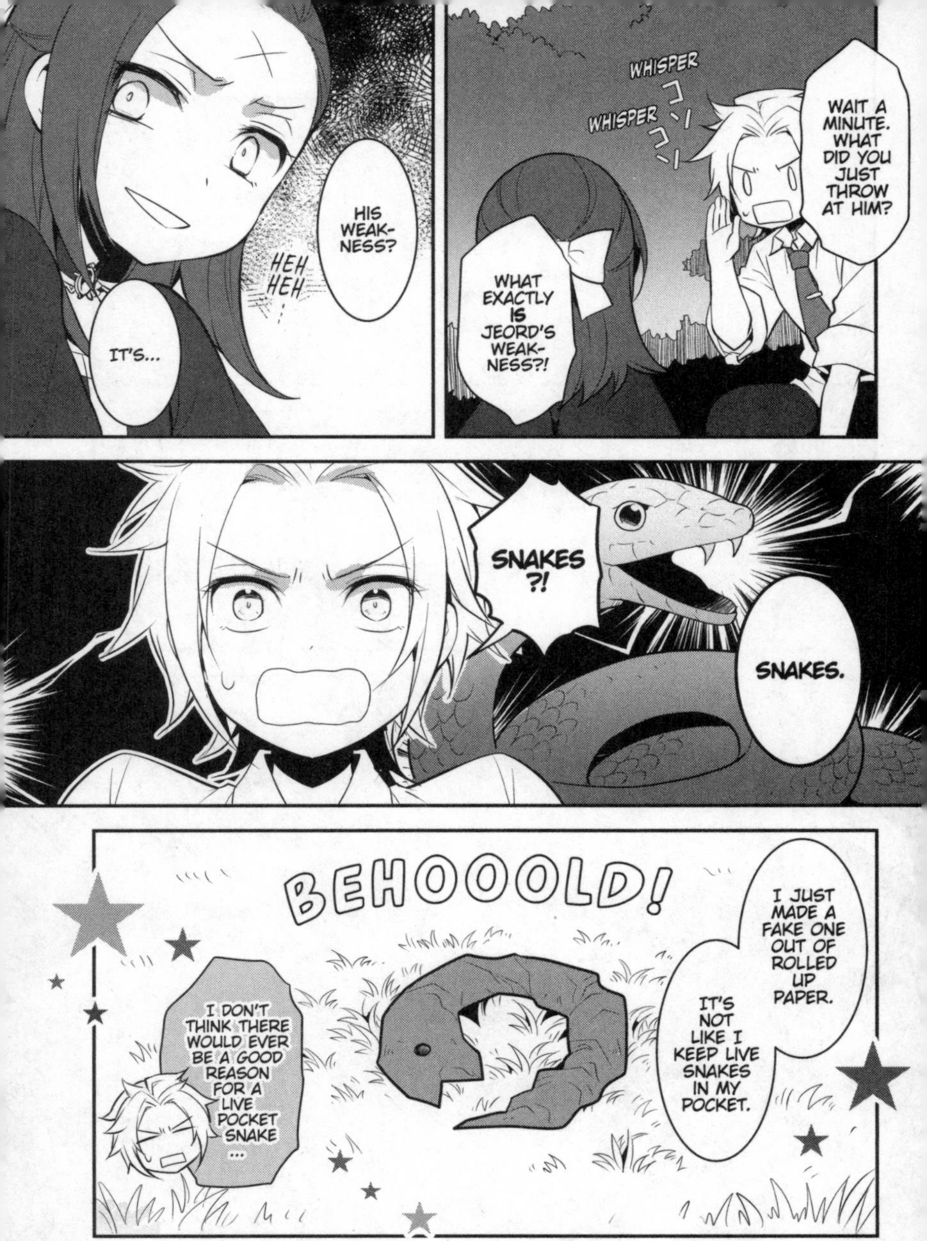
WHISPER
WHISPER
WAIT A MINUTE. WHAT DID YOU JUST THROW AT HIM?
WHAT EXACTLY IS JEORD'S WEAKNESS?!
HIS WEAKNESS?
HEH HEH
IT'S...
SNAKES.
SNAKES?!
BEHOOOLD!
I JUST MADE A FAKE ONE OUT OF ROLLED UP PAPER.
IT'S NOT LIKE I KEEP LIVE SNAKES IN MY POCKET.
I DON'T THINK THERE WOULD EVER BE A GOOD REASON FOR A LIVE POCKET SNAKE...

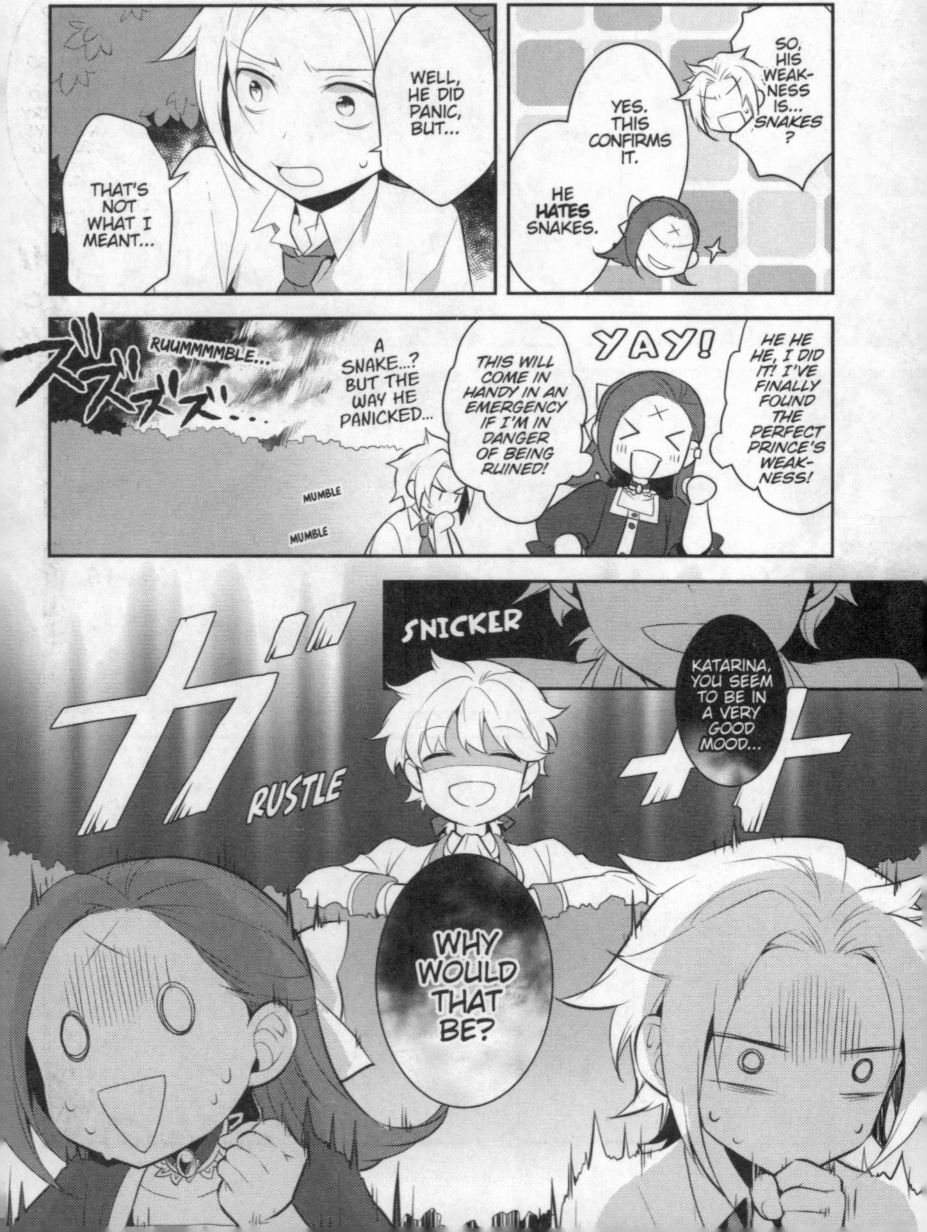
SO, HIS WEAK-NESS IS... SNAKES?
YES. THIS CONFIRMS IT.
HE HATES SNAKES.
WELL, HE DID PANIC, BUT...
THAT'S NOT WHAT I MEANT...
HE HE HE, I DID IT! I'VE FINALLY FOUND THE PERFECT PRINCE'S WEAK-NESS!
YAY!
THIS WILL COME IN HANDY IN AN EMERGENCY IF I'M IN DANGER OF BEING RUINED!
A SNAKE...? BUT THE WAY HE PANICKED...
RUUMMMMBLE...
MUMBLE
MUMBLE
SNICKER
KATARINA, YOU SEEM TO BE IN A VERY GOOD MOOD...
RUSTLE
WHY WOULD THAT BE?

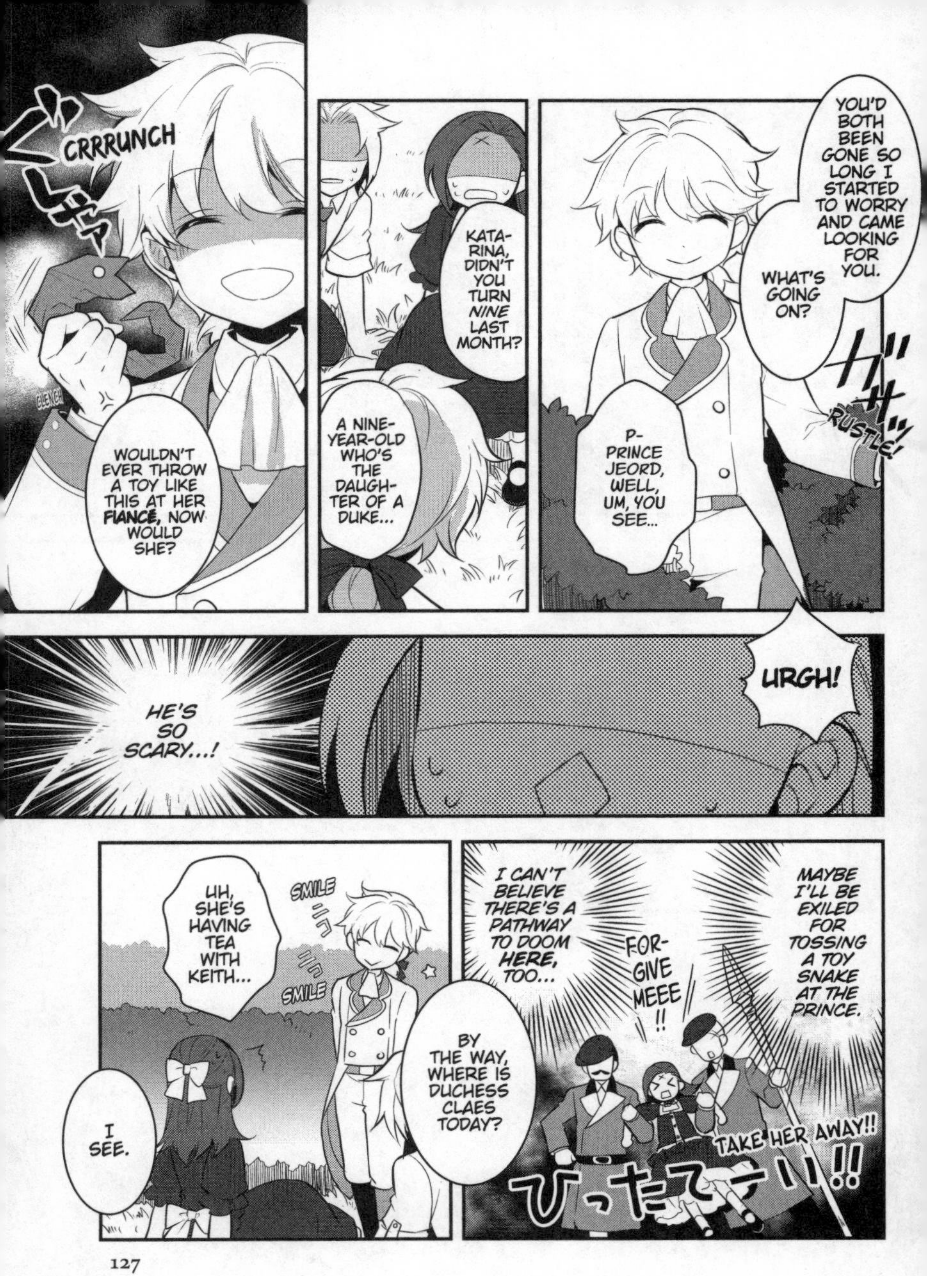

YOU'D BOTH BEEN GONE SO LONG I STARTED TO WORRY AND CAME LOOKING FOR YOU.
WHAT'S GOING ON?
RUSTLE!
P-PRINCE JEORD, WELL, UM, YOU SEE...
KATARINA, DIDN'T YOU TURN NINE LAST MONTH?
A NINE-YEAR-OLD WHO'S THE DAUGHTER OF A DUKE...
CRRRUNCH
WOULDN'T EVER THROW A TOY LIKE THIS AT HER FIANCÉ, NOW WOULD SHE?
CLENCH
URGH!
HE'S SO SCARY...!
MAYBE I'LL BE EXILED FOR TOSSING A TOY SNAKE AT THE PRINCE.
I CAN'T BELIEVE THERE'S A PATHWAY TO DOOM HERE, TOO...
FORGIVE MEEE!!
TAKE HER AWAY!!
ひったてーい!!
BY THE WAY, WHERE IS DUCHESS CLAES TODAY?
SMILE
SMILE
UH, SHE'S HAVING TEA WITH KEITH...
I SEE.

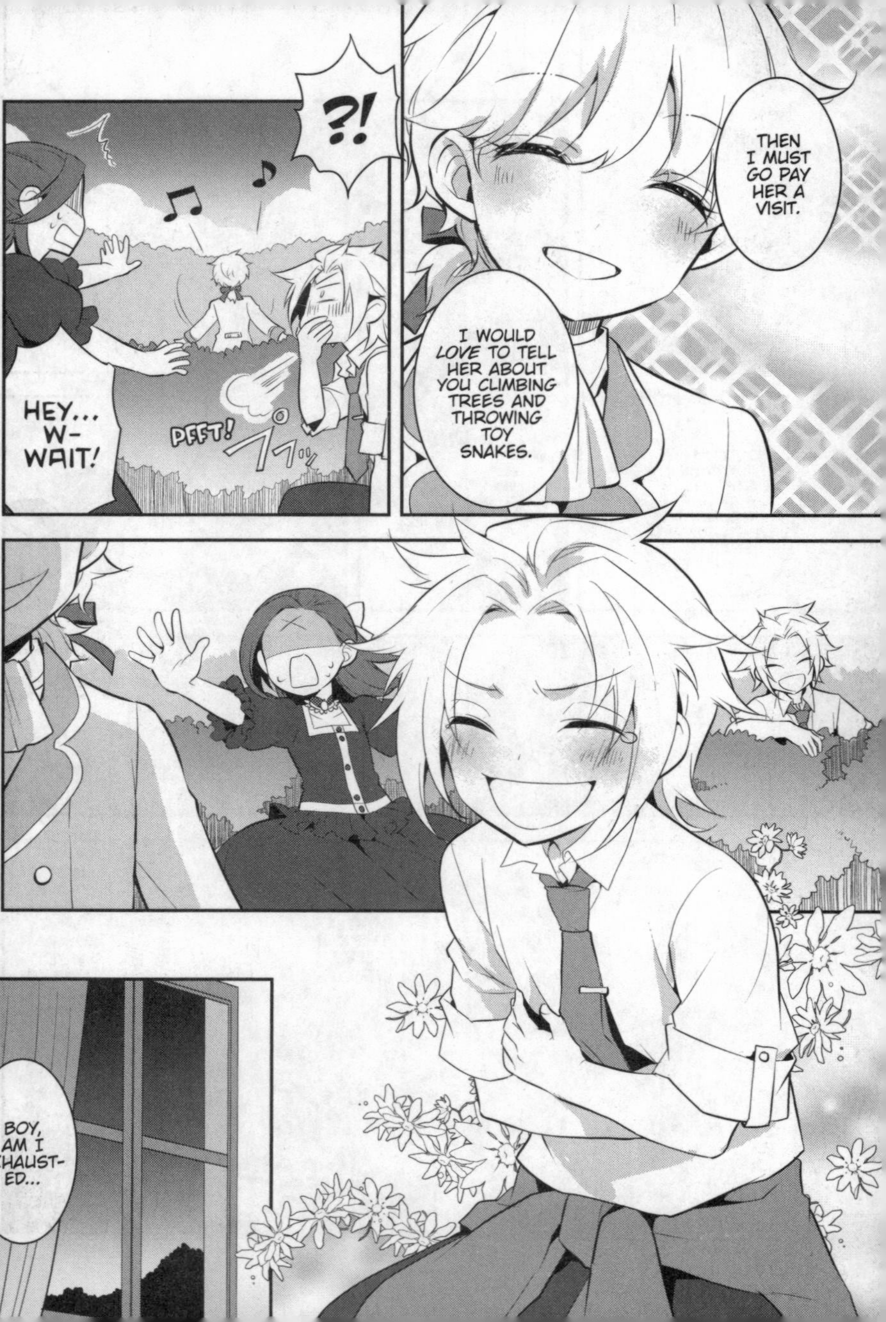
THEN I MUST GO PAY HER A VISIT.
I WOULD *LOVE* TO TELL HER ABOUT YOU CLIMBING TREES AND THROWING TOY SNAKES.
?!
HEY... W-WAIT!
PFFT!
BOY, AM I EXHAUST-ED...

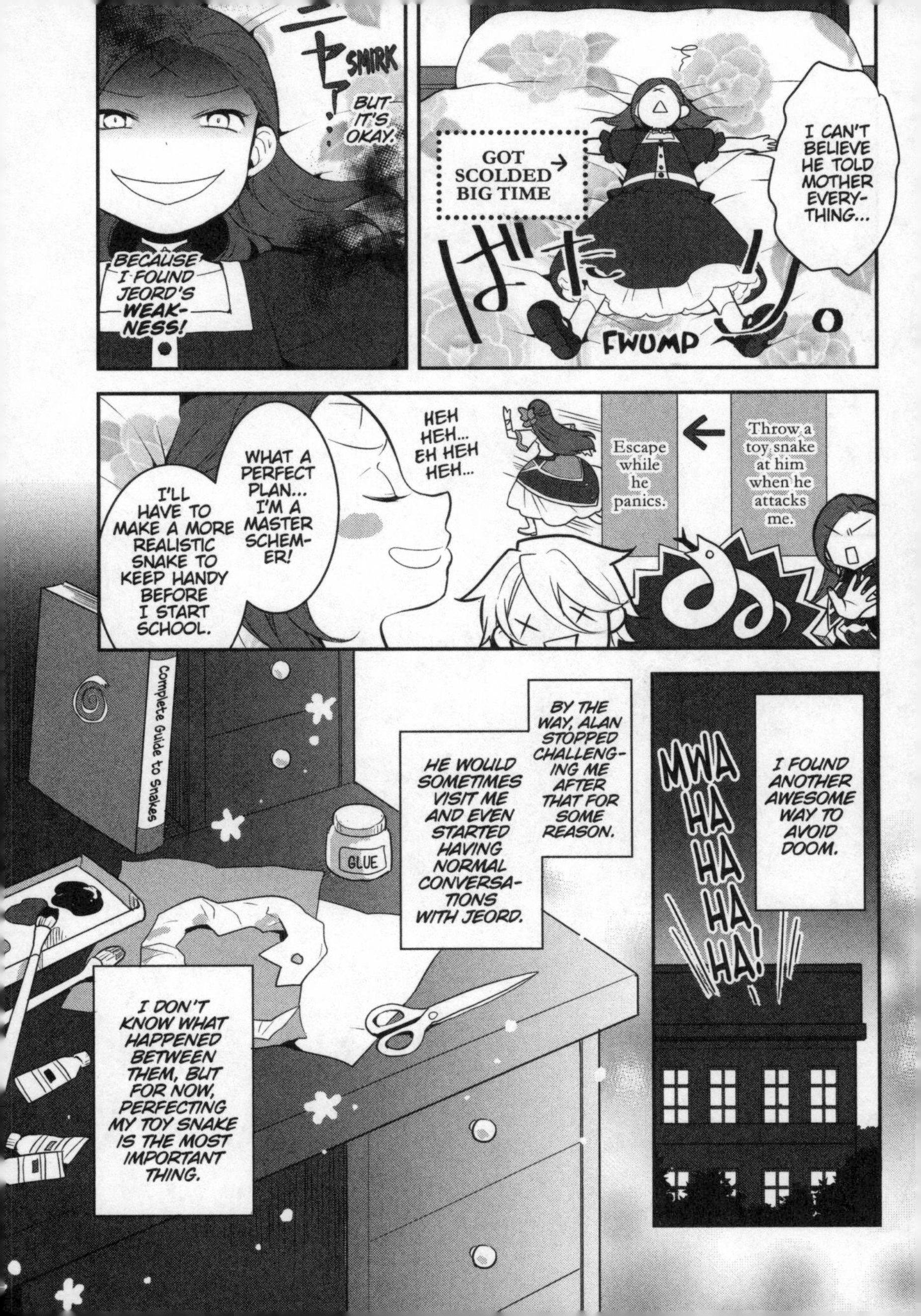
I CAN'T BELIEVE HE TOLD MOTHER EVERYTHING...
GOT SCOLDED BIG TIME
FWUMP
SMIRK
BUT IT'S OKAY.
BECAUSE I FOUND JEORD'S WEAKNESS!
Throw a toy snake at him when he attacks me.
Escape while he panics.
HEH HEH... EH HEH HEH...
WHAT A PERFECT PLAN... I'M A MASTER SCHEMER!
I'LL HAVE TO MAKE A MORE REALISTIC SNAKE TO KEEP HANDY BEFORE I START SCHOOL.
I FOUND ANOTHER AWESOME WAY TO AVOID DOOM.
MWA HA HA HA HA HA!
BY THE WAY, ALAN STOPPED CHALLENGING ME AFTER THAT FOR SOME REASON.
HE WOULD SOMETIMES VISIT ME AND EVEN STARTED HAVING NORMAL CONVERSATIONS WITH JEORD.
Complete Guide to Snakes
GLUE
I DON'T KNOW WHAT HAPPENED BETWEEN THEM, BUT FOR NOW, PERFECTING MY TOY SNAKE IS THE MOST IMPORTANT THING.

My Next Life
as a **VILLAINESS:**
ALL ROUTES
LEAD
TO **DOOM!**

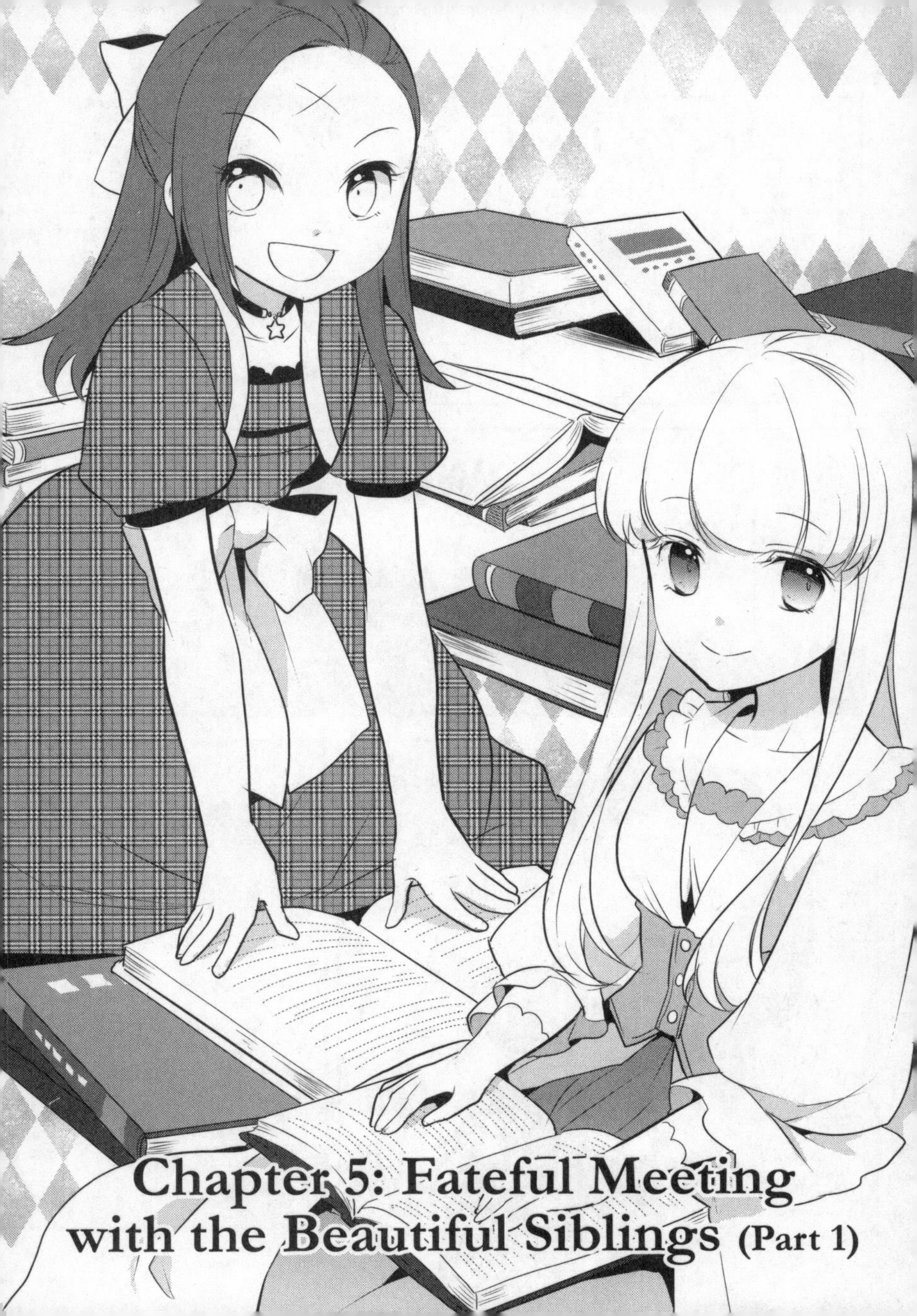

Chapter 5: Fateful Meeting with the Beautiful Siblings (Part 1)

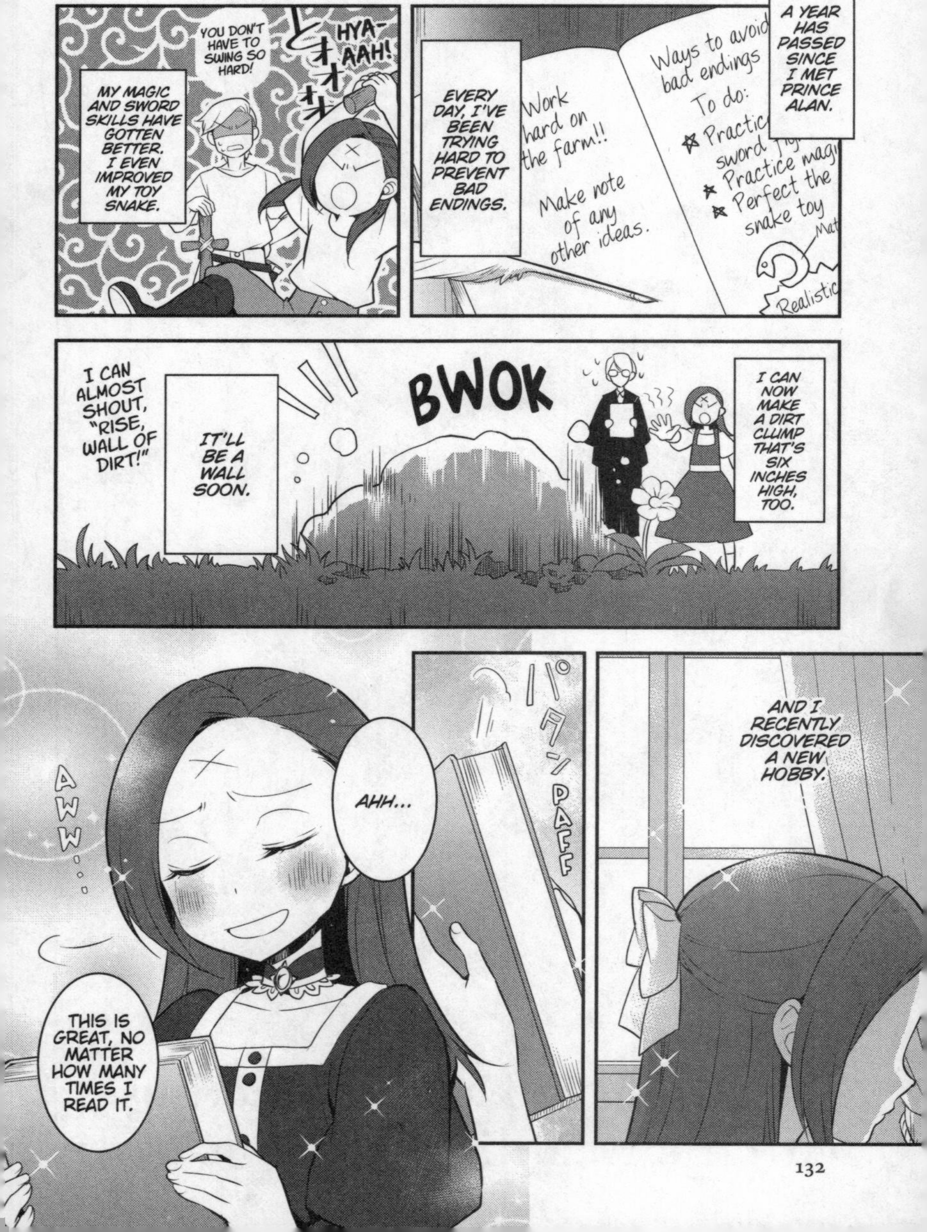
A YEAR HAS PASSED SINCE I MET PRINCE ALAN.
Ways to avoid bad endings
To do:
Practic sword fig
Practice magi
Perfect the snake toy
Mat
Realistic
Work hard on the farm!!
Make note of any other ideas.
EVERY DAY, I'VE BEEN TRYING HARD TO PREVENT BAD ENDINGS.
HYA-AAH!
YOU DON'T HAVE TO SWING SO HARD!
MY MAGIC AND SWORD SKILLS HAVE GOTTEN BETTER. I EVEN IMPROVED MY TOY SNAKE.
I CAN NOW MAKE A DIRT CLUMP THAT'S SIX INCHES HIGH, TOO.
BWOK
IT'LL BE A WALL SOON.
I CAN ALMOST SHOUT, "RISE, WALL OF DIRT!"
AND I RECENTLY DISCOVERED A NEW HOBBY.
PAFF
AHH...
AWWW...
THIS IS GREAT, NO MATTER HOW MANY TIMES I READ IT.

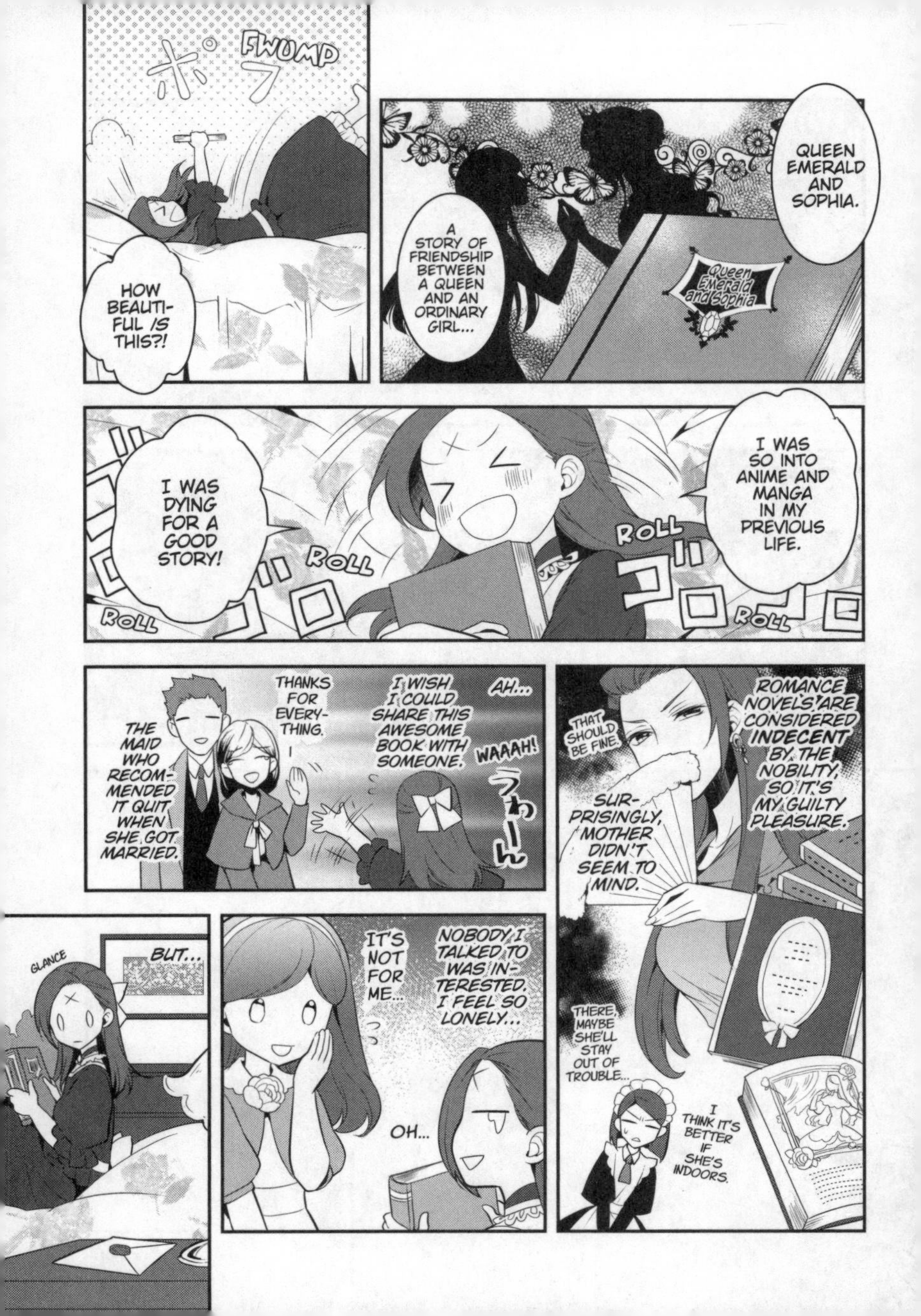
QUEEN EMERALD AND SOPHIA.
A STORY OF FRIENDSHIP BETWEEN A QUEEN AND AN ORDINARY GIRL...
Queen Emerald and Sophia
FWUMP
HOW BEAUTI-FUL IS THIS?!
I WAS SO INTO ANIME AND MANGA IN MY PREVIOUS LIFE.
ROLL
ROLL
ROLL
ROLL
I WAS DYING FOR A GOOD STORY!
ROMANCE NOVELS ARE CONSIDERED INDECENT BY THE NOBILITY, SO IT'S MY GUILTY PLEASURE.
THAT SHOULD BE FINE.
SUR-PRISINGLY, MOTHER DIDN'T SEEM TO MIND.
THERE, MAYBE SHE'LL STAY OUT OF TROUBLE...
I THINK IT'S BETTER IF SHE'S INDOORS.
AH...
I WISH I COULD SHARE THIS AWESOME BOOK WITH SOMEONE.
WAAAH!
THANKS FOR EVERY-THING.
THE MAID WHO RECOM-MENDED IT QUIT WHEN SHE GOT MARRIED.
NOBODY I TALKED TO WAS IN-TERESTED. I FEEL SO LONELY...
IT'S NOT FOR ME...
OH...
BUT...
GLANCE

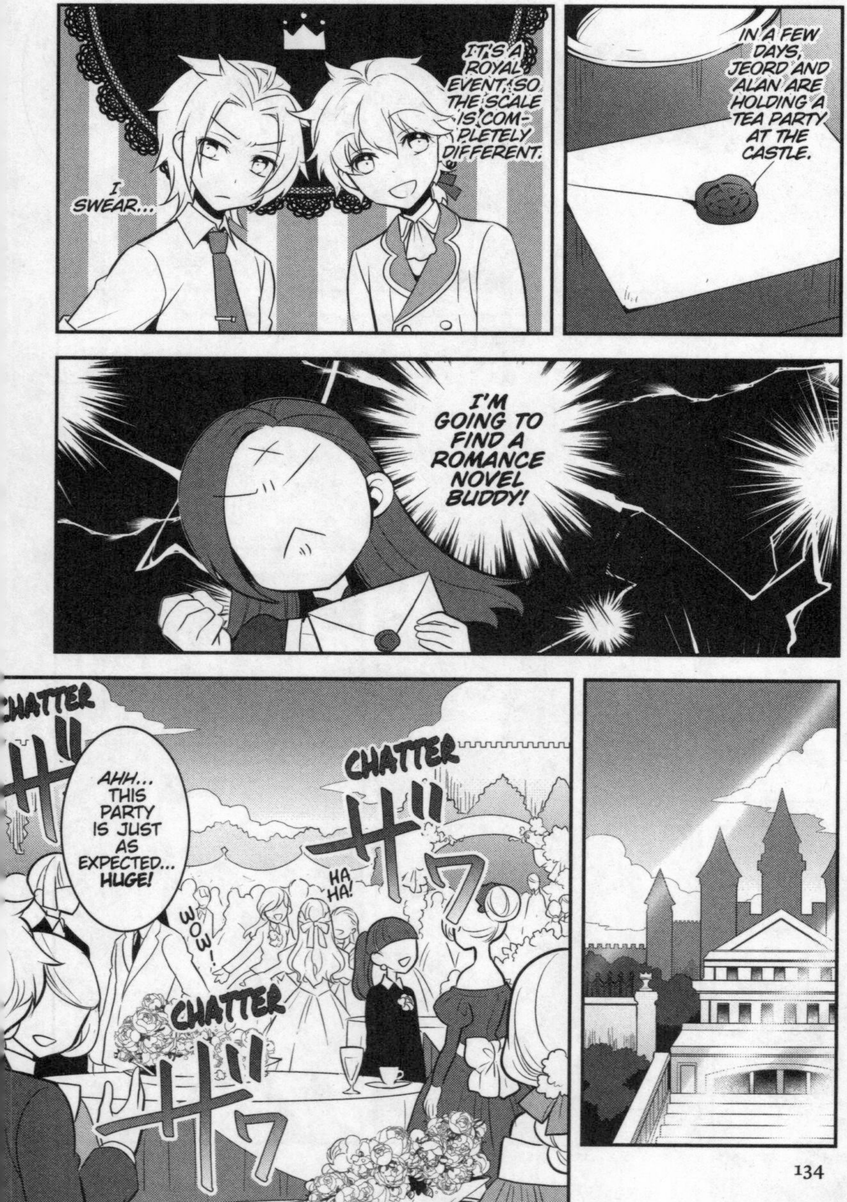
IN A FEW DAYS, JEORD AND ALAN ARE HOLDING A TEA PARTY AT THE CASTLE.
IT'S A ROYAL EVENT, SO THE SCALE IS COM-PLETELY DIFFERENT.
I SWEAR...
I'M GOING TO FIND A ROMANCE NOVEL BUDDY!
CHATTER
ザワ
CHATTER
ザワ
AHH... THIS PARTY IS JUST AS EXPECTED... **HUGE!**
HA HA!
WOW!
CHATTER
ザワ

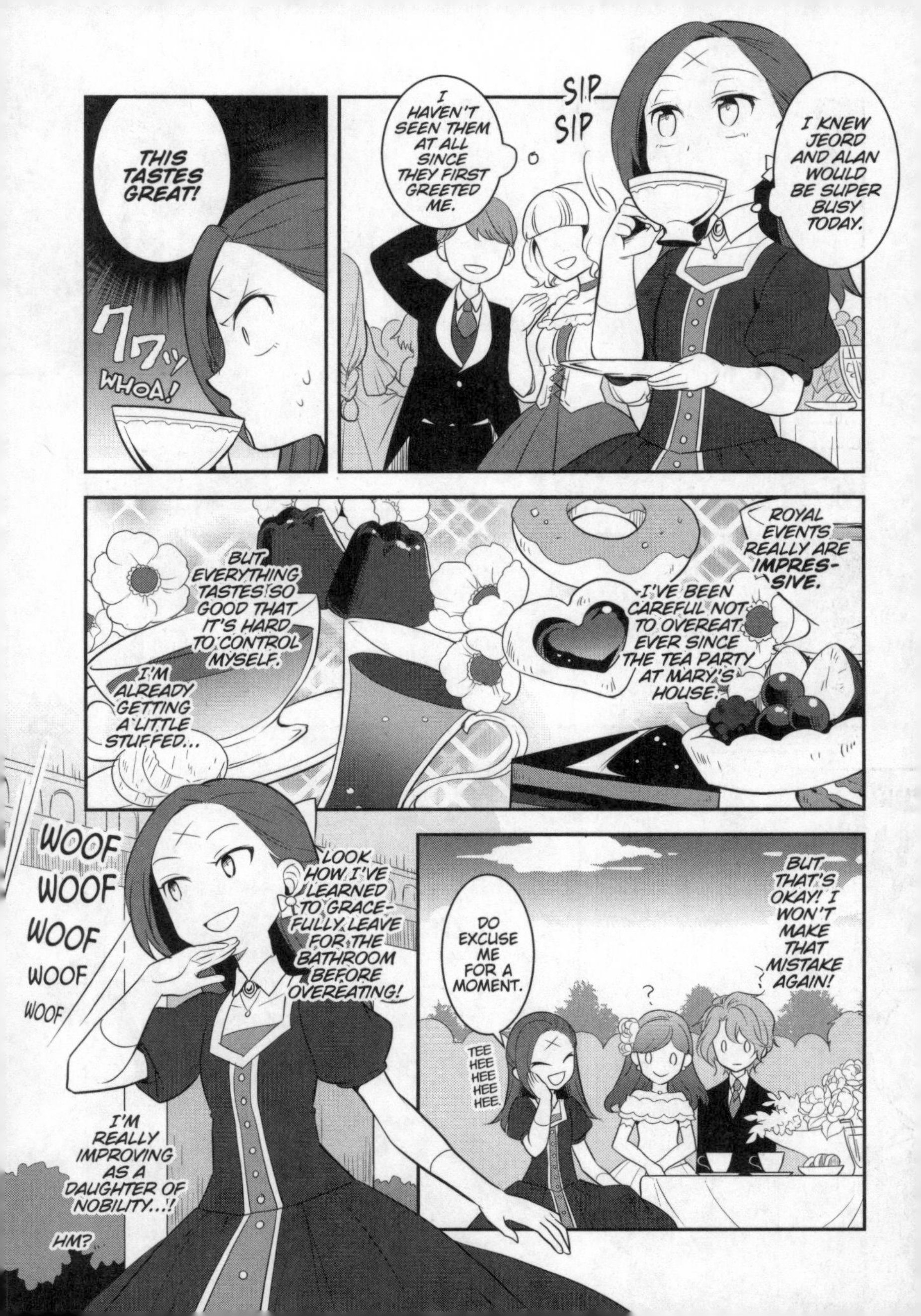
SIP SIP
I KNEW JEORD AND ALAN WOULD BE SUPER BUSY TODAY.
I HAVEN'T SEEN THEM AT ALL SINCE THEY FIRST GREETED ME.
THIS TASTES GREAT!
WHOA!
ROYAL EVENTS REALLY ARE IMPRESSIVE.
I'VE BEEN CAREFUL NOT TO OVEREAT EVER SINCE THE TEA PARTY AT MARY'S HOUSE.
BUT EVERYTHING TASTES SO GOOD THAT IT'S HARD TO CONTROL MYSELF.
I'M ALREADY GETTING A LITTLE STUFFED...
BUT THAT'S OKAY! I WON'T MAKE THAT MISTAKE AGAIN!
?
DO EXCUSE ME FOR A MOMENT.
TEE HEE HEE HEE HEE.
LOOK HOW I'VE LEARNED TO GRACEFULLY LEAVE FOR THE BATHROOM BEFORE OVEREATING!
WOOF WOOF WOOF WOOF WOOF
I'M REALLY IMPROVING AS A DAUGHTER OF NOBILITY...!
HM?

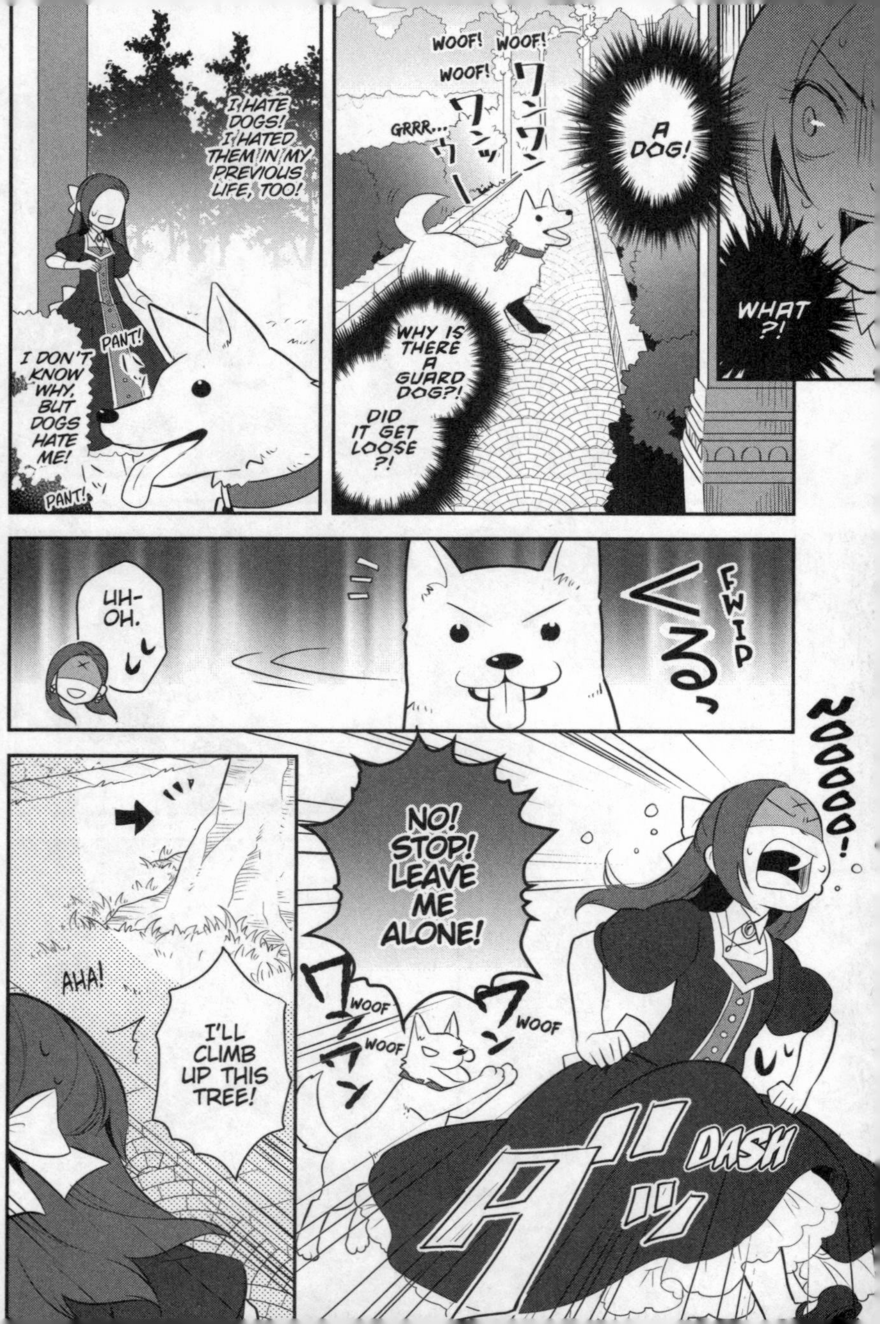
WHAT ?!
WOOF! WOOF!
WOOF!
ワンワン
ワンッ
GRRR...
ウーー
A DOG!
WHY IS THERE A GUARD DOG?!
DID IT GET LOOSE ?!
I HATE DOGS! I HATED THEM IN MY PREVIOUS LIFE, TOO!
PANT!
I DON'T KNOW WHY, BUT DOGS HATE ME!
PANT!
FWIP
くるっ
UH-OH.
NOOOOOO!
NO! STOP! LEAVE ME ALONE!
WOOF
WOOF
WOOF
DASH
ダッ
AHA!
I'LL CLIMB UP THIS TREE!

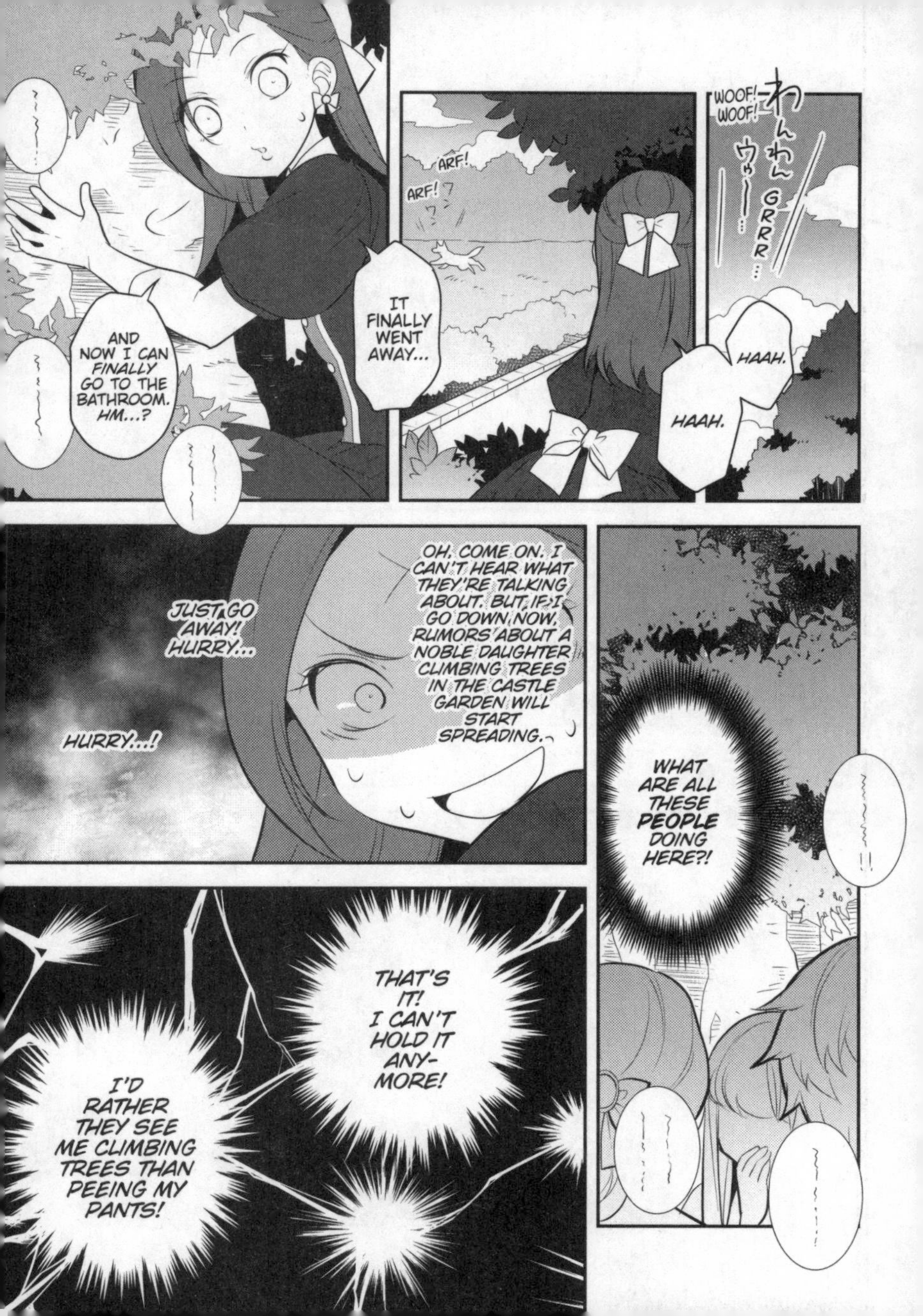
WOOF! WOOF!
わんわん
GRRR...
ウゥ〜〜…
HAAH.
HAAH.
ARF!
ARF!
IT FINALLY WENT AWAY...
AND NOW I CAN FINALLY GO TO THE BATHROOM. HM...?
WHAT ARE ALL THESE PEOPLE DOING HERE?!
OH, COME ON. I CAN'T HEAR WHAT THEY'RE TALKING ABOUT. BUT IF I GO DOWN NOW, RUMORS ABOUT A NOBLE DAUGHTER CLIMBING TREES IN THE CASTLE GARDEN WILL START SPREADING.
JUST GO AWAY! HURRY...
HURRY...!
THAT'S IT! I CAN'T HOLD IT ANYMORE!
I'D RATHER THEY SEE ME CLIMBING TREES THAN PEEING MY PANTS!

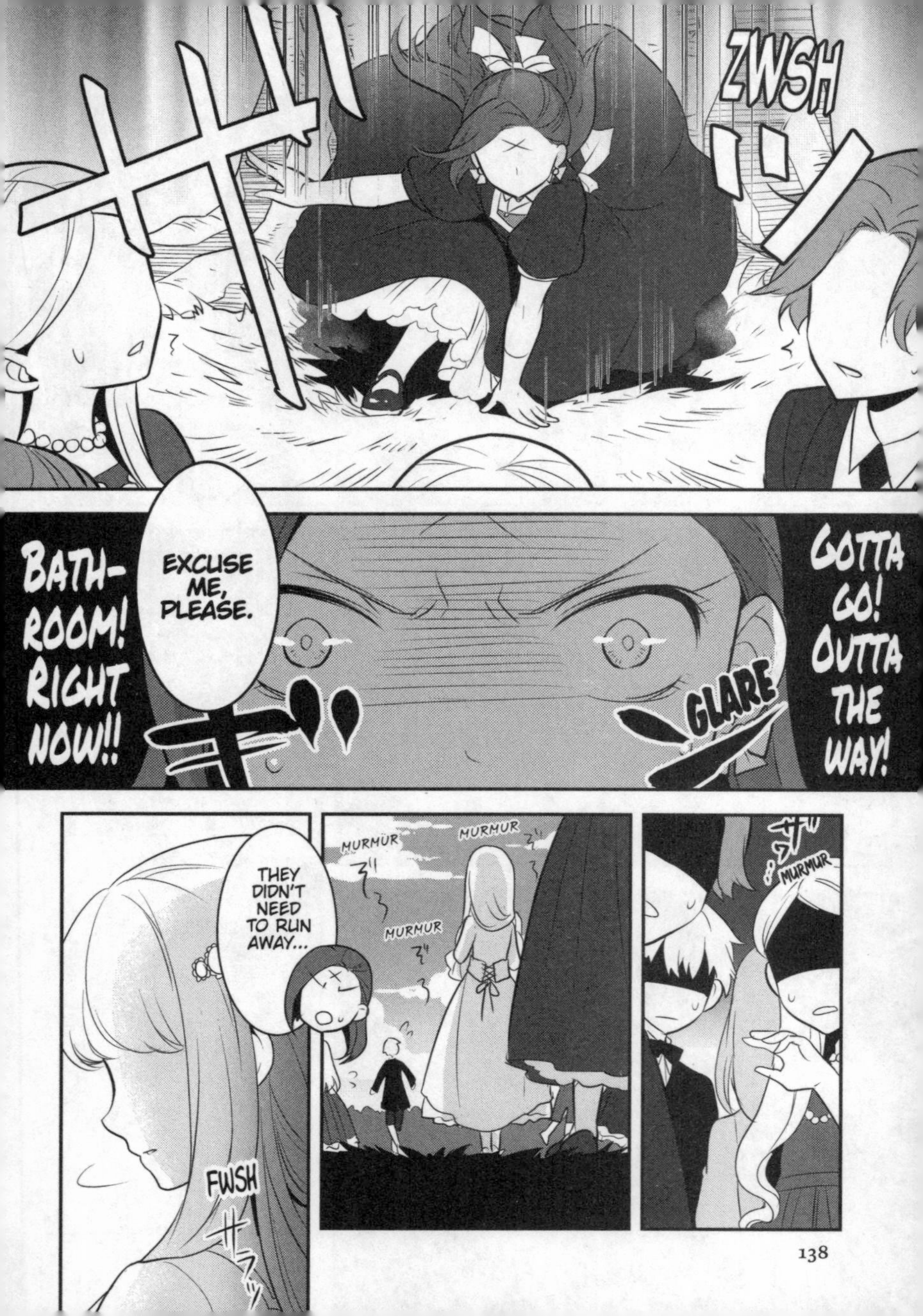
ZWSH
GOTTA GO! OUTTA THE WAY!
GLARE
EXCUSE ME, PLEASE.
BATH-ROOM! RIGHT NOW!!
MURMUR
MURMUR
MURMUR
MURMUR
THEY DIDN'T NEED TO RUN AWAY...
FWSH

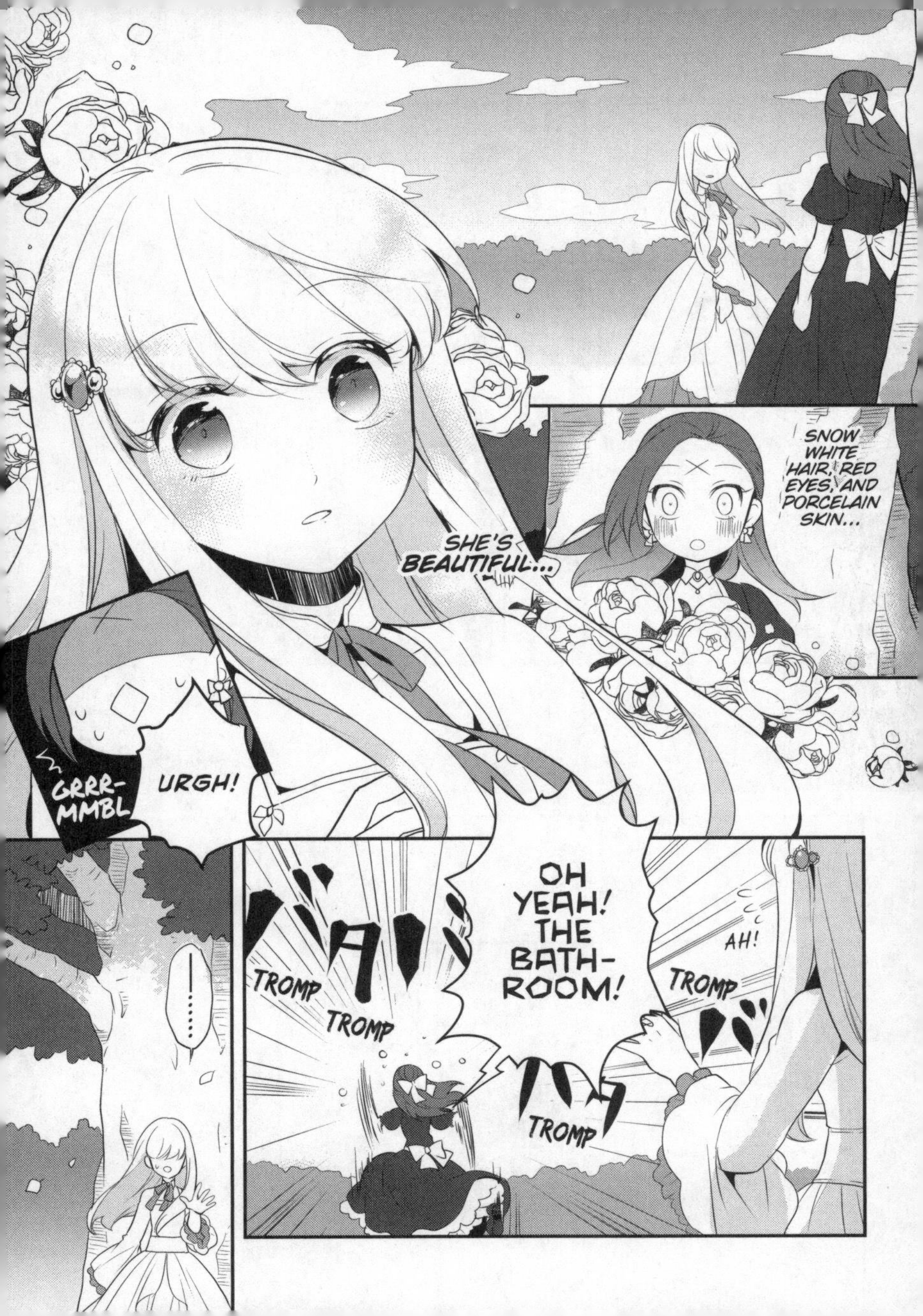
SNOW WHITE HAIR, RED EYES, AND PORCELAIN SKIN...
SHE'S BEAUTIFUL...
URGH!
GRRR-MMBL
AH!
TROMP
OH YEAH! THE BATH-ROOM!
TROMP
TROMP
TROMP
......!

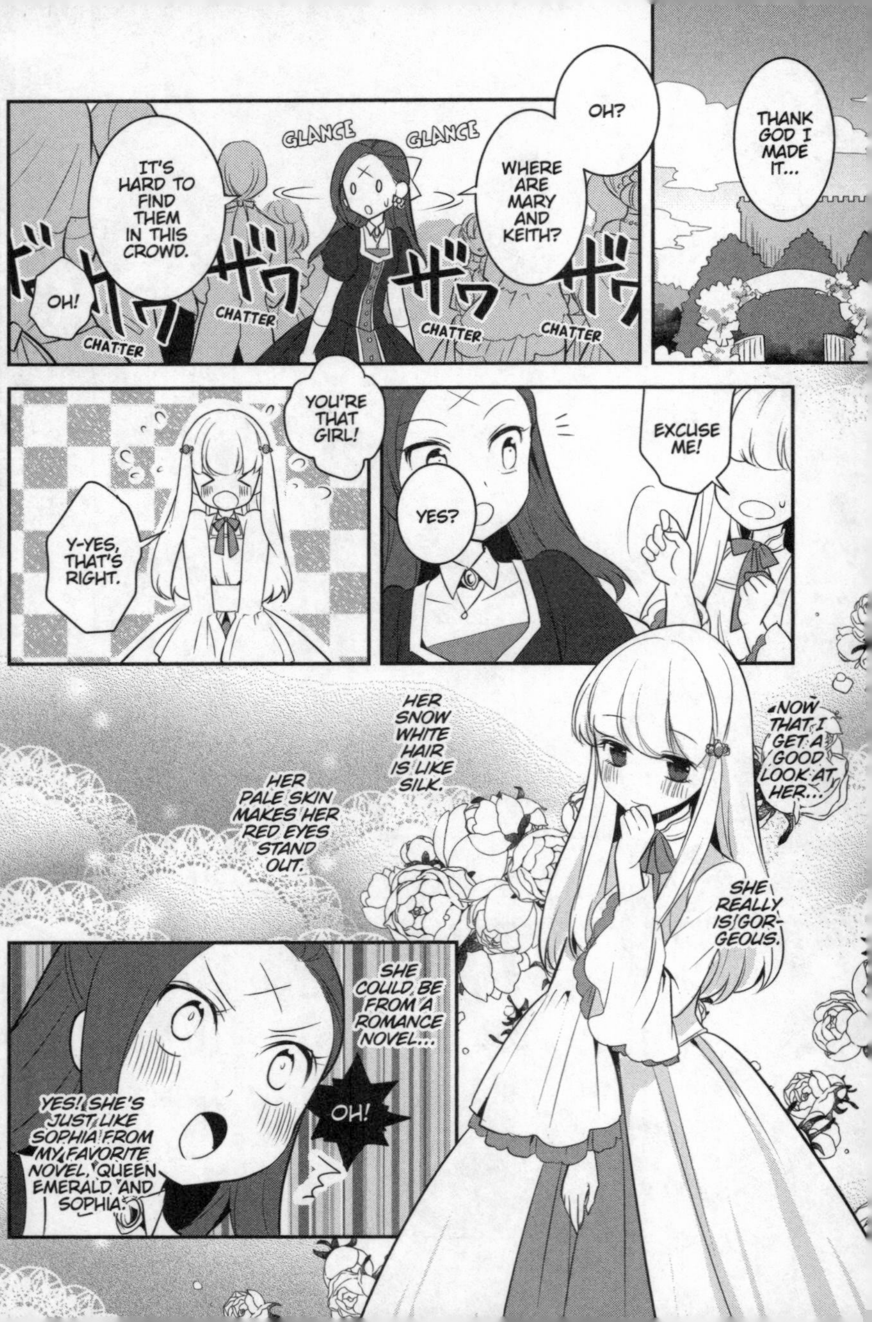
THANK GOD I MADE IT...
OH?
WHERE ARE MARY AND KEITH?
GLANCE
GLANCE
IT'S HARD TO FIND THEM IN THIS CROWD.
ザワ
ザワ
CHATTER
CHATTER
CHATTER
OH!
CHATTER
EXCUSE ME!
YES?
YOU'RE THAT GIRL!
Y-YES, THAT'S RIGHT.
NOW THAT I GET A GOOD LOOK AT HER...
SHE REALLY IS GORGEOUS.
HER SNOW WHITE HAIR IS LIKE SILK.
HER PALE SKIN MAKES HER RED EYES STAND OUT.
SHE COULD BE FROM A ROMANCE NOVEL...
OH!
YES! SHE'S JUST LIKE SOPHIA FROM MY FAVORITE NOVEL, QUEEN EMERALD AND SOPHIA.

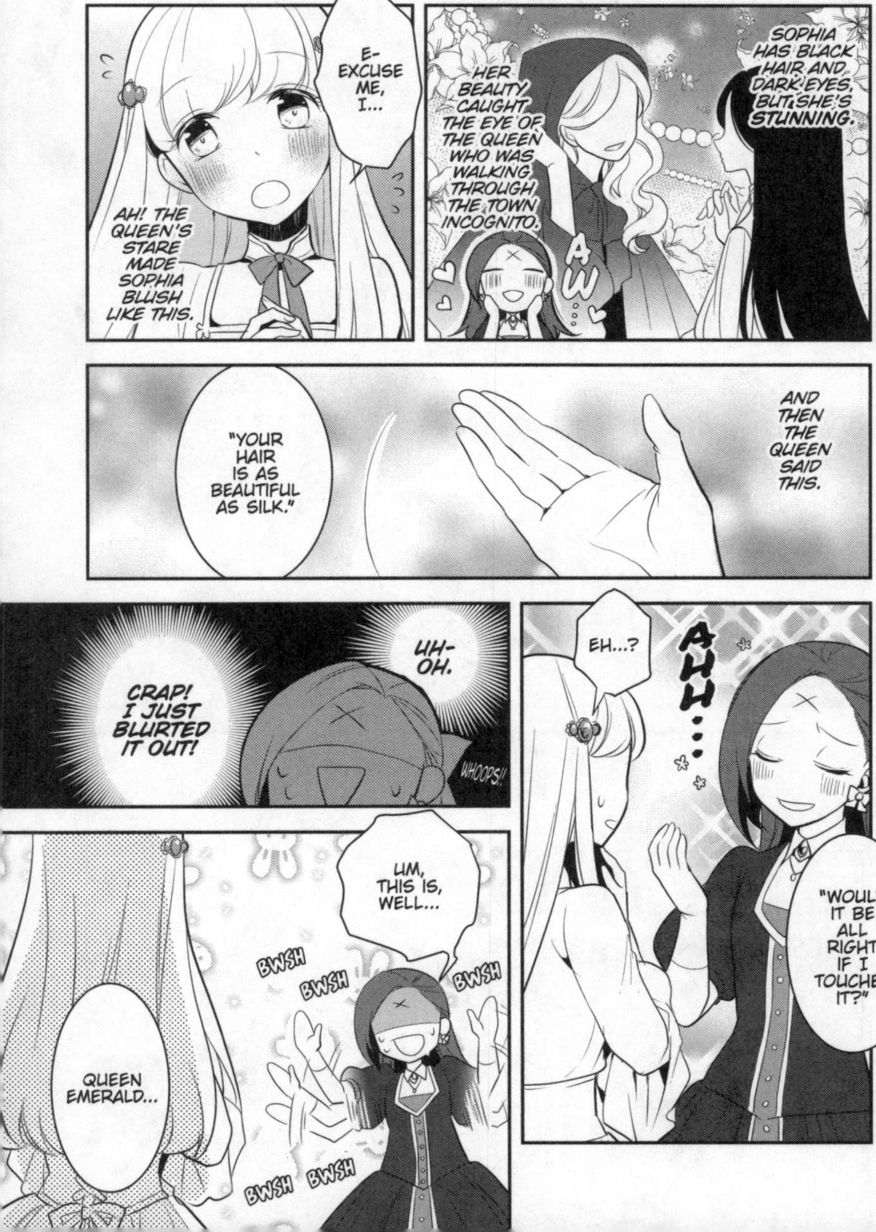
SOPHIA HAS BLACK HAIR AND DARK EYES, BUT SHE'S STUNNING.
HER BEAUTY CAUGHT THE EYE OF THE QUEEN WHO WAS WALKING THROUGH THE TOWN INCOGNITO.
AW
E-EXCUSE ME, I...
AH! THE QUEEN'S STARE MADE SOPHIA BLUSH LIKE THIS.
AND THEN THE QUEEN SAID THIS.
"YOUR HAIR IS AS BEAUTIFUL AS SILK."
EH...?
AHH...
"WOULD IT BE ALL RIGHT IF I TOUCHED IT?"
UH-OH.
CRAP! I JUST BLURTED IT OUT!
WHOOPS!!
UM, THIS IS, WELL...
BWSH
BWSH
BWSH
BWSH
BWSH
QUEEN EMERALD...

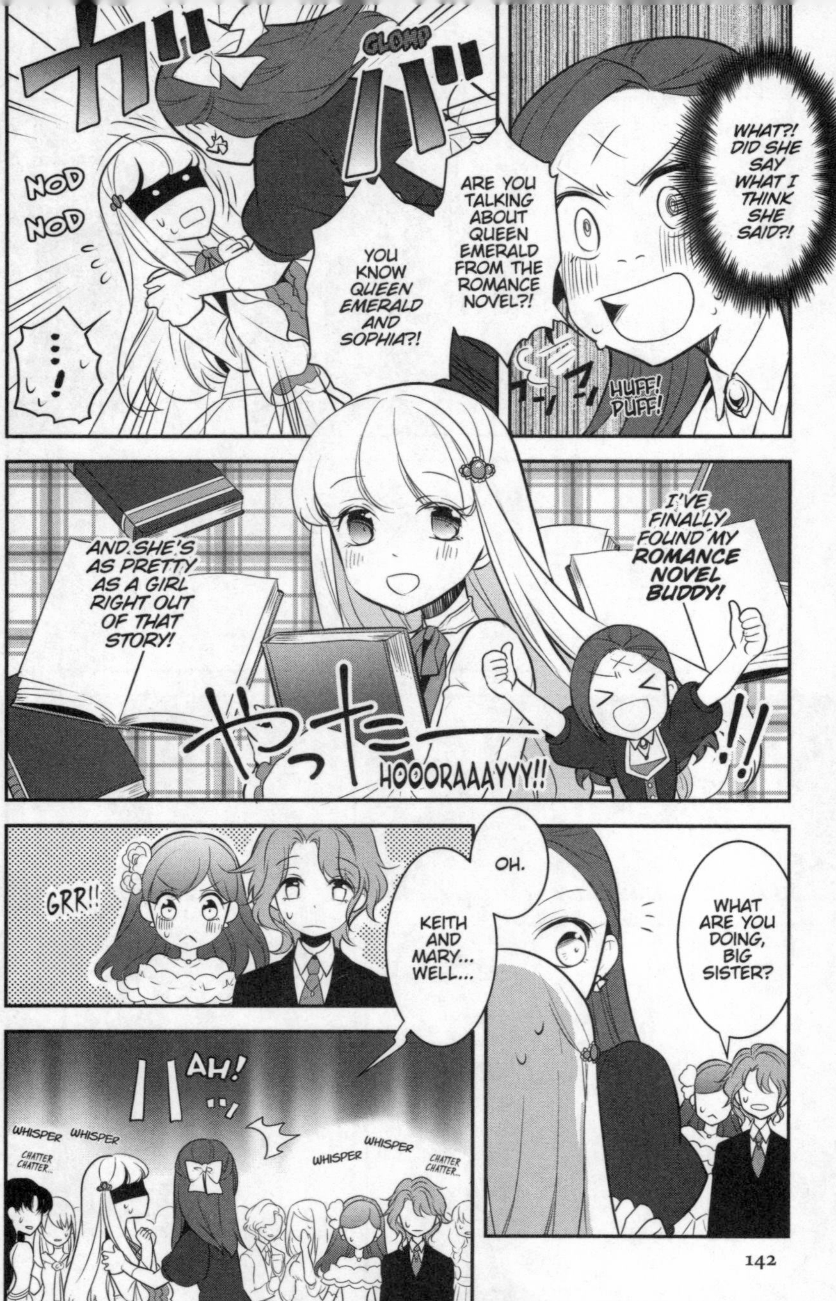
WHAT?! DID SHE SAY WHAT I THINK SHE SAID?!
ARE YOU TALKING ABOUT QUEEN EMERALD FROM THE ROMANCE NOVEL?!
YOU KNOW QUEEN EMERALD AND SOPHIA?!
HUFF! PUFF!
GLOMP
NOD NOD
...!
I'VE FINALLY FOUND MY ROMANCE NOVEL BUDDY!
AND SHE'S AS PRETTY AS A GIRL RIGHT OUT OF THAT STORY!
HOOORAAAYYY!!
WHAT ARE YOU DOING, BIG SISTER?
OH.
KEITH AND MARY... WELL...
GRR!!
AH!
WHISPER WHISPER
WHISPER WHISPER
CHATTER CHATTER...
CHATTER CHATTER...

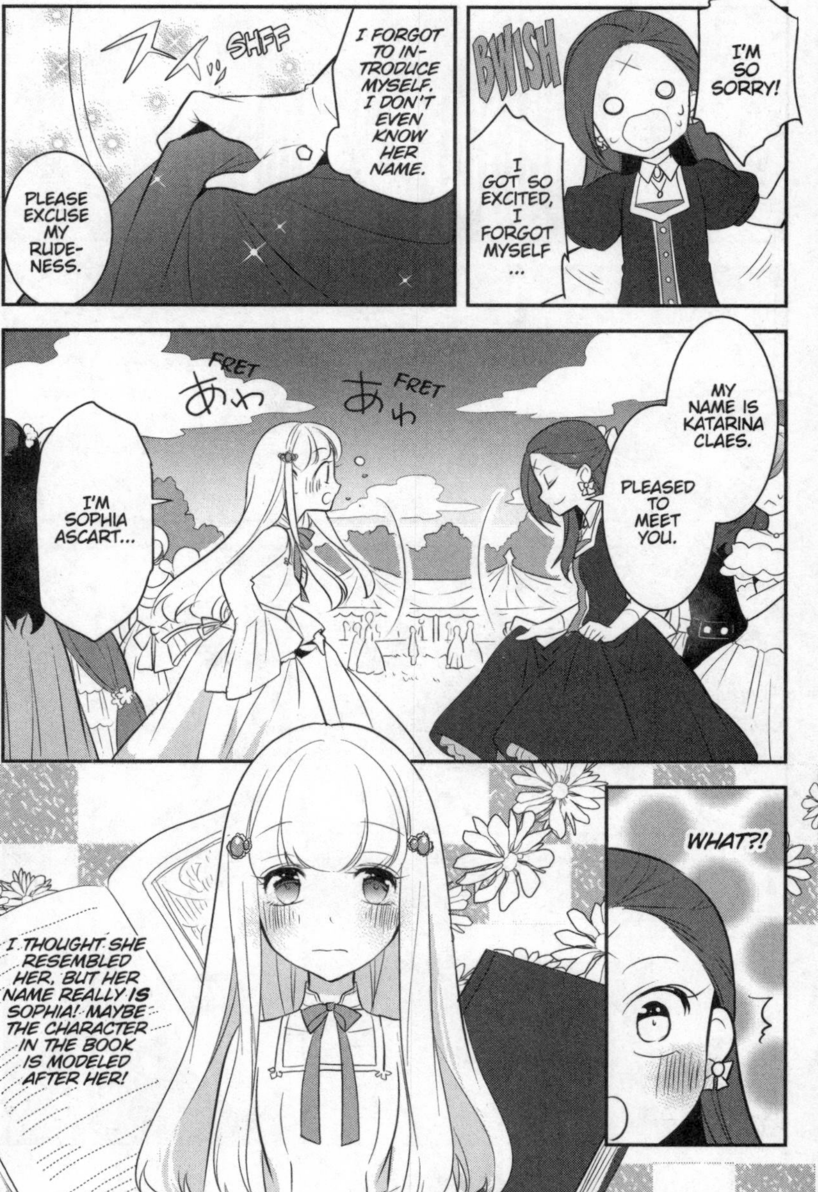
BWISH
I'M SO SORRY!
I GOT SO EXCITED, I FORGOT MYSELF...
SHFF
I FORGOT TO INTRODUCE MYSELF. I DON'T EVEN KNOW HER NAME.
PLEASE EXCUSE MY RUDENESS.
MY NAME IS KATARINA CLAES.
PLEASED TO MEET YOU.
FRET
FRET
I'M SOPHIA ASCART...
WHAT?!
I THOUGHT SHE RESEMBLED HER, BUT HER NAME REALLY IS SOPHIA! MAYBE THE CHARACTER IN THE BOOK IS MODELED AFTER HER!

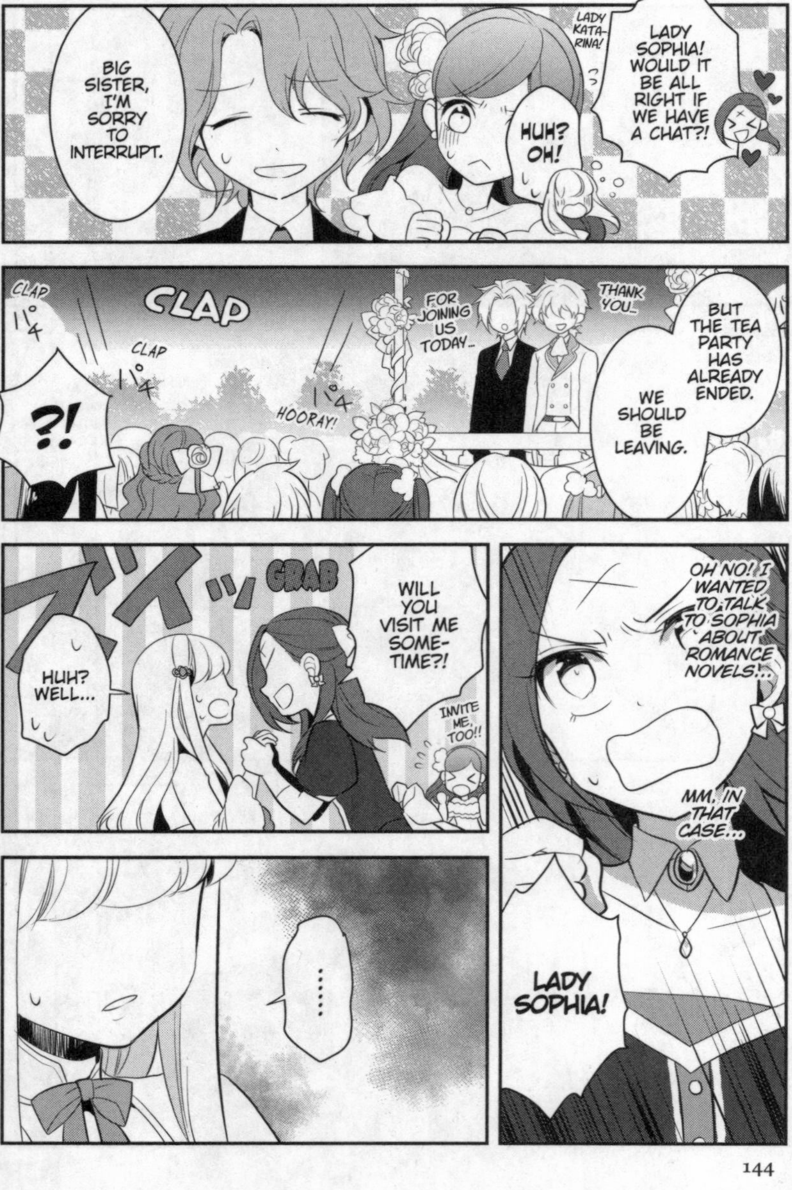
LADY SOPHIA! WOULD IT BE ALL RIGHT IF WE HAVE A CHAT?!
LADY KATA-RINA!
HUH? OH!
BIG SISTER, I'M SORRY TO INTERRUPT.
BUT THE TEA PARTY HAS ALREADY ENDED.
WE SHOULD BE LEAVING.
THANK YOU...
FOR JOINING US TODAY...
CLAP
CLAP
CLAP
HOORAY!
?!
OH NO! I WANTED TO TALK TO SOPHIA ABOUT ROMANCE NOVELS...
MM. IN THAT CASE...
LADY SOPHIA!
GRAB
WILL YOU VISIT ME SOME-TIME?!
INVITE ME, TOO!!
HUH? WELL...
......

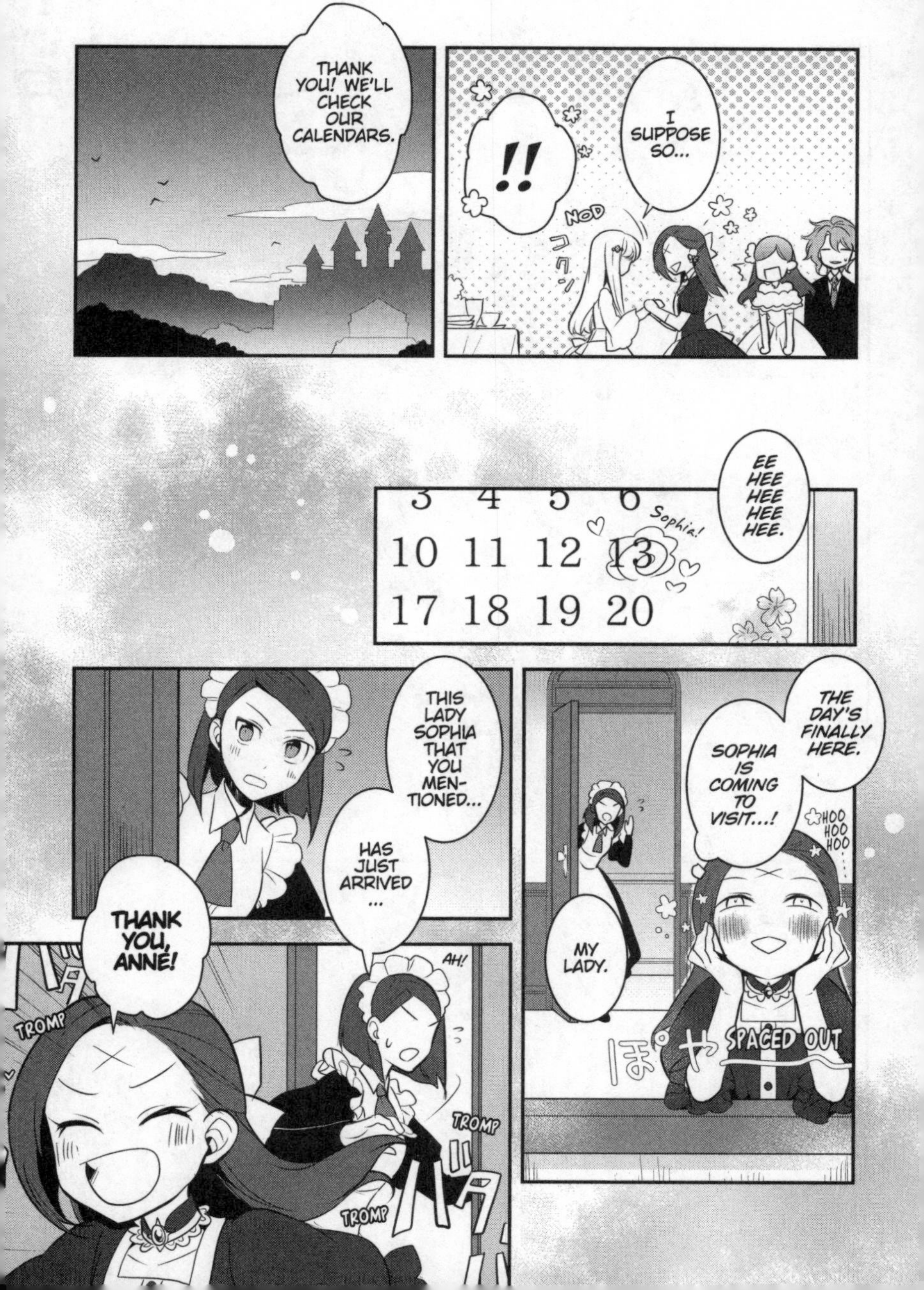
I SUPPOSE SO...
!!
NOD
THANK YOU! WE'LL CHECK OUR CALENDARS.
EE HEE HEE HEE HEE.
3 4 5 6
10 11 12 13
17 18 19 20
Sophia!
THE DAY'S FINALLY HERE.
SOPHIA IS COMING TO VISIT...!
HOO HOO HOO...
SPACED OUT
MY LADY.
THIS LADY SOPHIA THAT YOU MENTIONED...
HAS JUST ARRIVED...
AH!
THANK YOU, ANNE!
TROMP
TROMP
TROMP

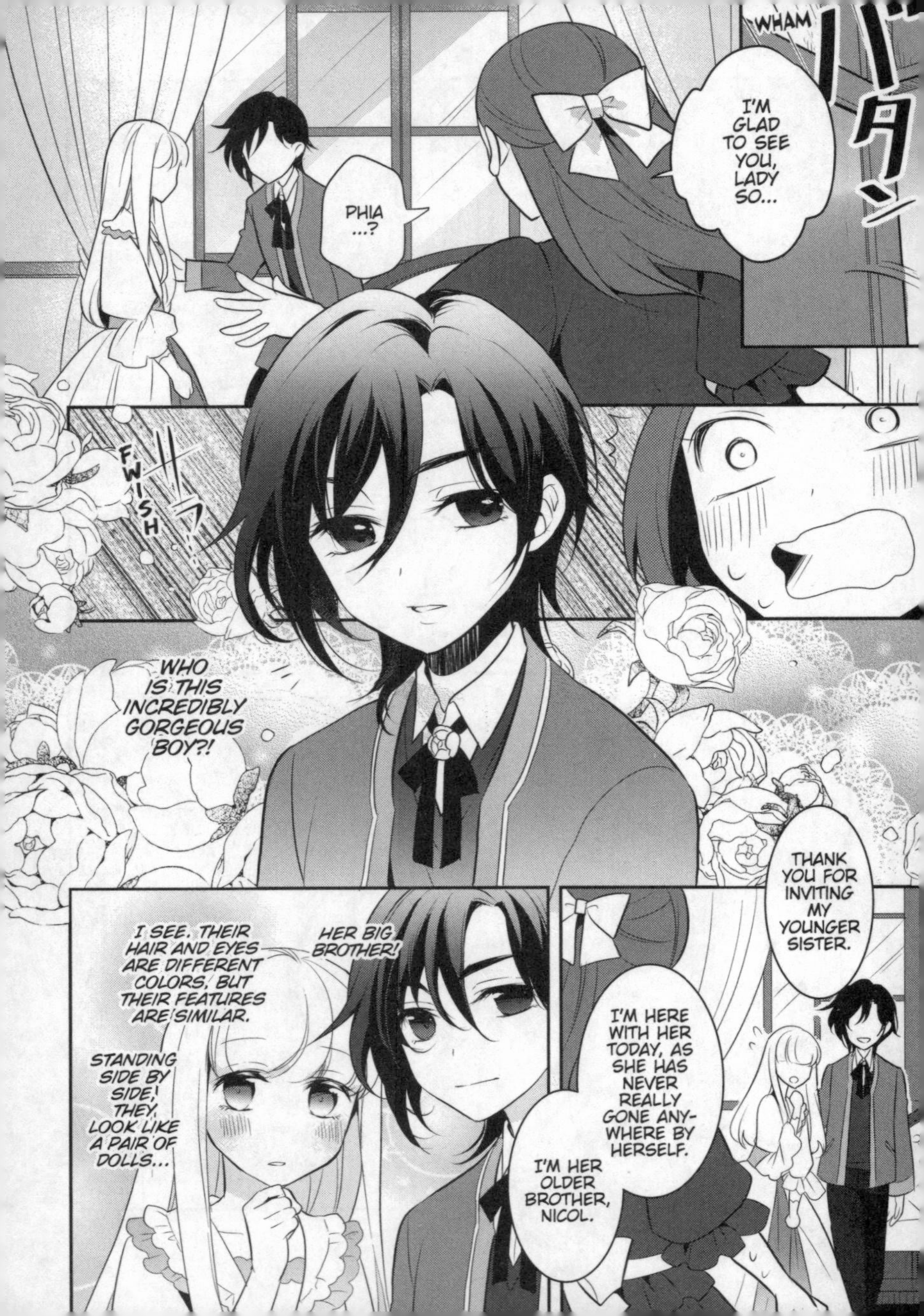
WHAM
バタン
I'M GLAD TO SEE YOU, LADY SO...
PHIA ...?
FWISH
WHO IS THIS INCREDIBLY GORGEOUS BOY?!
THANK YOU FOR INVITING MY YOUNGER SISTER.
I'M HERE WITH HER TODAY, AS SHE HAS NEVER REALLY GONE ANYWHERE BY HERSELF.
I'M HER OLDER BROTHER, NICOL.
HER BIG BROTHER!
I SEE. THEIR HAIR AND EYES ARE DIFFERENT COLORS, BUT THEIR FEATURES ARE SIMILAR.
STANDING SIDE BY SIDE, THEY LOOK LIKE A PAIR OF DOLLS...

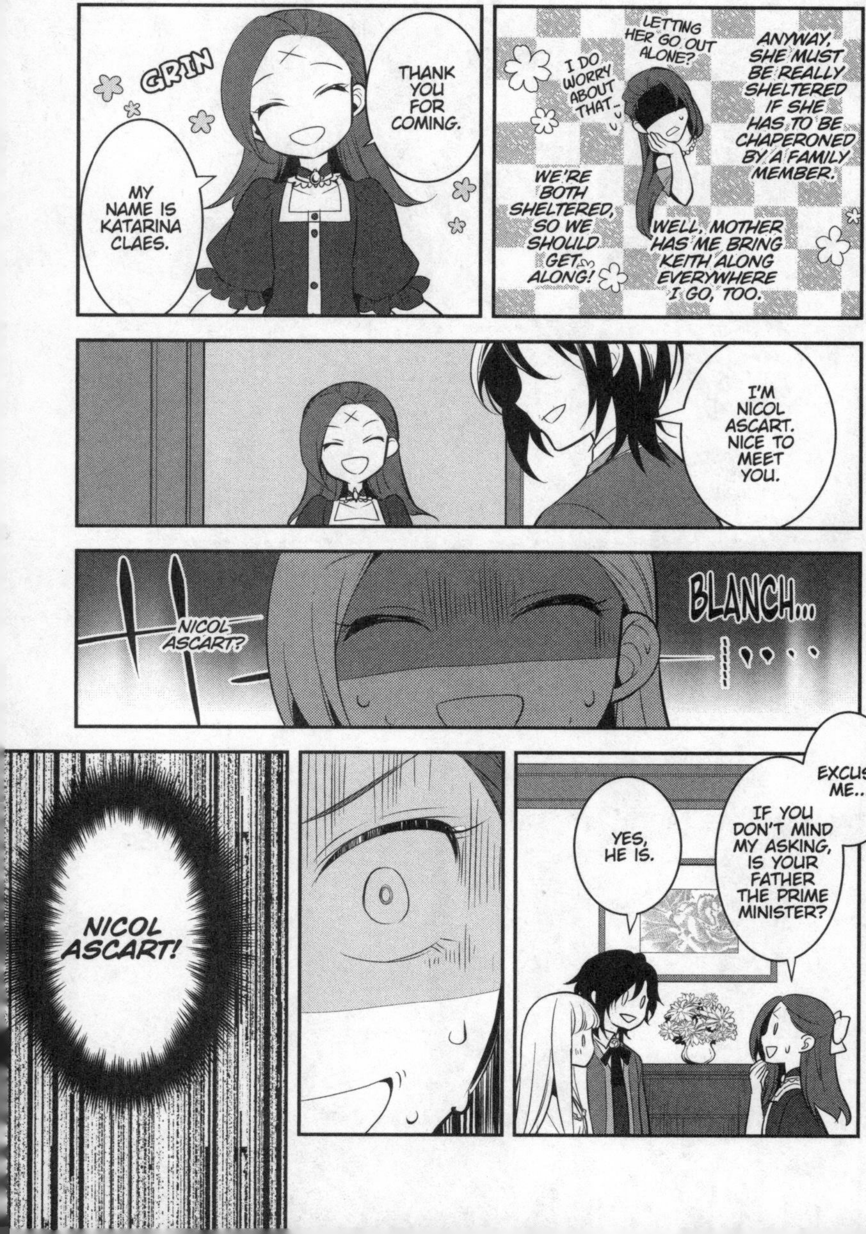
ANYWAY, SHE MUST BE REALLY SHELTERED IF SHE HAS TO BE CHAPERONED BY A FAMILY MEMBER.
LETTING HER GO OUT ALONE?
I DO WORRY ABOUT THAT...
WELL, MOTHER HAS ME BRING KEITH ALONG EVERYWHERE I GO, TOO.
WE'RE BOTH SHELTERED, SO WE SHOULD GET ALONG!
THANK YOU FOR COMING.
GRIN
MY NAME IS KATARINA CLAES.
I'M NICOL ASCART. NICE TO MEET YOU.
BLANCH...
NICOL ASCART?
EXCUSE ME... IF YOU DON'T MIND MY ASKING, IS YOUR FATHER THE PRIME MINISTER?
YES, HE IS.
NICOL ASCART!

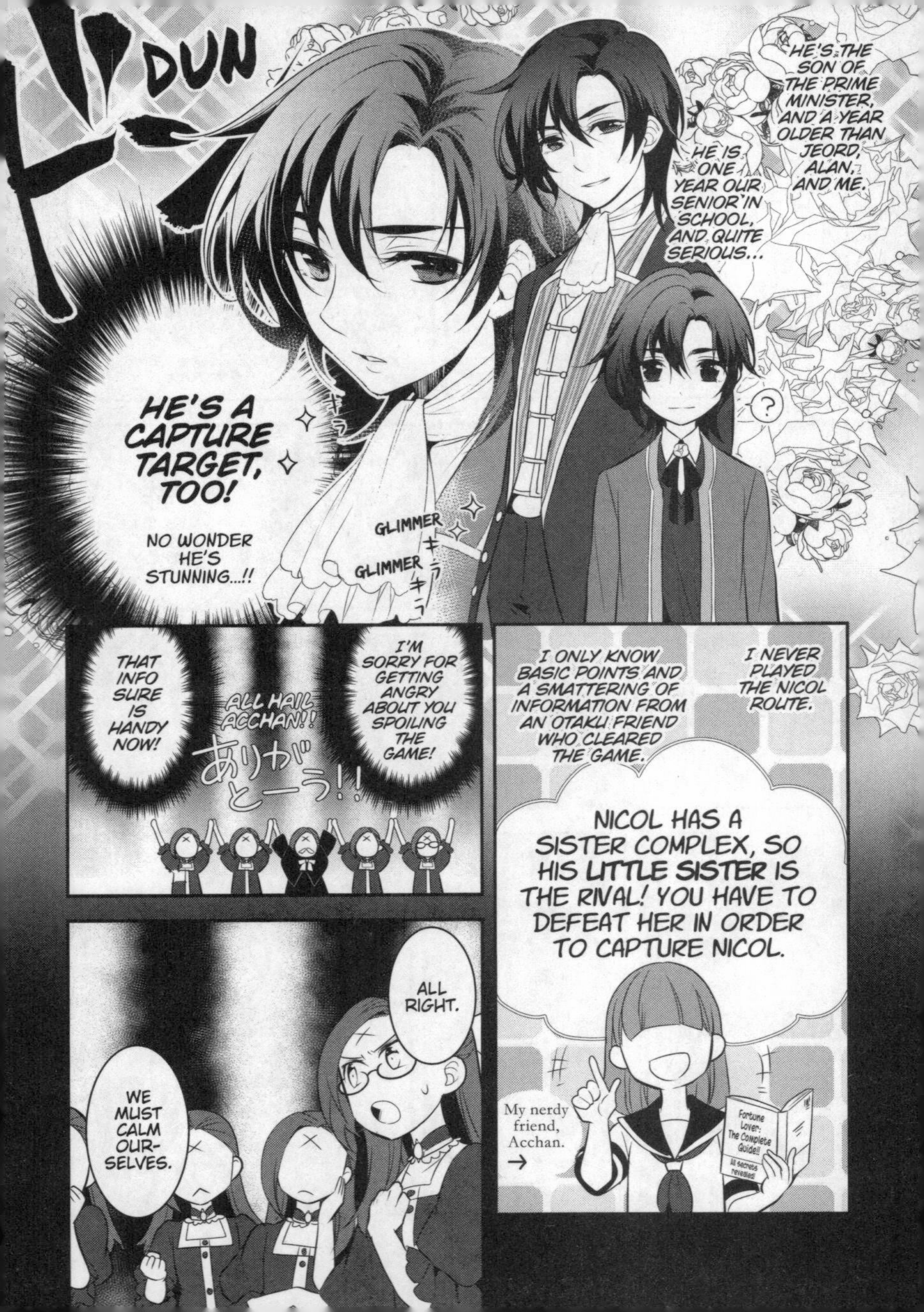
DUN
HE'S THE SON OF THE PRIME MINISTER, AND A YEAR OLDER THAN JEORD, ALAN, AND ME.
HE IS ONE YEAR OUR SENIOR IN SCHOOL, AND QUITE SERIOUS...
?
HE'S A CAPTURE TARGET, TOO!
NO WONDER HE'S STUNNING...!!
GLIMMER
GLIMMER
I NEVER PLAYED THE NICOL ROUTE.
I ONLY KNOW BASIC POINTS AND A SMATTERING OF INFORMATION FROM AN OTAKU FRIEND WHO CLEARED THE GAME.
NICOL HAS A SISTER COMPLEX, SO HIS LITTLE SISTER IS THE RIVAL! YOU HAVE TO DEFEAT HER IN ORDER TO CAPTURE NICOL.
My nerdy friend, Acchan.
Fortune Lover: The Complete Guide!!
All secrets revealed!
I'M SORRY FOR GETTING ANGRY ABOUT YOU SPOILING THE GAME!
ALL HAIL ACCHAN!!
ありがとーう!!
THAT INFO SURE IS HANDY NOW!
ALL RIGHT.
WE MUST CALM OURSELVES.

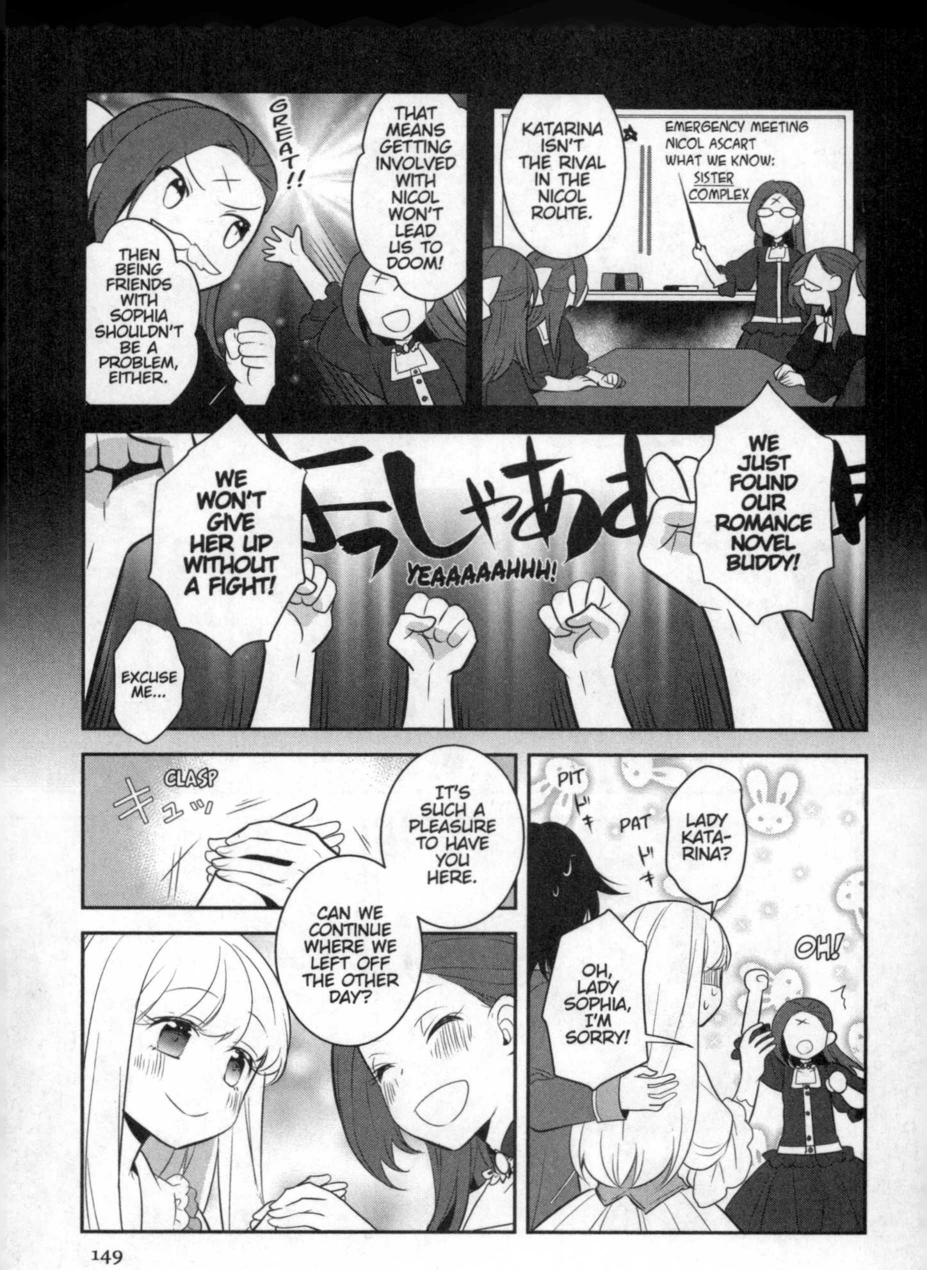
KATARINA ISN'T THE RIVAL IN THE NICOL ROUTE.
EMERGENCY MEETING
NICOL ASCART
WHAT WE KNOW:
SISTER COMPLEX
THAT MEANS GETTING INVOLVED WITH NICOL WON'T LEAD US TO DOOM!
GREAT!!
THEN BEING FRIENDS WITH SOPHIA SHOULDN'T BE A PROBLEM, EITHER.
WE JUST FOUND OUR ROMANCE NOVEL BUDDY!
YEAAAAAHHH!
WE WON'T GIVE HER UP WITHOUT A FIGHT!
EXCUSE ME...
PIT
ドキ
PAT
ドキ
LADY KATA-RINA?
OH!
OH, LADY SOPHIA, I'M SORRY!
CLASP
キュッ
IT'S SUCH A PLEASURE TO HAVE YOU HERE.
CAN WE CONTINUE WHERE WE LEFT OFF THE OTHER DAY?

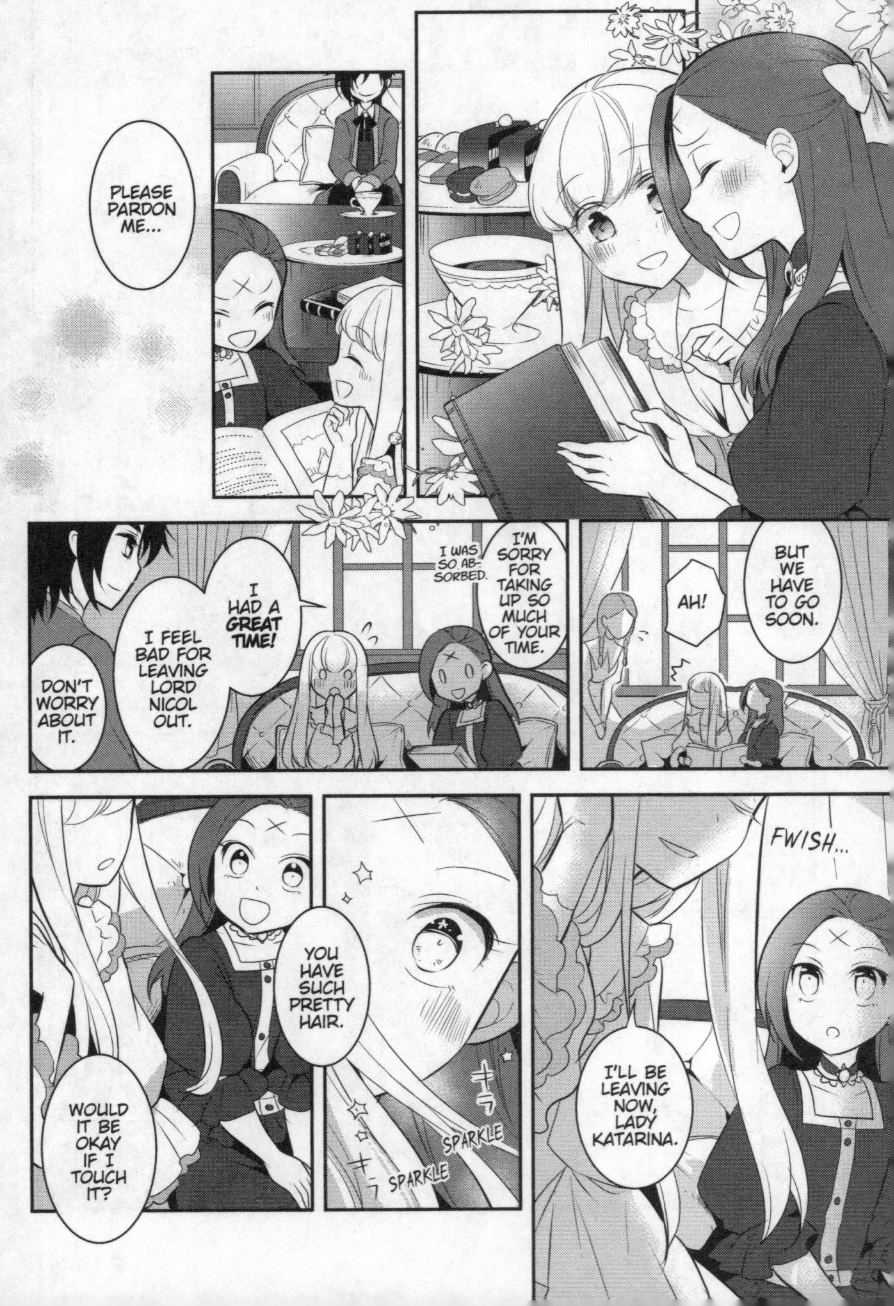
PLEASE PARDON ME...
BUT WE HAVE TO GO SOON.
AH!
I'M SORRY FOR TAKING UP SO MUCH OF YOUR TIME.
I WAS SO ABSORBED.
I HAD A GREAT TIME!
I FEEL BAD FOR LEAVING LORD NICOL OUT.
DON'T WORRY ABOUT IT.
FWISH...
I'LL BE LEAVING NOW, LADY KATARINA.
SPARKLE
SPARKLE
YOU HAVE SUCH PRETTY HAIR.
WOULD IT BE OKAY IF I TOUCH IT?

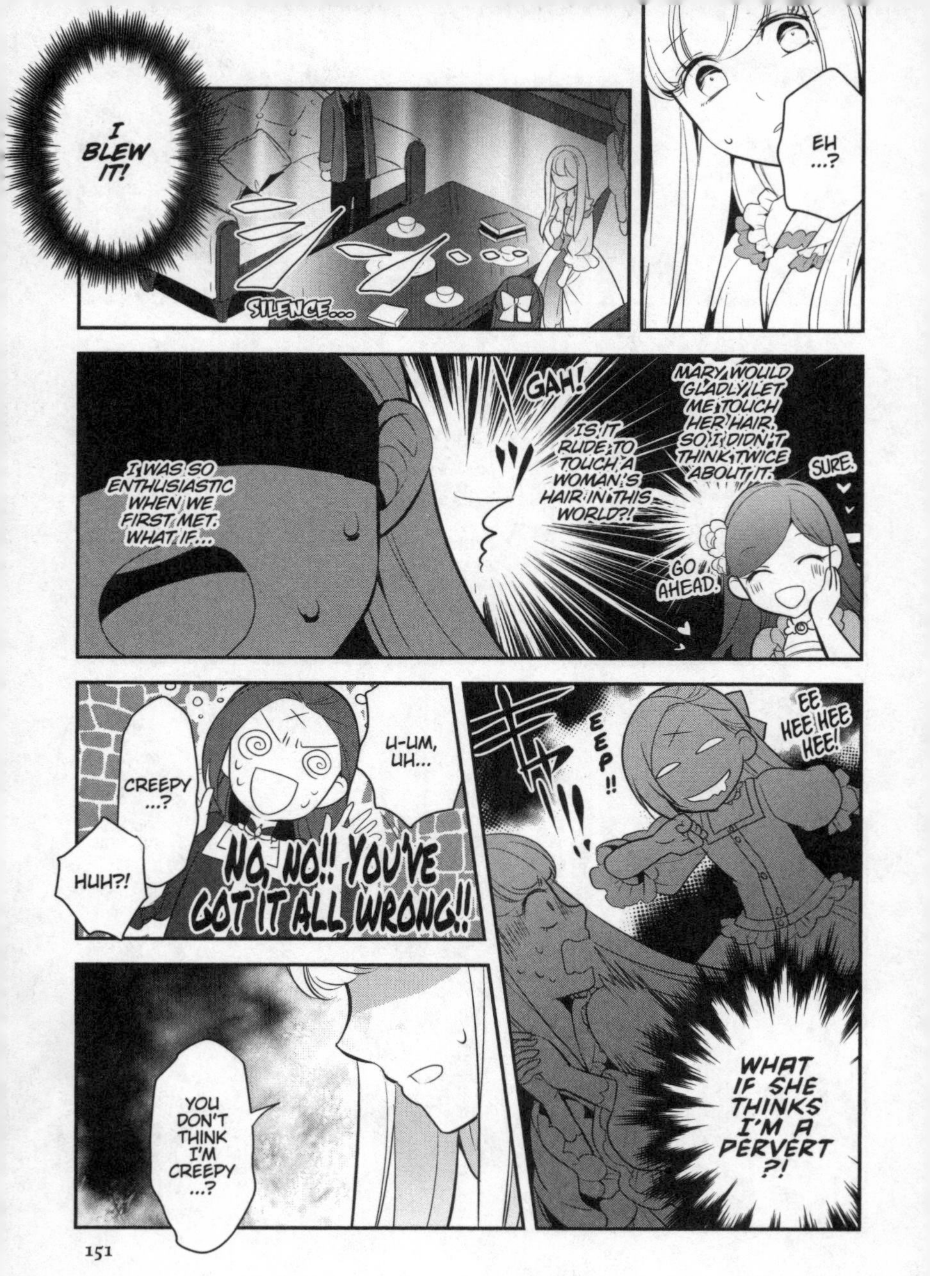
EH ...?
I BLEW IT!
SILENCE...
SURE.
GO AHEAD.
MARY WOULD GLADLY LET ME TOUCH HER HAIR, SO I DIDN'T THINK TWICE ABOUT IT.
GAH!
IS IT RUDE TO TOUCH A WOMAN'S HAIR IN THIS WORLD?!
I WAS SO ENTHUSIASTIC WHEN WE FIRST MET. WHAT IF...
EE HEE HEE HEE!
EEP!!
WHAT IF SHE THINKS I'M A PERVERT?!
U-UM, UH...
CREEPY ...?
NO, NO!! YOU'VE GOT IT ALL WRONG!!
HUH?!
YOU DON'T THINK I'M CREEPY ...?

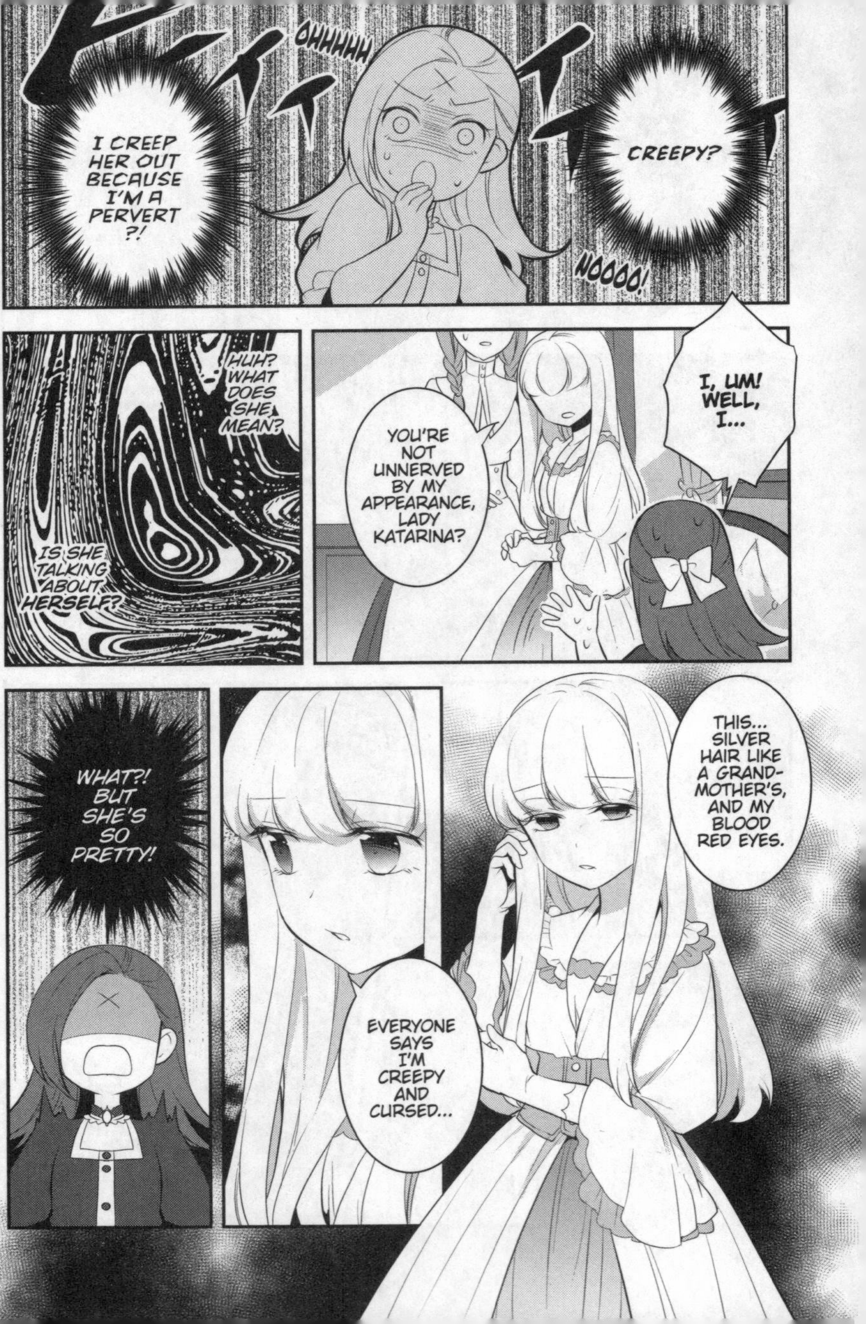
OHHHHH
CREEPY?
I CREEP HER OUT BECAUSE I'M A PERVERT ?!
NOOOO!
I, UM! WELL, I...
YOU'RE NOT UNNERVED BY MY APPEARANCE, LADY KATARINA?
HUH? WHAT DOES SHE MEAN?
IS SHE TALKING ABOUT HERSELF?
THIS... SILVER HAIR LIKE A GRAND-MOTHER'S, AND MY BLOOD RED EYES.
EVERYONE SAYS I'M CREEPY AND CURSED...
WHAT?! BUT SHE'S SO PRETTY!

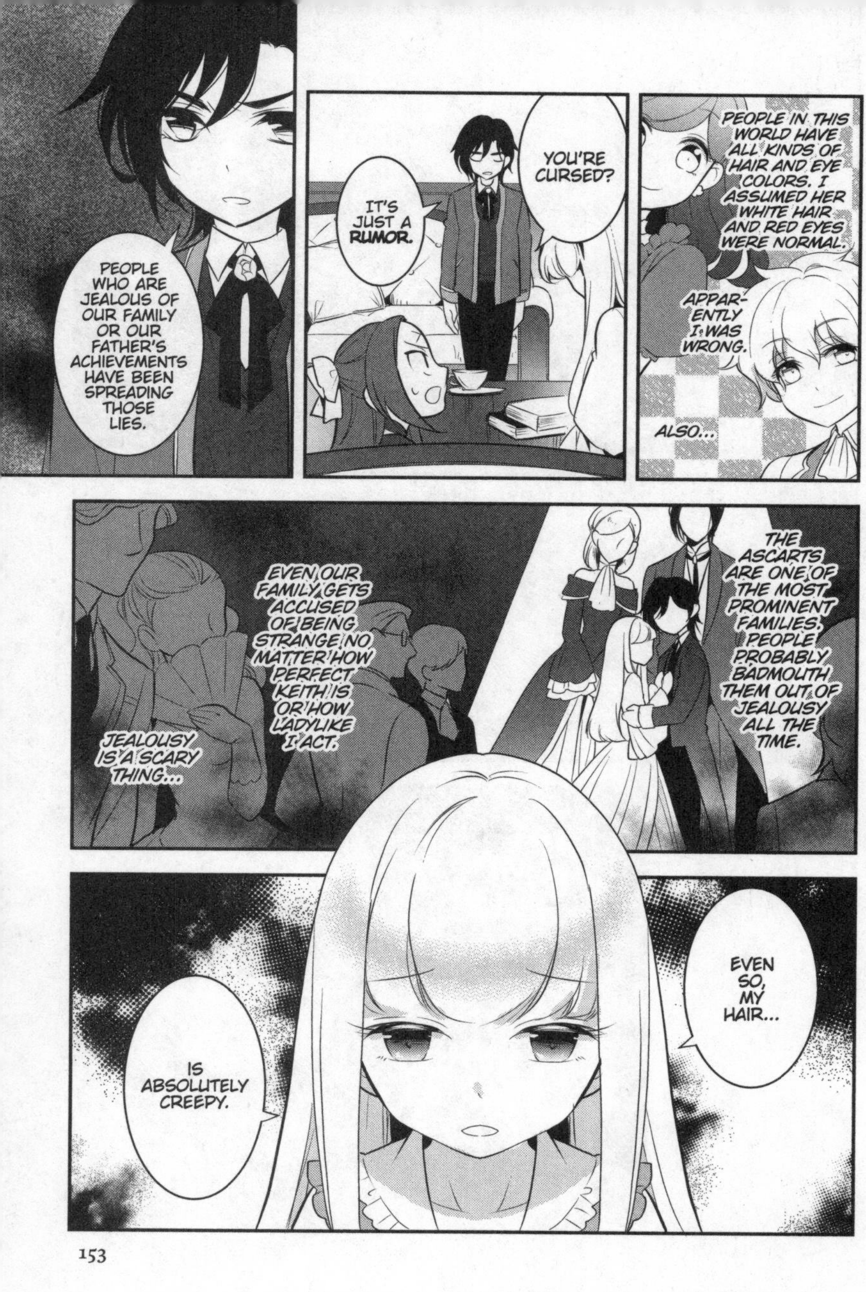
PEOPLE IN THIS WORLD HAVE ALL KINDS OF HAIR AND EYE COLORS. I ASSUMED HER WHITE HAIR AND RED EYES WERE NORMAL.
APPARENTLY I WAS WRONG.
ALSO...
YOU'RE CURSED?
IT'S JUST A RUMOR.
PEOPLE WHO ARE JEALOUS OF OUR FAMILY OR OUR FATHER'S ACHIEVEMENTS HAVE BEEN SPREADING THOSE LIES.
THE ASCARTS ARE ONE OF THE MOST PROMINENT FAMILIES. PEOPLE PROBABLY BADMOUTH THEM OUT OF JEALOUSY ALL THE TIME.
EVEN OUR FAMILY GETS ACCUSED OF BEING STRANGE NO MATTER HOW PERFECT KEITH IS OR HOW LADYLIKE I ACT.
JEALOUSY IS A SCARY THING...
EVEN SO, MY HAIR...
IS ABSOLUTELY CREEPY.

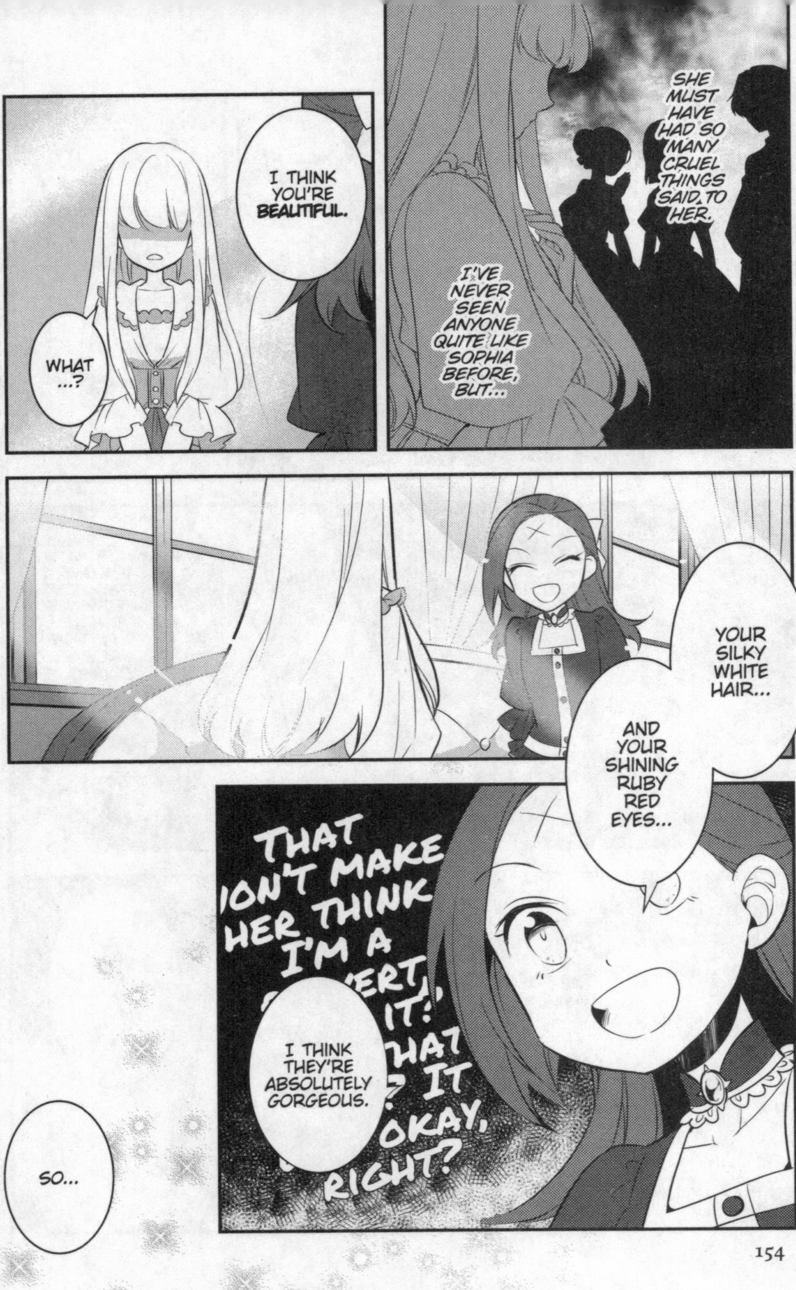
SHE MUST HAVE HAD SO MANY CRUEL THINGS SAID TO HER.
I'VE NEVER SEEN ANYONE QUITE LIKE SOPHIA BEFORE, BUT...
I THINK YOU'RE BEAUTIFUL.
WHAT ...?
YOUR SILKY WHITE HAIR...
AND YOUR SHINING RUBY RED EYES...
THAT
HER THINK I'M A
OKAY, RIGHT?
I THINK THEY'RE ABSOLUTELY GORGEOUS.
SO...

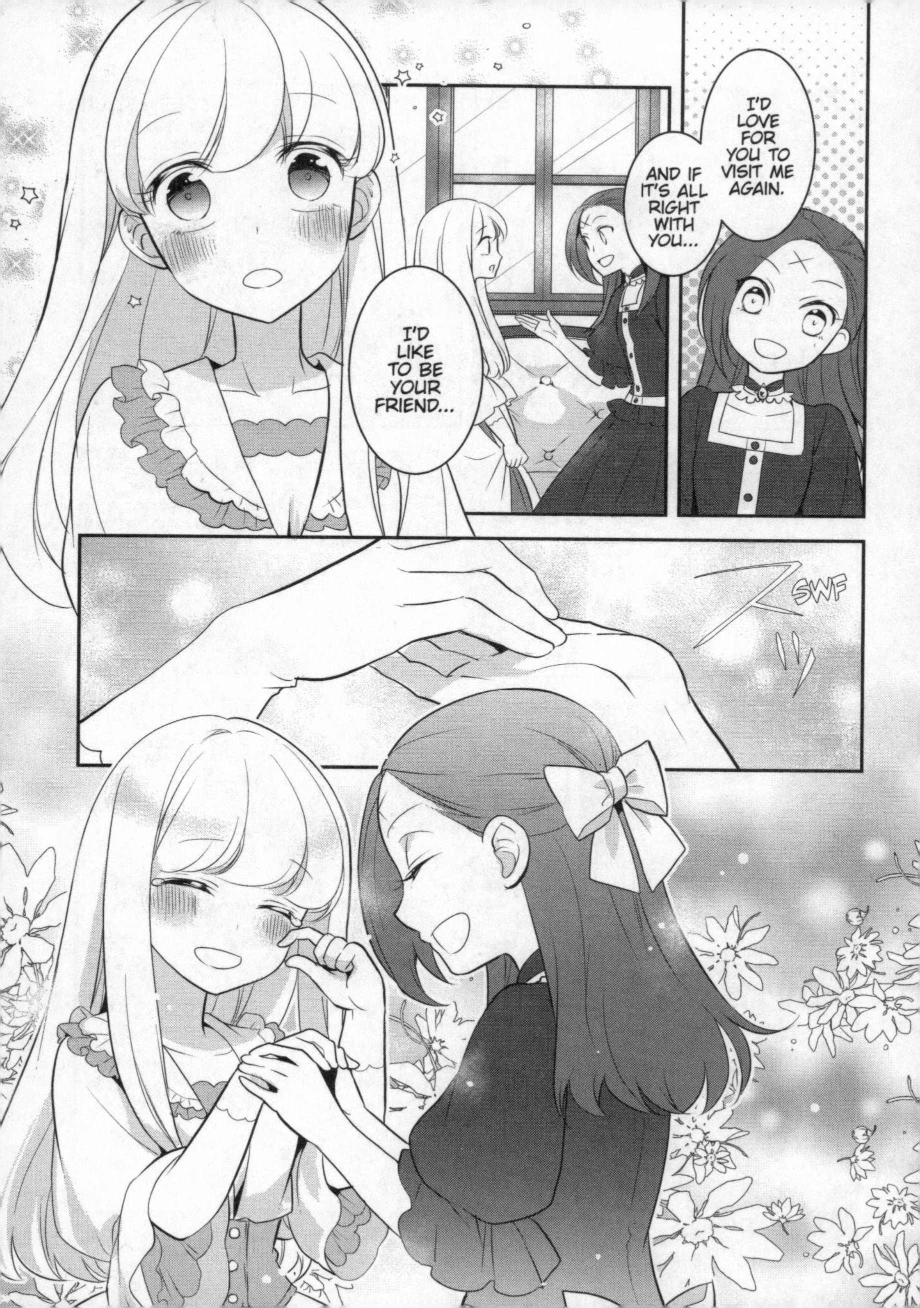
I'D LOVE FOR YOU TO VISIT ME AGAIN.
AND IF IT'S ALL RIGHT WITH YOU...
I'D LIKE TO BE YOUR FRIEND...
SWF

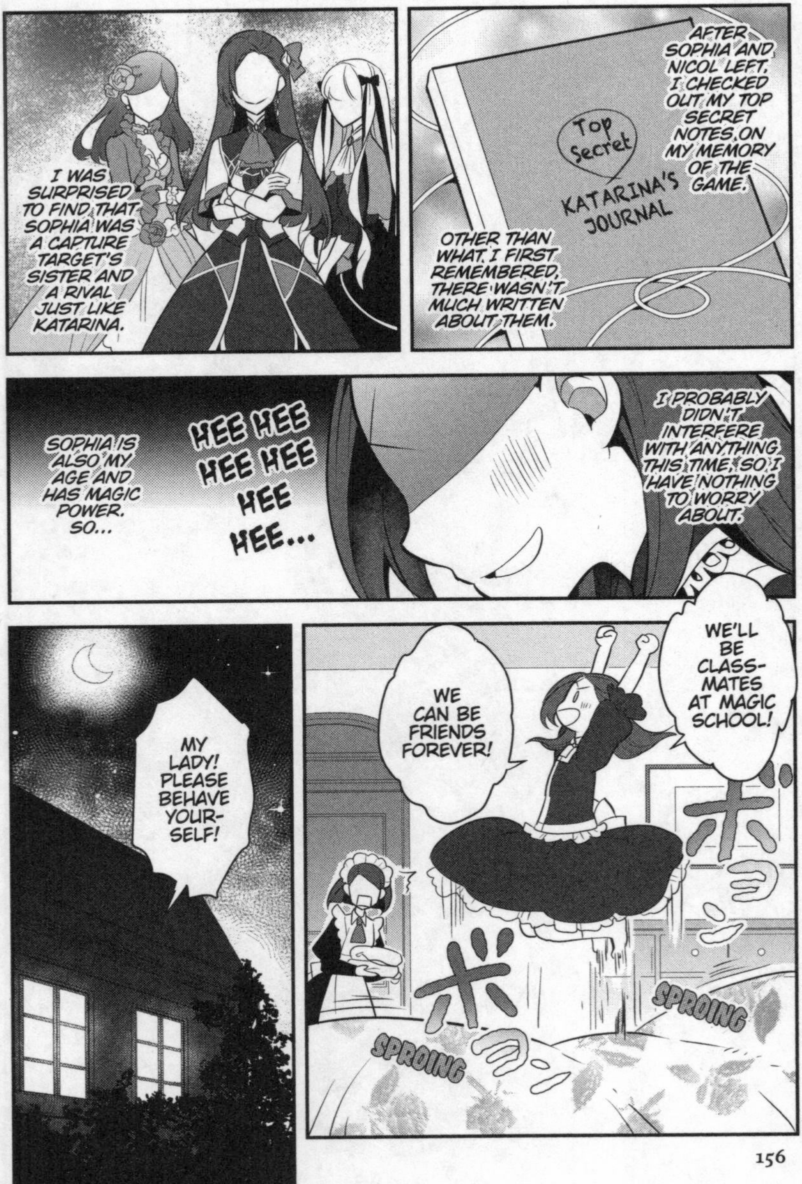
AFTER SOPHIA AND NICOL LEFT, I CHECKED OUT MY TOP SECRET NOTES ON MY MEMORY OF THE GAME.
Top Secret
KATARINA'S JOURNAL
OTHER THAN WHAT I FIRST REMEMBERED, THERE WASN'T MUCH WRITTEN ABOUT THEM.
I WAS SURPRISED TO FIND THAT SOPHIA WAS A CAPTURE TARGET'S SISTER AND A RIVAL JUST LIKE KATARINA.
I PROBABLY DIDN'T INTERFERE WITH ANYTHING THIS TIME, SO I HAVE NOTHING TO WORRY ABOUT.
SOPHIA IS ALSO MY AGE AND HAS MAGIC POWER. SO...
HEE HEE HEE HEE HEE HEE...
WE'LL BE CLASSMATES AT MAGIC SCHOOL!
WE CAN BE FRIENDS FOREVER!
ボッ
ボッ
SPROING
SPROING
MY LADY! PLEASE BEHAVE YOURSELF!

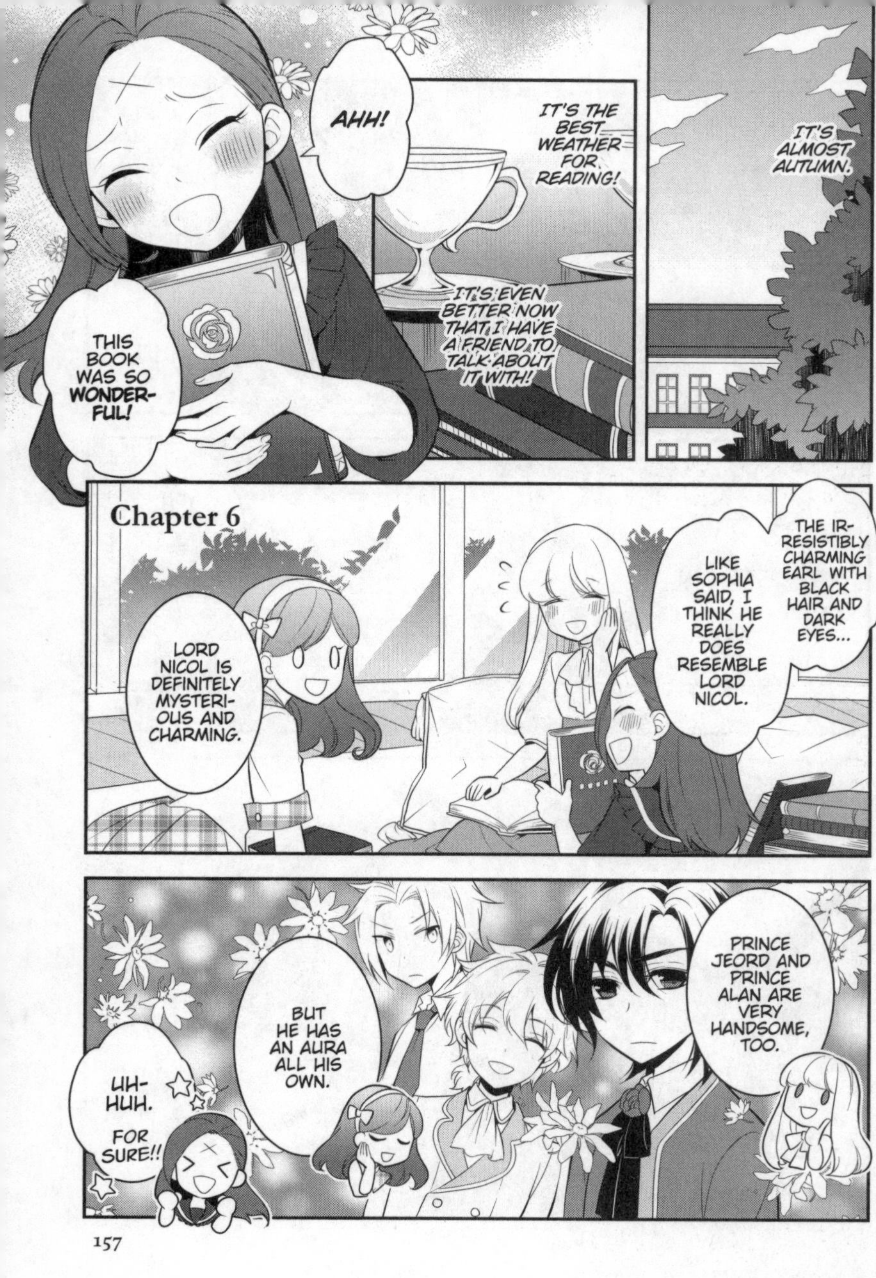
IT'S ALMOST AUTUMN.
IT'S THE BEST WEATHER FOR READING!
IT'S EVEN BETTER NOW THAT I HAVE A FRIEND TO TALK ABOUT IT WITH!
AHH!
THIS BOOK WAS SO WONDERFUL!
Chapter 6
THE IRRESISTIBLY CHARMING EARL WITH BLACK HAIR AND DARK EYES...
LIKE SOPHIA SAID, I THINK HE REALLY DOES RESEMBLE LORD NICOL.
LORD NICOL IS DEFINITELY MYSTERIOUS AND CHARMING.
PRINCE JEORD AND PRINCE ALAN ARE VERY HANDSOME, TOO.
BUT HE HAS AN AURA ALL HIS OWN.
UH-HUH.
FOR SURE!!

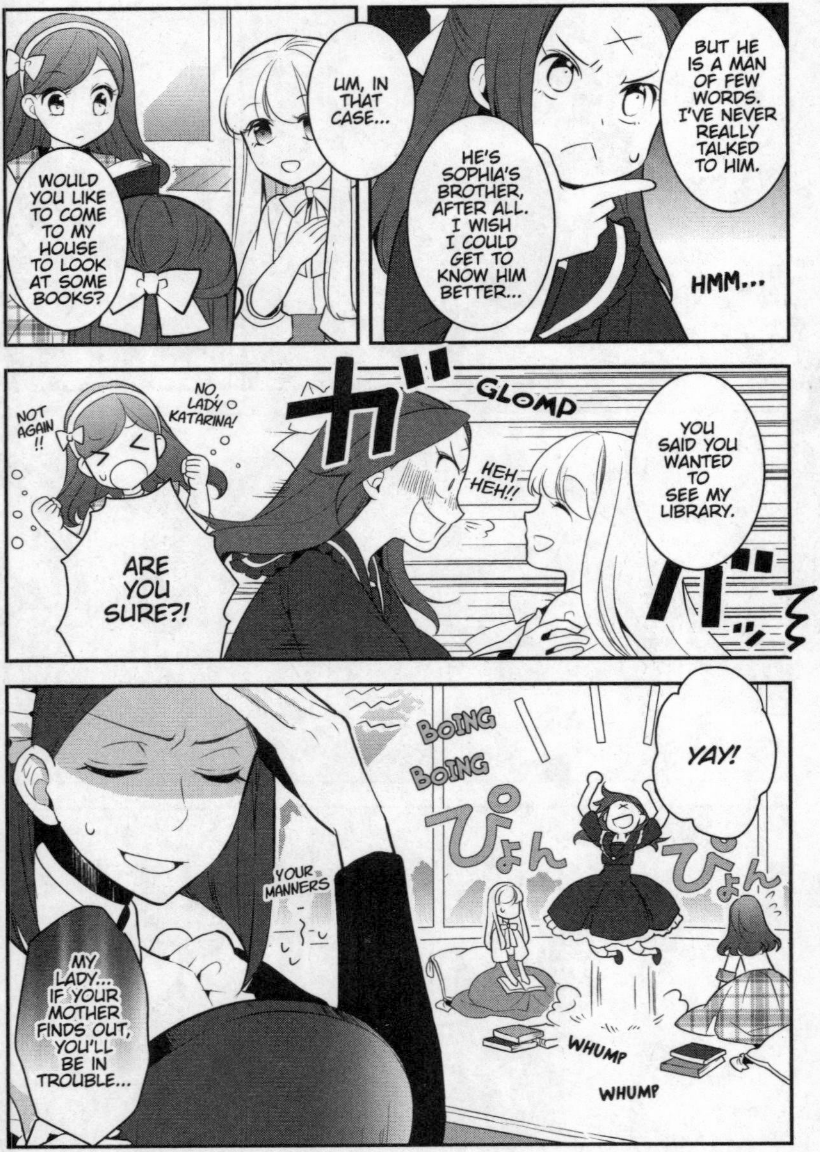
BUT HE IS A MAN OF FEW WORDS. I'VE NEVER REALLY TALKED TO HIM.
HMM...
HE'S SOPHIA'S BROTHER, AFTER ALL. I WISH I COULD GET TO KNOW HIM BETTER...
UM, IN THAT CASE...
WOULD YOU LIKE TO COME TO MY HOUSE TO LOOK AT SOME BOOKS?
YOU SAID YOU WANTED TO SEE MY LIBRARY.
バッ
GLOMP
ガ
HEH HEH!!
NO, LADY KATARINA!
NOT AGAIN!!
ARE YOU SURE?!
YAY!
BOING
BOING
ぴょん
ぴょん
WHUMP
WHUMP
YOUR MANNERS
MY LADY... IF YOUR MOTHER FINDS OUT, YOU'LL BE IN TROUBLE...

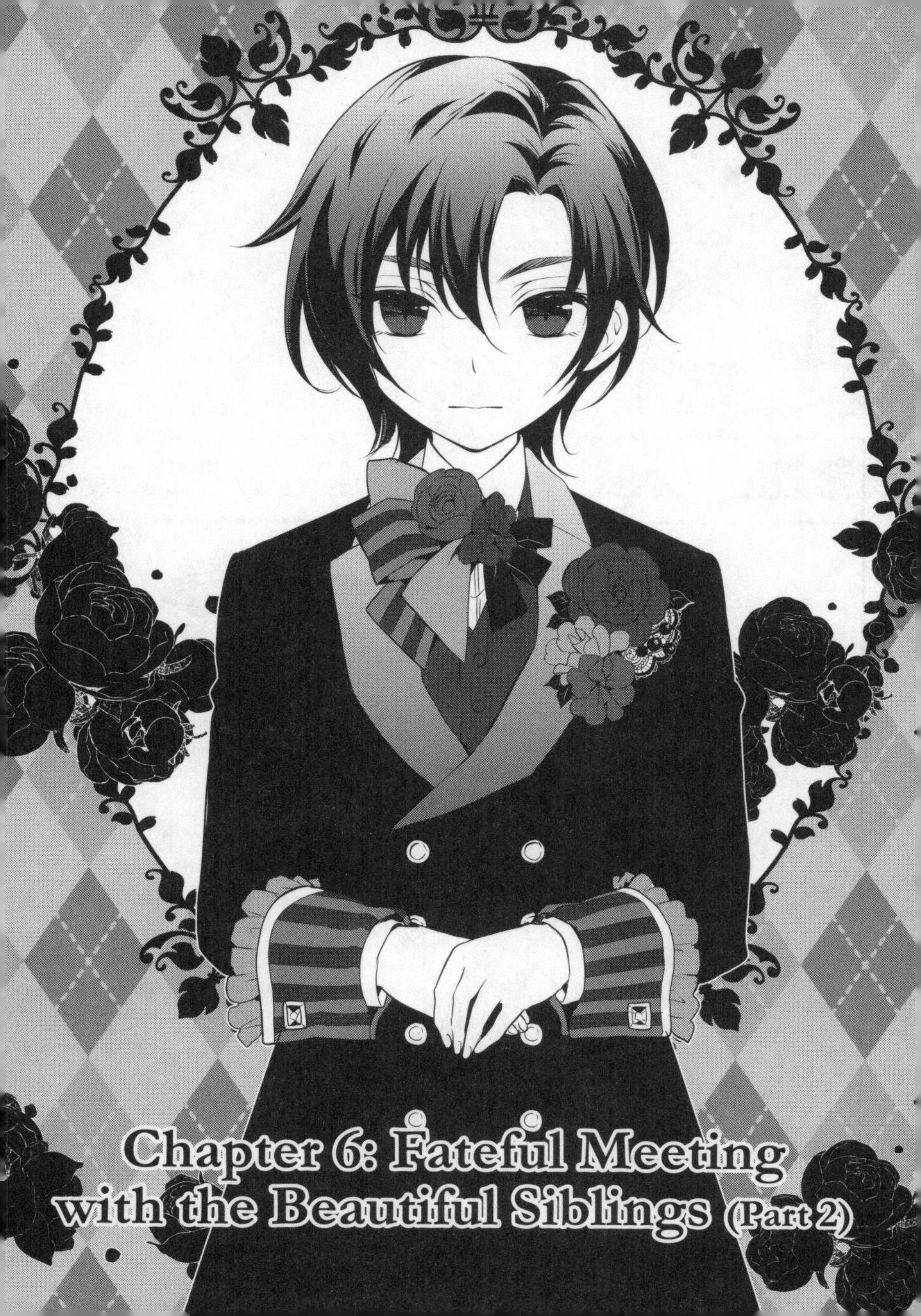

Chapter 6: Fateful Meeting with the Beautiful Siblings (Part 2)

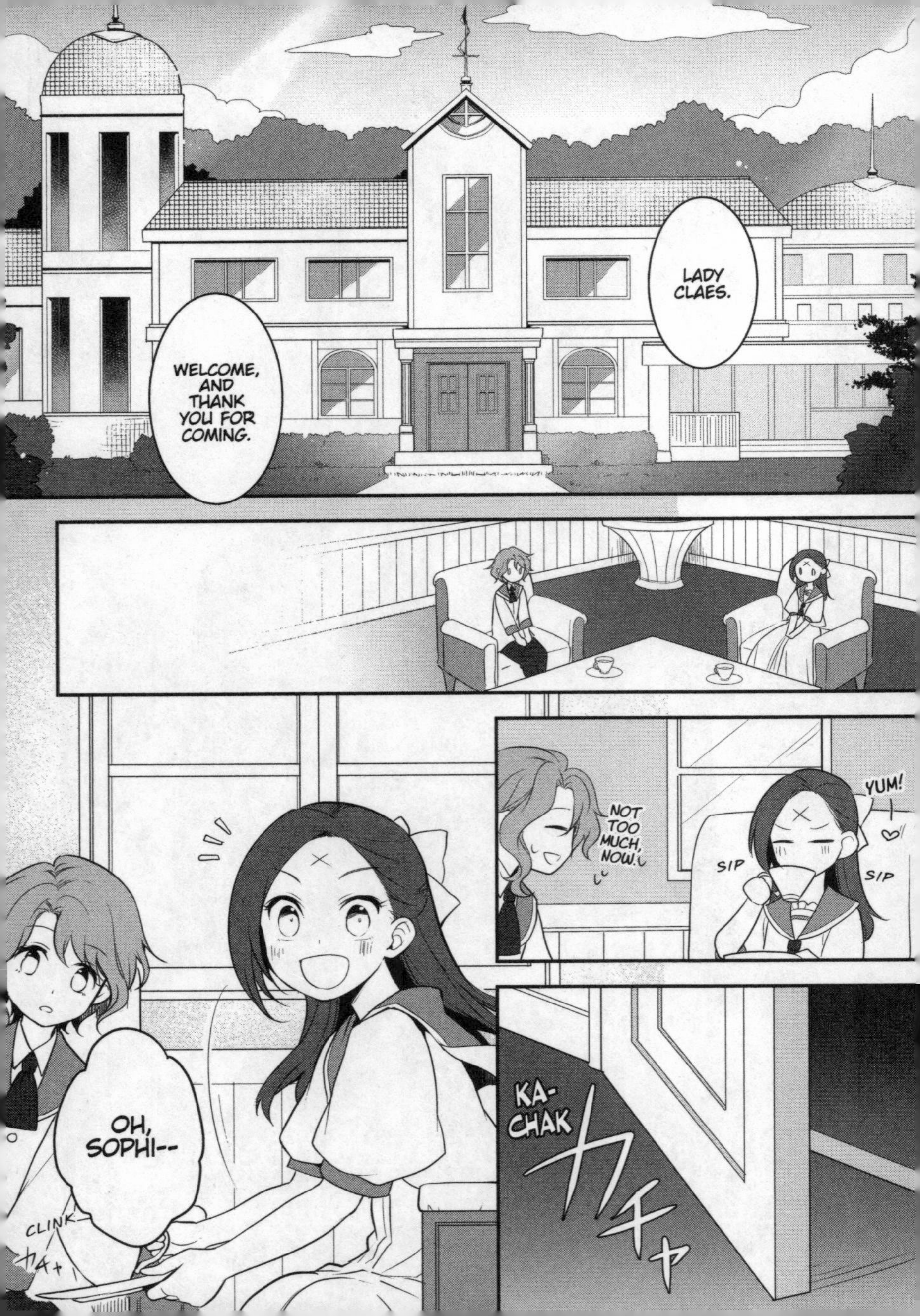
LADY CLAES.
WELCOME, AND THANK YOU FOR COMING.
YUM!
SIP
SIP
NOT TOO MUCH, NOW.
KA-CHAK
カチャ
OH, SOPHI--
CLINK

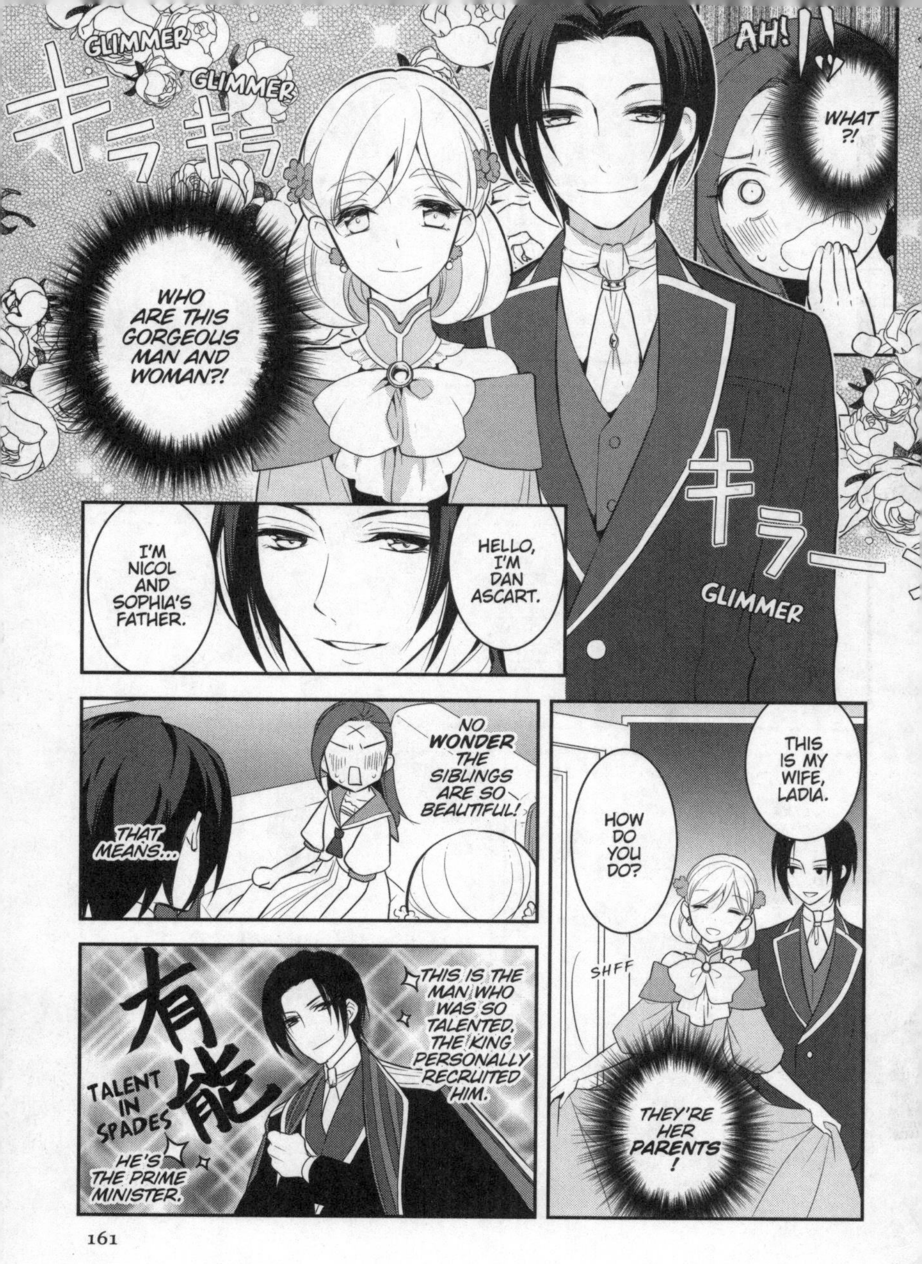
AH!
WHAT ?!
キラキラ
GLIMMER GLIMMER
WHO ARE THIS GORGEOUS MAN AND WOMAN?!
キラー
GLIMMER
HELLO, I'M DAN ASCART.
I'M NICOL AND SOPHIA'S FATHER.
THIS IS MY WIFE, LADIA.
HOW DO YOU DO?
SHFF
THEY'RE HER PARENTS!
NO WONDER THE SIBLINGS ARE SO BEAUTIFUL!
THAT MEANS...
有能
TALENT IN SPADES
THIS IS THE MAN WHO WAS SO TALENTED, THE KING PERSONALLY RECRUITED HIM.
HE'S THE PRIME MINISTER.

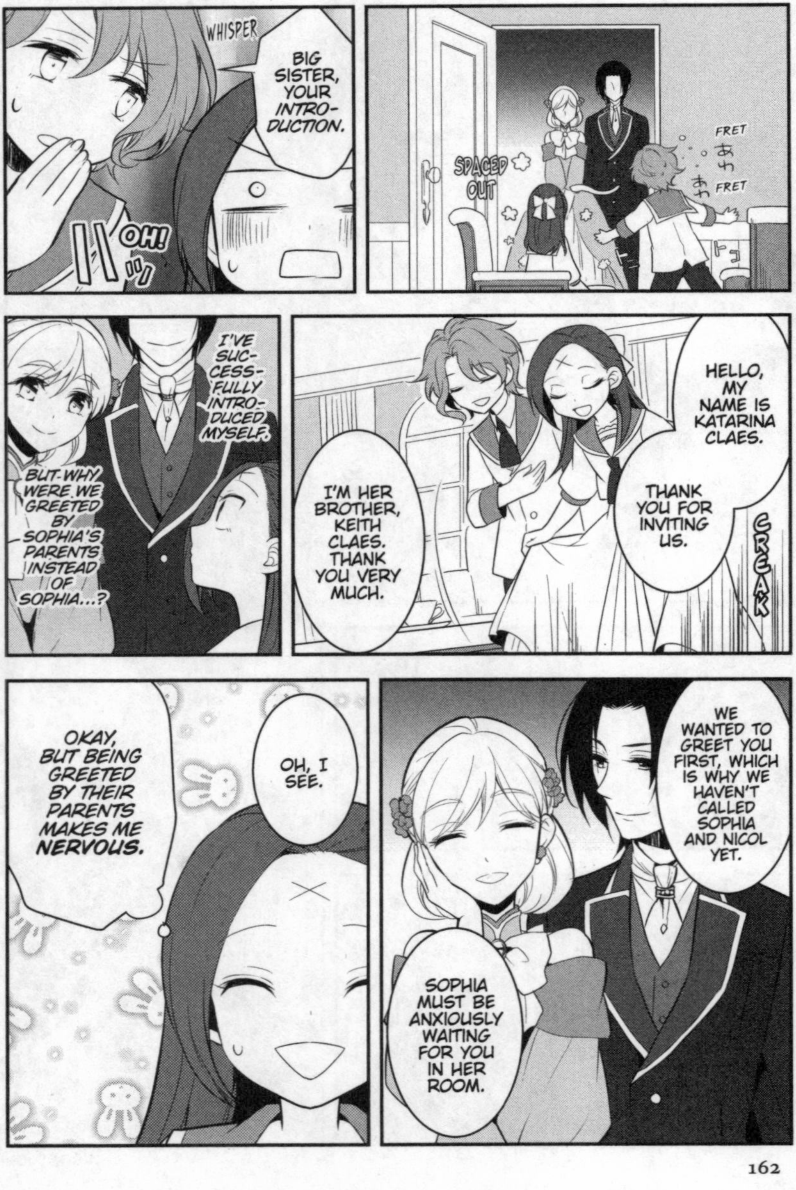
FRET
あわ
あわ
FRET
SPACED OUT
トコ
WHISPER
BIG SISTER, YOUR INTRODUCTION.
OH!
HELLO, MY NAME IS KATARINA CLAES.
THANK YOU FOR INVITING US.
CREAK
I'M HER BROTHER, KEITH CLAES. THANK YOU VERY MUCH.
I'VE SUCCESSFULLY INTRODUCED MYSELF.
BUT WHY WERE WE GREETED BY SOPHIA'S PARENTS INSTEAD OF SOPHIA...?
WE WANTED TO GREET YOU FIRST, WHICH IS WHY WE HAVEN'T CALLED SOPHIA AND NICOL YET.
SOPHIA MUST BE ANXIOUSLY WAITING FOR YOU IN HER ROOM.
OH, I SEE.
OKAY, BUT BEING GREETED BY THEIR PARENTS MAKES ME NERVOUS.

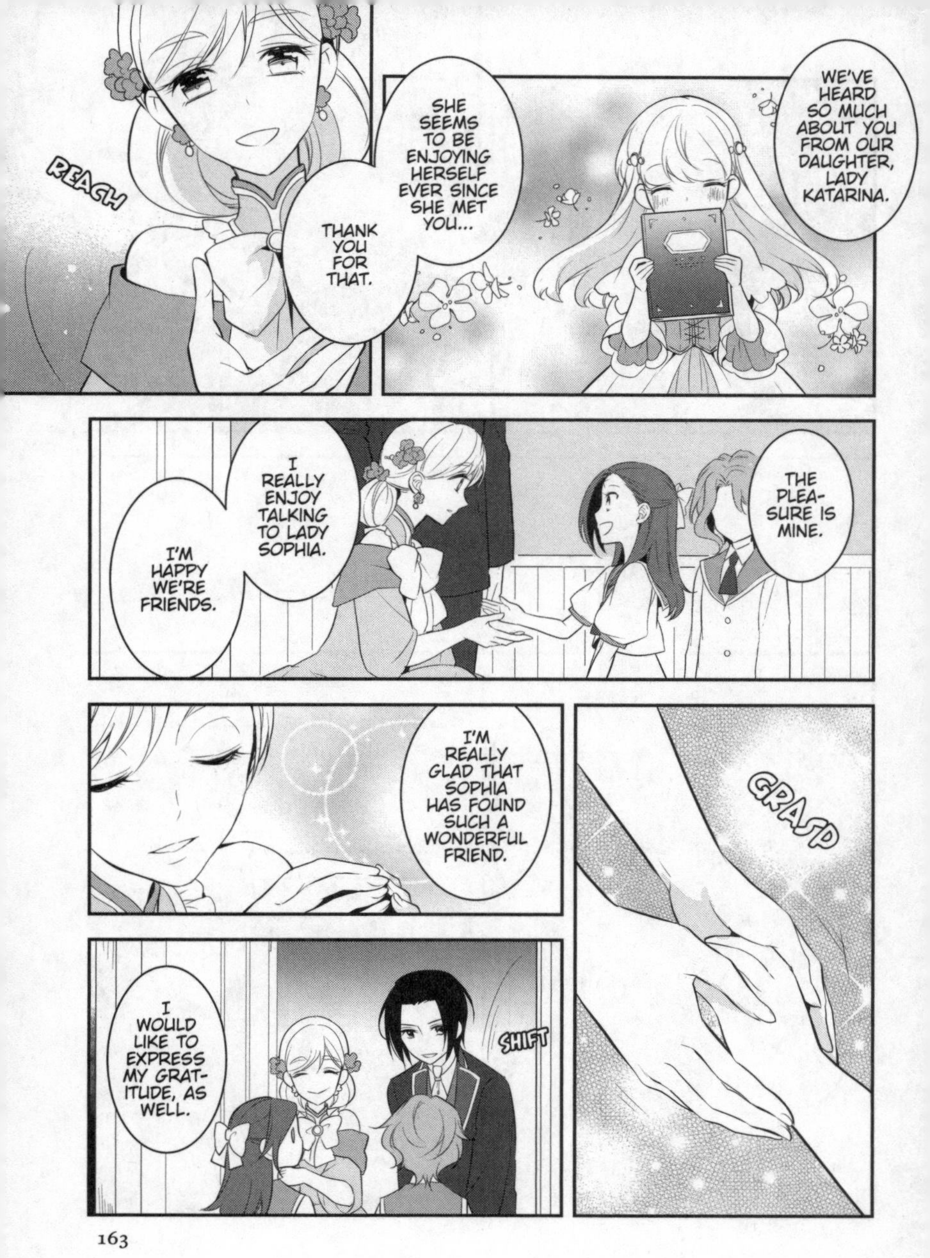
WE'VE HEARD SO MUCH ABOUT YOU FROM OUR DAUGHTER, LADY KATARINA.
SHE SEEMS TO BE ENJOYING HERSELF EVER SINCE SHE MET YOU...
THANK YOU FOR THAT.
REACH
THE PLEA-SURE IS MINE.
I REALLY ENJOY TALKING TO LADY SOPHIA.
I'M HAPPY WE'RE FRIENDS.
GRASP
I'M REALLY GLAD THAT SOPHIA HAS FOUND SUCH A WONDERFUL FRIEND.
SHIFT
I WOULD LIKE TO EXPRESS MY GRAT-ITUDE, AS WELL.

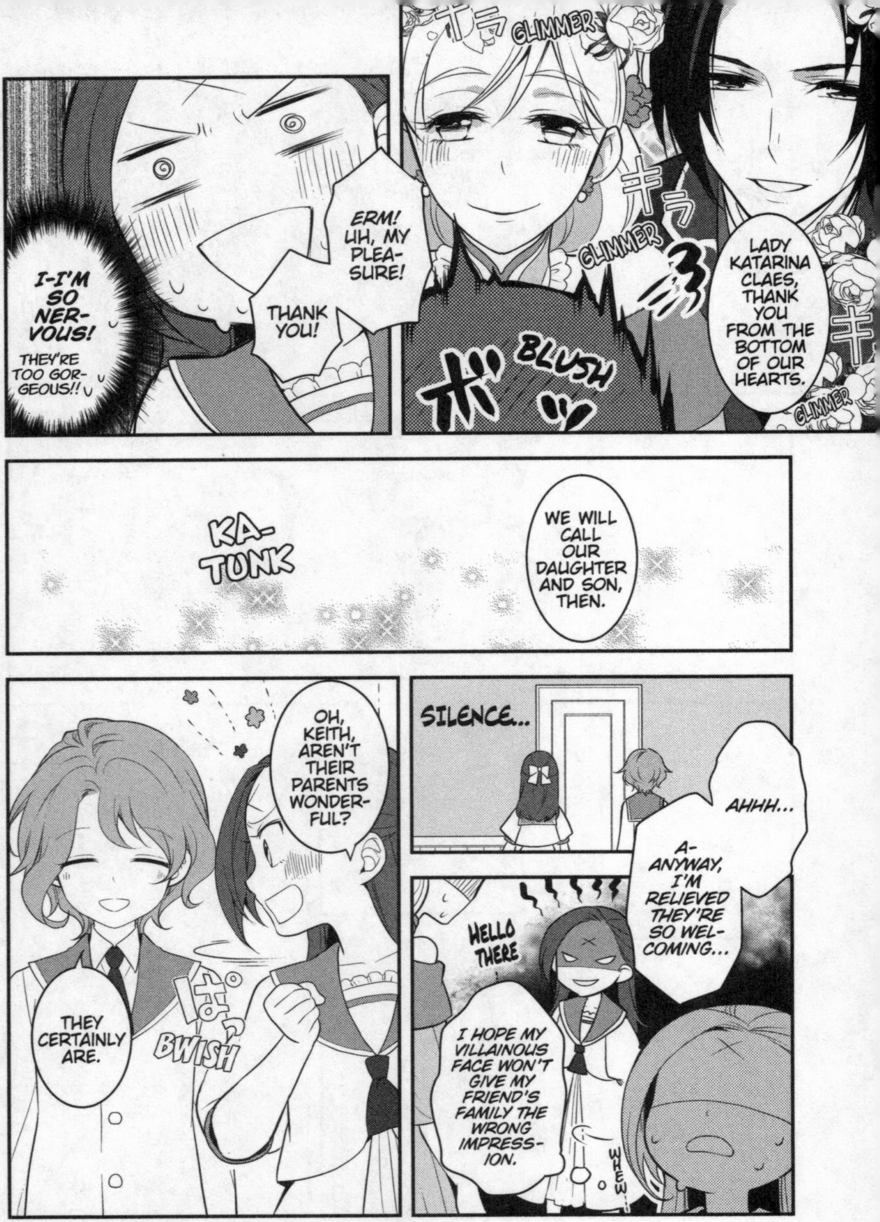
GLIMMER
GLIMMER
LADY KATARINA CLAES, THANK YOU FROM THE BOTTOM OF OUR HEARTS.
GLIMMER
BLUSH
ERM! UH, MY PLEASURE!
THANK YOU!
I-I'M SO NERVOUS!
THEY'RE TOO GORGEOUS!!
WE WILL CALL OUR DAUGHTER AND SON, THEN.
KA-TUNK
SILENCE...
AHHH...
A-ANYWAY, I'M RELIEVED THEY'RE SO WELCOMING...
HELLO THERE
I HOPE MY VILLAINOUS FACE WON'T GIVE MY FRIEND'S FAMILY THE WRONG IMPRESSION.
WHEW
OH, KEITH, AREN'T THEIR PARENTS WONDERFUL?
BWISH
THEY CERTAINLY ARE.

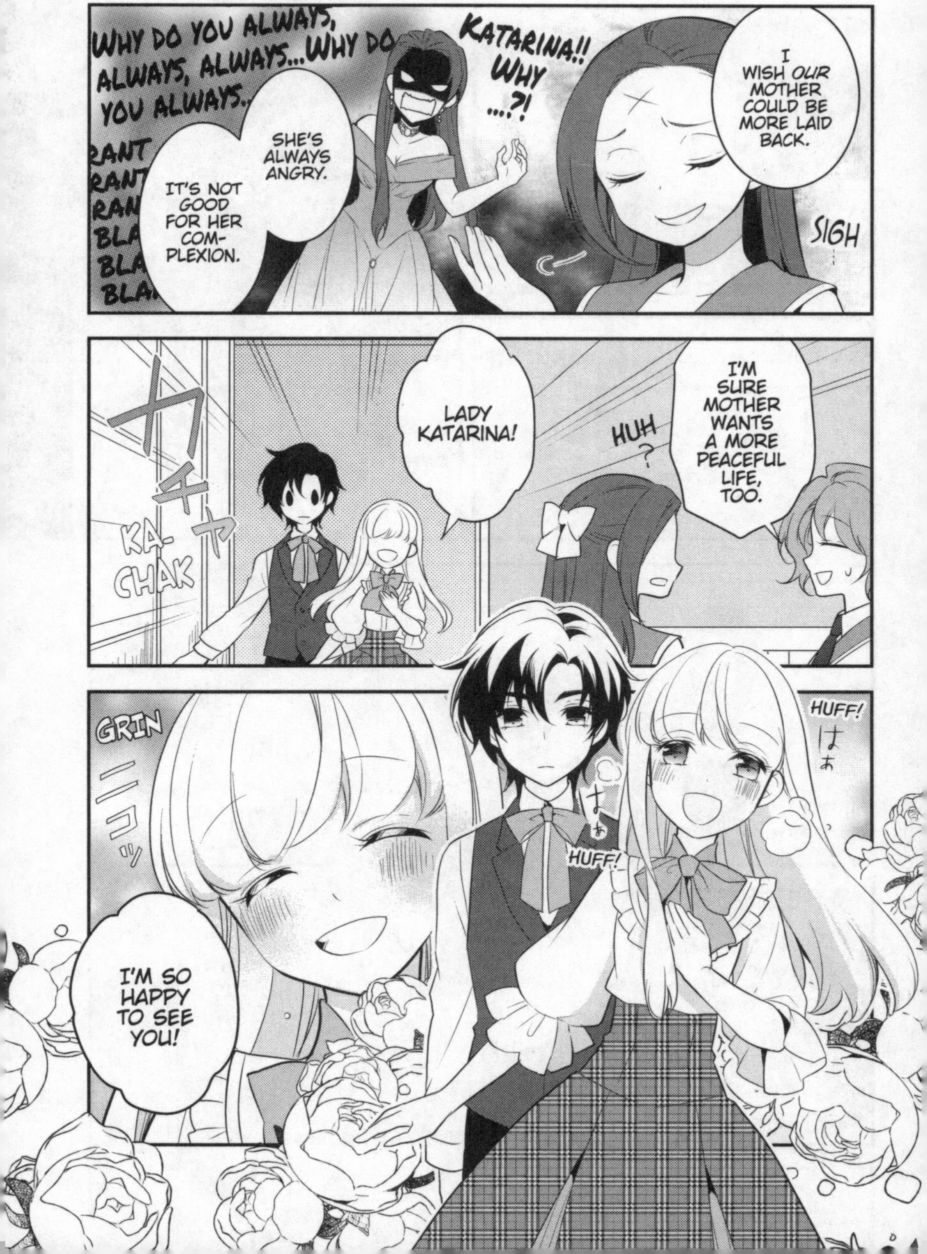
I WISH *OUR* MOTHER COULD BE MORE LAID BACK.
SIGH
KATARINA!! WHY ...?!
WHY DO YOU ALWAYS, ALWAYS, ALWAYS...WHY DO YOU ALWAYS...
SHE'S ALWAYS ANGRY.
IT'S NOT GOOD FOR HER COMPLEXION.
I'M SURE MOTHER WANTS A MORE PEACEFUL LIFE, TOO.
HUH?
LADY KATARINA!
KA-CHAK
HUFF!
はぁ
HUFF!
GRIN
ニコッ
I'M SO HAPPY TO SEE YOU!

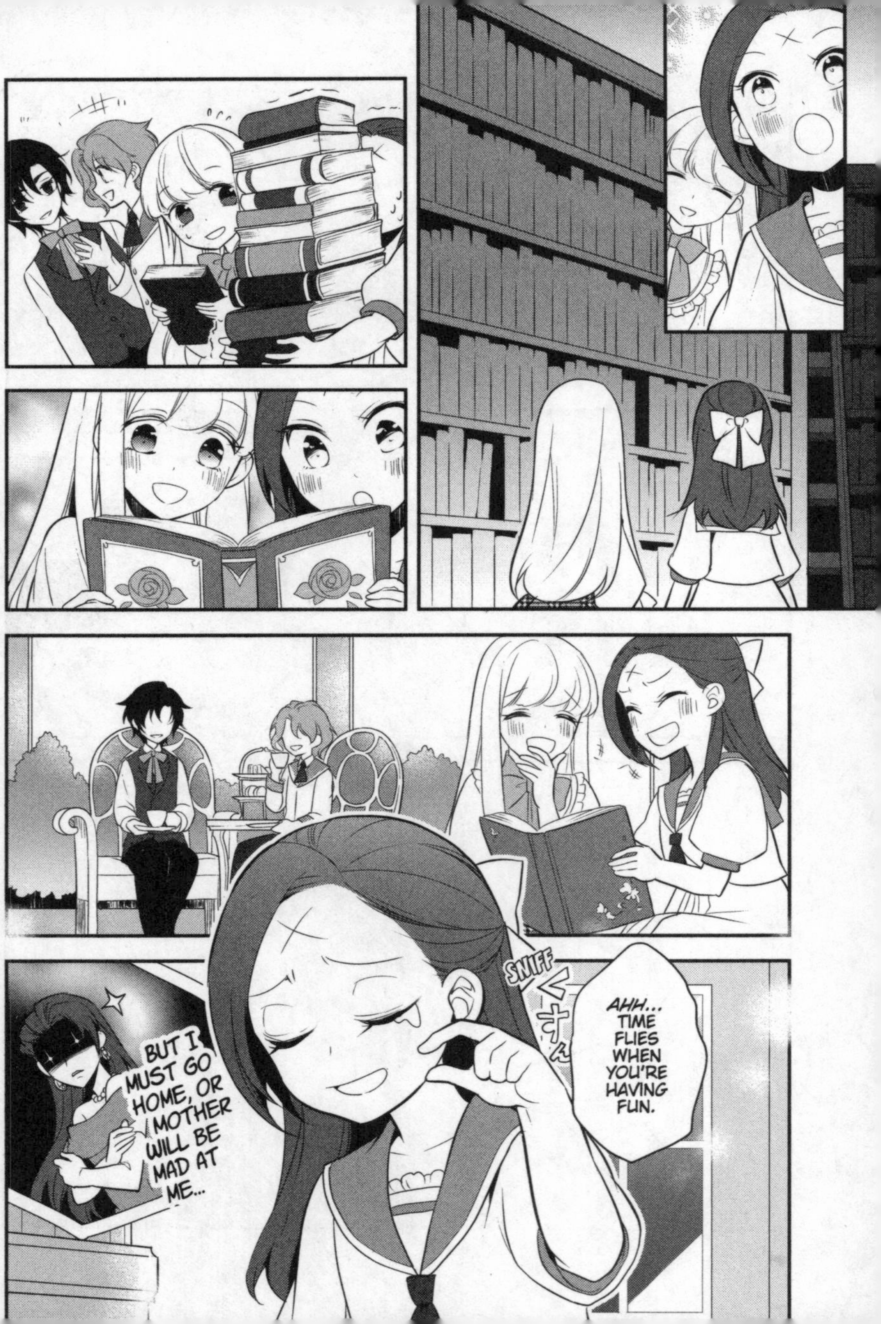
AHH... TIME FLIES WHEN YOU'RE HAVING FUN.
SNIFF
BUT I MUST GO HOME, OR MOTHER WILL BE MAD AT ME...

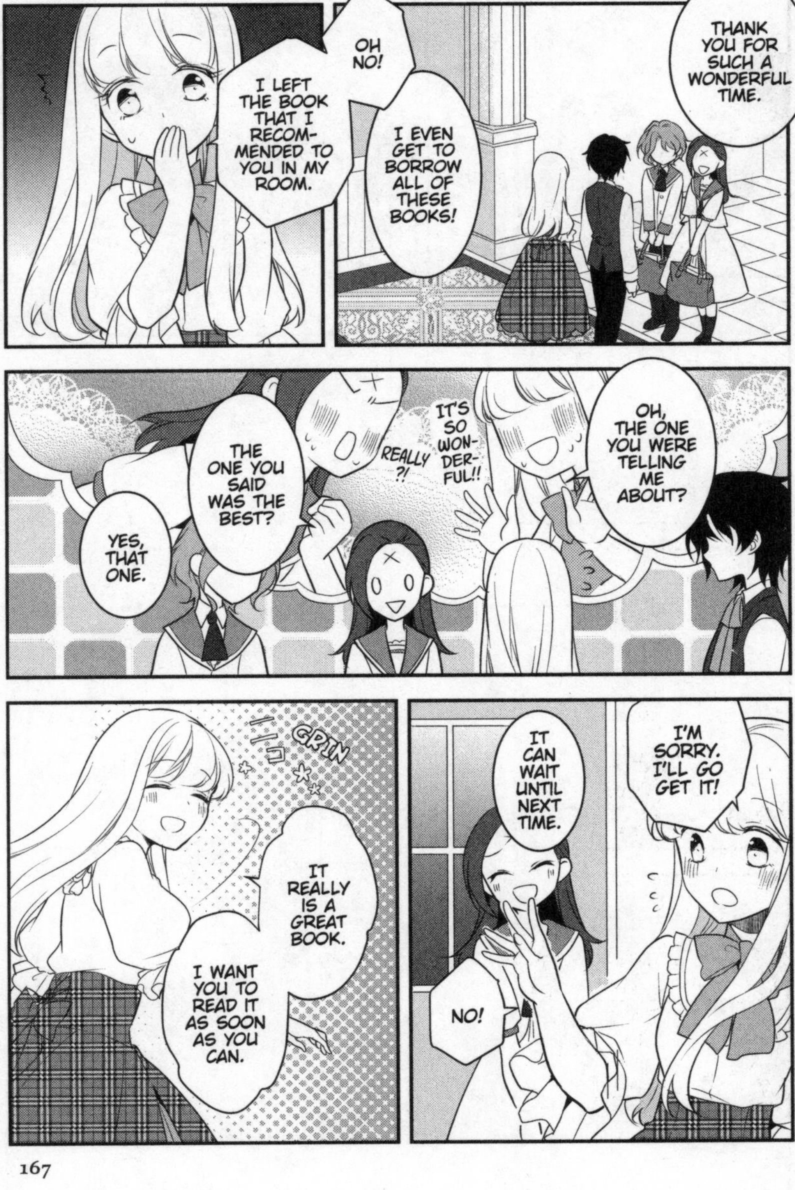
THANK YOU FOR SUCH A WONDERFUL TIME.
I EVEN GET TO BORROW ALL OF THESE BOOKS!
OH NO!
I LEFT THE BOOK THAT I RECOMMENDED TO YOU IN MY ROOM.
OH, THE ONE YOU WERE TELLING ME ABOUT?
IT'S SO WONDERFUL!!
REALLY?!
THE ONE YOU SAID WAS THE BEST?
YES, THAT ONE.
I'M SORRY. I'LL GO GET IT!
IT CAN WAIT UNTIL NEXT TIME.
NO!
ニコ
GRIN
IT REALLY IS A GREAT BOOK.
I WANT YOU TO READ IT AS SOON AS YOU CAN.

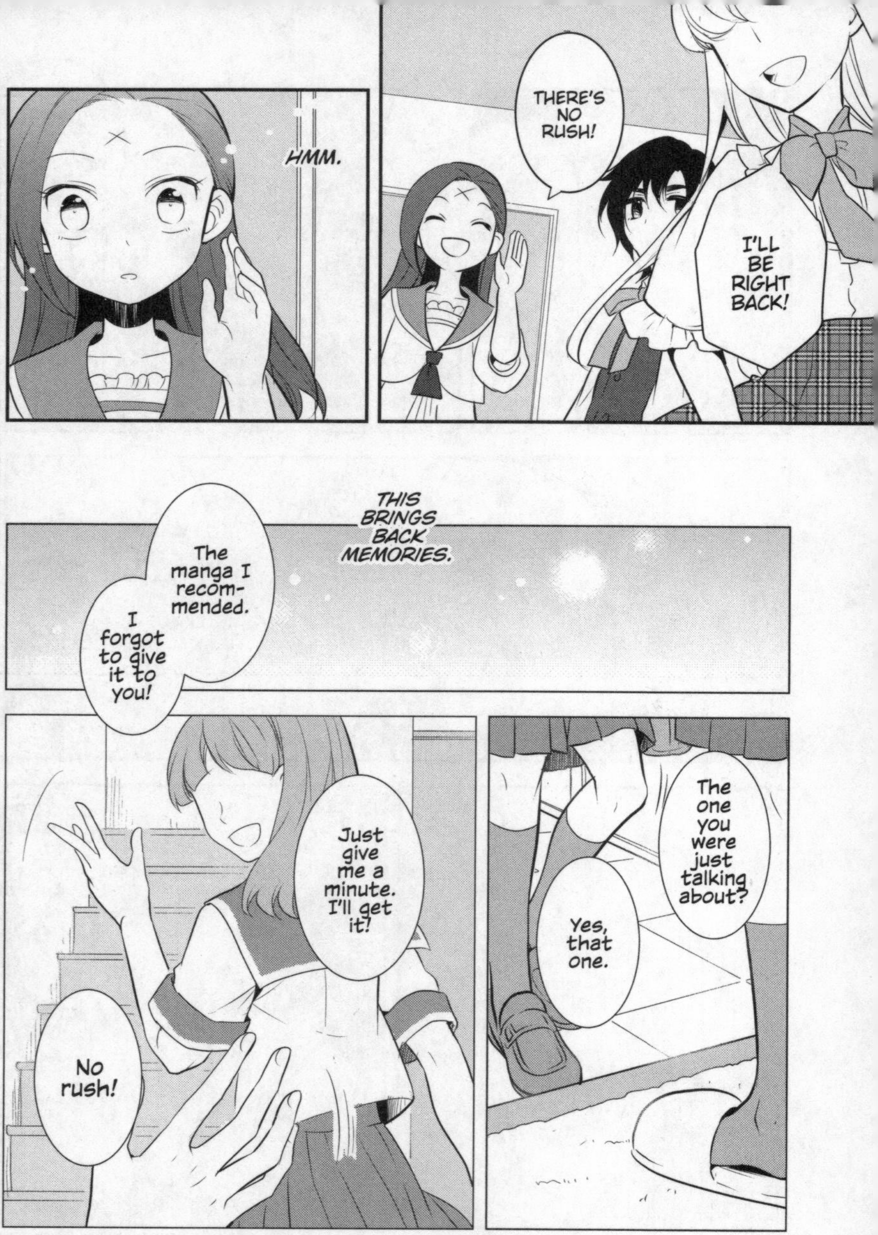
I'LL BE RIGHT BACK!
THERE'S NO RUSH!
HMM.
THIS BRINGS BACK MEMORIES.
The manga I recommended.
I forgot to give it to you!
The one you were just talking about?
Yes, that one.
Just give me a minute. I'll get it!
No rush!

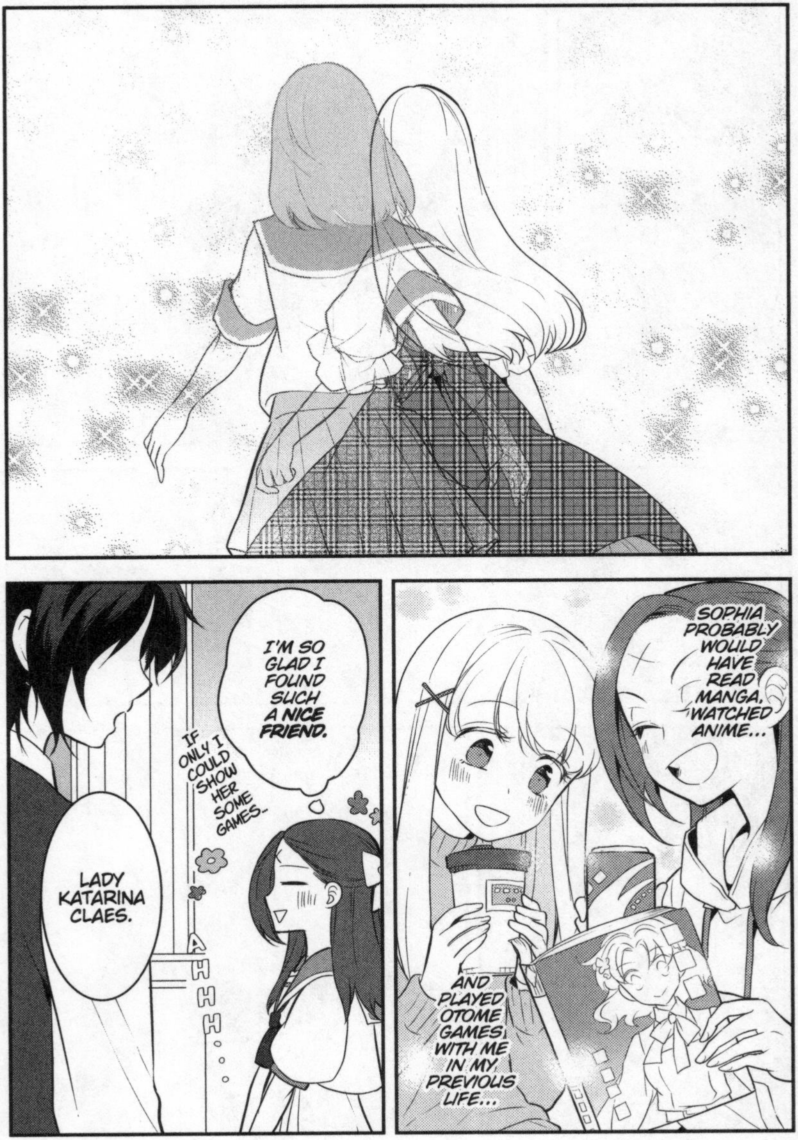
SOPHIA PROBABLY WOULD HAVE READ MANGA, WATCHED ANIME...
AND PLAYED OTOME GAMES WITH ME IN MY PREVIOUS LIFE...
I'M SO GLAD I FOUND SUCH A NICE FRIEND.
IF ONLY I COULD SHOW HER SOME GAMES...
AHHHH...
LADY KATARINA CLAES.

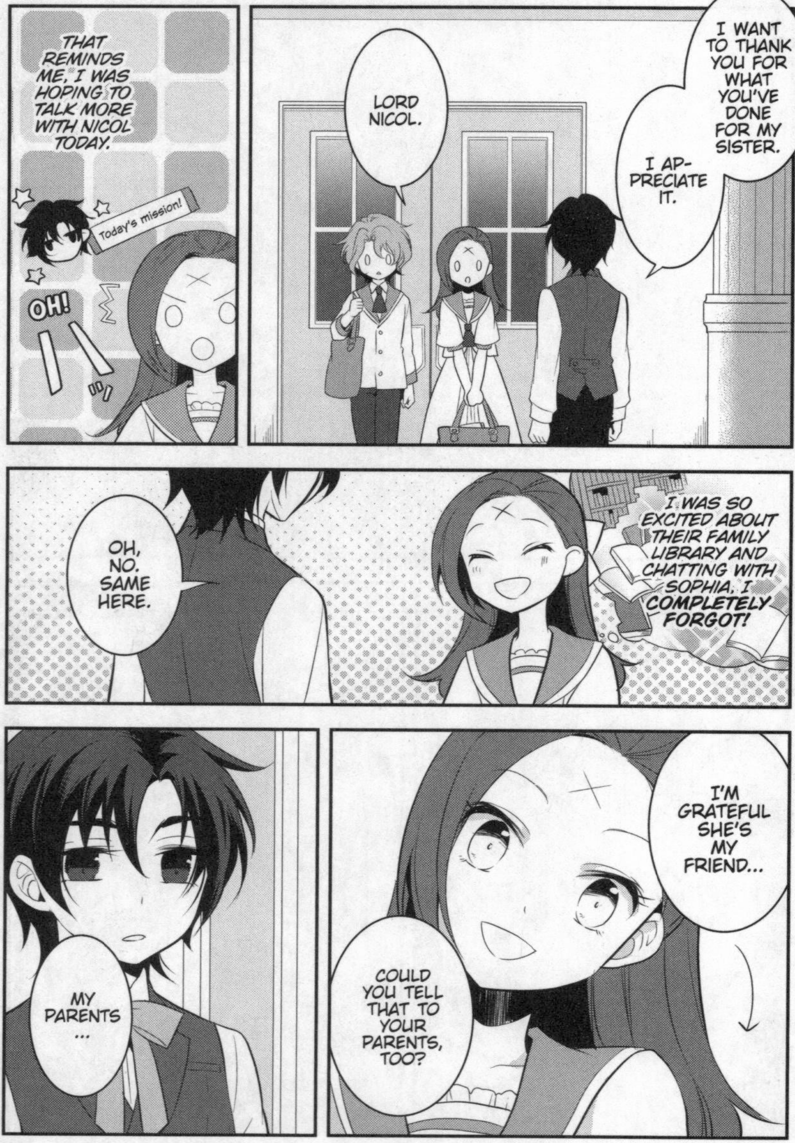
I WANT TO THANK YOU FOR WHAT YOU'VE DONE FOR MY SISTER.
I AP-PRECIATE IT.
LORD NICOL.
THAT REMINDS ME, I WAS HOPING TO TALK MORE WITH NICOL TODAY.
Today's mission!
OH!
I WAS SO EXCITED ABOUT THEIR FAMILY LIBRARY AND CHATTING WITH SOPHIA, I COMPLETELY FORGOT!
OH, NO. SAME HERE.
I'M GRATEFUL SHE'S MY FRIEND...
COULD YOU TELL THAT TO YOUR PARENTS, TOO?
MY PARENTS ...

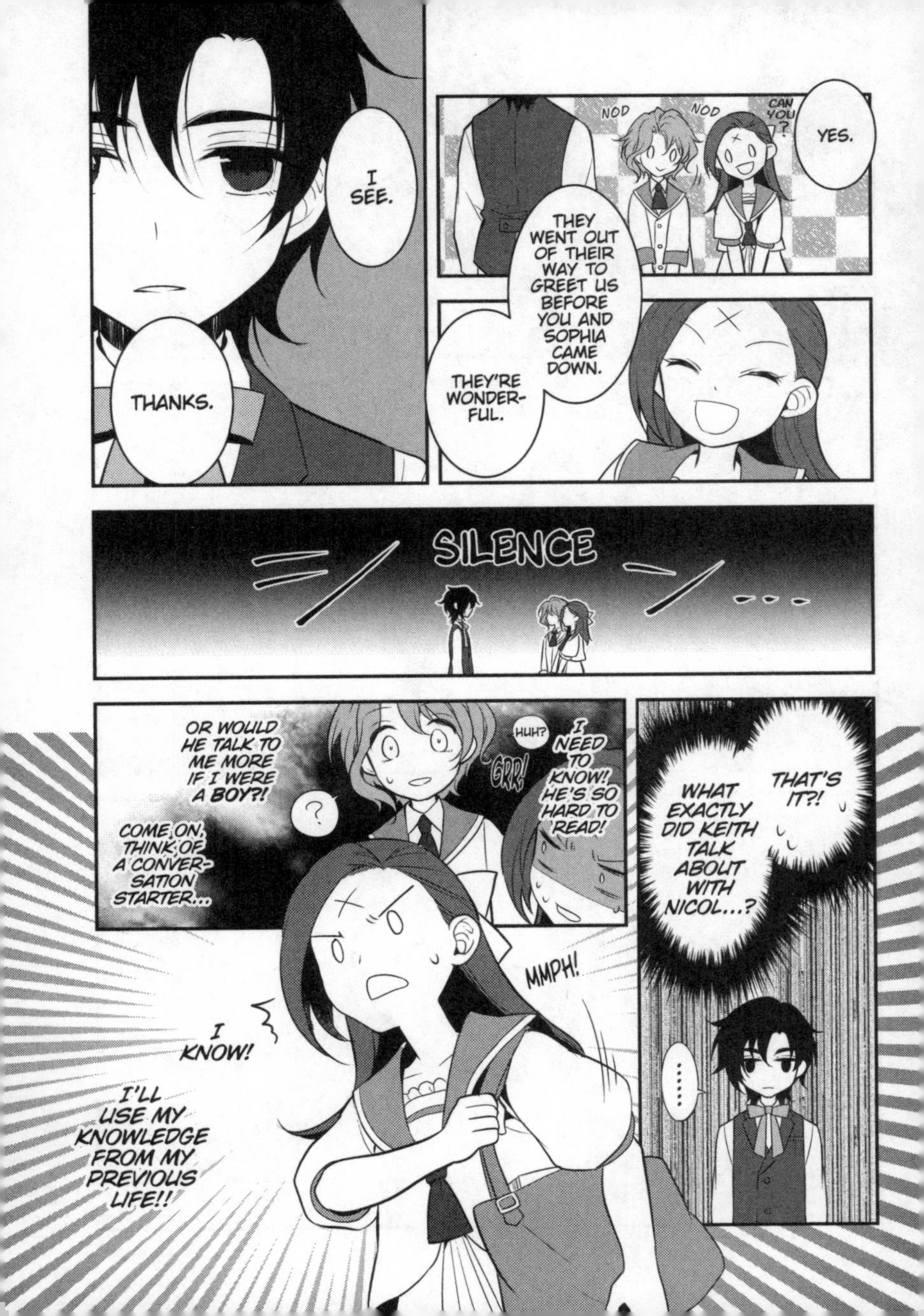
YES.
CAN YOU?
NOD
NOD
THEY WENT OUT OF THEIR WAY TO GREET US BEFORE YOU AND SOPHIA CAME DOWN.
THEY'RE WONDERFUL.
I SEE.
THANKS.
SILENCE
...
THAT'S IT?!
WHAT EXACTLY DID KEITH TALK ABOUT WITH NICOL...?
......
HUH?
I NEED TO KNOW! HE'S SO HARD TO READ!
GRR!
OR WOULD HE TALK TO ME MORE IF I WERE A BOY?!
?
COME ON, THINK OF A CONVERSATION STARTER...
MMPH!
I KNOW!
I'LL USE MY KNOWLEDGE FROM MY PREVIOUS LIFE!!

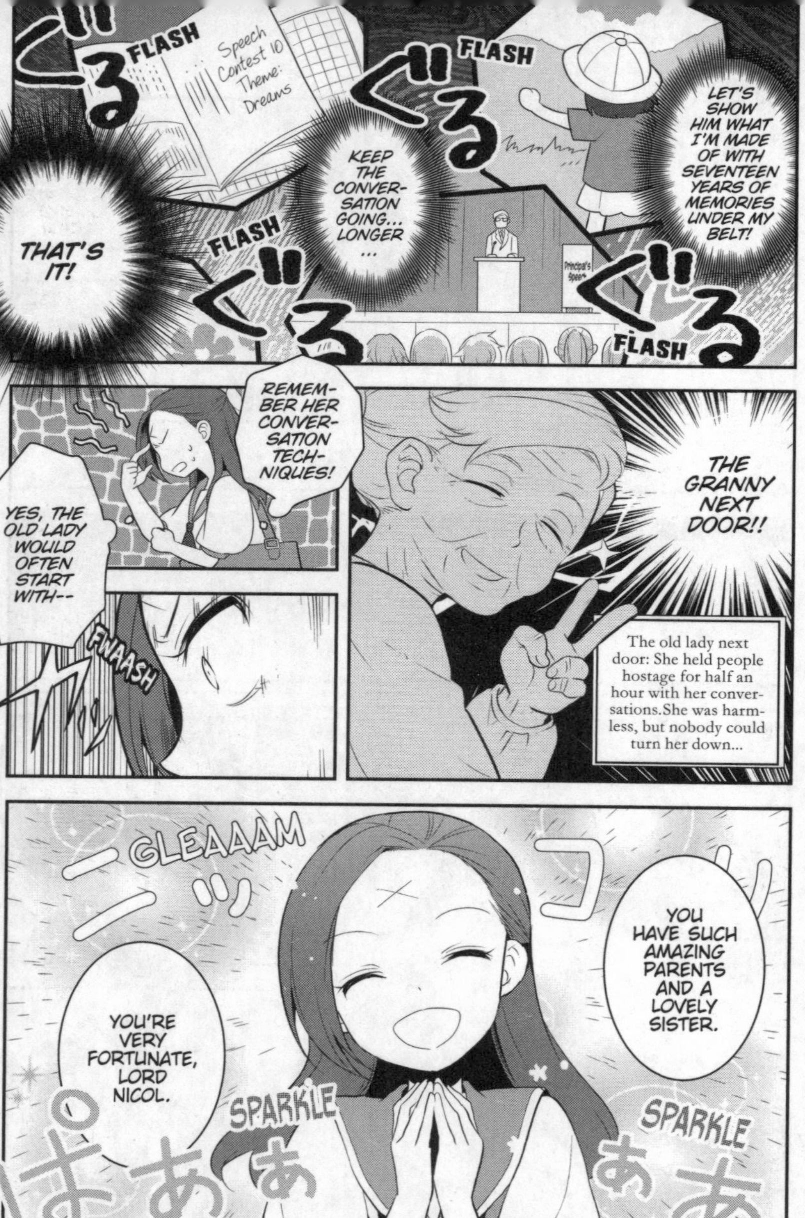
LET'S SHOW HIM WHAT I'M MADE OF WITH SEVENTEEN YEARS OF MEMORIES UNDER MY BELT!
FLASH
ぐる
FLASH
ぐる
Speech Contest 10 Theme: Dreams
FLASH
ぐる
KEEP THE CONVER-SATION GOING... LONGER ...
FLASH
ぐる
THAT'S IT!
THE GRANNY NEXT DOOR!!
The old lady next door: She held people hostage for half an hour with her conver-sations.She was harm-less, but nobody could turn her down...
REMEM-BER HER CONVER-SATION TECH-NIQUES!
YES, THE OLD LADY WOULD OFTEN START WITH--
FWAASH
GLEAAAM
YOU HAVE SUCH AMAZING PARENTS AND A LOVELY SISTER.
YOU'RE VERY FORTUNATE, LORD NICOL.
SPARKLE
SPARKLE
ぱあああ

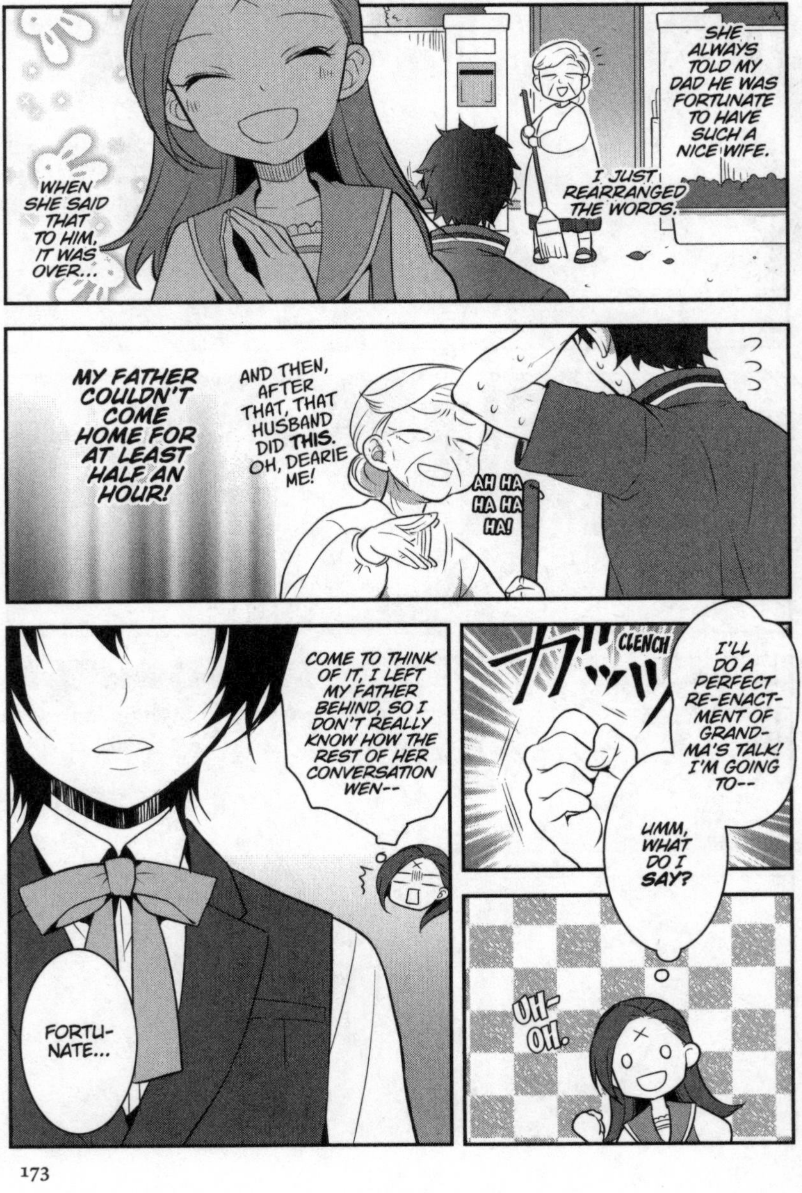
SHE ALWAYS TOLD MY DAD HE WAS FORTUNATE TO HAVE SUCH A NICE WIFE.
I JUST REARRANGED THE WORDS.
WHEN SHE SAID THAT TO HIM, IT WAS OVER...
AND THEN, AFTER THAT, THAT HUSBAND DID THIS. OH, DEARIE ME!
AH HA HA HA HA!
MY FATHER COULDN'T COME HOME FOR AT LEAST HALF AN HOUR!
CLENCH
I'LL DO A PERFECT RE-ENACTMENT OF GRANDMA'S TALK! I'M GOING TO--
UMM, WHAT DO I SAY?
UH-OH.
COME TO THINK OF IT, I LEFT MY FATHER BEHIND, SO I DON'T REALLY KNOW HOW THE REST OF HER CONVERSATION WEN--
FORTUNATE...

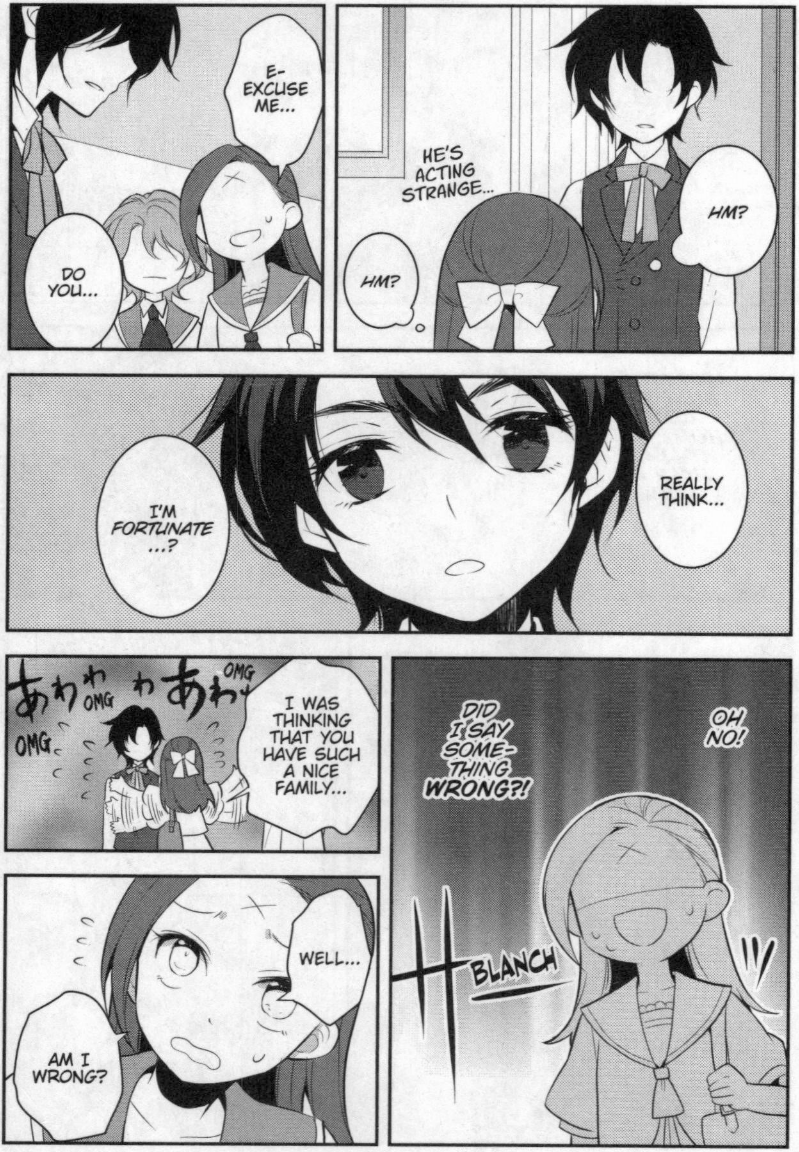
HM?
HE'S ACTING STRANGE...
HM?
E-EXCUSE ME...
DO YOU...
REALLY THINK...
I'M FORTUNATE ...?
OH NO!
DID I SAY SOME-THING WRONG?!
BLANCH
I WAS THINKING THAT YOU HAVE SUCH A NICE FAMILY...
OMG
あわわ
OMG
わ あわ
OMG
WELL...
AM I WRONG?

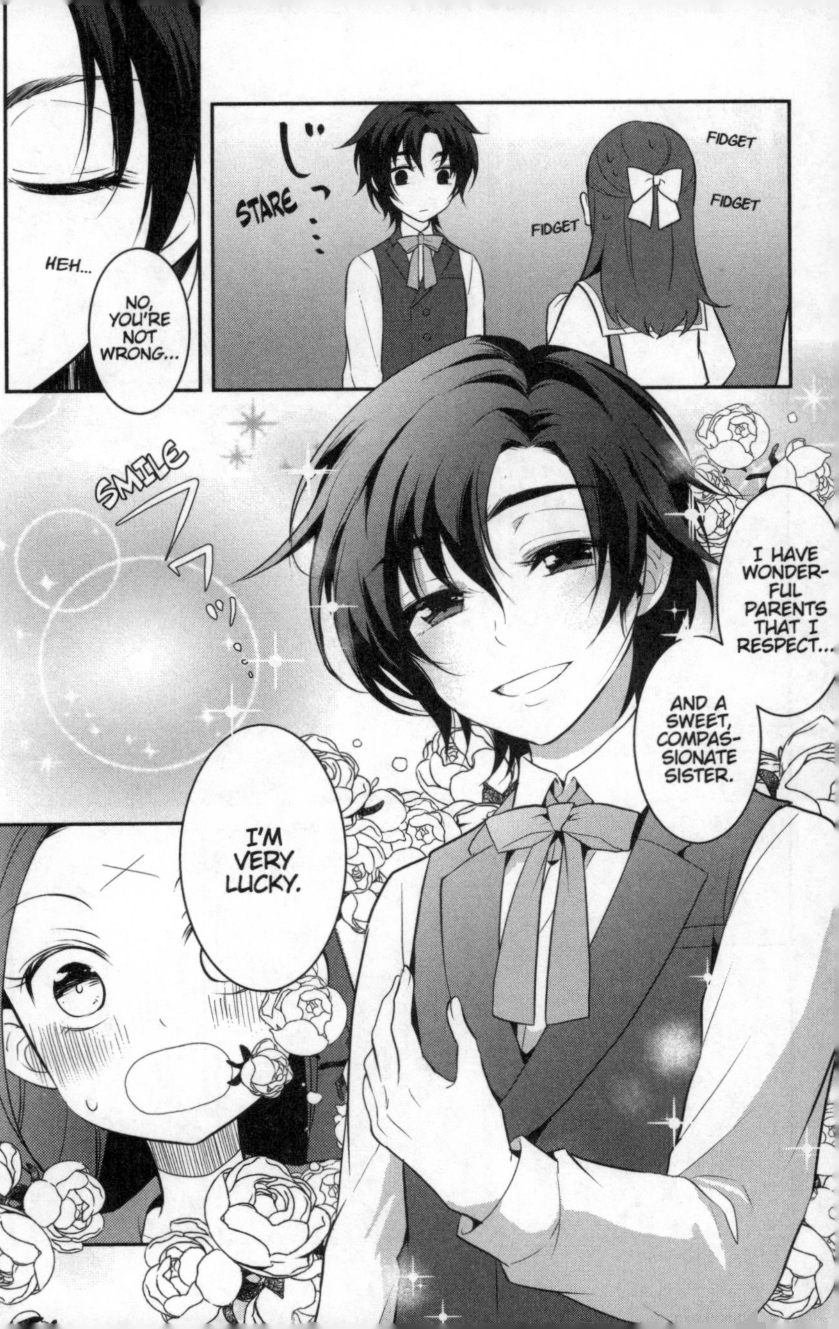
FIDGET
FIDGET
FIDGET
STARE
HEH...
NO, YOU'RE NOT WRONG...
I HAVE WONDER-FUL PARENTS THAT I RESPECT...
AND A SWEET, COMPAS-SIONATE SISTER.
SMILE
I'M VERY LUCKY.

HE'S LIKE SOMEONE FROM A FAIRY TALE...

AHA.

I THOUGHT HE WAS HANDSOME BEFORE.

BUT HIS SMILE IS JUST RADIANT!

A KILLER SMILE ON THE IRRESISTIBLY CHARMING EARL'S FACE FROM THAT NOVEL...

MUST LOOK LIKE THIS.

PANT!

PANT!

TUP

I'M SORRY TO KEEP YOU WAITING, LADY KATARINA.

TMP

TMP

TMP

TUP

LADY KATARINA!

AH!

EEK!

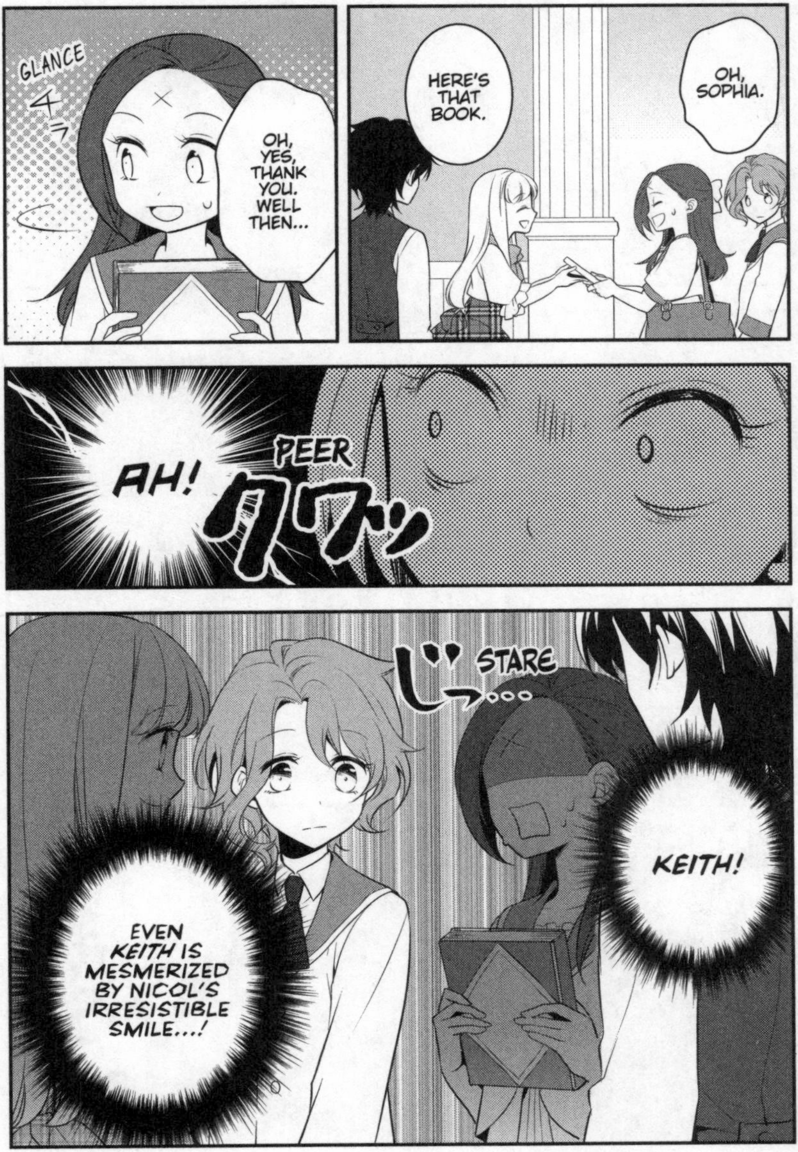
OH, SOPHIA.
HERE'S THAT BOOK.
GLANCE
OH, YES, THANK YOU. WELL THEN...
AH!
PEER
STARE
KEITH!
EVEN KEITH IS MESMERIZED BY NICOL'S IRRESISTIBLE SMILE...!

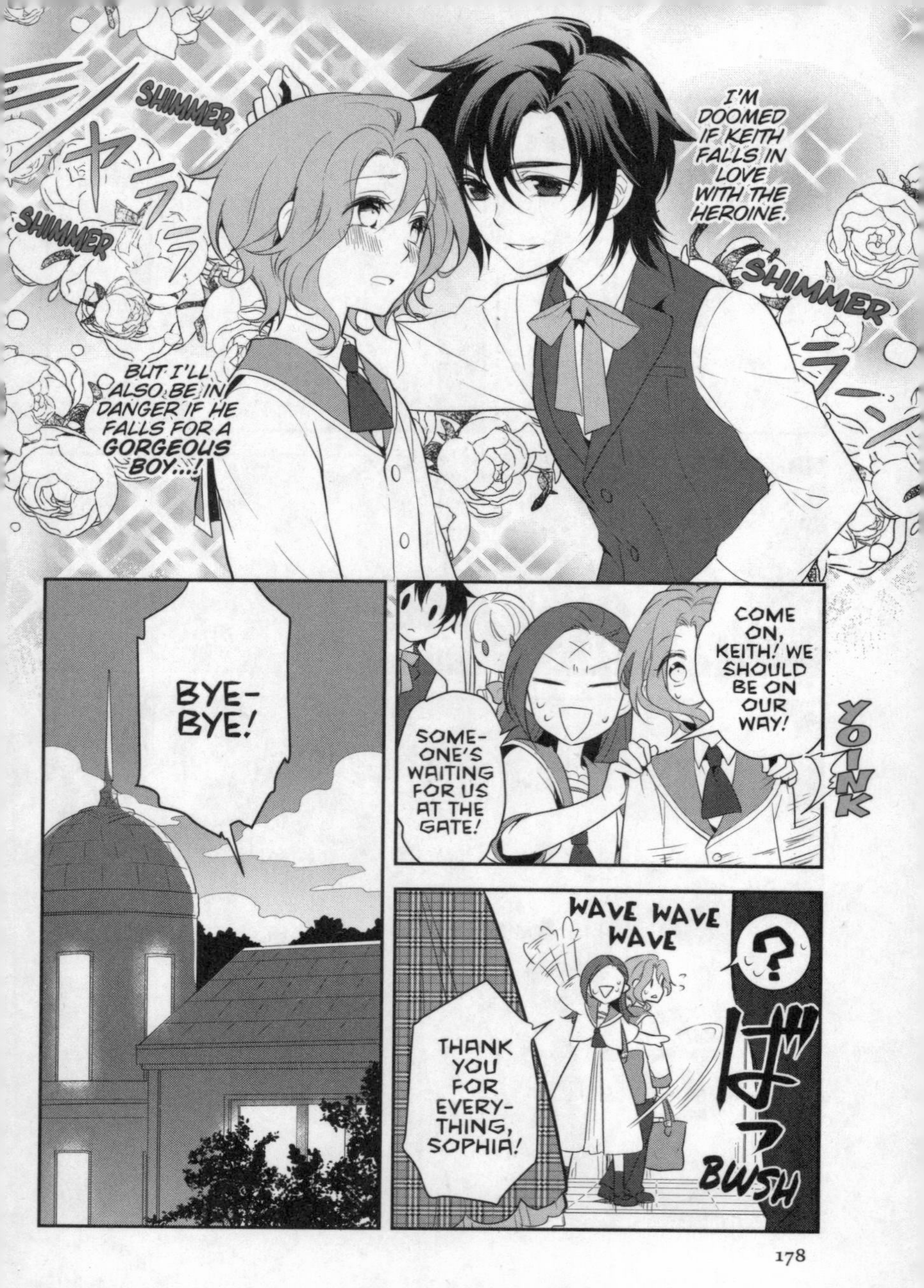
I'M DOOMED IF KEITH FALLS IN LOVE WITH THE HEROINE.
SHIMMER
SHIMMER
SHIMMER
BUT I'LL ALSO BE IN DANGER IF HE FALLS FOR A GORGEOUS BOY...!
COME ON, KEITH! WE SHOULD BE ON OUR WAY!
SOME-ONE'S WAITING FOR US AT THE GATE!
YOINK
WAVE WAVE WAVE
?
THANK YOU FOR EVERY-THING, SOPHIA!
BWSH
BYE-BYE!

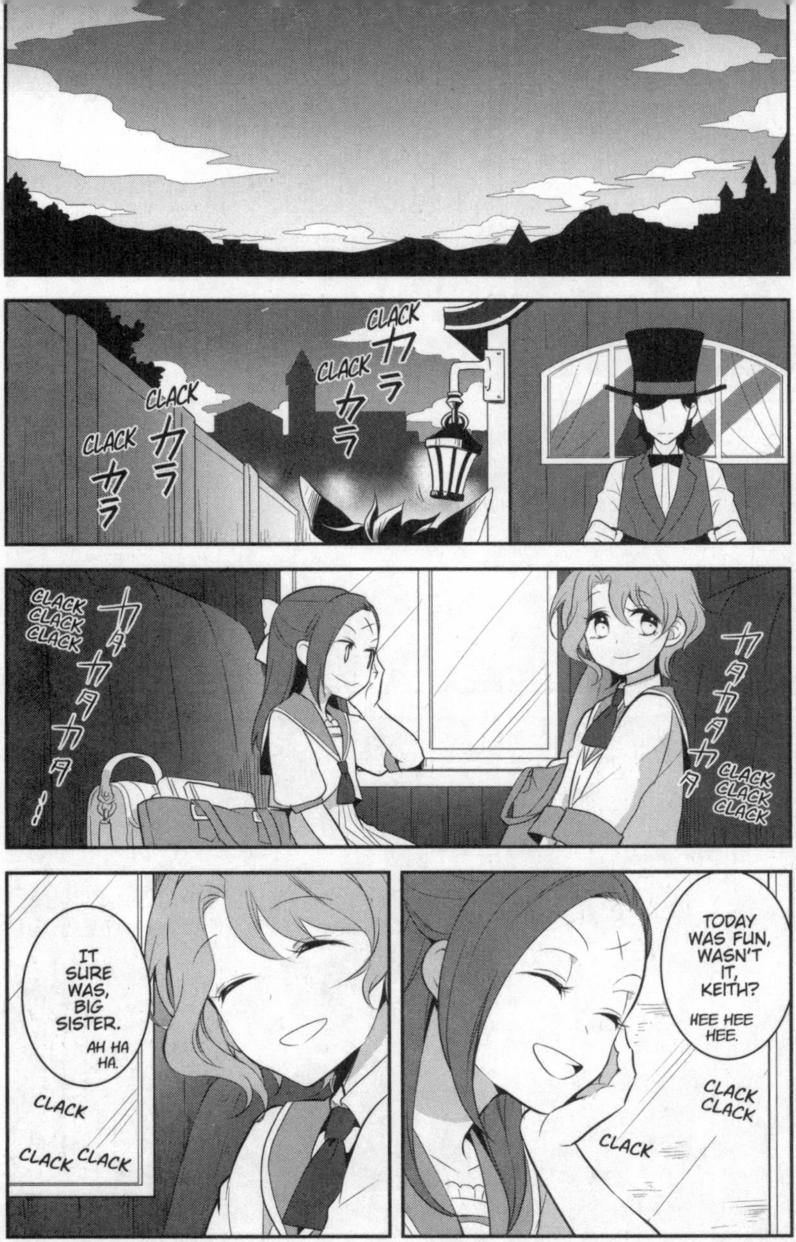
CLACK カラ
CLACK カラ
CLACK カラ
CLACK カラ
CLACK CLACK CLACK カタカタカタ
CLACK CLACK CLACK カタカタカタ…
TODAY WAS FUN, WASN'T IT, KEITH?
HEE HEE HEE.
CLACK CLACK
CLACK
IT SURE WAS, BIG SISTER.
AH HA HA.
CLACK
CLACK CLACK

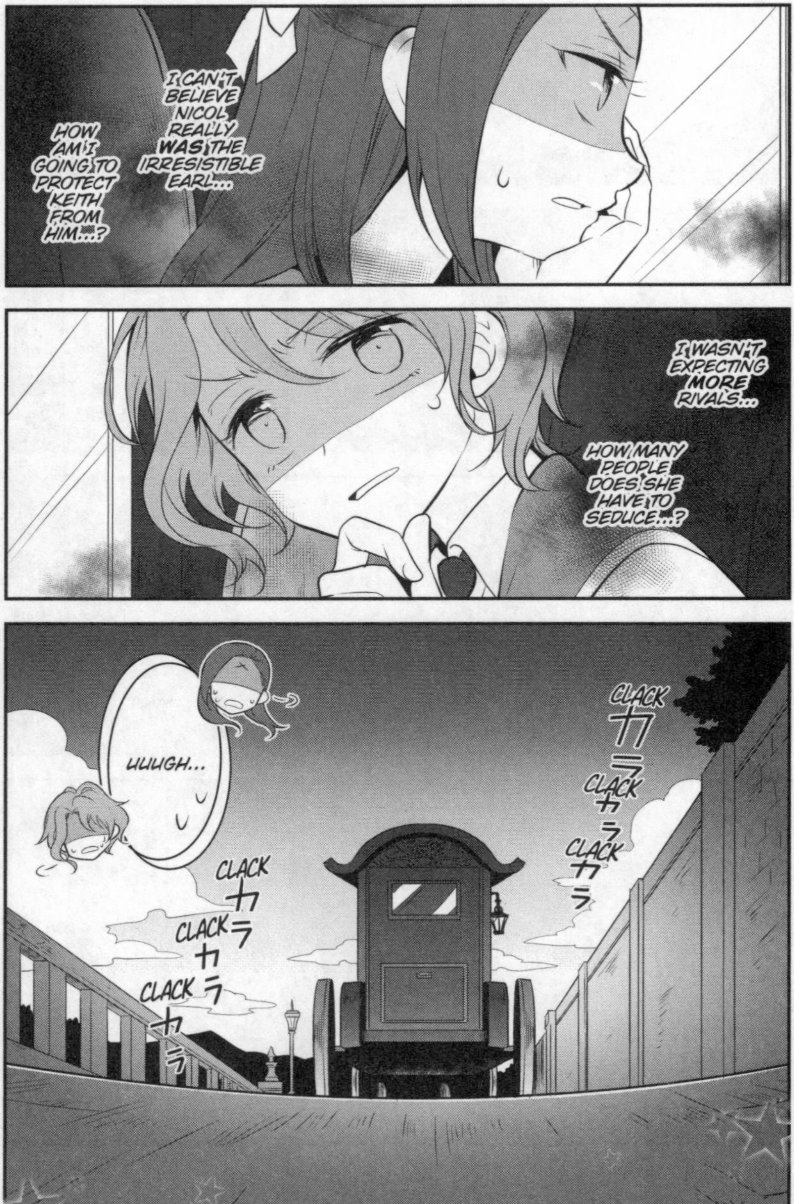
I CAN'T BELIEVE NICOL REALLY WAS THE IRRESISTIBLE EARL...
HOW AM I GOING TO PROTECT KEITH FROM HIM...?
I WASN'T EXPECTING MORE RIVALS...
HOW MANY PEOPLE DOES SHE HAVE TO SEDUCE...?
CLACK カラ
CLACK カラ
CLACK カラ
UUUGH...
CLACK カラ
CLACK カラ
CLACK カラ

Chapter 7

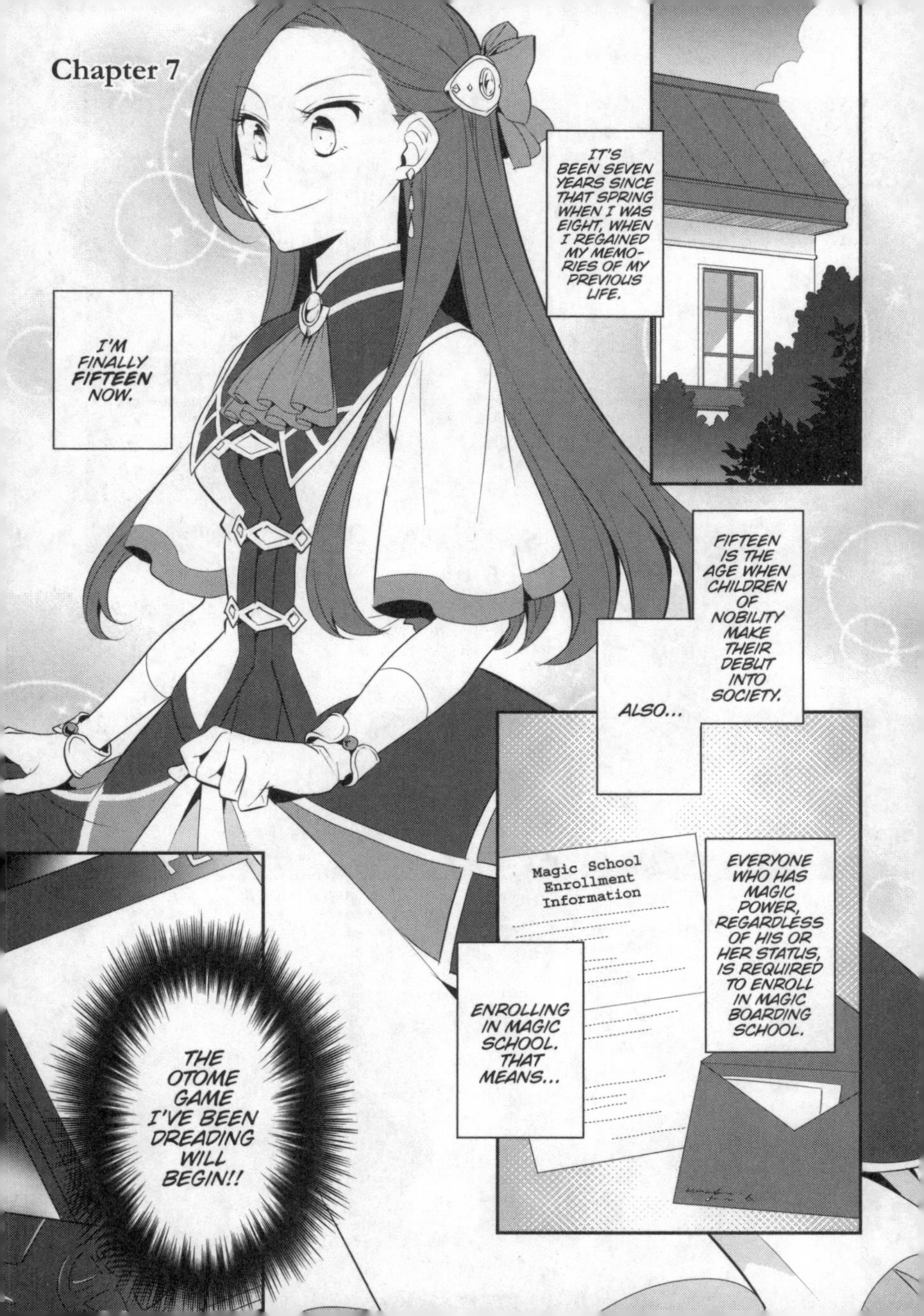
IT'S BEEN SEVEN YEARS SINCE THAT SPRING WHEN I WAS EIGHT, WHEN I REGAINED MY MEMO-RIES OF MY PREVIOUS LIFE.
I'M FINALLY FIFTEEN NOW.
FIFTEEN IS THE AGE WHEN CHILDREN OF NOBILITY MAKE THEIR DEBUT INTO SOCIETY.
ALSO...
EVERYONE WHO HAS MAGIC POWER, REGARDLESS OF HIS OR HER STATUS, IS REQUIRED TO ENROLL IN MAGIC BOARDING SCHOOL.
Magic School Enrollment Information
ENROLLING IN MAGIC SCHOOL. THAT MEANS...
THE OTOME GAME I'VE BEEN DREADING WILL BEGIN!!

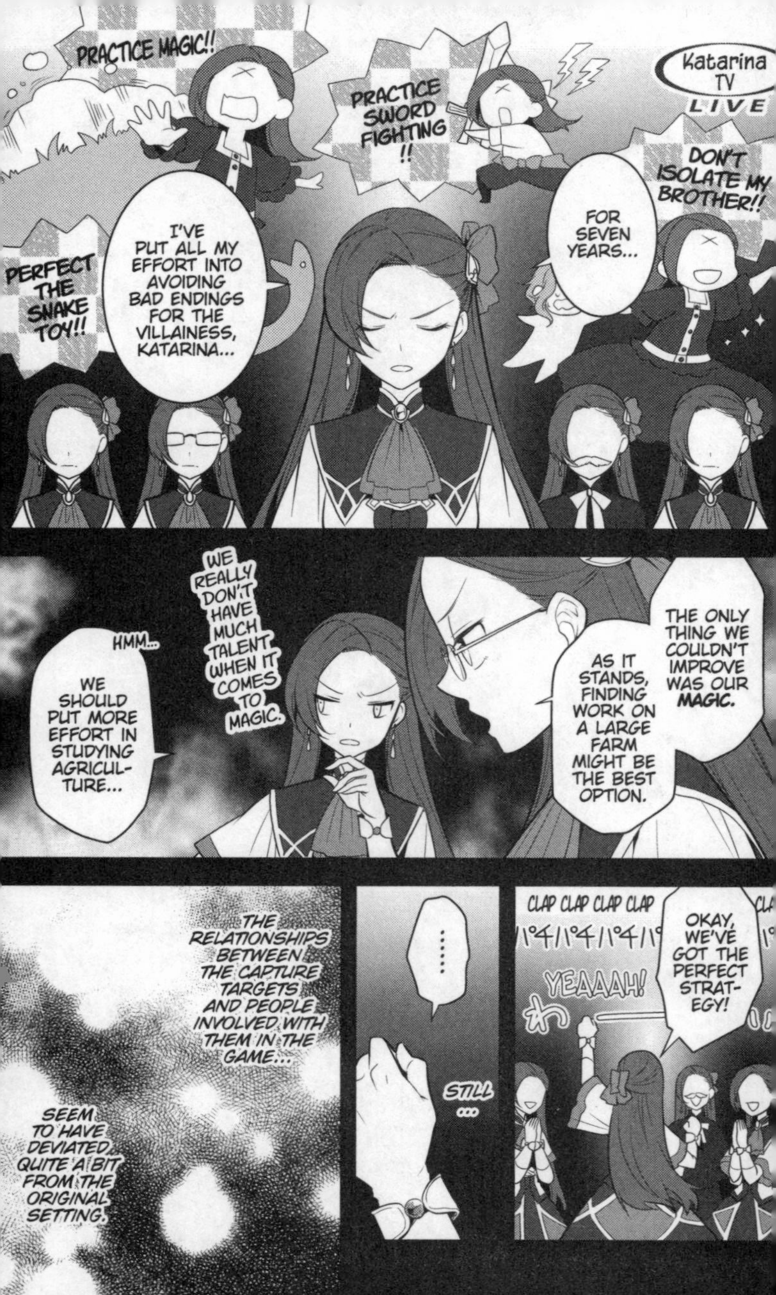
Katarina TV LIVE
DON'T ISOLATE MY BROTHER!!
FOR SEVEN YEARS...
PRACTICE SWORD FIGHTING!!
PRACTICE MAGIC!!
I'VE PUT ALL MY EFFORT INTO AVOIDING BAD ENDINGS FOR THE VILLAINESS, KATARINA...
PERFECT THE SNAKE TOY!!
THE ONLY THING WE COULDN'T IMPROVE WAS OUR **MAGIC.**
AS IT STANDS, FINDING WORK ON A LARGE FARM MIGHT BE THE BEST OPTION.
WE REALLY DON'T HAVE MUCH TALENT WHEN IT COMES TO MAGIC.
HMM...
WE SHOULD PUT MORE EFFORT IN STUDYING AGRICULTURE...
CLAP CLAP CLAP CLAP
OKAY, WE'VE GOT THE PERFECT STRATEGY!
YEAAAH!
......
STILL...
THE RELATIONSHIPS BETWEEN THE CAPTURE TARGETS AND PEOPLE INVOLVED WITH THEM IN THE GAME...
SEEM TO HAVE DEVIATED QUITE A BIT FROM THE ORIGINAL SETTING.

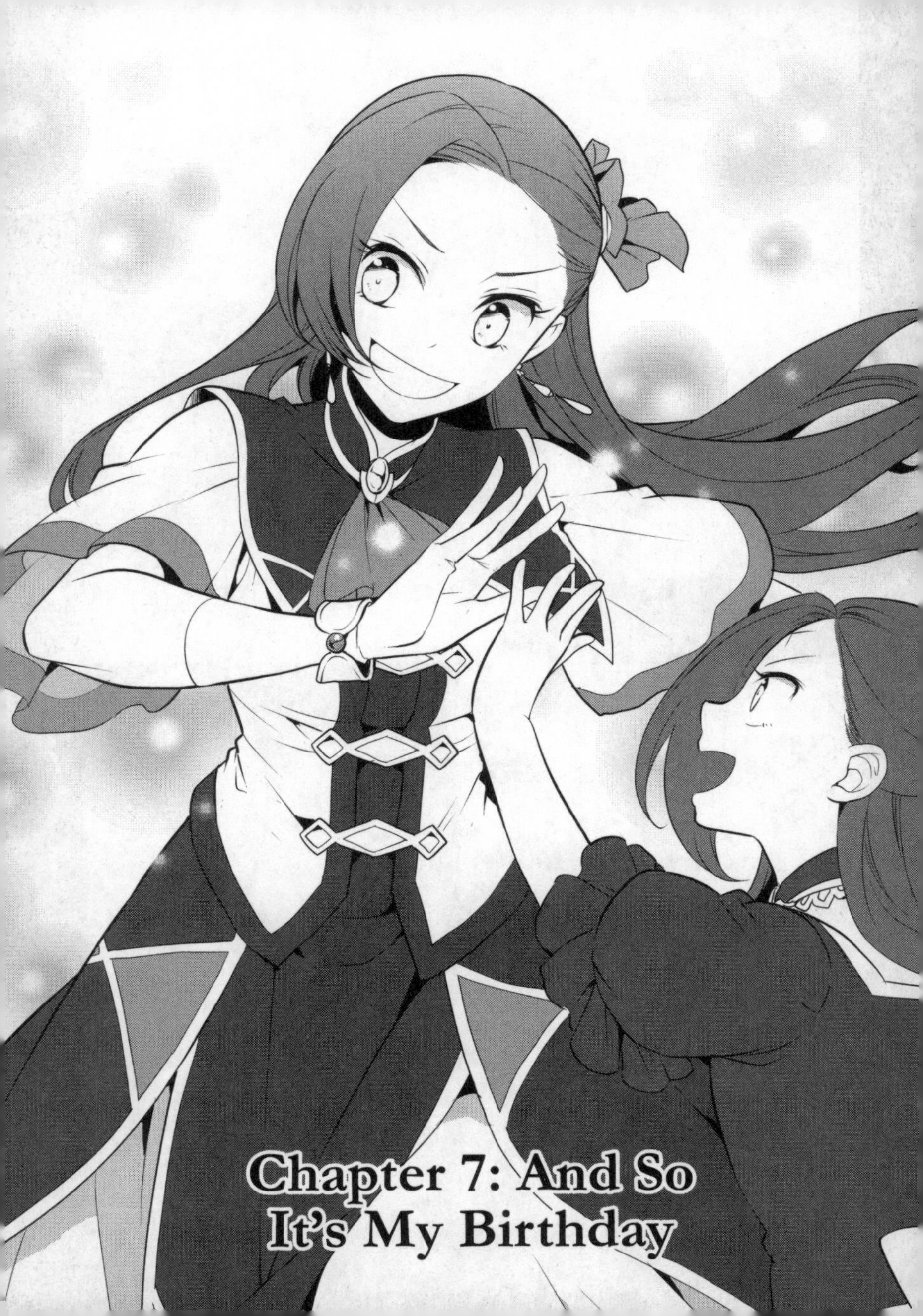

Chapter 7: And So It's My Birthday

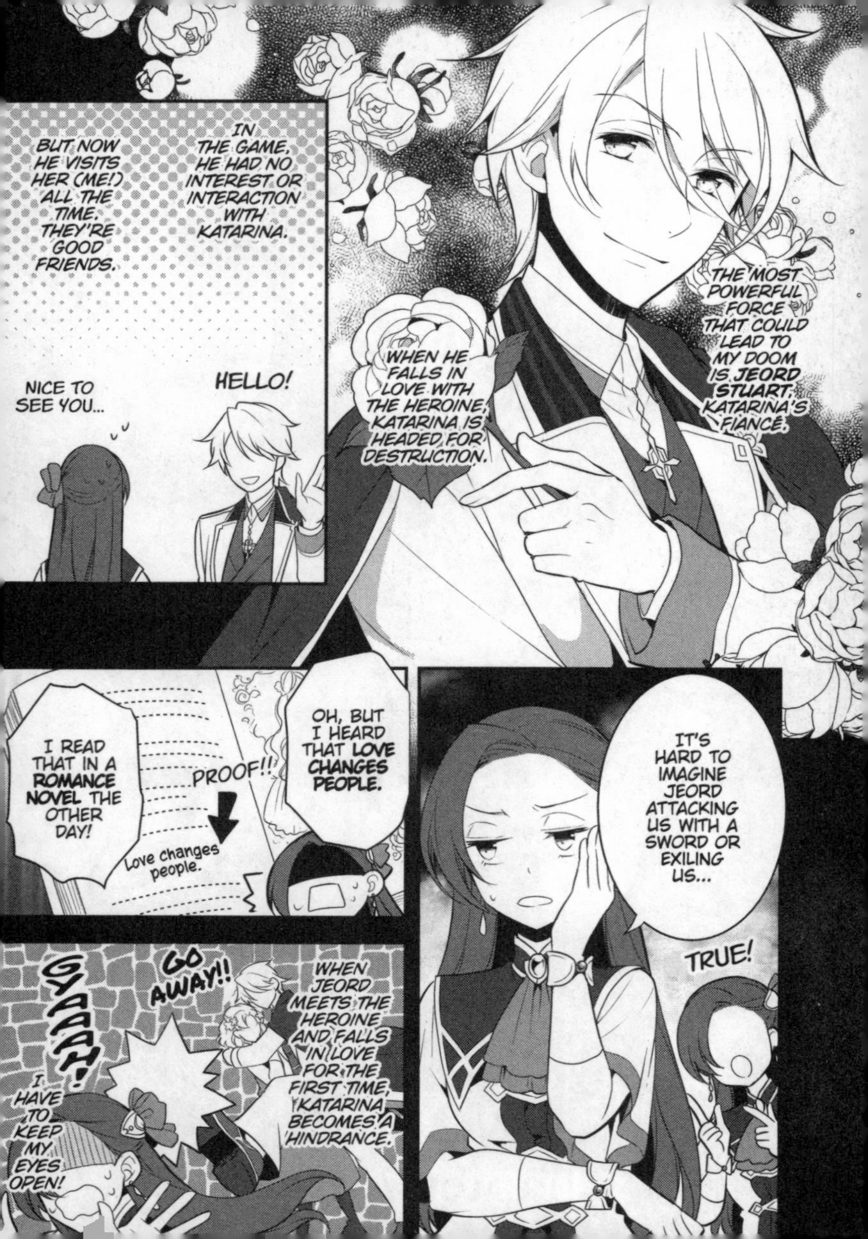
THE MOST POWERFUL FORCE THAT COULD LEAD TO MY DOOM IS JEORD STUART, KATARINA'S FIANCÉ.
WHEN HE FALLS IN LOVE WITH THE HEROINE, KATARINA IS HEADED FOR DESTRUCTION.
IN THE GAME, HE HAD NO INTEREST OR INTERACTION WITH KATARINA.
BUT NOW HE VISITS HER (ME!) ALL THE TIME. THEY'RE GOOD FRIENDS.
HELLO!
NICE TO SEE YOU...
IT'S HARD TO IMAGINE JEORD ATTACKING US WITH A SWORD OR EXILING US...
TRUE!
OH, BUT I HEARD THAT LOVE CHANGES PEOPLE.
I READ THAT IN A ROMANCE NOVEL THE OTHER DAY!
PROOF!!
Love changes people.
WHEN JEORD MEETS THE HEROINE AND FALLS IN LOVE FOR THE FIRST TIME, KATARINA BECOMES A HINDRANCE.
GO AWAY!!
GAAAAH!
I HAVE TO KEEP MY EYES OPEN!

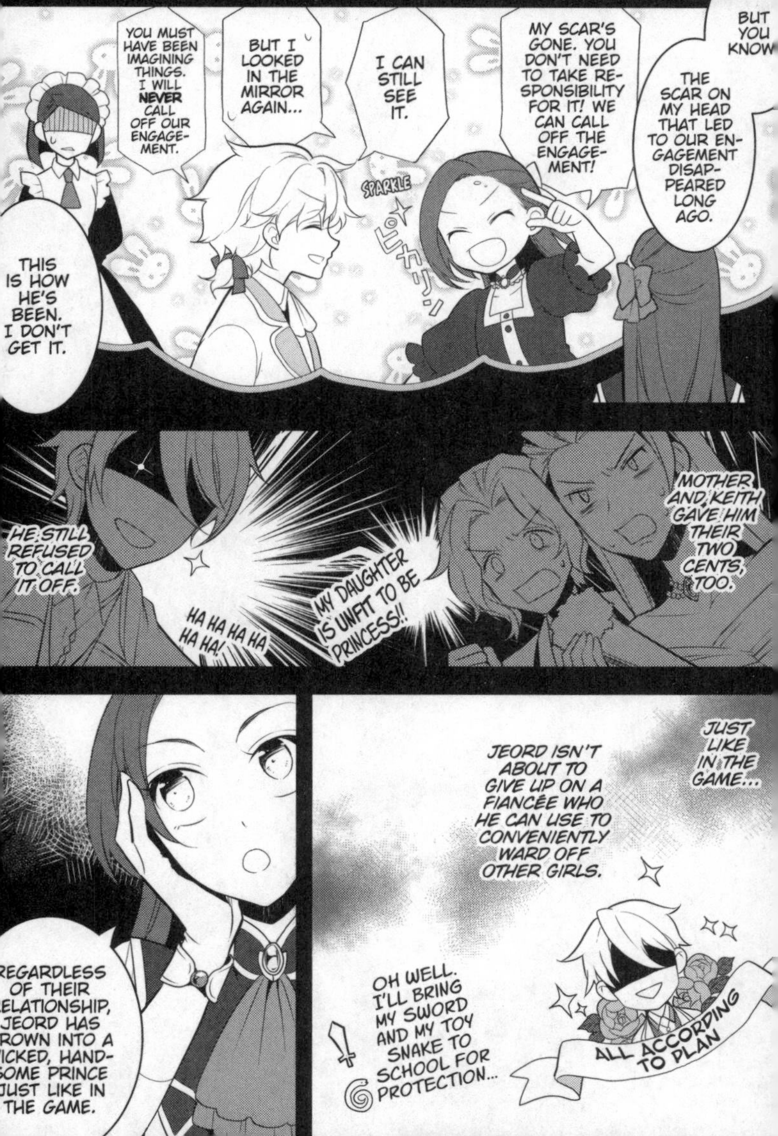
BUT YOU KNOW
THE SCAR ON MY HEAD THAT LED TO OUR ENGAGEMENT DISAPPEARED LONG AGO.
MY SCAR'S GONE. YOU DON'T NEED TO TAKE RESPONSIBILITY FOR IT! WE CAN CALL OFF THE ENGAGEMENT!
SPARKLE
I CAN STILL SEE IT.
BUT I LOOKED IN THE MIRROR AGAIN...
YOU MUST HAVE BEEN IMAGINING THINGS. I WILL NEVER CALL OFF OUR ENGAGEMENT.
THIS IS HOW HE'S BEEN. I DON'T GET IT.
MOTHER AND KEITH GAVE HIM THEIR TWO CENTS, TOO.
MY DAUGHTER IS UNFIT TO BE PRINCESS!!
HA HA HA HA HA HA!
HE STILL REFUSED TO CALL IT OFF.
JUST LIKE IN THE GAME...
JEORD ISN'T ABOUT TO GIVE UP ON A FIANCÉE WHO HE CAN USE TO CONVENIENTLY WARD OFF OTHER GIRLS.
ALL ACCORDING TO PLAN
OH WELL. I'LL BRING MY SWORD AND MY TOY SNAKE TO SCHOOL FOR PROTECTION...
REGARDLESS OF THEIR RELATIONSHIP, JEORD HAS ROWN INTO A ICKED, HANDSOME PRINCE JUST LIKE IN THE GAME.

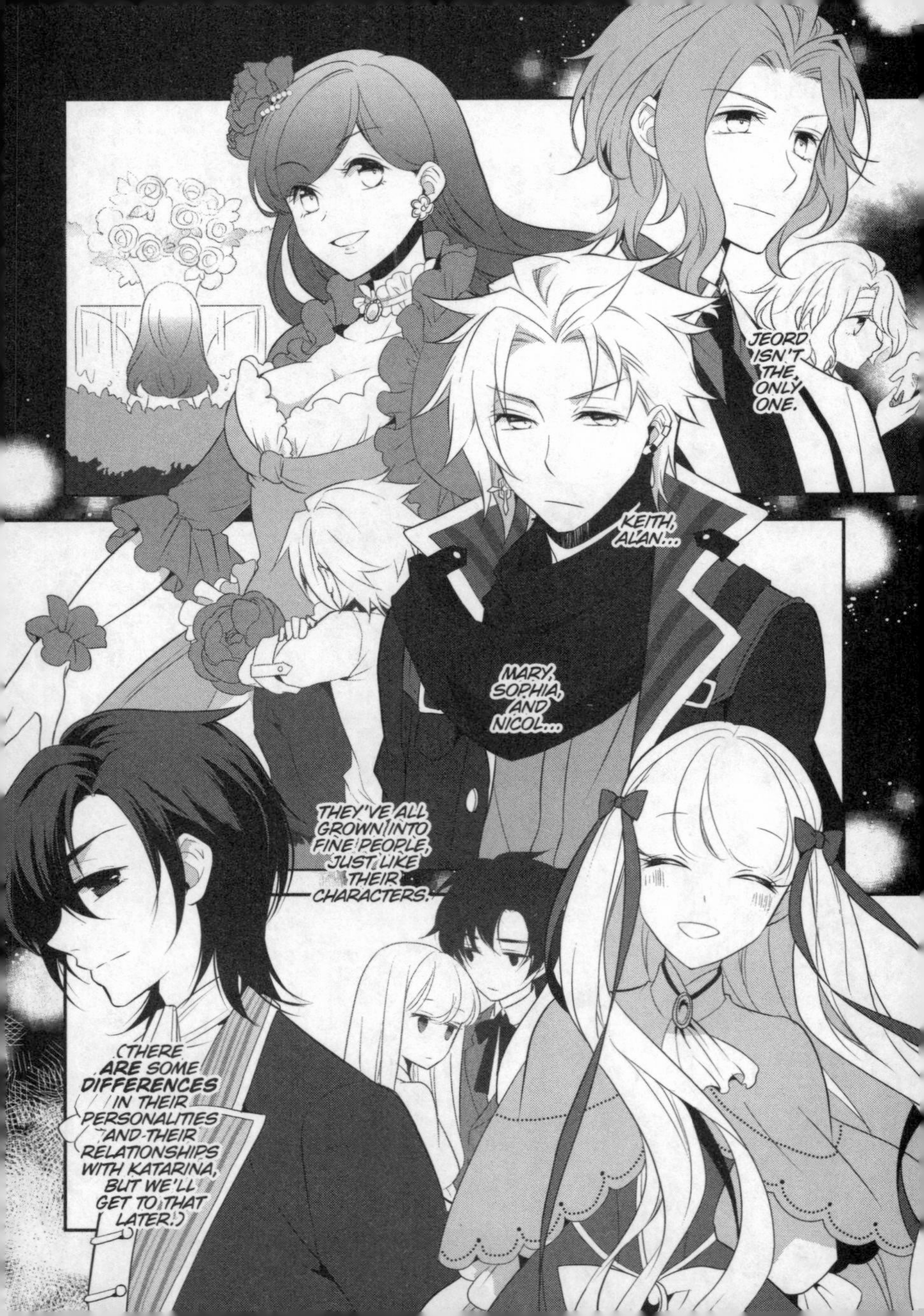
JEORD ISN'T THE ONLY ONE.
KEITH, ALAN...
MARY, SOPHIA, AND NICOL...
THEY'VE ALL GROWN INTO FINE PEOPLE, JUST LIKE THEIR CHARACTERS.
(THERE ARE SOME DIFFERENCES IN THEIR PERSONALITIES AND THEIR RELATIONSHIPS WITH KATARINA, BUT WE'LL GET TO THAT LATER.)

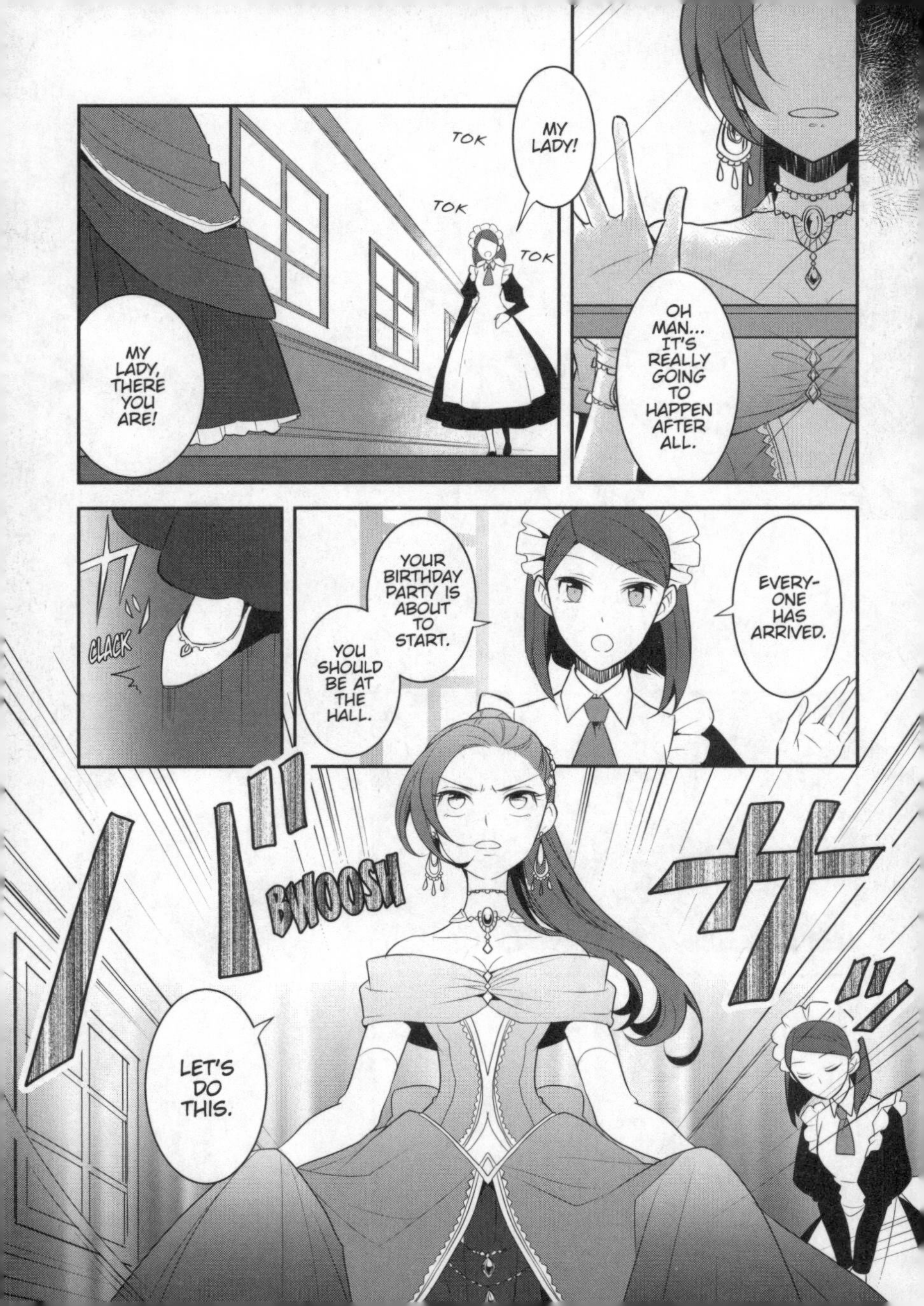
OH MAN... IT'S REALLY GOING TO HAPPEN AFTER ALL.
MY LADY!
TOK
TOK
TOK
MY LADY, THERE YOU ARE!
EVERY-ONE HAS ARRIVED.
YOUR BIRTHDAY PARTY IS ABOUT TO START.
YOU SHOULD BE AT THE HALL.
CLACK
BWOOSH
LET'S DO THIS.

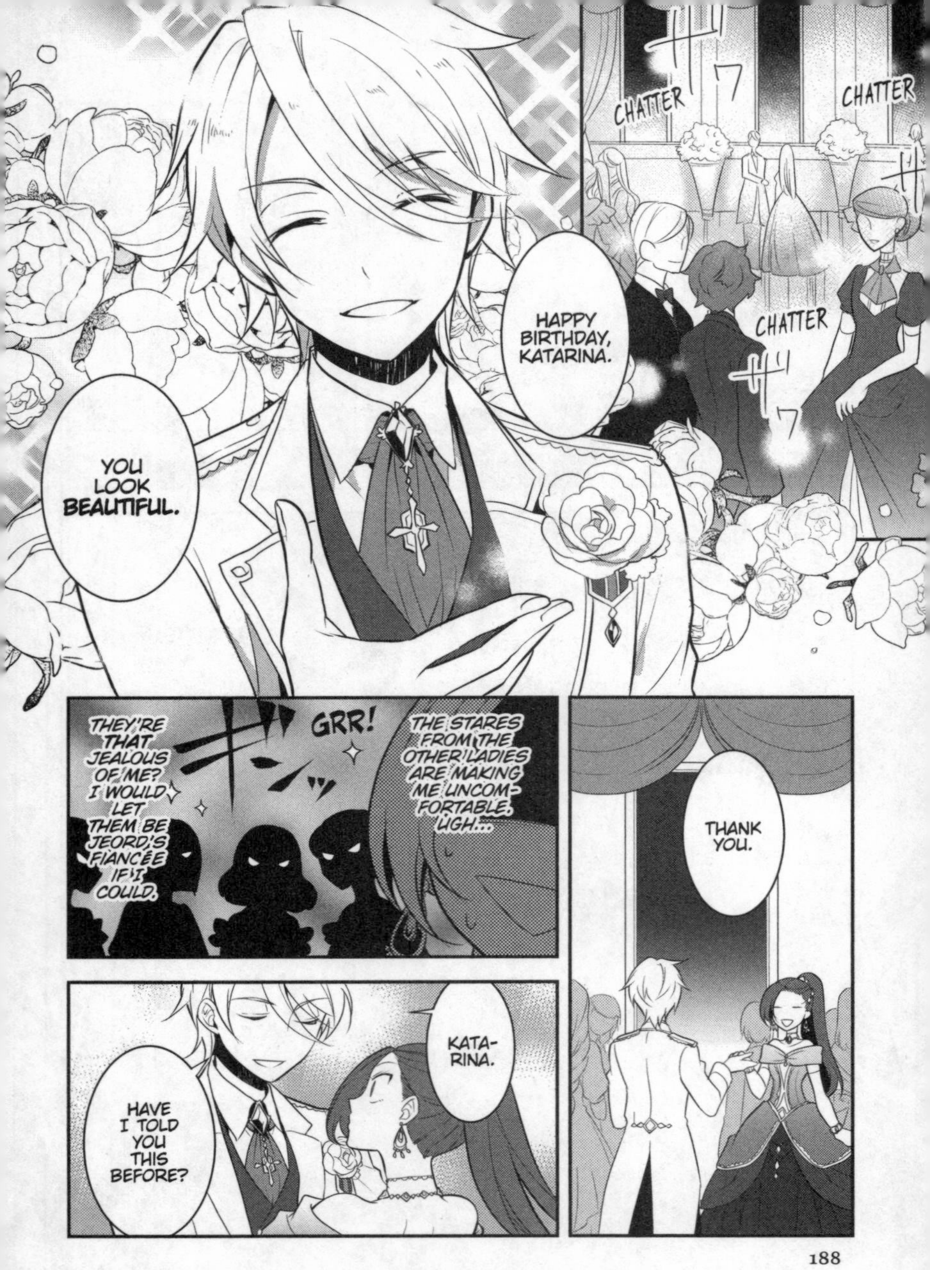
CHATTER
CHATTER
CHATTER
HAPPY BIRTHDAY, KATARINA.
YOU LOOK BEAUTIFUL.
THANK YOU.
THE STARES FROM THE OTHER LADIES ARE MAKING ME UNCOMFORTABLE. UGH...
GRR!
THEY'RE THAT JEALOUS OF ME? I WOULD LET THEM BE JEORD'S FIANCÉE IF I COULD.
KATARINA.
HAVE I TOLD YOU THIS BEFORE?

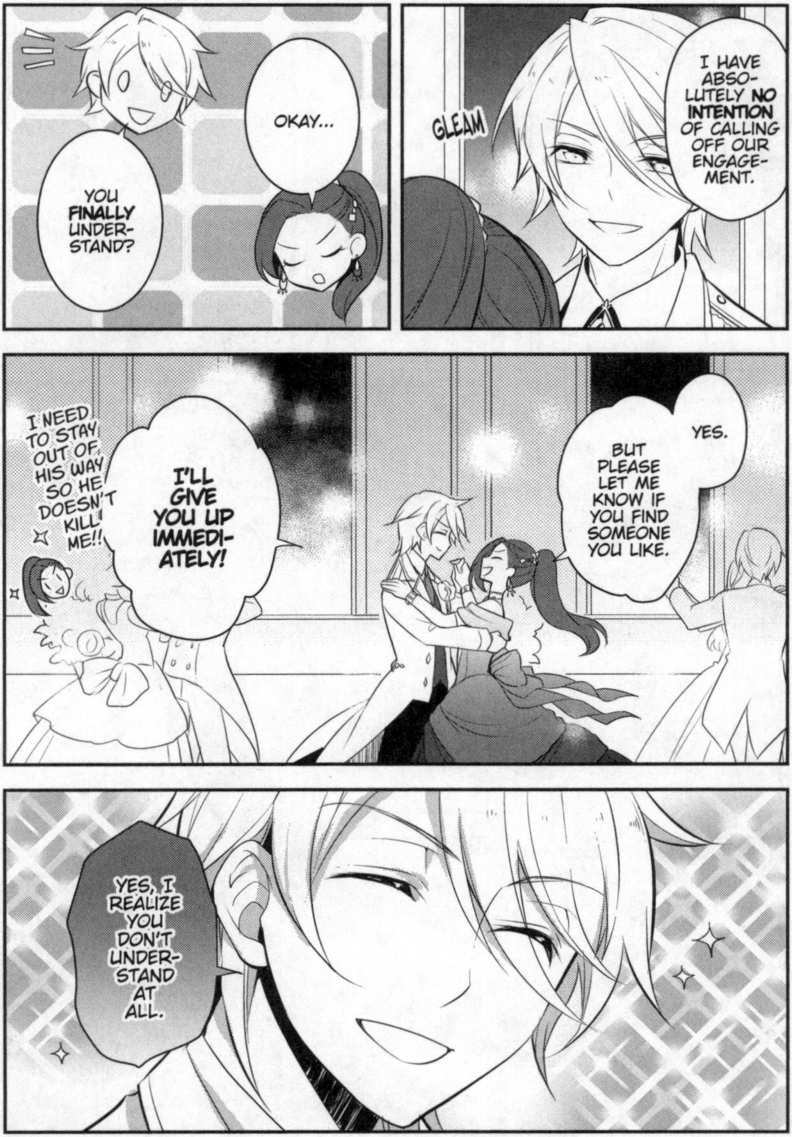
GLEAM
I HAVE ABSOLUTELY NO INTENTION OF CALLING OFF OUR ENGAGEMENT.
OKAY...
YOU FINALLY UNDERSTAND?
YES.
BUT PLEASE LET ME KNOW IF YOU FIND SOMEONE YOU LIKE.
I'LL GIVE YOU UP IMMEDIATELY!
I NEED TO STAY OUT OF HIS WAY SO HE DOESN'T KILL ME!!
YES, I REALIZE YOU DON'T UNDERSTAND AT ALL.

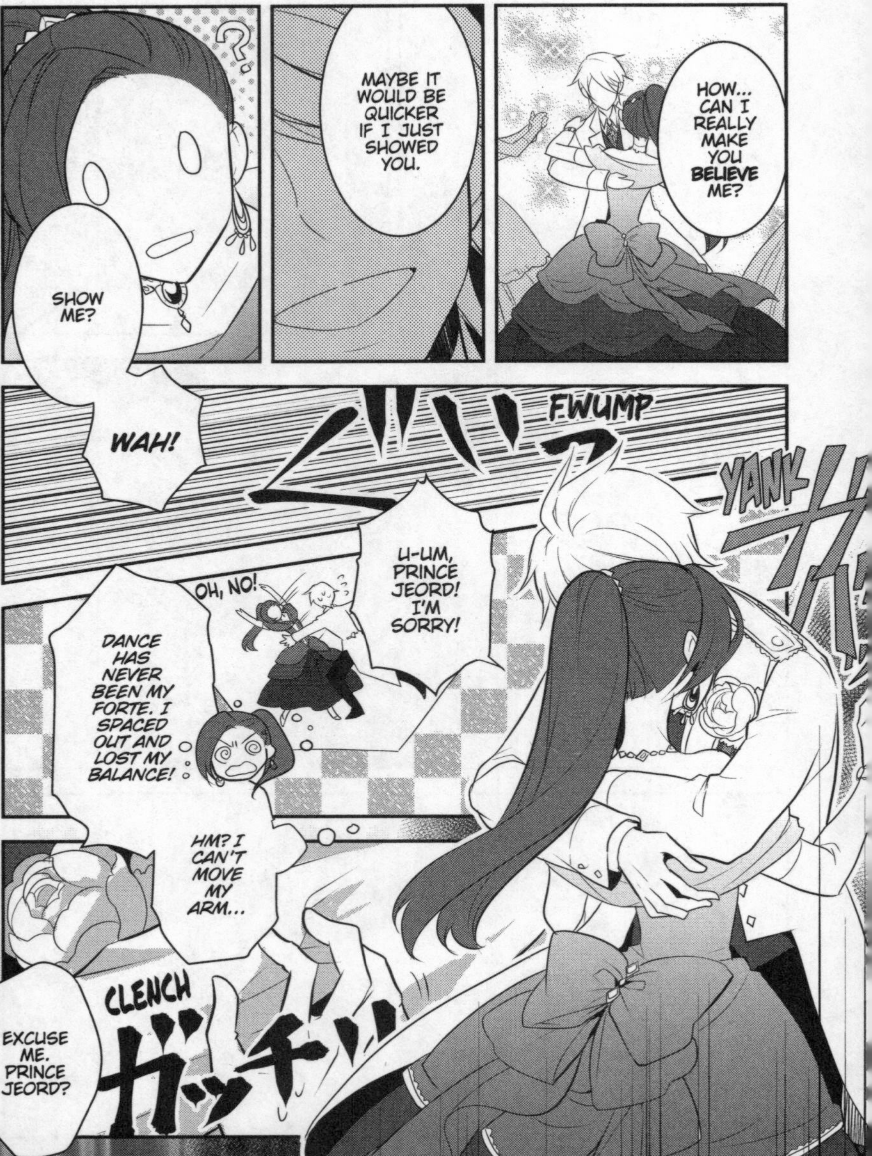
HOW... CAN I REALLY MAKE YOU **BELIEVE** ME?
MAYBE IT WOULD BE QUICKER IF I JUST SHOWED YOU.
SHOW ME?
FWUMP
WAH!
YANK
U-UM, PRINCE JEORD! I'M SORRY!
OH, NO!
DANCE HAS NEVER BEEN MY FORTE. I SPACED OUT AND LOST MY BALANCE!
HM? I CAN'T MOVE MY ARM...
CLENCH
ガッチ
EXCUSE ME. PRINCE JEORD?

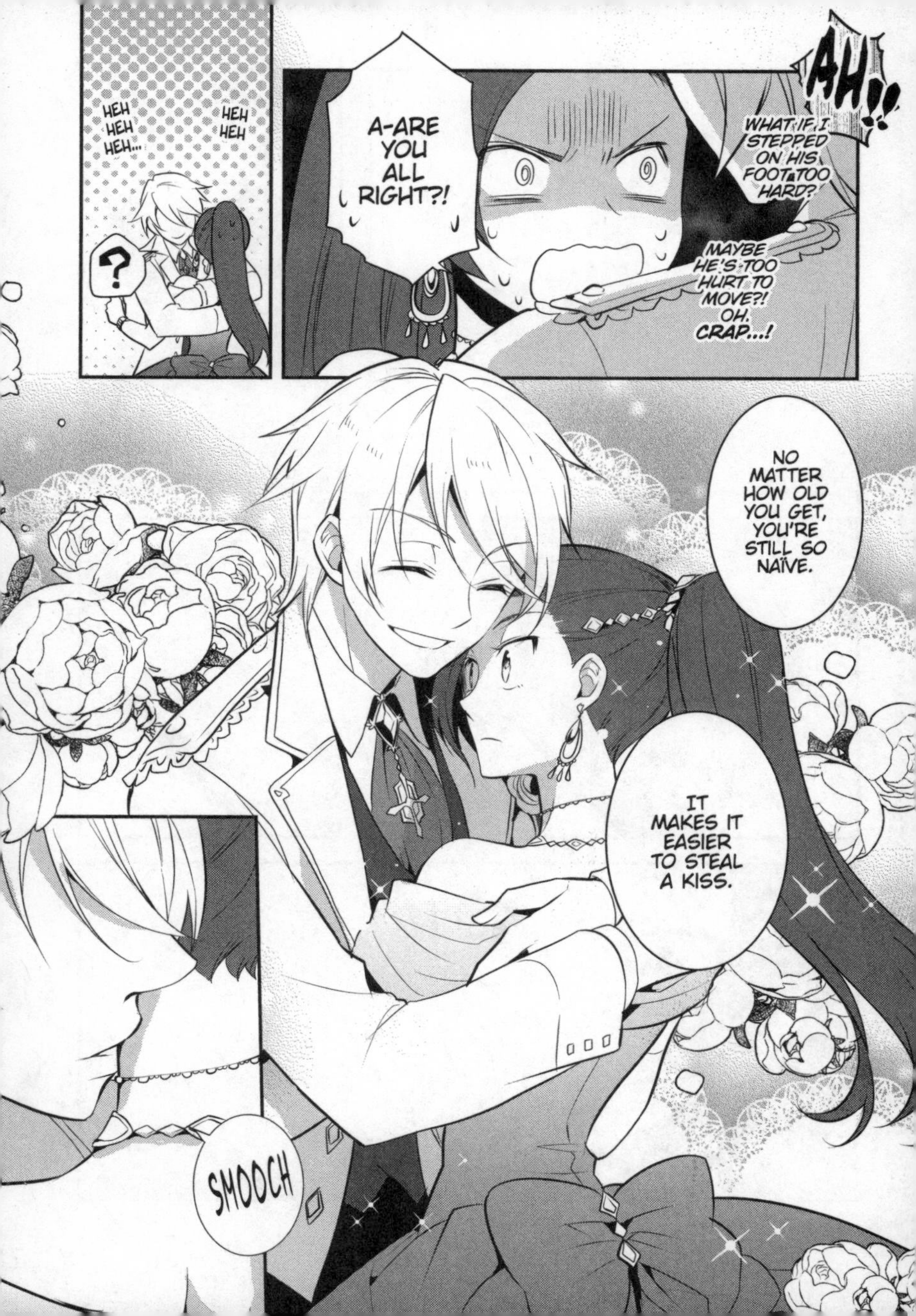
AH!!
WHAT IF I STEPPED ON HIS FOOT TOO HARD?
MAYBE HE'S TOO HURT TO MOVE?! OH. CRAP...!
A-ARE YOU ALL RIGHT?!
HEH HEH
HEH HEH HEH...
?
NO MATTER HOW OLD YOU GET, YOU'RE STILL SO NAÏVE.
IT MAKES IT EASIER TO STEAL A KISS.
SMOOCH

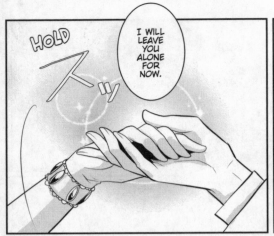

HOLD
ズッ

I WILL LEAVE YOU ALONE FOR NOW.

BWSH

KISS ♡

BECAUSE SOMEDAY I'LL HAVE ALL OF YOU.

?

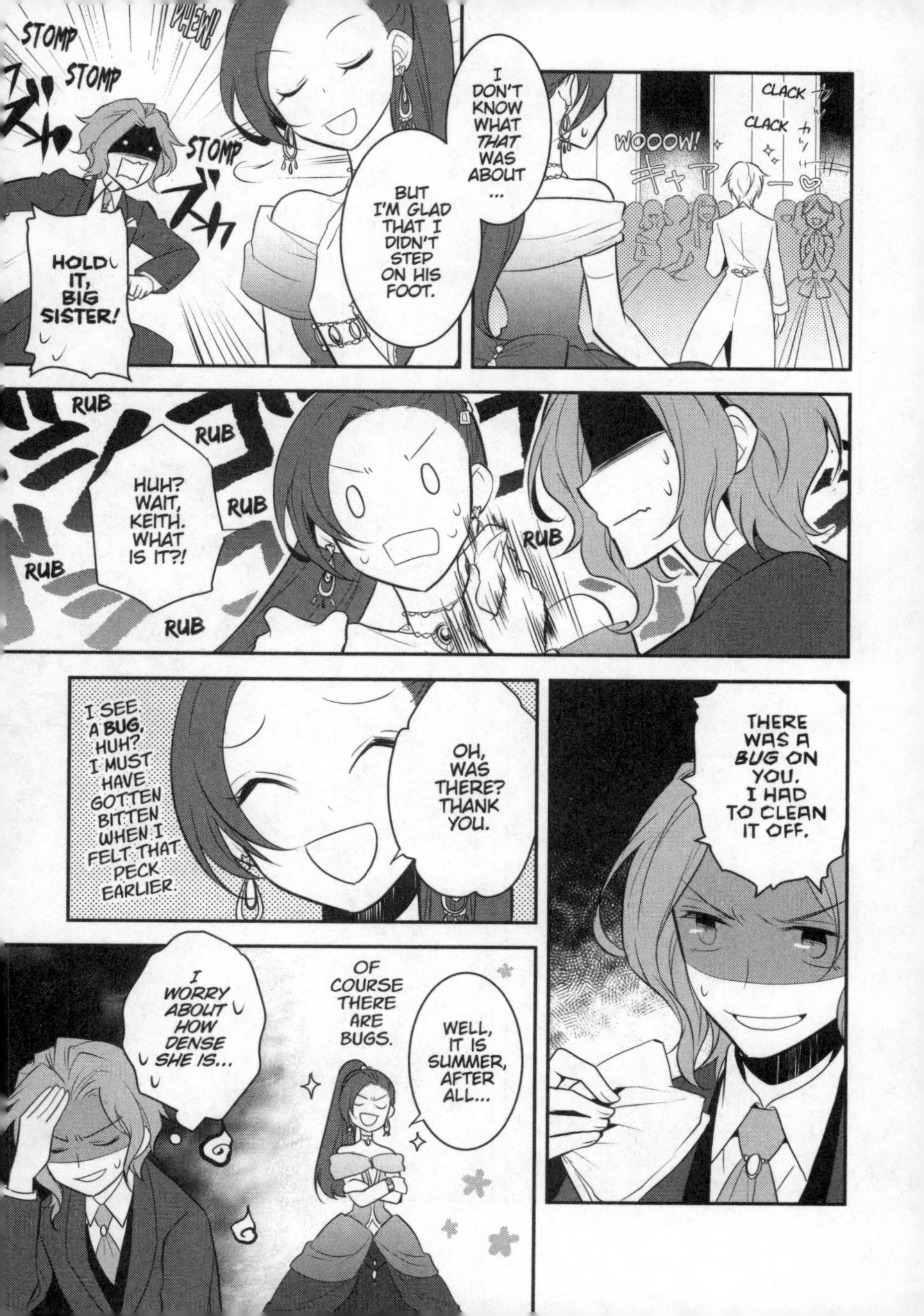
CLACK
CLACK
WOOOW!
キャアー
I DON'T KNOW WHAT THAT WAS ABOUT...
BUT I'M GLAD THAT I DIDN'T STEP ON HIS FOOT.
WHEW!
STOMP
STOMP
STOMP
HOLD IT, BIG SISTER!
RUB
RUB
RUB
RUB
RUB
RUB
HUH? WAIT, KEITH. WHAT IS IT?!
THERE WAS A BUG ON YOU. I HAD TO CLEAN IT OFF.
OH, WAS THERE? THANK YOU.
I SEE. A BUG, HUH? I MUST HAVE GOTTEN BITTEN WHEN I FELT THAT PECK EARLIER.
WELL, IT IS SUMMER, AFTER ALL...
OF COURSE THERE ARE BUGS.
I WORRY ABOUT HOW DENSE SHE IS...

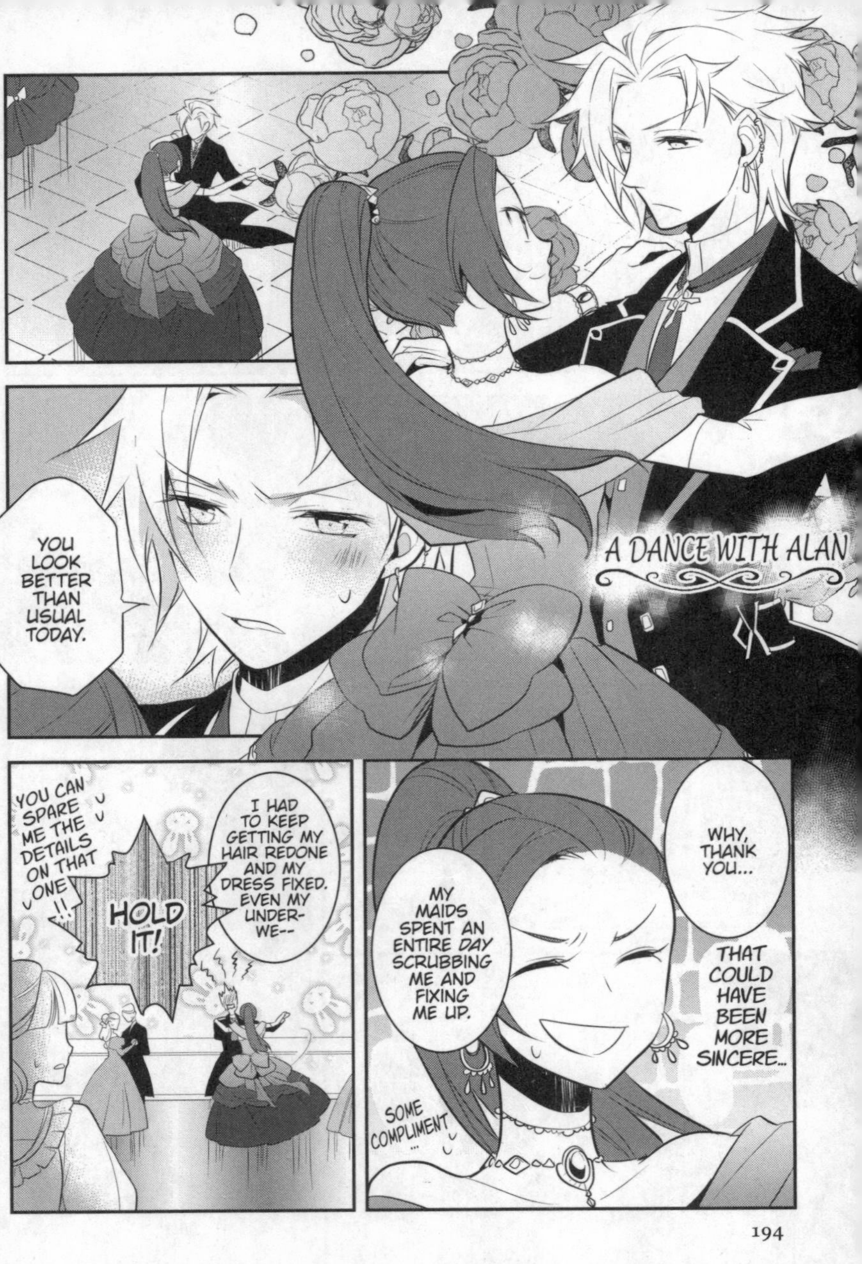
A DANCE WITH ALAN
YOU LOOK BETTER THAN USUAL TODAY.
WHY, THANK YOU...
THAT COULD HAVE BEEN MORE SINCERE...
MY MAIDS SPENT AN ENTIRE *DAY* SCRUBBING ME AND FIXING ME UP.
SOME COMPLIMENT...
I HAD TO KEEP GETTING MY HAIR REDONE AND MY DRESS FIXED. EVEN MY UNDER-WE--
HOLD IT!
YOU CAN SPARE ME THE DETAILS ON THAT ONE!!

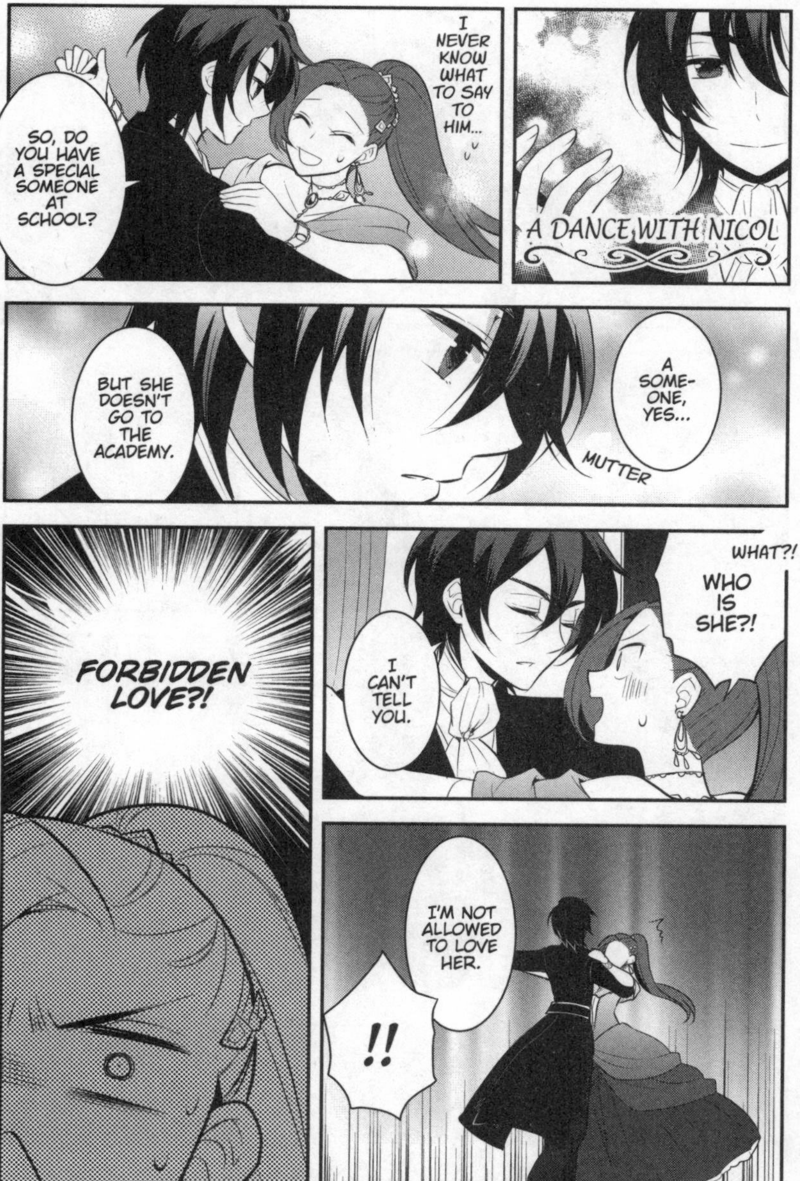
A DANCE WITH NICOL
I NEVER KNOW WHAT TO SAY TO HIM...
SO, DO YOU HAVE A SPECIAL SOMEONE AT SCHOOL?
A SOME-ONE, YES...
MUTTER
BUT SHE DOESN'T GO TO THE ACADEMY.
WHAT?!
WHO IS SHE?!
I CAN'T TELL YOU.
I'M NOT ALLOWED TO LOVE HER.
!!
FORBIDDEN LOVE?!

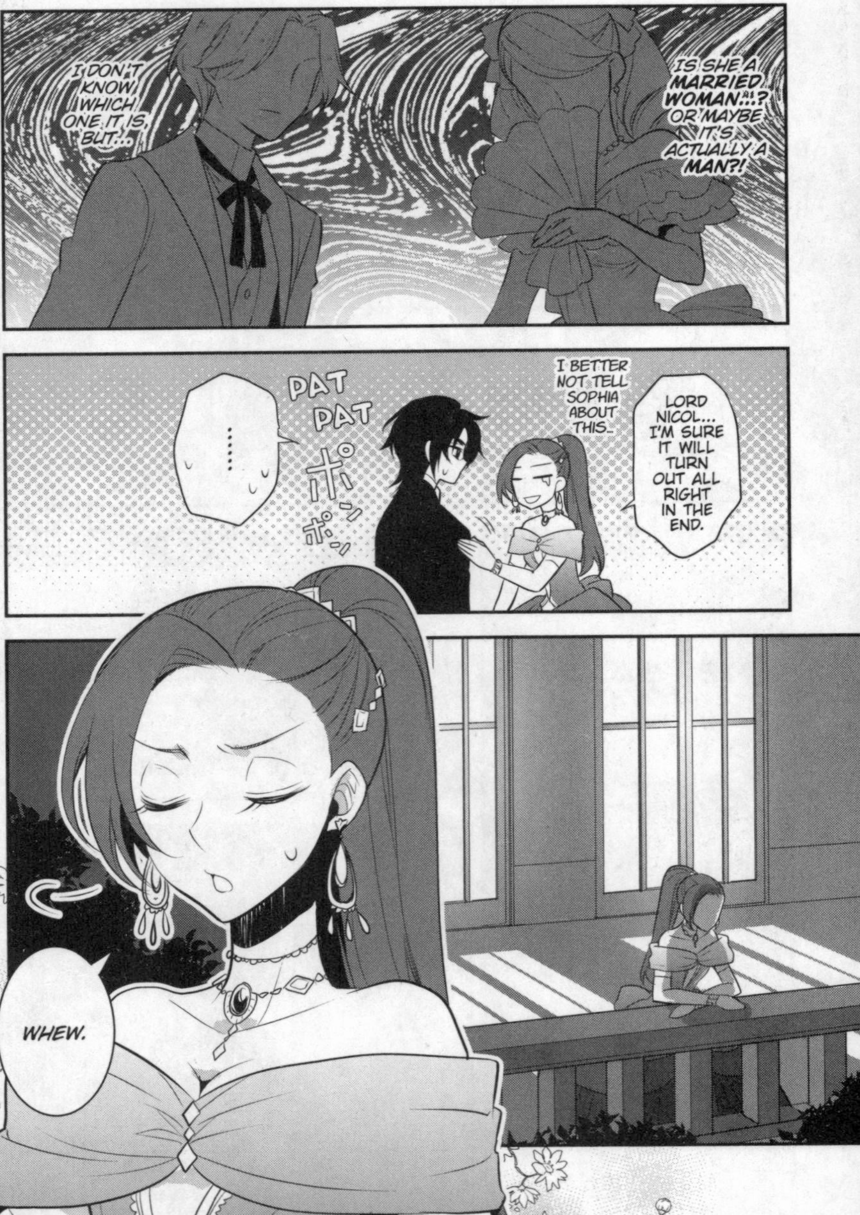
IS SHE A MARRIED WOMAN...? OR MAYBE IT'S ACTUALLY A MAN?!
I DON'T KNOW WHICH ONE IT IS, BUT...
LORD NICOL... I'M SURE IT WILL TURN OUT ALL RIGHT IN THE END.
I BETTER NOT TELL SOPHIA ABOUT THIS...
PAT PAT
......
WHEW.

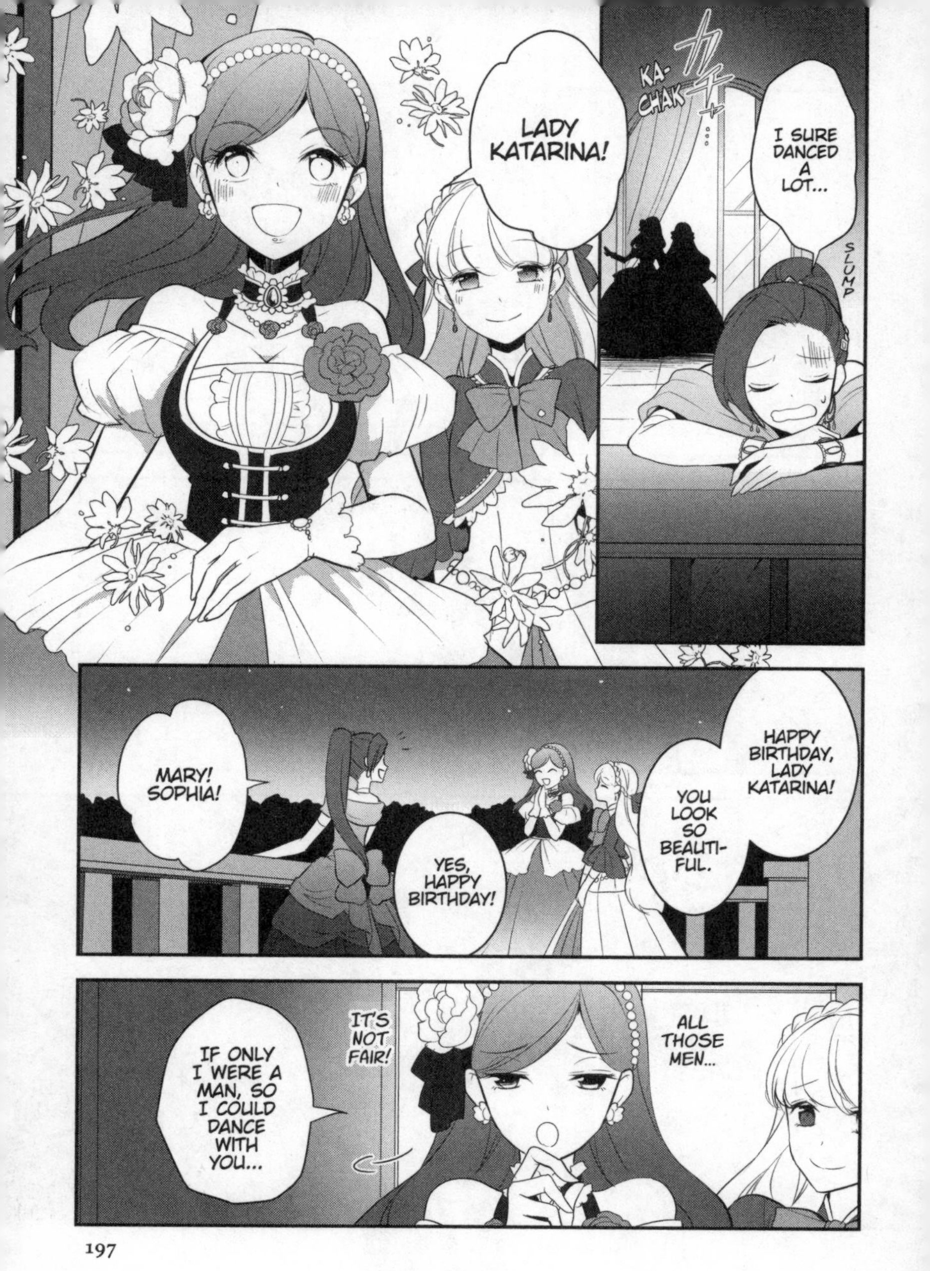
KA-CHAK
カチャ
I SURE DANCED A LOT...
SLUMP
LADY KATARINA!
HAPPY BIRTHDAY, LADY KATARINA!
YOU LOOK SO BEAUTI-FUL.
YES, HAPPY BIRTHDAY!
MARY! SOPHIA!
ALL THOSE MEN...
IT'S NOT FAIR!
IF ONLY I WERE A MAN, SO I COULD DANCE WITH YOU...

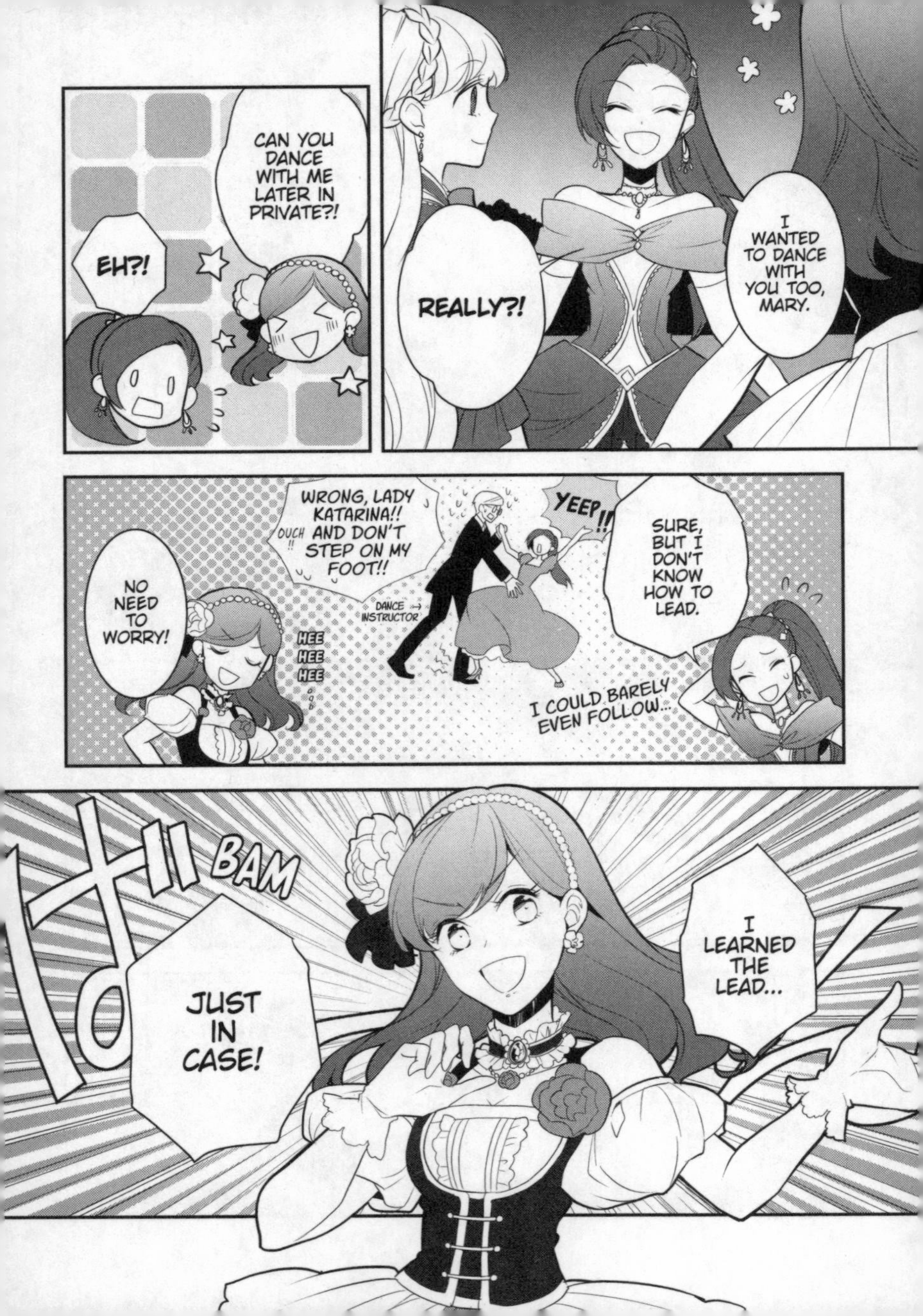
I WANTED TO DANCE WITH YOU TOO, MARY.
REALLY?!
CAN YOU DANCE WITH ME LATER IN PRIVATE?!
EH?!
SURE, BUT I DON'T KNOW HOW TO LEAD.
I COULD BARELY EVEN FOLLOW...
YEEP!!
WRONG, LADY KATARINA!! AND DON'T STEP ON MY FOOT!!
OUCH!!
DANCE INSTRUCTOR
HEE HEE HEE
NO NEED TO WORRY!
I LEARNED THE LEAD...
BAM
JUST IN CASE!

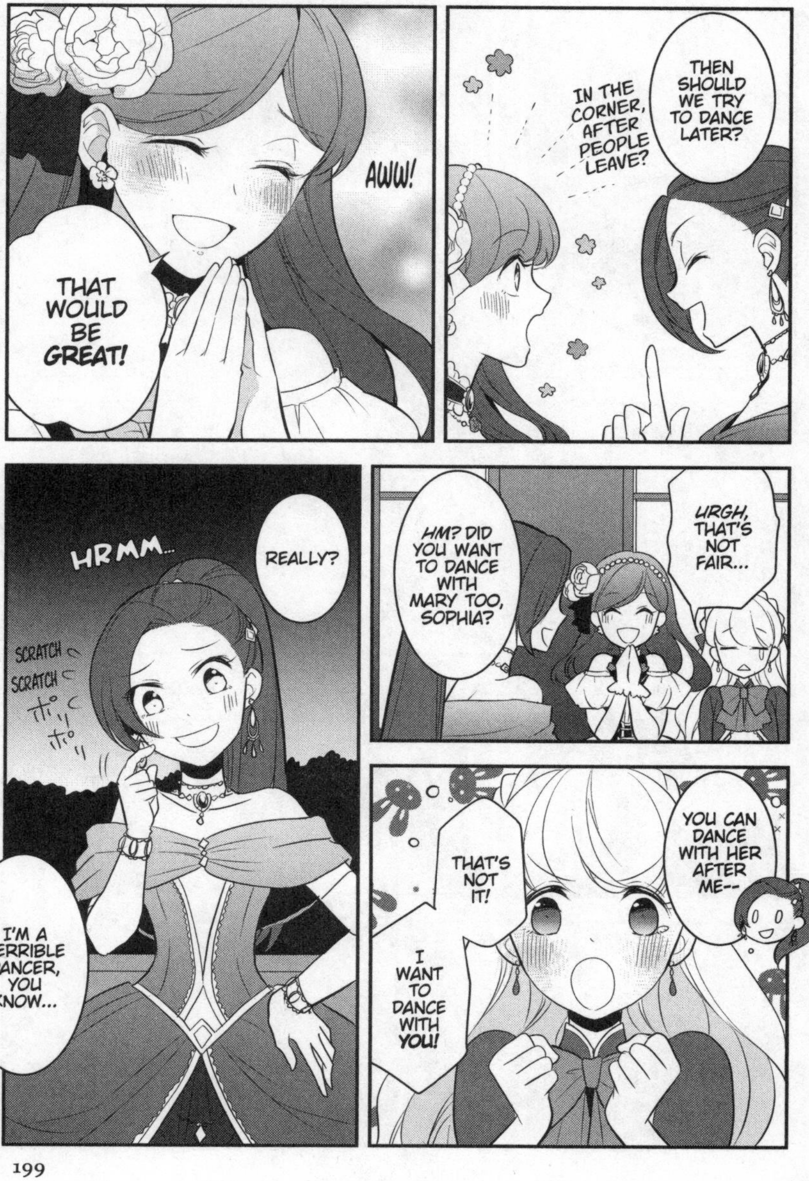
THEN SHOULD WE TRY TO DANCE LATER?
IN THE CORNER, AFTER PEOPLE LEAVE?
AWW!
THAT WOULD BE GREAT!
URGH, THAT'S NOT FAIR...
HM? DID YOU WANT TO DANCE WITH MARY TOO, SOPHIA?
YOU CAN DANCE WITH HER AFTER ME--
THAT'S NOT IT!
I WANT TO DANCE WITH YOU!
REALLY?
HRMM...
SCRATCH
SCRATCH
ポリポリ
I'M A TERRIBLE DANCER, YOU KNOW...

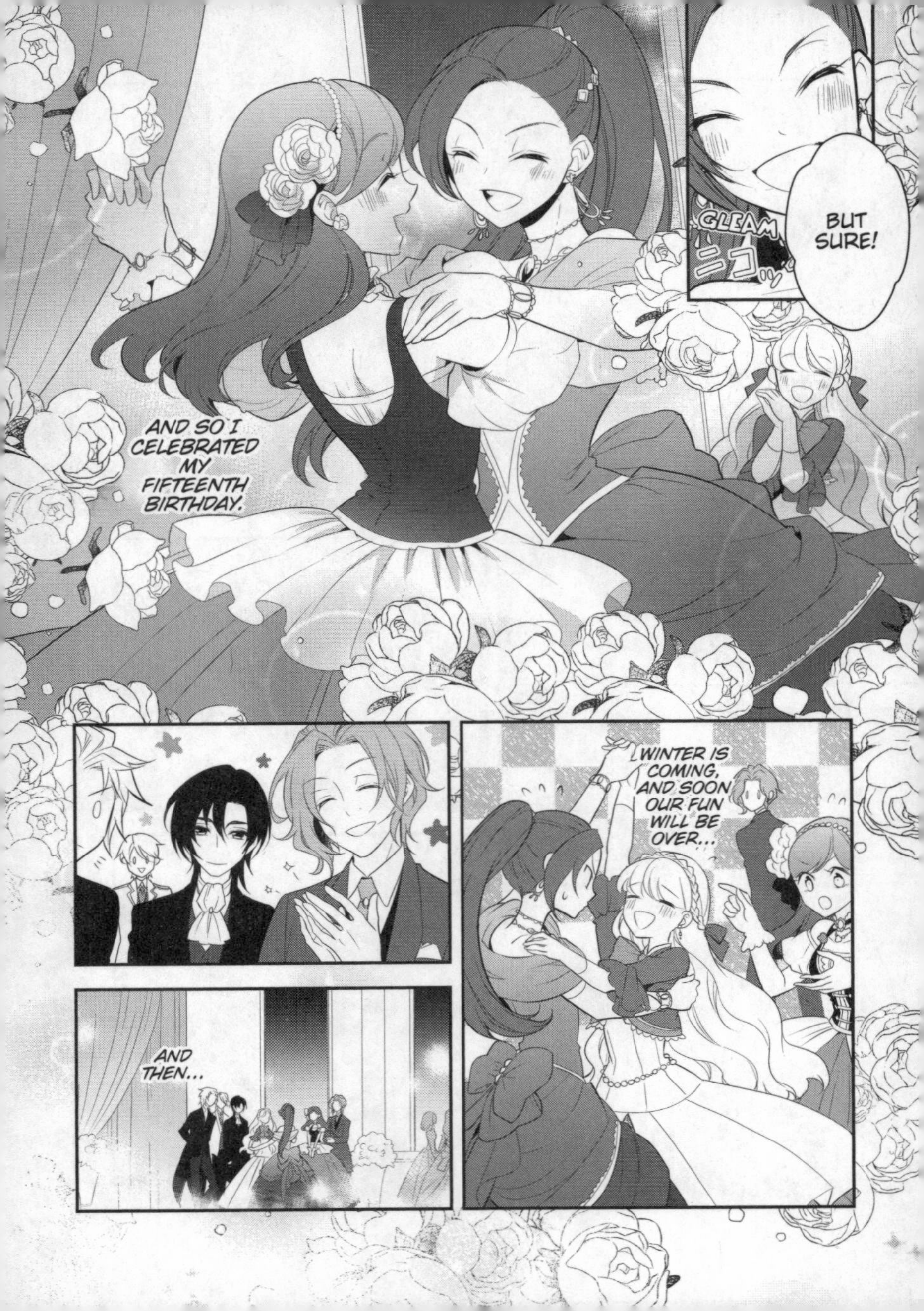
GLEAM
ニコッ
BUT SURE!
AND SO I CELEBRATED MY FIFTEENTH BIRTHDAY.
WINTER IS COMING, AND SOON OUR FUN WILL BE OVER...
AND THEN...

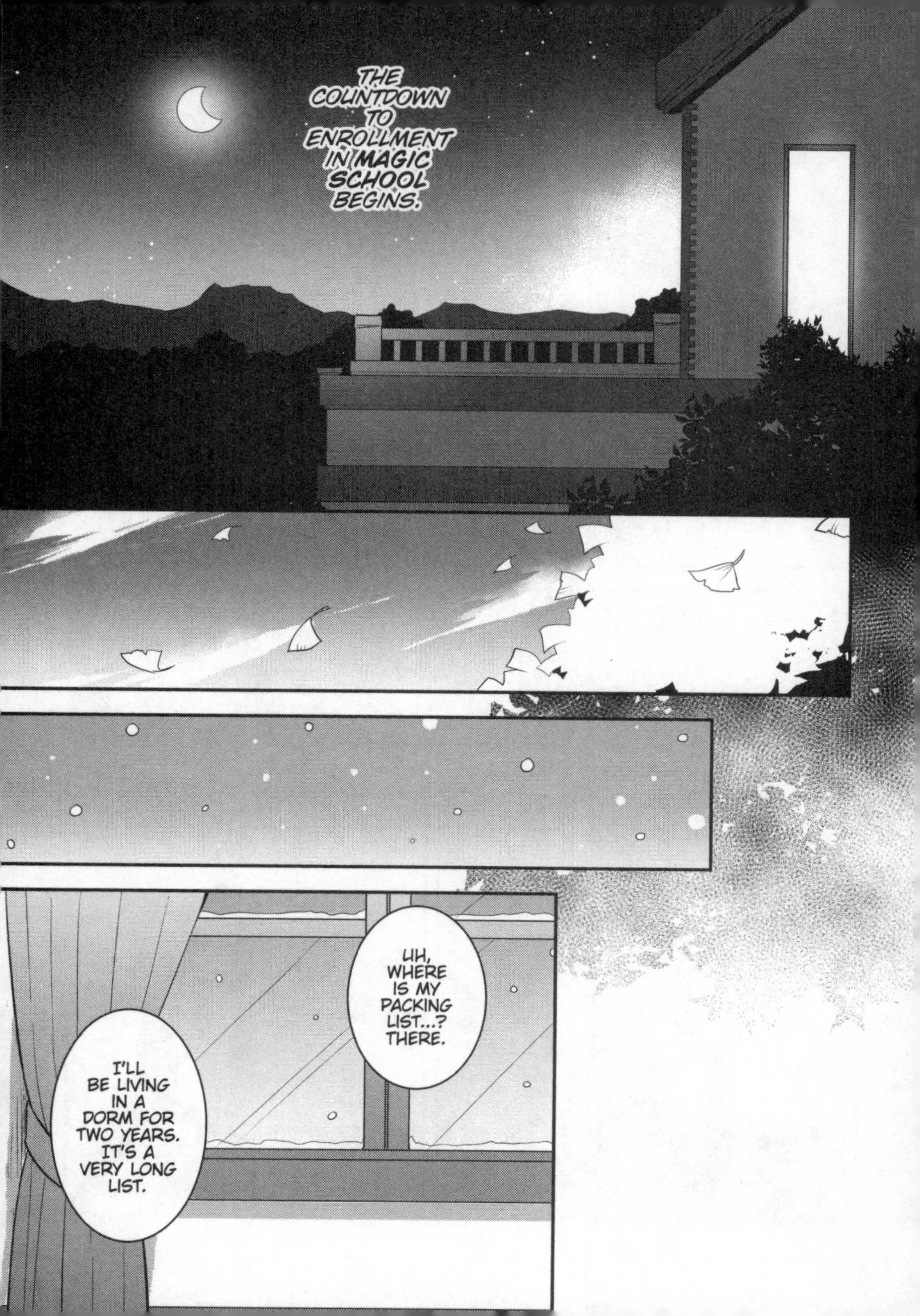
THE COUNTDOWN TO ENROLLMENT IN MAGIC SCHOOL BEGINS.
UH, WHERE IS MY PACKING LIST...? THERE.
I'LL BE LIVING IN A DORM FOR TWO YEARS. IT'S A VERY LONG LIST.

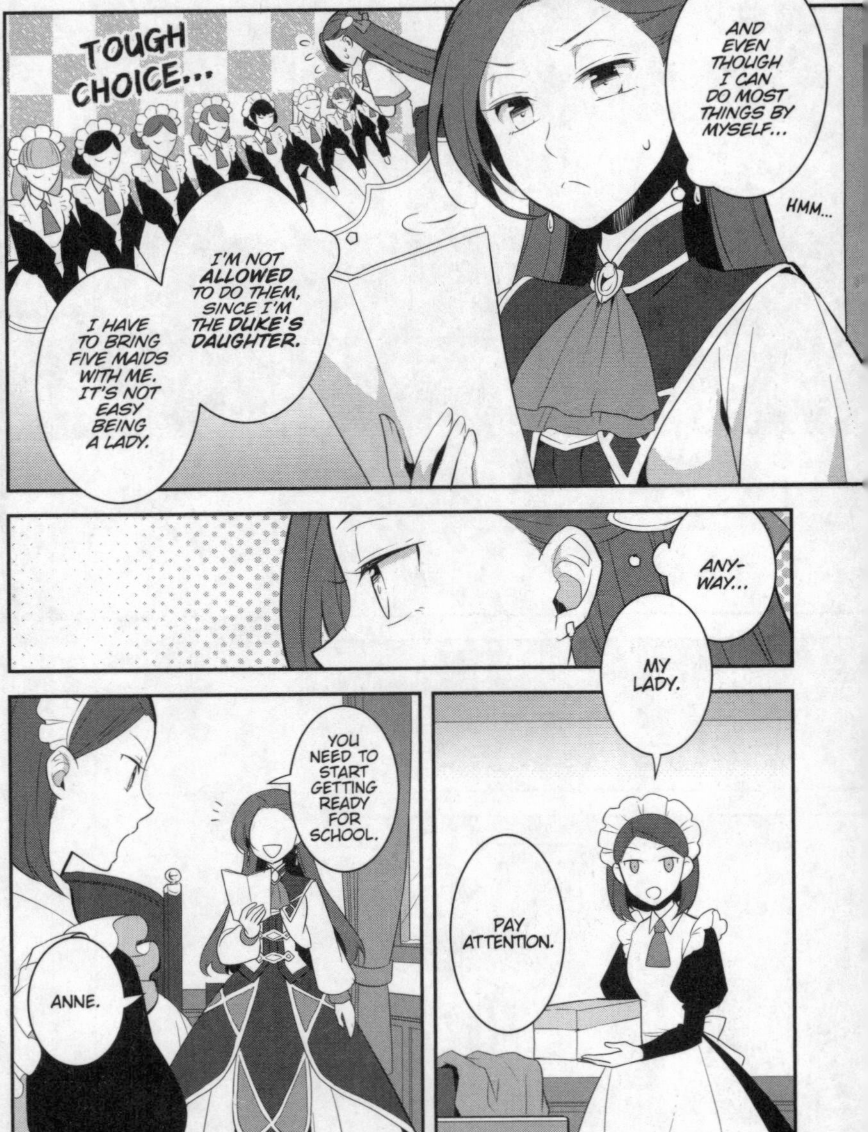
AND EVEN THOUGH I CAN DO MOST THINGS BY MYSELF...
HMM...
I'M NOT **ALLOWED** TO DO THEM, SINCE I'M THE **DUKE'S DAUGHTER.**
I HAVE TO BRING FIVE MAIDS WITH ME. IT'S NOT EASY BEING A LADY.
TOUGH CHOICE...
ANY-WAY...
MY LADY.
PAY ATTENTION.
YOU NEED TO START GETTING READY FOR SCHOOL.
ANNE.

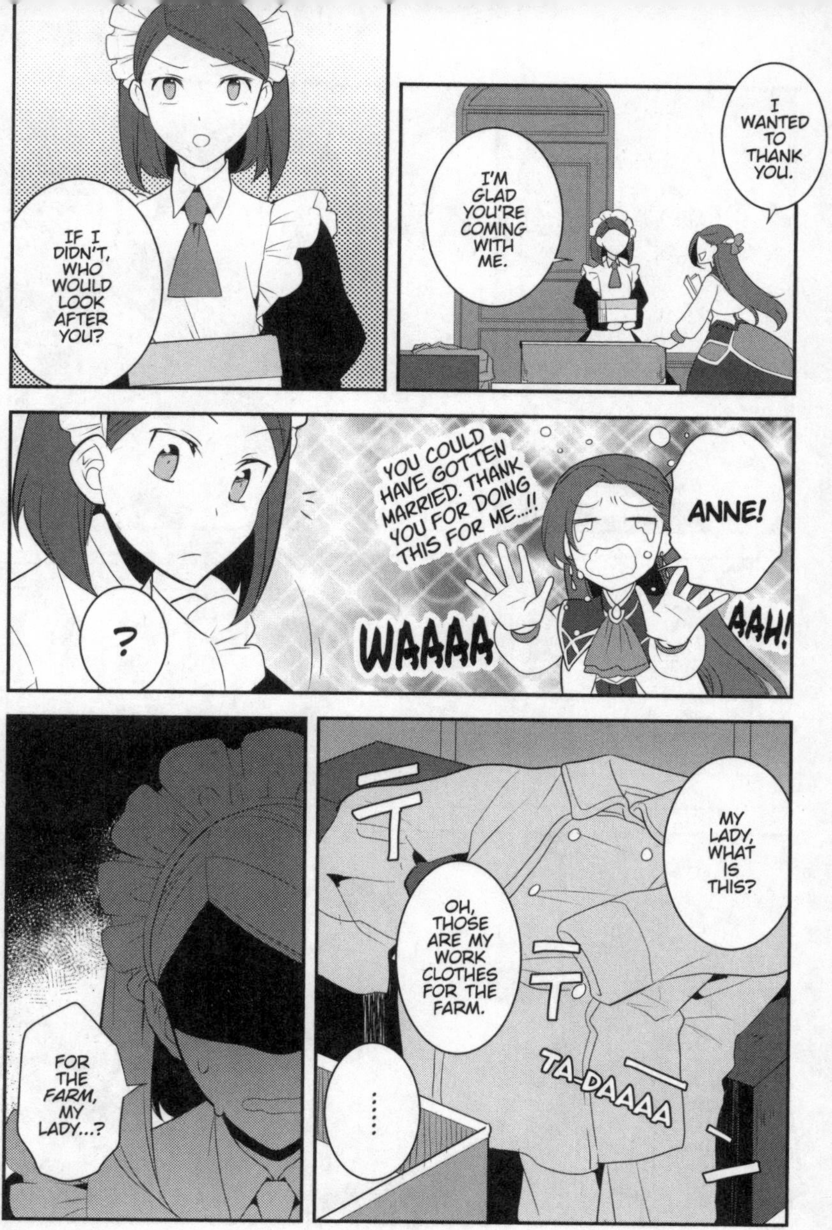
I WANTED TO THANK YOU.
I'M GLAD YOU'RE COMING WITH ME.
IF I DIDN'T, WHO WOULD LOOK AFTER YOU?
ANNE!
YOU COULD HAVE GOTTEN MARRIED. THANK YOU FOR DOING THIS FOR ME...!!
AAH!
WAAAA
?
MY LADY, WHAT IS THIS?
OH, THOSE ARE MY WORK CLOTHES FOR THE FARM.
TA-DAAAA
......
FOR THE *FARM*, MY LADY...?

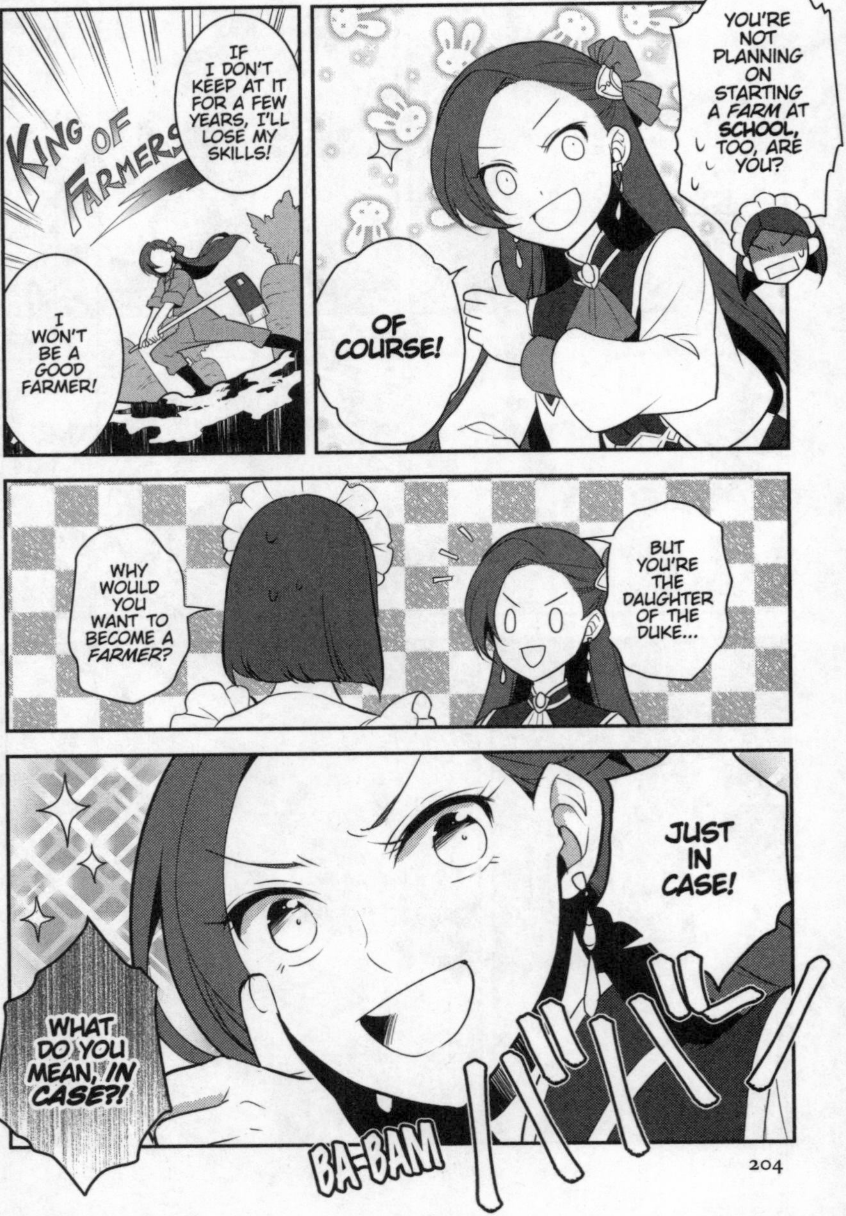
YOU'RE NOT PLANNING ON STARTING A *FARM* AT SCHOOL, TOO, ARE YOU?
OF COURSE!
KING OF FARMERS
IF I DON'T KEEP AT IT FOR A FEW YEARS, I'LL LOSE MY SKILLS!
I WON'T BE A GOOD FARMER!
BUT YOU'RE THE DAUGHTER OF THE DUKE...
WHY WOULD YOU WANT TO BECOME A *FARMER?*
JUST IN CASE!
WHAT DO YOU MEAN, *IN CASE?!*
BA-BAM

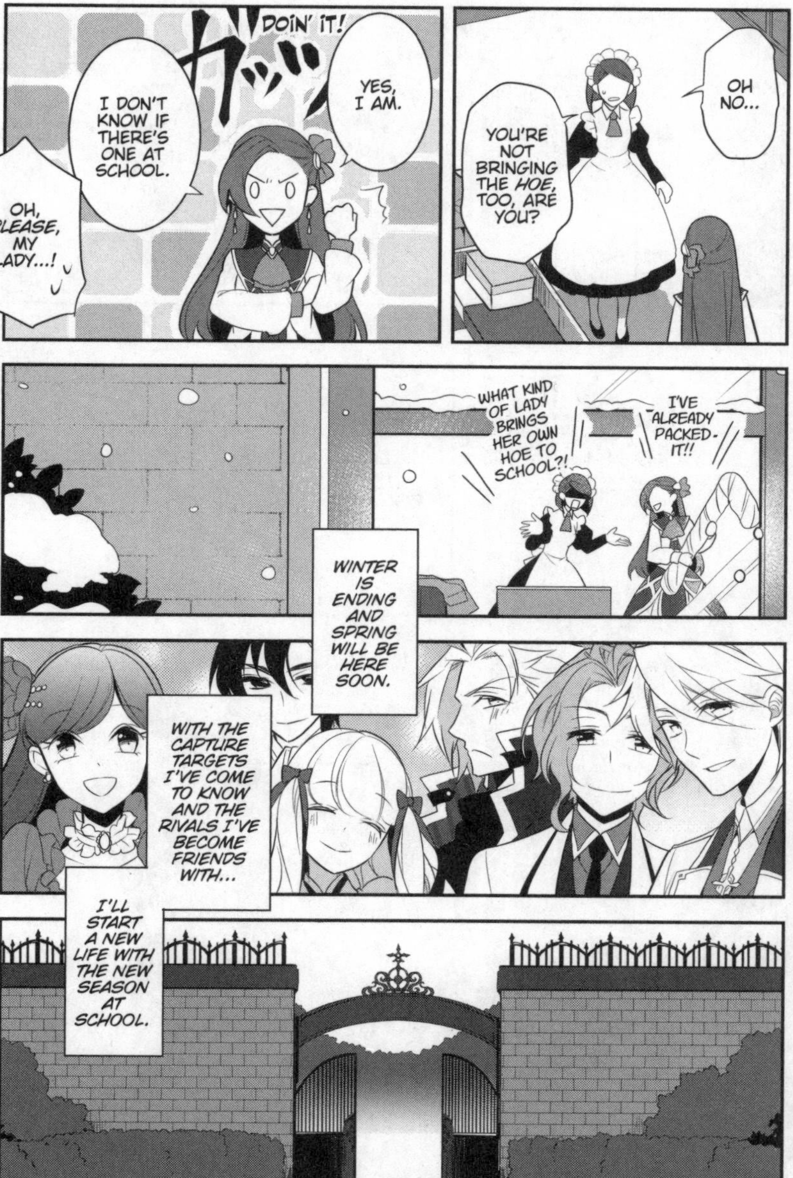
OH NO...
YOU'RE NOT BRINGING THE HOE, TOO, ARE YOU?
YES, I AM.
DOIN' IT!
I DON'T KNOW IF THERE'S ONE AT SCHOOL.
OH, PLEASE, MY LADY...!
I'VE ALREADY PACKED IT!!
WHAT KIND OF LADY BRINGS HER OWN HOE TO SCHOOL?!
WINTER IS ENDING AND SPRING WILL BE HERE SOON.
WITH THE CAPTURE TARGETS I'VE COME TO KNOW AND THE RIVALS I'VE BECOME FRIENDS WITH...
I'LL START A NEW LIFE WITH THE NEW SEASON AT SCHOOL.

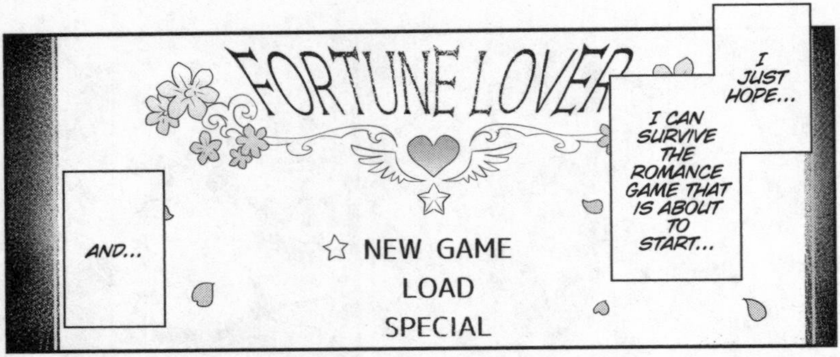
I JUST HOPE...
I CAN SURVIVE THE ROMANCE GAME THAT IS ABOUT TO START...
FORTUNE LOVER
☆ NEW GAME
LOAD
SPECIAL
AND...

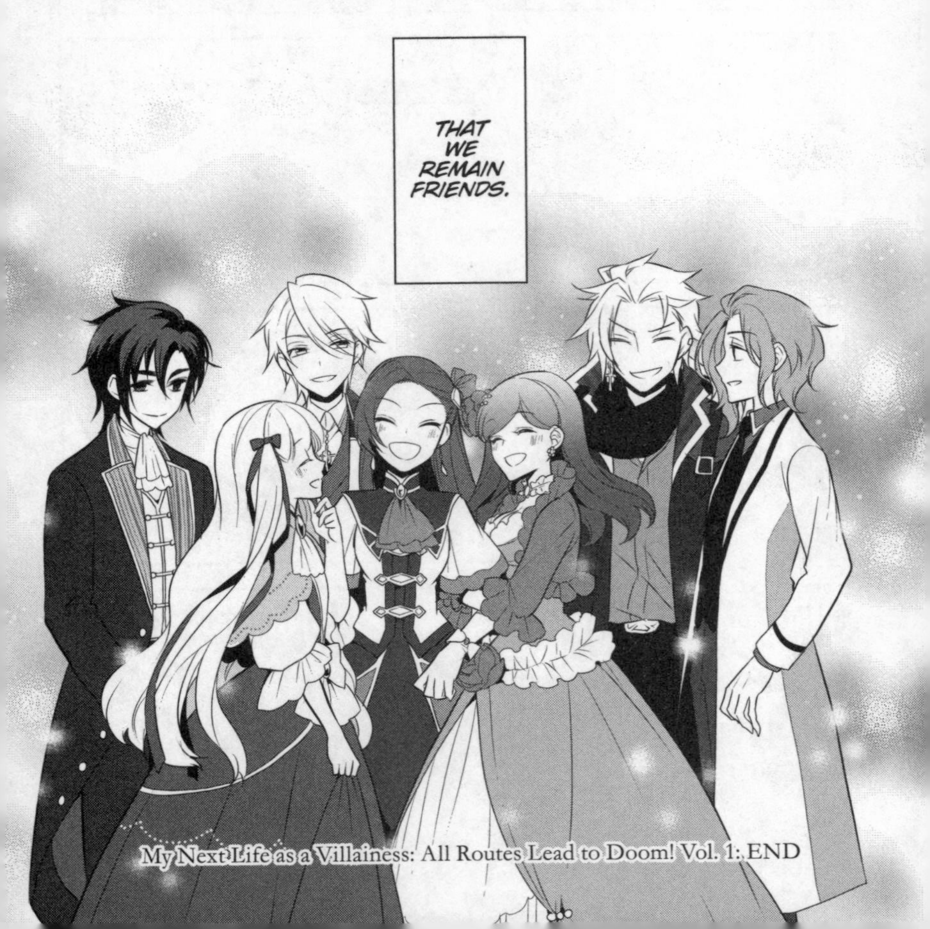
THAT WE REMAIN FRIENDS.
My Next Life as a Villainess: All Routes Lead to Doom! Vol. 1: END

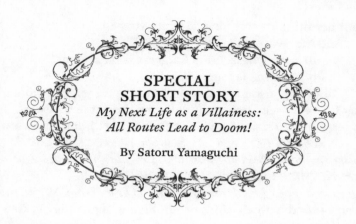

SPECIAL
SHORT STORY
My Next Life as a Villainess:
All Routes Lead to Doom!

By Satoru Yamaguchi

Hm? Where am I?

I opened my eyes to behold some kind of huge garden and a long stretch of green grass. It wasn't the Claes Estate garden that I'd become familiar with over the fifteen years of my life. It wasn't even a garden I'd visited at the castle, or at any of my friends' estates. I didn't know this place at all... and yet it looked strangely familiar. Also, why on Earth was I hustling forward so quickly, against my own will? *My body isn't listening to me. It's like I'm on autopilot.*

Is this some weird illusion? I panicked at first, but after a while, I realized that it was just a dream. It couldn't possibly be happening in reality. Besides, I knew I went to lay down on the bed that my maid, Anne, had just made for me. *Uh-huh, this* has *to be a dream.* But I had to wonder, why was my dream self moving through this unfamiliar place so fast?

Without finding any answers to my question, I continued to move forward. *It's as though someone's possessed my body. Or...hrmm...maybe I'm the one doing the possessing? Maybe this body isn't my own?* I entertained the thought, but the person I saw in the glass along the way was that villainess with whom I was so very familiar. There she was, with her thin lips and blue, almond-shaped eyes.

And that wasn't all.

"In all seriousness, Lady Katarina is marvelous."

"Lady Katarina is magnificent."

Following just a few steps behind me were some women that I'd never seen before. Judging by the name they used, it appeared that I'd possessed none other than Katarina Claes.

So, why am I, the girl who is supposed to be *Katarina, possessing myself? What in the world is going on? Could you even really call this a possession? It's like watching a scene from a film or a video game. It's too strange to be a dream.* While my head swirled with all kinds of jumbled thoughts, my vessel suddenly stopped moving.

Hm? What's happening? Did I get hungry? I certainly don't feel hungry—but maybe that's just because I'm only Katarina's spirit. Maybe the physical Katarina wants to grab a bite to eat. Just as I was thinking that, my vessel began to storm down the grassy field faster than ever before. Just a moment ago, she was walking at a stately pace down the paved path, as graceful as any woman in Mother's book of manners. But now she was pretty much zooming across the grass.

Hm, did she actually get an upset stomach? Is she heading towards the bathroom? However, over where my vessel is dashing, I saw...a girl. A girl with feathery blonde hair. I didn't know her, but she looked awfully familiar.

"What is a *commoner like you* doing here?" My vessel's sharp tongue spat the words out at the girl.

A commoner... Could she possibly be referring to the heroine of the romance game, *Fortune Lover*? No wonder she looked so familiar to me. She was in that video game that I'd played in my previous life. *I see, I see. That makes sense. I can see why she's a heroine. She's a sweet and pretty girl.*

However, the look this lovely girl turned up at me was one of abject fear.

"Uh, well, I was bringing some food for the Student Council..." She spoke timidly, cradling her basket against her chest, as if to hide it.

It...it pains me to see this. To terrify such a sweet girl like this, it wounded my heart, even though it wasn't my own doing. *Wait, the body I'm possessing belongs to Katarina, so doesn't this concern me, too? Or does it?*

Unlike my vessel, who seemed to have a very different attitude from my own, I just wanted to say, "Don't be afraid. See? I may look villainous, but I won't hurt you."

"You're bringing food to the Student Council? How dreadful! Don't you get too comfortable, you commoner!" My vessel grabbed the basket from the girl and threw it on the ground—much to my dismay!

Hey, you! How could you do this to her?! Deep down inside, I was enraged at her for what she'd just done.

Out from the basket fell what looked like a pile of very tasty muffins. At the sight of such scrumptiousness, my inner voice complete forgot the situation. I practically squealed at the sight of it all.

What?! Those look absolutely YUMMY! I want some! However, of all the things she could have done, my vessel crushed those delicious treats under her booted heel. When I saw that, something inside me snapped.

What the hell are you doing?! I can't believe it! You smashed all that scrumptiousness! You...you...muffin-mutilator! I couldn't believe her! *Now I'm FURIOUS! This is outrageous!* I wanted to attack my vessel...but I couldn't move my body at all. Of course. I was just a spirit in a body. I would have doled out a few dozen spanks as punishment, but I was truly powerless, which made me even more enraged.

While I ground my nonexistent teeth in frustration, my vessel went even further. She trampled more treats into the ground, spitting still-harsher words at the heroine.

What the hell is wrong with her?! I don't care who it is. Can someone please beat up this arrogant evil woman for me? And no sooner had I wished that, when...

"What in the world are you doing?"

A beautiful but piercing voice rang out. Two boys appeared.

"Prince Jeord... Keith..." My vessel muttered in shock.

They were boys that I knew very well: Katarina Claes's fiancé (*my* fiancé) and the third prince of this country, Jeord Stuart; and my adoptive younger brother, Keith Claes. They both looked sternly at my vessel.

What a relief! Here come the heroes. Come on, Jeord and Keith. Come kick this villainess's ass! There I was, a spirit who couldn't do anything but bite my intangible lip, cheering them on. It's not as if they heard my cheers, but...

"Are you all right?" Keith placed his hand on the girl's shoulder and hid her behind him.

Seeing my brother make such a slick move for the first time took me by surprise. He seemed different from the brother I knew. But that wasn't important just then.

Okay, my vessel shouldn't be able to do any more harm if someone is here to defend the girl like this. I breathed a sigh of relief, but my vessel, caught in the act by those heroes, began to tremble in fear. And then...

"I'm asking you! What were you doing harassing another student? Please answer my question, Lady Katarina Claes." The cold tone in Jeord's voice made my vessel jump.

She spoke in a quivering murmur, stammering, unable to muster up a sufficiently credible excuse. "...W-well, I was..."

Humph, that's what you get for your misdeeds! Or so I thought at first, but, for some reason, I started to have this indescribable, unbearable feeling. Even though I was angry at my vessel a moment ago, I began to want to apologize to the heroine myself. Probably because of the way Jeord and Keith were looking at me. I felt as though they were giving *me* their cold stares, and it made me feel terrible. *But I'm just a spirit in Katarina's body. Wait, the one who is possessing her body is Katarina, too. We're both Katarina!* Maybe they were staring at *me* after all.

I'd never once received such cold stares from them before. Nor had I ever seen such expressionless masks on their faces. Even my brother Keith treated me like a complete stranger with the way he called me "Lady Katarina." *I can't stand this.* It pained me to stand like that with them. *It's just so sad. It breaks my heart.*

Just as I was about to cry, my vessel seemed to reach her own limit.

"I-I must be going." She said in a shaky voice, before swiftly walking away. The looks on the boys' faces remained cold, even as she left.

* * * * * * * * *

"L-Lady Katarina, are you all right?" One of the girls following my vessel asked, when they finally reached a safe building, some time later.

My vessel replied, "I'm fine," without hesitation. I couldn't believe she said so, when she was shaking like a leaf just a moment ago. "That woman had Prince Jeord defending her like that again. Her, who dared even to make advances towards the duke's son! She's just a commoner. Who does she think she is?"

It seemed she still hadn't learned her lesson.

"Next time I'll pick somewhere less noticeable, and put her in her place." What an outrageous suggestion that was. *What the hell is she saying? She can't do that! Come on, you're supposed to be her friends. Why don't you guys stop her?*

"Yes, let's do that."

"You're absolutely right." Believe it or not, they agreed with her!

Are you kidding me? What are you guys thinking? You just did a terrible thing, got caught by the prince, and were forced to flee. You haven't learned a single thing! If they kept this up...

"You'll be doomed!" I cried out, jumping out of my bed. Then I realized that I was finally in a familiar room. Near me was my maid, Anne, with her eyes wide open.

"Oh, where are Katarina and her friends?"

As I muttered this, Anne looked at me, puzzled. "Lady Katarina, are you all right?" She asked me. She was holding the clothes I needed to wear today.

"Is it already time to go to school?"

"Lady Katarina, you won't be going to school until you're enrolled this spring. Please wake up," Anne replied flatly to me, while I lay there, half-awake.

"You're absolutely right." I hadn't enrolled in magic school yet. I'd celebrated my fifteenth birthday just before summer, and was planning to enroll after this winter. It seemed I'd dreamed about a future event.

I hadn't ever been to that school, not in person. How could the image of its landscape come from my memory of playing the game? Was that dream really a recollection of some game scene, or something else entirely? I tried to reexamine my dream, but I could only remember it vaguely. It was so vivid while I was in it, but it soon gradually faded away until it was mostly forgotten. How typical of a dream.

Although it hasn't remained in my memory, there is one thing I can recall clearly. It's that cold stare I got from Jeord and Keith. It remained imprinted in my mind even after having woken up.

In the game, Jeord used me as a way to ward off other women, and Keith hated me for being an annoying older sister. But right now, in reality, I've been getting along with both of them well.

Jeord visits me frequently and even helps me out at my farm at times. He's very kind to me. He must think of me as a good friend. Even Keith—who always takes care of me and backs me up whenever I get into trouble—is kind as well. He must see me as a big sister he loves dearly. For these reasons, they've never once looked at me so coldly. I'd gone so far as to believe our relationships would always stay the same, so long as things stayed peaceful.

What if they enroll in school and meet that heroine? Can we continue to stay this way? Jeord might see me, his fiancée, as a nuisance. Keith might simply find me annoying. If that happens, they might look at me just like they did in my dream.

As I began to think of such things, sadness overtook me.

"...Bi... ...Hello...? ...Big sister?"

They might even tell me never to show my face around them again...

"Big Sister, are you listening?"

"Oh my goodness! You scared me! Keith, when did you get here?"

His voice had come out of nowhere. Startled, I turned to look towards him. There he was—my brother Keith, looking puzzled.

"What do you mean, 'When did I get here?' I came in after I knocked at your door. How come you didn't you notice? Are you still half-asleep?"

"Uh, well, I was thinking about all kinds of things..."

"Thinking? Are you hungry? Or did you get an upset stomach?"

No, Little Brother. Why must you assume a lady always thinks of hunger or an upset stomach? Who would do that? I wish Keith would learn how to be smoother with ladies, like the game version of himself.

I looked intently at Keith in front of me while I thought. Whatever his remarks were about, he'd been staring at me with concern. I didn't see any of the coldness he had in my dream at all. *I don't know what's going to happen, but we're still okay.*

"Keith, I'll always be on your side, and I'll never get in your way." That's what I swore to Keith, standing there in front of me.

"Huh? What's this about? I'm lost." As Keith widened his eyes, I embraced him tightly.

"I'm just saying I care about you *so much,* Keith." *So please don't hate me for being annoying, even when you fall in love with that girl.* I hugged Keith with all the sisterly affection I possessed, waiting for him to respond in kind... but there was no sign of it. *That's odd.* I unwrapped my arms from around him and looked into his face. He was completely frozen, his face completely red. Why? I didn't think I gave him *that* tight a hug. Was I stronger than I thought? Strength is sort of a questionable virtue for a lady, but my concern for Keith was the more important thing.

"Uh, Keith, are you all—"

"I waited patiently for you to bring back Katarina, but it's been taking you ages." Before I could finish my sentence, it was Jeord's turn to enter my room. "So I came up to have a look myself. ...Keith, what in the world have you been doing?"

Jeord was a cute little prince when I first met him, but he'd grown into such a handsome young man these last seven years. Even though he stood just as tall as me at the beginning, he surpassed my height before I knew it. I can't find even a trace of his sweet little old self in him anymore.

Once Jeord came in, Keith quickly stepped away from me. "Oh no! This wasn't my doing..." He began to stammer something.

I don't know what that was about, but I'm glad that he got his complexion back to normal. I'll be careful not to hug him too tight next time.

After checking on Keith, I turned towards Jeord. "Good morning, Prince Jeord." I greeted him with my most ladylike disposition. A proper greeting is basic etiquette, an expectation I must fulfill—even if I'm in my pajamas with messy hair in my own room. I've truly become more like a noblewoman. It must be the result of so many years of my mother's strict instruction.

"Good morning, Katarina. Forgive me for barging into your room. Keith took so long that it had me worried." Jeord beamed a smile. "So tell me, what were you and Keith embracing each other for?" Jeord asked.

It made me wonder. He had such a big smile on his face, yet I could feel the anger simmering in the air around him. "Uh, well, a sister is free to hug her brother, is she not?"

"Perhaps so, but you're fifteen years old now. An adult. You should refrain from embracing any man in your chambers alone—even if he is family." He wore his most charming smile.

When I become an adult, I'm not allowed to give any men any hugs, even if they're relatives? I had to wonder why no one had ever told me *that* before. Ultimately, with Jeord being so assertive about it, I decided to just nod and agree. I had a feeling he'd have a lot to say if I objected. As if to praise me for nodding so obediently, Jeord smiled...and then opened his arms to me for some odd reason.

"Eh?"

When I tilted my head in confusion, Jeord spoke without any hesitation. "Might I not have the favor of a loving embrace as well?"

"Oh, but you just said not to hug *any* men..."

"Yes, but *I* am your fiancé. It should be no problem."

The smile he put on made it all pretty convincing to me. Jeord came up to me suddenly, pulled me into his arms, and hugged me close.

"Eh? Uh...!"

While I panicked, Keith interjected. "Excuse me, Prince Jeord. Just what are you doing to her?!"

I was busy getting squeezed against Jeord's manly chest, and I have to say that I felt his "loving embrace" was a bit one-sided.

Then I realized I'd done exactly the same thing to Keith, and felt a little abashed.

While I was absorbed in thought, Keith forced Jeord to open his arms and pried me away. Seeing Keith's desperate act made me realize just how tight my embrace must have been for him. That was surely why he came so frantically to my rescue.

I decided to be careful from then on.

Jeord and Keith fussed at each other, vivacious, pleasant.

I'll do everything I can to fight off all the routes that lead to doom. I never want to see those cold stares from them ever again.

My Next Life
as a VILLAINESS:
ALL ROUTES
LEAD TO DOOM!

AFTERWORD

Hi, good afternoon, good evening,
and good morning, everyone! My name is
Nami Hidaka. This is my first-ever
comment in one of my books, so I had to give
it some thought on what to write. But first,
I want to express my gratitude: Thank you
so much for picking up this book!

When I was first offered the chance to do
the manga adaptation of this light novel,
I thought...

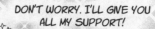

OH NO! I'VE NEVER REALLY DONE
MANGA BEFORE. THERE'S NO WAY
I CAN DO THIS!

So I freaked out, but my editor said...

DON'T WORRY. I'LL GIVE YOU
ALL MY SUPPORT!

With those encouraging words,
I managed to put this book together. I was
able to work without any worries, knowing
everything would be run past Yamaguchi-
sensei, the author of the light novel. I really
owe a lot to the help I got from everyone!

Volume one focuses on
Katarina and her friends' childhood.
It was fun drawing lots of women
and little kids!

KATARINA'S HAIRSTYLE

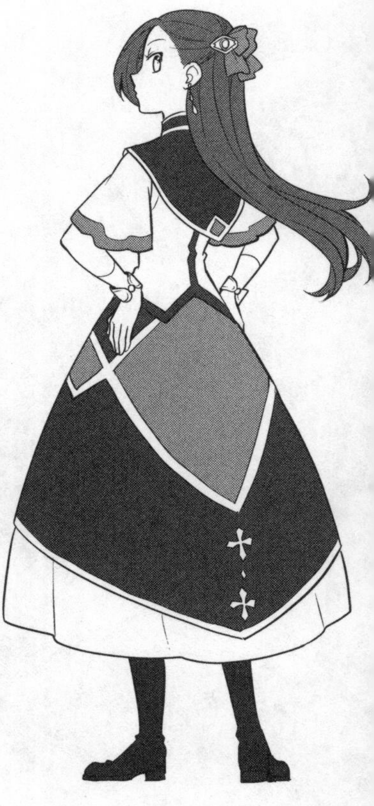

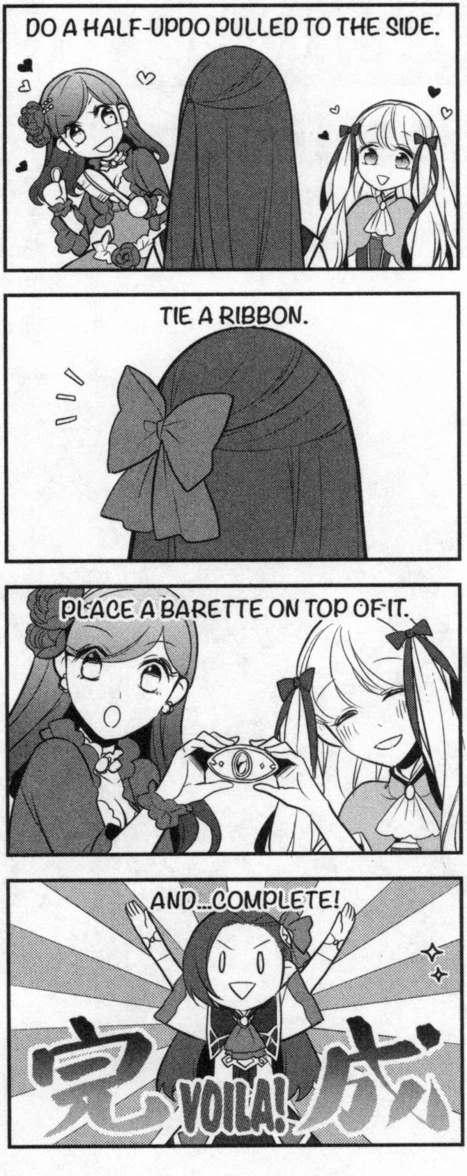
DO A HALF-UPDO PULLED TO THE SIDE.
TIE A RIBBON.
PLACE A BARETTE ON TOP OF IT.
AND...COMPLETE!
完成
VOILA!

MAGIC SCHOOL NEWSPAPER
- EXTRA EDITION -

Enrolls in Magic School Soon!!

Expanding Circle of Friends

Lady Katarina Makes Grand Entrance to Magic School with Capture Targets and Rivals She Befriended

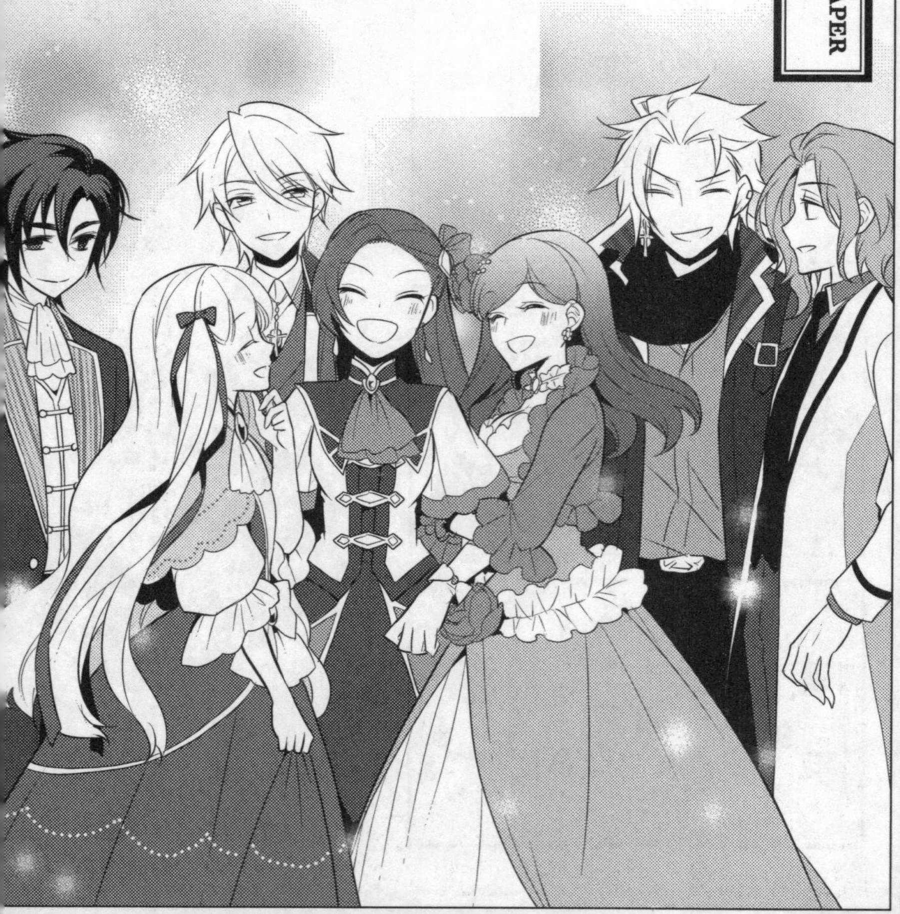

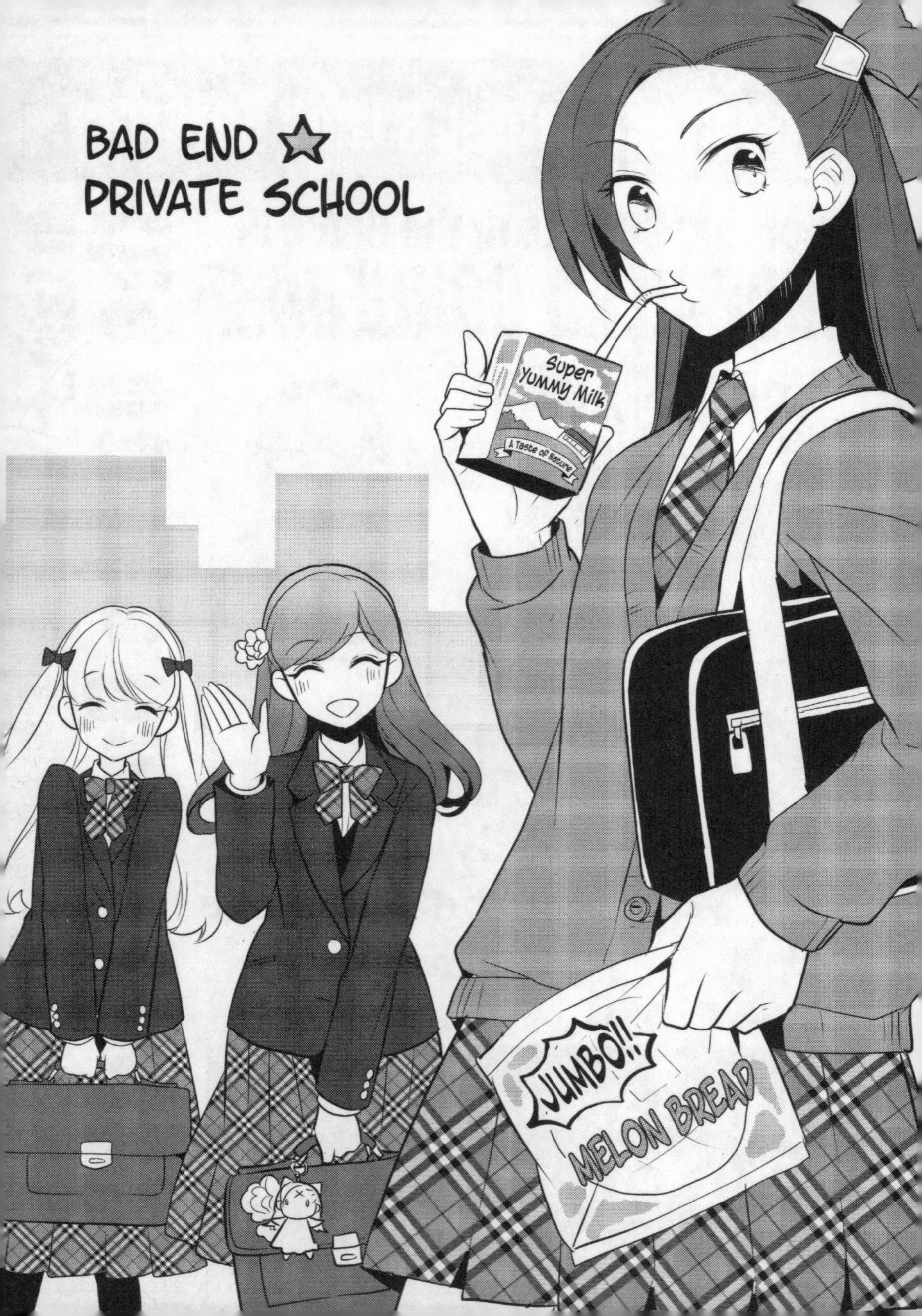
BAD END ☆ PRIVATE SCHOOL
Super Yummy Milk
A Taste of Nature
JUMBO!!
MELON BREAD

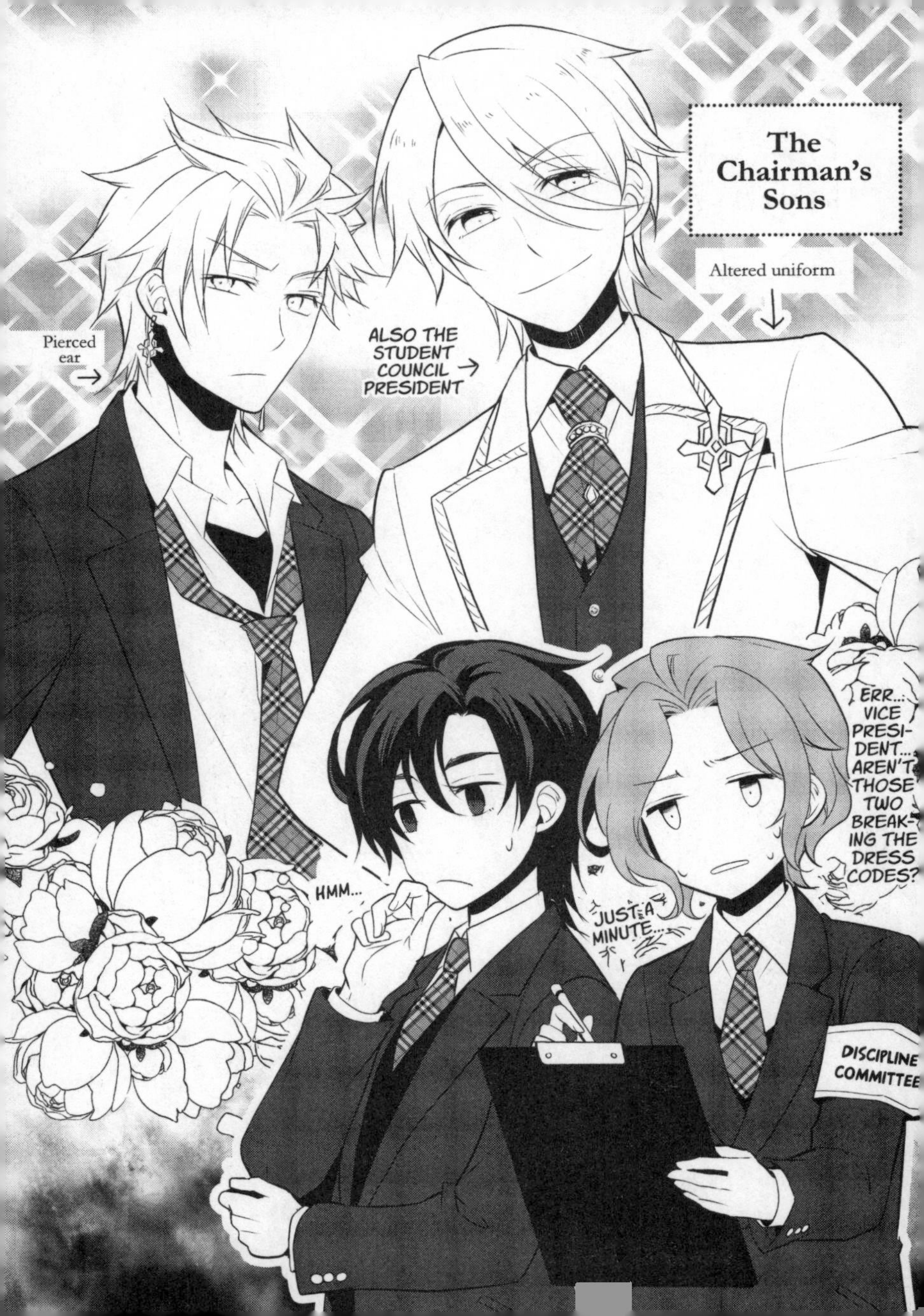
The Chairman's Sons
Altered uniform
ALSO THE STUDENT COUNCIL PRESIDENT
Pierced ear
ERR... VICE PRESIDENT... AREN'T THOSE TWO BREAKING THE DRESS CODES?
DISCIPLINE COMMITTEE
JUST A MINUTE...
HMM...

My Next Life
as a VILLAINESS:
ALL ROUTES
LEAD TO DOOM!